THE BIBLE DOCTRINE OF GRACE

THE BIBLE DOCTRINE OF GRACE

and Related Doctrines

By

C. RYDER SMITH, B.A., D.D.

*Formerly Professor of Theology in the
University of London*

'Where sin abounded, grace did much more abound.'
(ROMANS 5:20)

WIPF & STOCK · Eugene, Oregon

Wipf and Stock Publishers
199 W 8th Ave, Suite 3
Eugene, OR 97401

The Bible Doctrine of Grace
By Smith, C. Ryder
Copyright©1956 Epworth Press
ISBN 13: 978-1-60899-120-4
Publication date 10/20/2009
Previously published by Epworth Press, 1956

Copyright © Epworth Press 1956
First English edition1956 by Epworth Press
This edition published by arrangement with Epworth Press

TABLE OF CONTENTS

INTRODUCTION	. . . .	1
1. THE SCOPE AND ARRANGEMENT OF THE BOOK	. .	5
2. OLD TESTAMENT ANTECEDENTS	. . . . .	8
3. FROM HEBREW INTO GREEK	. . . . .	33
4. THE NEW TESTAMENT DOCTRINE OF GRACE	. . .	56
5. TRIAL, TEMPTATION, AND DISCIPLINE	. . . .	100
6. THE CO-EXISTENCE OF GRACE AND SIN	. . .	124
7. THE DOCTRINE OF ELECTION	. . . . .	141
8. THE FELLOWSHIP OF GOD WITH MAN IN CHRIST	. .	187
INDEX OF HEBREW, GREEK, AND ENGLISH TERMS	.	225
INDEX OF TEXTS	. . . .	229

ABBREVIATIONS

for the names of

BOOKS OF THE BIBLE

Old Testament

Gn—Genesis
Ex—Exodus
Lv—Leviticus
Nu—Numbers
Dt—Deuteronomy
Jos—Joshua
Jg—Judges
Ru—Ruth
1 S, 2 S—1 and 2 Samuel
1 K, 2 K—1 and 2 Kings
1 Ch, 2 Ch—1 and 2 Chronicles
Ezr—Ezra
Neh—Nehemiah
Est—Esther
Job
Ps—Psalms
Pr—Proverbs
Ec—Ecclesiastes
Ca—Canticles
Is—Isaiah
Jer—Jeremiah
La—Lamentations
Ezk—Ezekiel
Dn—Daniel
Hos—Hosea
Jl—Joel
Am—Amos
Ob—Obadiah
Jon—Jonah
Mic—Micah
Nah—Nahum
Hab—Habakkuk
Zeph—Zephaniah
Hag—Haggai
Zec—Zechariah
Mal—Malachi

Apocrypha

1 Es, 2 Es—1 and 2 Esdras
Ad. Est—Additions to Esther
Wis—Wisdom
Sir—Sirach or Ecclesiasticus
Bar—Baruch
Three—Song of the Three Holy Children
To—Tobit
Jth—Judith
Sus—Susanna
Bel—Bel and the Dragon
Pr. Man—Prayer of Manasses
1 Mac, 2 Mac—1 and 2 Maccabees

New Testament

Mt—Matthew
Mk—Mark
Lk—Luke
Jn—John
Ac—Acts of the Apostles
Ro—Romans
1 Co, 2 Co—1 and 2 Corinthians
Gal—Galatians
Eph—Ephesians
Ph—Philippians
Col—Colossians
1 Th, 2 Th—1 and 2 Thessalonians
1 Ti, 2 Ti—1 and 2 Timothy
Tit—Titus
Philem—Philemon
He—Hebrews
Ja—James
1 P, 2 P—1 and 2 Peter
1 Jn, 2 Jn, 3 Jn—1, 2, and 3 John
Jude
Rev—Revelation of John

INTRODUCTION

As is explained in the first chapter below, it is difficult to define the scope of a book on 'Grace'. This volume is the fourth in a series, and, if the word be taken in a wide sense, all the three earlier volumes are on this subject. The titles of two of these, *The Bible Doctrine of Salvation, a Study in the Atonement* and *The Bible Doctrine of Sin and of the Ways of God with Sinners*, sufficiently show this. The books are clearly about the Grace of God in Christ. Under the remaining book, *The Bible Doctrine of Man*, it seemed to me that the subject 'What a man ought to be', should be included, as well as 'What a man is', and, for example, the Bible teaches that a man ought to be 'holy' or 'sanctified', and 'sanctification' is the work of Grace. To examine the doctrines of Man, Sin and Grace separately is as difficult as to take the ear, nose and throat separately in medicine. In consequence, there is need in each of the four volumes to refer to the others. In the earlier volumes I have kept the number of cross-references down to the minimum so that, as nearly as possible, each of them might be complete in itself. In the present volume the number of such references is greater because, if the word 'grace' be taken in a wide sense, the number of subjects already examined is large. If, however, it be taken in a narrow sense, the case is different. To devote a whole book to the subject is comparatively rare, but it is frequently discussed in articles written for encyclopedias and journals. In the latter the discussion is usually confined to an examination of the use and meaning of the Greek word for 'grace' (*charis*) and its Old Testament antecedents. Under this definition I think that I may claim that Chapters 2, 3 and 4 below include an account that is reasonably complete in itself. For the rest, I can only ask my readers, like myself, to take the consequences of the writing of books in an organically connected series. At the same time, I hope that they will agree that there are advantages in the inclusion in this volume of subjects that are not commonly considered under Grace, though they are, in fact, organically connected with it. This applies particularly, though not exclusively, to the later chapters.

The doctrine of Grace, like those of Man and Sin, has to be

collected from a very large number of passages. Usually these include a *term* relevant to the subject, and I have not very often referred to passages that contain a relevant *idea* without a relevant word, though in the last Chapter the *phrases* 'in Christ' and its companions take the place of single terms. Other notes, similar to those in earlier books, may be added. Under the discussion of most of the terms the number of times that each occurs is usually added in brackets on its first use. Especially with the commonest terms, it is not likely that the number is exact to a digit, if only because of variant 'readings' in the manuscripts, but it is sufficiently near for the present purpose. I have used the rendering of the Revised Version (or of its margin) in quotations, except when I have given a more nearly literal translation. Under the Apocrypha I have confined myself to the books found in the English Bible. I have used 'Sirach' instead of 'Ecclesiasticus', giving references to it before those from the Book of Wisdom, which usually illustrates a later development in doctrine. Following the example of the Revisers I have generally used 'the LORD' (in capitals) for JHVH (Jahveh), the Hebrews' personal name for God. In passages from the Pentateuch I have added the customary letters, J, E, D and P, where the date of the document is pertinent to the discussion. For those who do not read Hebrew and Greek I may add that in the transliteration of terms ' and ' stand for two Hebrew gutturals that are often left unpronounced, and that in Hebrew words *ch* is to be pronounced as in 'loch' and in Greek words as in 'chasm'. As in earlier books, I have gone back to the Bible itself without discussing the findings of other writers. Here again, of course, there is room for criticism, but in a book on so large a subject the inclusion of such discussions would have swollen the volume to inordinate bulk. Besides, at a time when there is a return of interest in biblical theology, there seem to me to be advantages in looking at the original sources, as far as may be, 'with a fresh eye', and examining them apart from the distractions of current discussion. For good or for ill, there is an example of this in the chapter on 'The Co-existence of Grace and Sin'.

Finally, I have again to thank my friends, the Revs. G. W. Anderson, M.A., and T. Francis Glasson, M.A., D.D., for reading the typescript and making a number of suggestive and valuable comments, and to my friend, the Rev. Frank H. Cumbers, B.A., B.D., the Book Steward of the Epworth Press, for his sustained and kindly help with the publication of the book. I am also in debt to the Rev. Frederic A. Tomlinson for undertaking the tedious task of making a 'fair copy', and to Mr William Jackson for preparing the long index of texts.

November 1954   C. RYDER SMITH

CHAPTER ONE

THE SCOPE AND ARRANGEMENT OF THE BOOK

THERE IS something arbitrary in defining the scope of a study in any branch of Biblical Theology, for, on examination, the latter is found to be an integrated whole, every part implying every other. It is as if a botanist set out to study the roots of trees by themselves, or their trunks or flowers. Such subjects can only be isolated artificially. Under some doctrines, however, the limits of treatment are fairly well fixed by custom—for instance, 'The Person of Christ' or 'The Work of Christ' or 'The Holy Spirit'. As already seen, so far as there are agreed limits in the case of 'Grace', discussion is usually limited to the Greek word, *charis*, with its cognates in the New Testament and its Hebrew antecedents in the Old. To the present writer this seems to narrow the subject overmuch. But how far shall it be widened? It may be said that in the New Testament the *idea*, as distinct from the *word*, includes the whole *kerugma*. For instance, the text 'God so loved the world that he gave his only begotten Son that whosoever believeth on him should not perish but have everlasting life' (Jn 3[16]) just describes 'grace'. But under this account the doctrine of the Incarnation would need to be included and the doctrine of 'everlasting life', to go no farther. Clearly this is too wide an account. The writer has taken a middle course. It seems to him that in the New Testament there is a cluster of words, each of which describes an ingredient in the concept of 'grace'. Or, to use a metaphor, 'grace' is like a jewel with many facets, each facet, however, having its own colour. But how many facets has the jewel of grace? To abandon the metaphor, how many aspects has grace? The writer has selected eleven—mercy or pity, justification, forgiveness, reconciliation, salvation, the 'new creation', 'comfort' (or rather *paraclēsis*, which is more than 'comfort'), holiness, blessedness, peace, love. The list includes words not usually included under the exegesis of *charis*, but, as the writer thinks, involved in it. Yet he admits too that the selection is arbitrary, for other words—such as 'patience' and 'hope' and 'life'—might be included. At any rate, the selection does not lack range.

Here, however, another difficulty, already noted in the Introduction, emerges. In earlier volumes of the series four of these terms have already been discussed at length—salvation and reconciliation in *The Bible Doctrine of Salvation,* holiness (or sanctification) in *The Bible Doctrine of Man,* and justification in *The Bible Doctrine of Sin.* Of these four the first, salvation, is considered again in this volume, but from a different point of view. In *The Bible Doctrine of Salvation,* which is 'a Study in the Atonement', the subject was discussed on its God-ward side, but in this volume on its man-ward side—i.e. as a part of the Christian experience. The discussion of the other three subjects—justification, reconciliation, and holiness—is not repeated in this book, though, of course, they are sometimes referred to. It may prevent misunderstanding if it is added that for the present writer 'to justify' does not mean 'to treat a man as if he were already what he is to be —righteous', but 'to treat a man as righteous because he has already, through a "new creation", begun to be this'. Chapter 4, then, on 'The New Testament Doctrine of Grace', consists of an account, first, of *charis* itself, and then of mercy, forgiveness, salvation, the 'new creation', *paraclesis,* blessedness, peace, and love.

In the chapters on the Old Testament and LXX the subjects are taken in the same order, two Hebrew terms, *chen* and *chesed,* being taken together as the Hebrew antecedents of *charis.* This explains why 'mercy' (*eleos*) is taken immediately after *charis* in the New Testament, for, while LXX almost always uses *charis* for *chen* and *eleos* for *chesed,* it uses cognates of *eleos* under the cognates of *both* Hebrew terms. This means that for Greek-speaking Jews and Christians the ideas under *chen* and *chesed* more or less fused, for LXX was their Bible.

As for the *order* in which the other terms are taken, they seem to have a fairly natural order in the New Testament. Forgiveness and salvation come next to *charis* and *eleos* because, since they include the forgiveness of *past* sins and salvation from them, they look backwards as well as forwards. The 'new creation' follows, since it is the initial outcome of grace; next comes *paraclesis,* for it denotes the 'help' that is constant throughout a Christian's life; blessedness and peace are taken next, as being results of grace; love comes last, as the underlying principle of the manifold experience called 'grace'. Having adopted this order for the New Testament, the writer has for convenience, followed it also

THE SCOPE AND ARRANGEMENT OF THE BOOK 7

in the Old, though, particularly under 'love', it is not so easy to justify it there. It is an advantage that this brings out a difference of emphasis in the two Testaments.

After three chapters on 'Grace', there are four on 'related doctrines'. In the New Testament the 'men of grace' continually experience 'Trial, Temptation and Discipline' and a chapter follows on these subjects. The three go together throughout the Bible, the Old Testament again providing the background for the New. One of the salient *phenomena* is that in *one and the same experience* God may be trying a man and the Devil tempting him. In Chapter 6, on 'The Co-existence of Grace and Sin', an attempt is made to deal with two subjects for which the New Testament evidence is sparse and wholly implicit—'righteousness in sinners' and 'sin in believers'. Chapter 7 is given to 'the Doctrine of Election', for in the New Testament believers are 'the elect'. Here again there are antecedent Old Testament doctrines. It is argued that in the Bible the doctrine that a man is 'elect' *if he is willing* to be 'elect', gradually works itself clear and that nothing in Paul, not even Romans 9-11, contradicts this. No one will be surprised that this is a long chapter. Finally, there is a chapter entitled 'The Fellowship of God with Man in Christ'. The ultimate source of grace is the fact that God made man to live in fellowship with Himself and that He seeks fellowship even with sinful men. To examine all the evidence for this would require a volume. Some of it appears in this and earlier books. In Chapter 8 the doctrine is illustrated by three great examples—the word for 'fellowship', *koinōnia*, and its cognates; the phrase 'to know God'; and the phrase 'in Christ', with its parallels.

CHAPTER TWO

OLD TESTAMENT ANTECEDENTS

IN THE previous chapter 'grace' is defined in New Testament terms and the definition centres in Christ. Under this definition, of course, there can be no doctrine of 'grace' in the Old Testament, for in its time Christ had not yet come. Yet, on this subject as on others, the Old Testament prepares the way for Christ, and the word 'antecedents' is apposite. There is another difference between the Testaments. The subject of the New Testament chapter might be defined as 'The Ways of God with Believers in Christ'. The subject of this chapter is 'The Ways of God with Good Men (and with penitents who seek to be good)'. Behind the difference there lie two contrary assumptions. In the New Testament it is taken for granted that all men are sinners (even though occasionally particular men are called 'righteous' in a relative sense), and that it is believers and believers alone who begin to be truly righteous. In it, therefore, 'the Ways of God with the Good' becomes 'The Ways of God with Believers'. In the Old Testament, on the other hand, it is assumed that all men are not sinners and that there are good men as well as bad men in the world, or at any rate in Israel (though here too there are a few exceptional texts). The phrase 'The Ways of God with the Good', therefore, suits the Old Testament. In the volume on *The Bible Doctrine of Sin* 'the Ways of God with Sinners' were examined; here there is a complementary study on His 'Ways with the Righteous'. As already indicated, the discussion proceeds chiefly by the examination of *terms* (and, where need be, of their context), but sometimes passages are taken into account where an *idea* is found without the term.

Under the arrangement traced in the previous chapter, the first Old Testament term to be considered is *chēn*. It is one of the words formed from the root *chnn* (*225*). These words usually (though not always) imply that one man, having some kind of superiority or advantage over another man, shows him favour. Of the two common English renderings of *chen* itself, 'favour' and 'grace', the former is nearly always preferable. The *differentia* of *chen* is that the recipient has *no claim* to favour—that is, it is undeserved. There is a verb of the same root, an adjective, and an adverb (or adverbial noun). The usual renderings of the verb and adjective are 'to show favour' or 'grace' or 'pity', and 'gracious'. The adverb has the same meaning as the Latin *gratis*. Such phrases as 'If now I have found favour in the eyes of . . .' occur over fifty times in the historical books. Of the showing of 'favour' by *man to man*, there are instances when Job cries out 'Have *chen* upon me, O ye my friends' (Job 19^{21}; cf. Jg 21^{22}, Ps 37$^{21, 26}$), and when Joseph's brothers confess that 'when he asked their *chen*' they 'would not hear' (Gn 12^{21} E; cf. Est 4^8). As just noted, the noun occurs frequently in such phrases as 'find *favour* in the eyes of' and 'find *favour* with' this man or that (e.g. Gn 30^{27} J; Ru 2$^{2, 10, 13}$; Pr 28^{23}), and it may be used of the beauty that gives a woman *favour* with a man (e.g. Pr 31^{30}; cf. Ps 22^{11}). There are good examples of the use of the adverbial noun (*gratis*) in Jonathan's appeal to Saul on behalf of David, 'Wherefore wilt thou . . . slay David gratuitously?' (1 S 19^5), and in the proverb 'the curse that is gratuitous lighteth not' (Pr 26^2). When the *chen* of *God* is in question there is such a heightening and deepening of meaning as befits the Almighty. The verb usually relates to deliverance from evil or affliction—for instance, Amos says, 'It may be that the LORD, the God of hosts, will show *chen* unto the remnant of Jacob', the writer of the Fifty-first Psalm begins his plea by crying, 'Have *chen* upon me, O God' (51^1; cf. 57^1), and Moses speaks of 'asking *chen* of the LORD' (Dt 3^{23}). Similarly there are passages where men seek or find *'favour* in the eyes of' God or 'with' God—e.g. a passage of several verses tells how Moses 'found *favour* in (God's) eyes' (Ex 33$^{12-17}$ J), and Jeremiah declares that Israel 'found *favour* in the wilderness' (Jer 31^2). There are instances of the use of the adverbial noun in 'Doth Job serve God *for nought*?' (Job 1^9), and in 'ye shall be redeemed *without money*' (Is 52^3). There are repeated examples of a derivative noun (*techinnah*) under the rendering 'supplication'—e.g. in Solomon's Prayer (1 K 8$^{38-54}$), and in the Psalms (e.g. Ps 28$^{2, 6}$; cf. Jer 31^9). The word denotes a plea for an undeserved boon. The adjective 'gracious' (*13*) is not used except of God. It is frequent in the phrase 'merciful and gracious' (e.g. Ps 103^8; 145^8; Ex 34^6; Neh 9^{16}). Finally, while the terms do not themselves require the concept of 'covenant', there are passages where *the context* adds it—for instance in the High Priestly benediction (Nu 6^{25}), and in Ezra's prayer

(Ezr 9⁸⁻¹⁰). In one of the great chapters of the Covenant the prelude to the words 'I make a covenant' (Ex 34¹⁰ J; cf. vv. 1, 28) begins with the phrase 'merciful and *gracious*' (v. 6). There are two passages in Jeremiah, in one of which God repudiates *chen* to His covenanted people (16¹⁻¹³), and in the other promises the renewal of *chen* to the true Israel that is to be (31¹⁻⁹). These two passages illustrate what is everywhere implicit—that it is to the righteous or to sinners who are now prepared to be righteous that God shows *chen*. In the great majority of cases *chen* is shown to individuals (or groups of individuals), and not to the nation Israel. Its characteristic notion is a *personal* 'favour'. No man, of course, shows *chen* to God, for none can do Him a favour.

The next term in the New Testament list is *eleos*, 'mercy', the regular rendering in LXX of the Hebrew word *chesed*. For this word, however, *eleos* is quite inadequate. In English 'loving-kindness' is the nearest equivalent, but, as no English word expresses the exact meaning, the Hebrew term will be transliterated here. It is the noun from the root *chsd* (*275*), and occurs about two hundred and fifty times. The experts differ about the origin of the root, some referring it to the 'kindly' temper of those of the same kin, and some to a Semitic root meaning 'desire'. In its use, as distinct from its origin, both ideas are usually present, though, while there is *chesed* between those of the same kin, the temper that it denotes sometimes spreads to others. As it has been argued that the *chesed* of God always means His 'covenant love' to Israel, it will be helpful first to examine briefly the range of the concept of 'the *chesed* of *man*'. Here it is sometimes used in connexion with human *covenant* (made, of course, before God)—notably of that between David and Jonathan, which may itself be called 'the *chesed* of God' (1 S 20⁸ᐧ ¹⁴ᶠ; 2 S 9¹ᐧ ³ᐧ ⁷). Covenant, of course, implies oath, and even when the word is used of a promise given under oath to a *Gentile*—for instance, the promise of the two spies to Rahab (Jos 2¹²; cf. Gn 21²³ E), or of the behaviour of David to an allied nation (2 S 10²)—it may be argued that covenant of some kind is implied. But there are a number of passages about the *chesed* shown by one Hebrew to another where this does not seem to be so. For instance, a friend may show *chesed* to a friend (2 S 16¹⁷; Job 6¹⁴), or a mistress to her household (Pr 31²⁶). Here there is neither oath nor covenant. *Chesed*, again, marks the 'desirable' kind of man (Pr 19²²), and it is the temper of a true king (Pr

20²⁸). While the wicked show no *chesed* to the poor (Ps 109¹⁶), a blow from the righteous may be *chesed* (Ps 141⁵), and God requires that men shall practise *chesed* with each other (Mic 6⁸; Hos 4¹; Zec 7⁹). It may, of course, be suggested that when the dealings of Hebrew with Hebrew are in question, the idea that they are both in the same covenant with God is always in the background, but some of the passages named hardly require this implication, and the word can be used of the treatment of *Gentiles* without any mention of oath (Jg 1²⁴), and *Gentiles themselves* may practise *chesed* (Est 2⁹, ¹⁷; Dn 1⁹). In one passage it is compared to flowers and seems to be used of the 'kindliness' that binds men together in any true 'civilization' (Is 40⁶). It seems clear therefore, that, while covenant between men implies *chesed*, *chesed*, when shown by man to man, does not necessarily imply covenant—i.e. the concept of *chesed* is wider than that of covenant.

Is the meaning the same when the word *chesed* refers to God, or is it then confined to 'covenant love'? As with the other words examined here, in the great majority of instances the reference undoubtedly is to God's relation to *Israel* or an *Israelite*, for 'God and Israel' is the main topic of the Old Testament. There are a number of passages where the 'covenant' with Israel is mentioned in the same context as *chesed* (e.g. Dt 7⁹, ¹²; 1 K 8²³; Mic 7²⁰; Neh 1⁶; Ps 103¹⁷), but these are not numerous; usually the idea of covenant, even when undoubtedly present, is *implied* (e.g. Ex 20⁶). But under other terms than *chesed* it is the *context* that implies covenant, and not the terms *per se*. Examples occur in texts quoted later under *ahabah*, 'love'. It is the same with 'truth', for instance, and 'faithfulness' and 'righteousness'. It does not follow that these terms refer *only* to 'covenant truth', 'covenant faithfulness', and so on. In Ps 25¹⁰ the text 'all the paths of the LORD are *chesed* and truth unto such as keep his covenant and his testimonies' shows how the *context* may relate 'truth' to 'covenant'; may it not be the same with *chesed*? Again, there is a passage in Job which speaks of the *chesed* of the rain (Job 37¹³), and this, of course, was not limited to Israel. The text might be related to the covenant with Noah (Gn 9⁸⁻¹⁷ P; cf. 8²⁰ J), but the suggestion now under discussion is that *chesed* always means God's 'covenant love' to *Israel*. It seems to follow from these instances taken together that when the *chesed* of God is named, it does not mean 'God's covenant love to Israel', though 'covenant' always implies *chesed*.

Under *chesed* certain *phenomena* occur which are repeated under other terms. While there are early passages where God shows *chesed* to Israel, merely *qua* Israel, as in the Song of Moses (Ex 15^{13}), there is nearly always some reference to righteousness or its equivalent in the context. For instance, in a passage describing the ancient '*chasādim* of the LORD', Trito-Isaiah suggests that God had set Himself to bless the Children of Israel because He took them to be 'children that will not deal falsely' (Is 63$^{7-19}$). In such Psalms as 89, which begins 'I will sing of the *chasadim* of the LORD for ever', and the Shepherd Psalm, which ends, 'Surely goodness and *chesed* shall follow me all the days of my life', the writers are plainly faithful Hebrews, though they do not say so (Ps 89^1; 23^6). Under the Temple refrain 'For his *chesed* endureth for ever' (Ps 136, etc.) there is the postulate that the worshippers are loyal. In a few passages, however, God's *chesed* continues even to the *sinful*. For instance, this is promised to the House of David even if it sins (2 S 7^{15}; Ps 18^{50}). Similarly, when Deutero-Isaiah compares God's promise of *chesed* to Israel to His pledge to Noah, it is implied that His *chesed* will continue whatever men do (Is 54$^{5-10}$; cf. Jer 31^3). These passages are important because they are Old Testament anticipations of New Testament teaching, but they are few and far between. The prevalent idea, at any rate after the Prophets had proclaimed the righteousness of the one God, is that He shows *chesed* to the righteous (or, occasionally, to penitents, who long to be righteous—Ps 6^4; 25^7; 51^1; 130^7). While, however, the use of *chesed* is largely parallel to that of other terms, it has its own distinction. It occurs frequently on the lips of the 'poor', the 'distressed', 'the afflicted'. While this use of the term was ancient (cf. Gn 39^{21} J), it became common in the days when Israel had lost its independence and forlorn Hebrews were multitudinous. For instance, the whole of Chapter 3 of Lamentations centres in the cry: 'It is of the LORD's *chasadim* that we are not consumed, because his compassions fail not' (v. 22). In the Psalms, when 'the poor' speak *for themselves* to God, there are passages where they praise Him because He has shown His *chesed* to them—for instance, 'I will be glad and rejoice in thy *chesed*; For thou hast seen my affliction; Thou hast known the adversities of my soul' (Ps 31^7; cf. 59^{16}; Jer 31^3). Again, there are passages where 'the poor' confidently await the *chesed* of God—e.g. the writer of Psalm 130, beginning 'Out of the depths have I cried unto thee', rises to the sure and certain cry 'O Israel, hope in the

LORD; For with the LORD there is *chesed*' (v. 7; cf. Ps 32^{10}; 86^5). There are also passages where the suffering 'poor' *plead* with God for the *chesed* that He has promised to the righteous—for instance, 'I trusted in thee, O LORD; I said, Thou art my God. My times are in thy hand . . . Save me in thy *chesed*' (Ps 31$^{14\text{ff}}$; cf. 44^{26}). Indeed sometimes the plea almost rises to reproach—'Is his *chesed* clean gone for ever?' (Ps 77^8). Yet the ruling idea is not that the righteous have themselves an intrinsic claim to *chesed* but that it is *God's* nature to bless the faithful for this in the way of a true King—'Thou, LORD, art good, and ready to forgive, And plenteous in *chesed* unto all them that call upon thee' (Ps 86^5).

Chesed is used once by Jeremiah to denote Israel's *chesed to God*— 'Thus saith the LORD, I remember for thee the *chesed* of thy youth, the love of thine espousals; how, thou wentest after me in the wilderness' (Jer 2^2). The passage bases on the *chesed* of a bride to her husband. There seem to be two other Prophetic texts where Israel's *chesed* to God is named (Hos 6$^{4,\ 6}$; Is 57^1). In later days the plural was used of a faithful Hebrew's 'good deeds' toward God (Neh 13^{14}; 2 Ch 32^{32}, etc.). These passages are enough to show that the rendering 'mercy' only denotes one particular aspect of the exercise of *chesed*, for men cannot show mercy to God. It also brings us to the term *chāsīd* (*30*) Most experts hold that this term denotes one who exercises *chesed* toward God rather than one who receives it from Him. For instance, the ostrich is not *chasid*, for she forsakes her eggs (Job 34^{13}). *Chasid* is used twice to describe God Himself (Jer 3^{12}; Ps 145^{17}). The first of these texts runs: 'I am *chasid*, saith the LORD, I will not keep anger for ever.' Probably the term *implies* mutual *chesed*. It generally denotes the faithful Hebrew, the rendering *hosios*, 'saint' (*19*) being usual (e.g. Ps 4^3, 145^{17}). A 'saint' shows *chesed* to God because he has received it from God. Perhaps the English terms 'liege-lord' and 'liege-man' come nearest to expressing the idea. Just as the Hebrew was bidden to '*love* the LORD (his) God', so he ought to show Him *chesed*. Micah declares that 'the *chasid* is perished out of the earth' (7^2), but the term is almost confined to the Psalms. It occurs there in the singular—for instance, in the phrases 'Know ye that the LORD hath set apart the *chasid* for himself' (Ps 4^3), and 'Preserve my soul, for I am *chasid*' (Ps 86^2)—but the prevalent use is plural and makes 'the saints' (*chasidim*) synonymous with 'the righteous'. The phrases 'thy *chasidim*', 'my *chasidim*' and 'his *chasidim*', all meaning 'God's *chasidim*', are more frequent than '*the* chasidim'.

The ruling ideas are that the liege LORD cares for his *chasidim* (e.g. Ps 37[28], 97[10]), and that his liege-men exult in Him (e.g. Ps 30[4], 149[5]). He and they are loyal to each other. Clearly all this could be related to God's covenant with Israel, but, whether the writers thought of it or not, the idea itself is intrinsically wider. It describes righteousness on its spiritual side. In Maccabean times, however, the phrase 'the *Chasidim*' became the name of those among the followers of Mattathias and his sons who were loyal at all costs to the whole 'law', ritual as well as moral (e.g. 1 Mac 2[42]). This means that the intrinsically universalist concept of this term, as of others, was not developed. Here, as often, the New Testament is the true heir of the nobler side of Old Testament teaching. In the Old Testament the *dominant* idea is that God shows *chesed* to the faithful Hebrew.

Eleos, and with it *oiktirmos*, 'compassion', are the normal renderings of the Hebrew word *rachamim* in LXX. For it they are the right renderings. When God is said to show a man *chesed*, the idea, of course, is that the Great is dealing with the small. But when one man is said to show love or *chesed* to another man, an equal might be dealing with an equal. It is different with *rachamim*, for under it, even when two *men* are in question, one of them is in some way 'superior' to the other. While *rachamim* derives from a term meaning 'womb' and is used about thirty-five times in this physical sense, its root (*rchm*) is used over a hundred times to denote 'mercy' or 'pity'. Its verb (*50*), noun (*40*) and adjective (*13*), are all found. There are a very few passages where 'pity' runs from man to man—e.g. 'All day long (the righteous) dealeth *pitifully* and lendeth' (Ps 37[26]; cf. Pr 12[10]; Jer 6[23])—but the overwhelming majority of the texts speak of 'pity' of *God* for men. The physical origin of the word is well shown in 'Where is thy zeal and thy mighty acts? The yearning of thy bowels and thy *mercies* are restrained toward me' (Is 63[15]). The 'mercies of the LORD' are 'many' (2 S 24[14]); 'mercy' is sometimes related to 'covenant' (e.g. Dt 4[31]); it is opposed to 'anger' (e.g. Dt 13[17]; Jer 13[14]); it is frequently put alongside *chesed* (e.g. Ex 33[19] J; Hos 2[19]; Ps 116[5]); God shows mercy to the righteous and the penitent (e.g. Ps 25[6], 51[1]; Hos 2[1]; cf. 1[6]). Two or three great texts will suffice to show the depth and wonder of the mercy of God—'The LORD, the LORD, a God full of compassion and gracious, slow to anger, and plenteous in *mercy* and truth'

(Ex 34⁶ J); 'Sing, O heavens; and be joyful, O earth; and break forth into singing, O mountains, for the LORD hath comforted his people, and will have *pity* upon his afflicted' (Is 49¹³); 'Like as a father pitieth his children, So the LORD *pitieth* them that fear him' (Ps 103¹³).

The next word in the New Testament series is 'forgiveness'. In both Testaments one of the marks of the Forgiveness of God is that He will forgive the wicked if only they will repent. There is no other condition. As a Psalmist puts it, God is 'ready to forgive' (Ps 86⁵). Here there are three principal Hebrew roots. The first of these (*slch*, *50*) is always used of *God's* forgiveness. There are several examples in the Deuteronomic prayer put upon the lips of Solomon (1 K 8³⁰·⁹); God forgives the 'murmurings' of Israel in the Wilderness on the intercession of Moses (Nu 14²⁰ J); there is a good example of the connexion between repentance and pardon in the text beginning 'Let the wicked forsake his way' (Is 55⁷). In Jeremiah, God, having failed to find one righteous man in Jerusalem, cries out 'How can I forgive thee?' (Jer 5¹·⁷), but a Psalmist rejoices in a God 'who forgiveth all (his) iniquities' (Ps 103³). The noun 'forgiveness' occurs once—'But there is forgiveness with thee, That thou mayest be feared' (Ps 13⁴). The second root (*ns'*, *655*) has a great many meanings, but its use for 'forgive' or 'pardon' is not frequent (*23*). Its original meaning is 'to carry', and it may be used either of an unforgiven man who must 'bear his iniquity' (e.g. Lv 5¹; Ezk 14¹⁰), or of a man who forgives another by 'lifting off' or/and 'bearing away' the burden of the wrong that the latter has done him (e.g. Gn 50¹⁷ E; Ex 10¹⁷ J). The word is used of the so-called 'scape-goat' when it 'carries away' the sin of Israel to Azazel (Lv 16²²), and of the Servant of the LORD who 'bare the sin of many'—both carrying it and carrying it away. Under this term, therefore, God 'forgives' sin by taking its burden off the shoulders of the sinner. At the crisis of the Golden Calf Moses makes a plea that is urgent because it is unfinished—'If thou wilt forgive their sin' (Ex 32³² E); one of the phrases that describes the character of the LORD in a passage already quoted runs, 'forgiving iniquity, transgression and sin' (Ex 34⁷ J); Micah, opposing forgiveness to anger, cries, 'Who is a God like unto thee, that pardoneth iniquity?' (Mic 7¹⁸); and a Psalmist exclaims, 'O the happiness of the man whose transgression is forgiven' (Ps 32¹). The third relevant Hebrew term is *kipper* (literally 'to cover' or perhaps to 'wipe away'). It varies in meaning between 'propitiation' and 'forgiveness'. This requires extended investigation, but this is best taken in the next chapter under the renderings of the word in LXX. Meanwhile, two points may be mentioned about the meaning of 'forgiveness'. First, it does not necessarily imply that the forgiven man escapes punishment. Indeed, some of the passages quoted require that God has *already* punished him—for instance, Micah bases his belief in forgiveness on the conviction that God 'retaineth not his anger for ever' (Mic 7[18]); Deutero-Isaiah declares that God 'will abundantly pardon' (Is 55[7]) people who had already suffered in Exile; and the Psalmist last quoted cries, 'Day and night thy hand was heavy upon me' (Ps 32[4]). Indeed, another Psalmist says roundly, 'Thou wast a God that forgavest (*slch*) them (Israel in the Desert), Though thou inflictest retribution for their doings' (Ps 99[8]). Again, punishment may be mitigated, not altogether annulled (Nu 14[11ff] JE). The best analogy is, once more, with Eastern monarchs. The Pharaoh, for instance, 'restored the chief butler unto his butlership again' (Gn 40[21] E) after punishment. But, second, 'forgiveness', as this parallel shows, did mean that the forgiven man was restored to the service of God and to fellowship with Him. For instance, in the text, 'There is forgiveness with thee That thou mayest be feared' (Ps 130[4]), the word 'fear', as often, means worship and reverence and service and such degree of fellowship as a true Hebrew knew with the LORD. Of course, there are notable texts that describe forgiveness which do not fall under the three terms here discussed (e.g. Mic 7[19]; Ps 79[8], 103[12]), but the list of passages is already long enough.

For 'salvation' there are four leading Hebrew words. By far the most frequent is the verb *yasha‛*, 'save', with its nouns *yesha‛* and *yeshū‛ah*, 'salvation', which occur well over three hundred times. The underlying idea is that a man who has been beset by enemies or troubles is 'set at large', i.e. the words look both backwards and forwards. In early songs, for instance, the words are used for God's 'victories' on behalf of Israel (Ex 15[2]; Dt 33[29]). It may be that here the idea is that the LORD saves Israel merely because He has chosen her to be His people, without any ethical reference at all, but this use is very rare. In the vast majority of texts the words 'save' and 'salvation' are related in some way to Israel's sin or righteousness. Here three different concepts dominate in turn, and a fourth finally emerges. The first is that God punishes His people when they sin, but, having so punished, 'saves' them by giving them another opportunity to be righteous and so to prosper. The idea is sufficiently illustrated by 'the Deuteronomic framework' of the Book of Judges. Here the uniform teaching is—If Israel sins, God gives her enemies victory over her and so she suffers punishment; when the period of punishment is over, God gives Israel victory, and so 'saves' her; unhappily she goes on to sin again, and is again punished (Jg 2^{11-23}, 3^{7-11}, 4^{1-3}, etc.). In Judges God 'saves' her time after time by raising up 'mighty men of valour' to be her 'saviours' (Jg $3^{9, 15}$), but fundamentally He is Himself the 'saviour'.

The second and third concepts draw out further the teaching that underlies the first. Under the second the ruling idea is that, if and when Israel is righteous, God will 'save' her from all troubles and give her prosperity. Here the 'leading instance' is the message of Deutero-Isaiah. He preaches to those of the exiles in Babylon who have been staunch throughout the Exile; he declares that Israel has more than expiated her past sin (Is 40^2); he admits, in effect, that the sufferings of the faithful in the Exile are a mystery (e.g. 40^{27}); but he declares that *now* God will show His righteousness by 'saving' them. Beside Him there is no 'saviour' (43^{11}), but for them He is Saviour indeed. In several passages 'righteousness' and 'salvation' go together. The heavens are to 'pour down righteousness' and the earth is thereby to yield the harvest of 'salvation' (45^8); since God is 'righteous', He will 'save' the loyal (51^5); since He 'reigns', the heralds will speed to Zion with the good news of 'salvation' ($52^{7, 10}$); for the faithful remnant this is a 'day of salvation' (49^8). There are parallel texts in Trito-Isaiah (e.g. 60^{18}, 61^{10}, 62^{11}).

The third concept is best illustrated from the Psalms of the Chasidim. Here it is *individual* salvation that is in question. On the one hand, the ruling idea is that, if a man is righteous, the righteous God will save him from enemies and troubles and bless him with prosperity, and, on the other, that this rule has many exceptions. In one Psalm God Himself defines the *chasid* and pledges Himself to 'show him salvation' (Ps 91^{14-16}). In another the writer, having defined a righteous man, declares, 'He shall receive a blessing from the LORD, And righteousness from the God of his salvation' (Ps 24$^{3\cdot 6}$). Here 'righteousness' clearly includes prosperity. In another a *chasid*, who has been nigh unto death and 'saved' from it, declares, 'I will take the cup of salvation and call upon the name of the LORD' (116$^{3,\ 6,\ 13}$). One singer is fearless, whatever betide, because 'The LORD is my light and my salvation' (27^1), and another testifies, 'This poor man cried, and the LORD heard him, And saved him out of all his troubles' (34^6). More often, however, it is the *chasid*, who is still beset by enemies or troubles, who cries unto God to 'save' him. This is the burden of a whole Psalm which begins 'O LORD, the God of my salvation' (88^1). Another Psalmist, persecuted by 'enemies', cries out 'I trusted in thee, O LORD, . . . save me in thy loving kindness' (31$^{14\cdot 16}$). Yet another, an old man now, beginning, 'Bow down thine ear unto me and save me' (71^2), pours out his plea for God's speedy help (v. 12) through thirteen verses before he goes on to declare his indomitable 'hope' in God. In all such Psalms the plea of the *chasid* is not so much 'Save me because *I* am righteous', as 'Save me because *Thou* art righteous and hast given a pledge to the righteous!' It is under this concept that the few Old Testament passages fall which teach salvation *after death* (without the word 'save'.) There came a time when Hebrews began to believe that dismal Sheol could not be God's last word for His *chasidim*, and that they would rise from the dead. This belief perhaps appears in Ps 16^{10}, more probably in Ps 49^{14f}, and certainly in two Apocalyptic texts (Is 26^{19}; Dn 12^2). For a dead *chasid* there is to be 'salvation by resurrection'. This subject will be fully examined in *The Bible Doctrine of the Hereafter*.

None of these three concepts teaches salvation *from sin*, though the idea of salvation from the *consequences* of sin is found, in one way or another, in them all. Under the Deuteronomic concept the people Israel is saved from the punishment that is the consequence of sin when she has for a number of years suffered for her sins. Here the idea is societary. In Deutero-Isaiah the people Israel has more than paid the price of her sins (40^2)—that is, suffered its consequences—and, as part of Israel, the faithful Israelites have suffered too, but now the faithful are to be saved from these consequences. Here individualism emerges, for each exile decided for himself whether he would be faithful. Under the third concept, which is wholly individualist, one of the underlying ideas is that the *chasid* is suffering the consequences of sins though he has not himself committed them. The fourth and most important Hebrew concept is that God saves men from *sin itself*. The first two passages where this concept clearly emerges, illustrate the idea, though the term itself is missing. The first is the story of the Call of Isaiah (Is 6¹⁻⁸). No doubt the young Isaiah was one of the best men in Jerusalem, but, when he 'sees the LORD' he is overwhelmed with the sense of his sinfulness, and, protesting that he is unfit to be a Prophet, cries, 'I am a man of unclean lips,' meaning, 'How can I use unclean lips to speak for God?' Then God, through one of the Seraphim, burns his lips pure—'Lo, this hath touched thy lips, and thine iniquity is taken away, and thy sin purged' (cf. 27⁹). The whole man is cleansed from sin, not his lips only. The word rendered 'purged' is *kipper*. At this point there is no need to discuss the vexed question of its origin and meaning, for the whole Vision shows, that, whatever else the word means, there is cleansing from sin. Among the Hebrews, of course, the arts of smelting and refining were both practised, and in both fire purifies and cleanses. Malachi uses the word 'refine' (*zaqaq*) to denote the 'purifying' and saving of the Sons of Levi (Mal 3³). In Isaiah the rendering of *kipper* by 'purge' best expresses the meaning of the passage. Jeremiah too teaches that God will 'cleanse' from sin men who 'call unto' Him (33³, ⁸), but his chief passage is his prophecy of the New Covenant (31³¹⁻⁴). In it the implicit teaching is that when God has written His 'law' on each Hebrew's heart, the latter will give up sinning—that is, he teaches that God will save men from *future sin*. Ezekiel has both ideas in a single passage (36²⁵⁻⁸). God will 'pour out clean water upon' sinners like a torrent, and so save them from all the uncleannesses of the past (cf. 37²³). He will also 'put (his) spirit within (them)' and 'give (them) a new heart' and 'a new spirit', so that they will walk in (his) statutes and keep (his) judgements' —i.e. give up sinning. The context depicts the prosperity that is integral to 'salvation'. These passages from Jeremiah and Ezekiel will be treated more at length later. Though the word 'salvation' does not occur in the last of 'The Songs of the Servant' (Is 52¹³-53¹²), it is the climax of the doctrine of 'salvation from sin'. As the present writer thinks, it is the 'kings' of the Gentiles (52¹⁵) who, standing for their peoples, describe the Servant and what he has done for them in the first nine verses of Chapter 53, but, whoever the speakers are, they confess with amazement that he has vicariously 'borne (their) griefs', 'carried (their) sorrows'—that he was 'wounded for their transgressions', 'bruised for (their) iniquities', and bore the lash that they might have 'peace' and be 'healed'. This 'peace' and 'healing' are salvation from past sin. When God speaks (v. 12) He declares that the Servant has 'made many righteous'—that is, they will not sin in future. There are texts in the Psalter. For instance, a Psalmist says, 'Help us, O God of our salvation, for the glory of thy name, And deliver us, and *purge* away (*kipper*) our sins, for thy name's sake' (Ps 79^9; cf. 65^3), and there are texts where a *chasid*, instead of protesting that he is righteous, admits his sin, as in 'O God, thou knowest my foolishness: And my guiltinesses are not hid from thee, . . . Answer me in the truth of thy salvation' (69$^{5, 13}$), and in 'Turn to us, O God of our salvation, and cause thine indignation towards us to cease, . . . grant us thy salvation. . . . He will speak peace unto his people and to his *saints*; But let them not turn again to folly' (85$^{4, 7f}$). The great example is Psalm 51, which recurs below. Here a man who knows that he has sinned from birth (v. 5), cries out 'O God, thou God of my salvation' (v. 14), 'Wash me throughly from mine iniquity, And cleanse me from my sin. . . . Purge me with hyssop and I shall be clean, Wash me and I shall be whiter than snow' (vv. 2, 7). The phrase 'purge me with hyssop' probably refers to the ritual under which lepers were cleansed (Lv 14$^{4-7}$), the word for 'purge' denoting 'sin' and meaning 'un-sin'. All this refers to salvation from past sin and from sinfulness (vv. 5f), but the concept of salvation from future sinning is there too—'Create in me a clean heart, O God, And renew a stedfast spirit within me' (v. 10). It is clear that, at any rate from the time of the great Prophets of Righteousness onwards, there emerged a doctrine, not merely of salvation from the consequences of sin, but from sin itself.

Under the three other Hebrew words that denote 'salvation', there are many examples of the meaning 'save from troubles', sometimes regarded as the consequences of sin, but few under the concept 'save from sin itself'. The most frequent of the three verbs is a form from the root *ntsl* (*212*), which may be rendered 'deliver', the original meaning being 'to snatch away' as in the phrase 'a brand plucked out of the burning' or 'fire' (Am 4^{11}; Zec 3^2). Here, at most, there are only four texts that denote 'salvation from sin'. Two of these belong to Psalms already quoted under *yasha'*—one of them (79^9) setting 'deliver' alongside 'purge' (*kipper*) and the other running, 'Deliver me from blood-guiltiness, O God, thou God of my salvation' (51^{14}). A third

Psalmist prays, 'Deliver me from all my transgressions' (39⁸), and the 'supplication' of a fourth, who has 'gone away like a lost sheep', runs 'Deliver me according to thy word' (119¹⁷⁰, ¹⁷⁶). The second word is *padah* with its cognates (*72*). Here the original idea is 'to pay a price (whether in money or kind) in exchange' (e.g. Ex 13¹³, 20⁸; Nu 3⁴⁶⁻⁵¹). Attention is fixed, however, on what is acquired in exchange, rather than on what is given. For instance, when 'the people ransomed Jonathan' from death, the price paid is not mentioned (1 S 14⁴⁵). It is this emphasis that justifies the rendering 'ransom'. In the majority of texts it is God who 'ransoms'. Here the idea of a price paid is quite in the background, if it is there at all—though there is an exception in the ironical phrase, 'Zion shall be ransomed with judgement' (Is 1²⁷). The prayer, 'Ransom Israel, O God, out of all his *troubles*' (Ps 25²²), expresses the dominant idea. It has three main illustrations—God ransoms such righteous men as Abraham and David and the *chasid* in time of need (Is 29²²; 2 S 4⁹; Ps 31⁵); the suffering *chasid* pleads with God to 'ransom' him (Ps 26¹¹); God will 'ransom' from trouble those who repent of their sin (Jer 15¹⁹⁻²¹; cf. Hos 7¹³). Probably in the difficult text Hosea 13¹⁴, the Prophet means 'If only the Ephraimites will repent, I will ransom them from the death that is at the door'. There is only one passage where *padah* is used with the meaning 'ransom *from sin*'—'O Israel, hope in the LORD, For with the LORD there is *chesed*, And with him is plenteous ransom, And he shall ransom Israel from all his iniquities' (Ps 130⁷ᶠ)—and even here the meaning may be 'ransom from the *consequences* of sin'. The third verb is *ga'al* (*120*), 'to do the part of a kinsman', a participle, *go'ēl*, being used as a noun meaning 'kinsman'. As there is no English verb 'to bekin', 'redeem' has to be used. It was the part of one kinsman to 'stand by' another, alive or dead—for instance, a true '*go'el*' would ransom his kinsman from slavery (Lv 25²⁷ᶠᶠ), and, as the Book of Ruth shows, if a kinsman died childless, a true '*go'el*' would marry his widow and 'raise up seed' to him. While the belief that God is the Goel of faithful Israel and the faithful Israelite has examples in several parts of the Old Testament (e.g. Gn 48¹⁶; Jer 50²⁰, ³⁴; Job 19²⁵; Ps 69¹⁸; Pr 23¹¹), this is a favourite term in Isaiah 40-66, where it, or a cognate, occurs twenty-three times. In Deutero-Isaiah the belief that the LORD is 'the Goel of Israel' is the glowing theme of more than one oracle. For instance, the passage from 41¹⁸ to 43¹³ is addressed to the loyal remnant in Babylon. It is the true Israel, for it is the 'servant of the LORD'—i.e. it does His will (42^{19}). The faithful exiles are very slow to believe the good news of the Prophet (42^{18-20}), for they, with the rest of the exiles, have been suffering the punishment of their sins (42^{21-5}) and see no sign of anything better, 'but now' God will show Himself their Goel and give then an unprecedented deliverance (43^{1-13}). Similarly, in 44^{6-23}, the great Goel declares that 'beside (him) there is no god' (vv. 6-8), ridicules the seemingly mighty idols of Babylon (vv. 9-20), and calls on His 'servant Israel' to break out into joy because 'the LORD hath redeemed Jacob' (vv. 21-3). There are shorter oracles with the same burden in Trito-Isaiah (56^{20f}, 62^{10-12}). In the first there comes a Goel to those who 'turn from transgression', and He makes with them a covenant of the Spirit, which is to be everlasting. In the second 'the holy people, the redeemed of the LORD', returning to Jerusalem, throng its gates with a tumult of joy. The concept of 'the covenant of the Spirit' is probably derived from Ezekiel's greatest oracle, examined below. As shown there, it involves the doctrine of salvation from sin itself. In Deutero-Isaiah the leading idea under Sin comes out in two texts— 'I, even I, am he that blotteth out thy transgressions for mine own sake; and I will not remember thy sins' (43^{25}); 'I have blotted out as a thick cloud, thy transgressions, and, as a cloud, thy sins: return unto me, for I have redeemed thee' (44^{22}). The word 'blot out' means that God will forget the sins of the past and that therefore the new Israel will escape any further *consequences* of these sins. The constant series of ideas in Deutero-Isaiah is—There is now a true Israel—that is, a faithful Servant of the LORD; God forgives her past sins; the great Goel leads her back in joy to her beloved city and land. There is no such word as 'cleanse' or 'purge'. The leading concept, under *ga'al* as under the other terms, is 'salvation from the consequences of sin', not 'salvation from sin itself'. There is a passage in Deutero-Isaiah, as already seen, that clearly teaches the latter, but it does not fall in the Oracles of the Goel, but in the last 'Servant Song' under the phrase, 'My righteous Servant shall make many righteous' (53^{11}). The conclusion of the examination of terms is that, so far as *they* go, there are only a few scattered texts that teach salvation from sin itself, which is the focal doctrine of the New Testament. There are, however, three Old Testament passages that, while they do not use the terms, not only require the idea, but make it crucial, and so anticipate the New Testament. Their subject is 'the new creation', which is the next in the series of ideas.

Before this is taken a question that arises under both forgiveness and salvation needs to be asked. Are they the monopoly of Israel or may penitent Gentiles too be forgiven and saved? The great majority of the passages under 'forgive' and 'save', being addressed to Israel, naturally ignore the Gentiles, but there is more than this. There were two phases in Hebrew thought about the Gentiles. Broadly speaking, before the rise of the written Prophets the current concept was that the Gentile neighbours of Israel were enemies of the LORD just in so far as they were His people's enemies, no question of their righteousness or wickedness or penitence arising, but, after the Prophets had established the belief that there is only one God and that He is righteous, this gave way to the belief that *all* Gentiles are sinners, if only because they are idolaters, and therefore all will at length be punished. But what if Gentiles repented? Would God then forgive, spare and save *them*? Probably the question never occurred to the ordinary Hebrew. He believed that the Gentiles were irretrievably sinners, and that therefore God would at last inevitably punish them. This belief was not unwelcome in the days when Israel had suffered oppression under one Gentile empire after another for centuries. It was a 'natural' attitude. But there were a few men who believed that the time would come when the wicked Gentiles would repent, and not only repent, but turn to the one true God. When this came to pass, He would forgive and save them. In the earlier part of the present Book of Isaiah there are two oracles which, whether pre-exilic or not, rejoice in this belief ($2^{2\text{-}4}$, $19^{19\text{-}25}$; cf. 11^9). In later days the author of Jonah taught that, if Nineveh herself, the capital of the hated Assyrian oppressor, repented, God would pity and spare her (Jon 4^{11}). In two of the Servant Songs God declares that He is sending the Servant to be 'a light to the Gentiles' (Is 42^6, 49^6), and, on one interpretation of the last and greatest Song, which the writer accepts, God so longs to forgive and save 'many nations' that He commissions the Servant to suffer and die for them (52^{13}-53^{12}). Behind all these universalist passages there is the glow of joy. The mass of the Jews, however, while they were now universalist under the doctrine of God, were particularist under the doctrine of man.

For the next New Testament concept—that when a bad man

becomes a good man there is a 'new creation' or 'new birth'—there is no Hebrew term, for the idea was not current in Hebrew thought. On the contrary, it is almost everywhere assumed that for a bad man to become a good man it is enough that he repent and set himself to be good. Even under the words 'cleanse' and 'purge' it is the past that is undone, not the future that is secured. Yet there are three great exceptions to the assumption that a man can be righteous if he will—one in Jeremiah, one in Ezekiel, and one in the Psalm 51. All these teach 'a new creation'.

The first passage is Jeremiah's prophecy of the New Covenant (31^{31-4}). In it a Hebrew writer sees that, if Israel is to be God's true people, it is necessary that in *every individual* Israelite there should be a change of 'heart'. He also sees that only God can so 'write his law upon (a man's) heart' as to turn a bad man into a good man. For Jeremiah, God is so determined that Israel shall be His people (vv. 1, 33) that He will make this change in every Israelite's character. Through it every Israelite will 'know' Him, the word 'know' here describing the way in which one person knows another person. As is shown in Chapter 8 below this means that every Israelite will live in fellowship with God. There is no distinctive word in the passage for this 'change of character'. The significant terms are 'heart' and 'know'. Feeling, thought and will are all ascribed to the 'heart' in Hebrew psychology, as has been shown in *The Bible Doctrine of Man*, but the emphasis is on thought more than on feeling and on will rather than thought. The fundamental change is a change in the will. Every Israelite is to will what God wills. Then he will 'know' God. The Hebrew concept has none of the rather cold meaning of the English 'know'. An Englishman knows his acquaintances and may even know his enemies, but it is not in such ways that the Hebrews 'shall all know me, and (so) they shall be my people and I will be their God'. Here there is intimate fellowship. It is the consummation of forgiveness. And, of course, it is individual, for every man's 'heart', in the Hebrew sense, is just his own unique 'self'. Jeremiah did not know *how* God would make bad men into good men, but he saw that this was the *only* way to save sinners, and that God, being what He is, *must* therefore take it. This passage is a Pisgah for the New Testament.

The second passage is in Ezekiel (36^{22-8}; cf. 11^{19}). Here the later Prophet repeats Jeremiah but, as usual, adds his own significant idea. The passage is part of a longer one (vv. 16-36), and it has a prelude in a word rendered 'pity' (*chamal*), but more exactly this means 'spare' in compassion. Saul was not to 'spare' a single Amalekite (1 S 15³), but Pharaoh's daughter 'spared' the infant Moses (Ex 2⁶ E). Ezekiel had declared that at the Exodus 'none eye spared' the infant Israel (16⁵; cf. Jer 15⁵). In the present passage LXX renders by *pheidesthai*, the word that Paul uses when he declares that 'God spared not his own son' (Ro 8³²). God is going to 'spare' the sin-laden 'house of Israel', but He can only do this by giving every Israelite 'a new heart' and 'a new *spirit*'. It is the word 'spirit' (*ruach*) that is new. Its uses, both of the 'spirit' of man and the 'Spirit' of God were explored in *The Bible Doctrine of Man*. Only a note or two is made here. There are two other Old Testament passages where there is mention of the gift of the *ruach* of the LORD to *every* Israelite, but in them the immediate idea is that the prophetic *ecstasy* should come upon all (Nu 11²⁹ JE; Jl 2²⁸), though there is the implication that every Hebrew is to be a devotee of the LORD. Again, in Ezekiel's next chapter (37) he foretells the *resurrection* of the people Israel by the might of the *ruach* of God. The *differentia* of the passage in Chapter 36 is that there Ezekiel speaks of the Spirit of the LORD as *turning bad men into good men*. God does so by giving every Israelite what may be called either a 'new heart' or a 'new spirit'. Once more there is the phrase 'and (so) ye shall be my people and I will be your God'. Israel had had so 'stony' a 'heart' that she had been rejecting God and so committing the Sin of Sins. Now she is to have a 'heart of flesh', sensitive to the fellowship of God. It is in this passage that for the first time 'water' and 'spirit' go together. There is no question, of course, of *literal* water. Unfortunately the English Versions have 'I will *sprinkle* clean water upon you', perhaps following LXX, which here, and here only, renders the Hebrew word *zaraq* by *rainein*. The usual rendering *proschein* (*19*—e.g. Ezk 43¹⁸) gives the right idea, for the Hebrew word means 'pour (lavishly) upon'. Ezekiel, like Jeremiah, sees that the one way in which God can 'cleanse' and 'save' (Ezk 36²⁹) sinners is by purifying and re-making their 'hearts'. To these two passages a phrase may be added from the last of the Servant Songs—'My righteous servant shall *make many righteous*' (Isa 53¹¹).

The third passage is Psalm 51. In some ways it is parallel to the passages in Jeremiah and Ezekiel, particularly the latter. The writer speaks both of the 'spirit' of man and the 'Spirit' of God. He speaks of a man's 'heart' as a synonym for his 'spirit'. He uses the metaphor of water under the term 'wash' (vv. 2, 7), adding 'blot out' (vv. 1, 9). His key phrase, 'Create in me a clean heart, O God, and make anew (*chaddesh*, LXX *enkainizein*) a stedfast spirit within me', epitomizes the two Prophets' master concept. The term for 'create' is *bara'* (LXX *ktizein*), a word that always relates in some way to the actions of *God*. It does not mean 'to make out of nothing', but 'to make something old into something new'. There is a notable instance in Genesis 1[1f], where God makes an ordered universe out of a watery chaos. The Psalmist pleads that his unclean 'heart' may be made into a 'clean' one and his uncertain 'spirit' into a 'stedfast' one. This introduces the contrasts with the Prophets. They promise a new 'heart' to every Israelite in the *future*; the Psalmist pleads for a new heart for *himself now*. There is nothing more individualistic in the Bible. He was, no doubt, one of the best men in the world, for it is the saints who are most sensitive to sin. He had known the 'joy of salvation' (v. 12) and he had not been without God's 'holy spirit' (v. 11), but now he has discovered that outward sin roots in inward sinfulness, and, when he considers this, he sees that its subtle horror has pervaded his nature all his life long. With another Psalmist (130), the likest to him, he appeals 'out of the depths' to God's 'mercy' and 'lovingkindness' (v. 1). His psalm is the Old Testament counterpart of Romans 7—except that he did not know Christ. But can anyone doubt that his prayer was answered? Surely God 'blotted out (his) iniquities' from His book of remembrance (vv. 1, 9; cf. Ex 32[32f]; Is 43[25]).

The Psalm is remarkable also because it uses the phrase 'Thy *holy* Spirit'. This only occurs in one other passage in the Old Testament (Is 63[10f]). This is not because it was a new idea, for it would always be taken for granted that the *Ruach of the Lord* is 'holy'. The adjective is inserted in these two passages to denote that the Spirit of God can have nothing to do with sin—that is, they illustrate the fact that after the teaching of the Prophets from Amos onwards, the concept of 'holiness' inevitably included the concept of 'righteousness'. Trito-Isaiah, to whom the second text belongs, has his own account of the past history of Israel. First, from the days of Moses, Israel had for a while been God's 'holy people' (v. 18), and therefore His 'holy spirit' had led them safely through the Wilderness and 'caused them to rest in Canaan' (vv. 11, 14). But the people 'grieved (God's) holy spirit' by their sin (v. 10). Perhaps this refers to the 'sin of Jeroboam' that 'caused

Israel to sin', for after what the Prophet calls 'a little while' (v. 18) God 'was turned to be their enemy' (v. 10), sending them at last into exile. Now, though they have returned—and it was the faithful who returned, at any rate *wanting* to be 'holy' again—they are still in misery—so much so that God may be said thereby to be 'making them to err' and to be 'hardening their heart' (v. 17). The Prophet therefore pleads that God, being their 'Father', will once again show His 'compassion' in a new deliverance. In effect he pleads that God will no longer 'visit' His people with punishment for their past sins, but forgive and be bountiful once more. The Psalmist, on the other hand, pleads, not for a return of prosperity, but for a 'cleansed' heart. In the phrase, 'Take not thy holy spirit from me', he implies that this gift had been given him and had not yet altogether forsaken him. He asks that God will 'cleanse' him *inwardly* so thoroughly that he will be a new man (vv. 6-10). He believes that there may be an immediate answer to his urgent plea, and that, when it comes, being 'upheld by (God's) noble Spirit', he will be able to preach to other sinners out of this new experience (vv. 12f). This is just what happened to Paul.

For the next Greek term, *parakalein* and its cognates, the Hebrew term is *nacham* (*107*). The experts trace it back to a Semitic root that relates it to the breath. This root may, for instance, mean 'pant hard' or describe a 'sigh'. It is to the latter idea that *nacham* attaches itself, and 'rue' expresses the primary meaning of the Hebrew term. When used reflexively (*Niphal*) the word is often rendered 'repent', in the sense 'change one's mind'. For instance, God 'rues' or 'repents' that He has made man and determines to 'blot him out' (Gn 6^{6f} J); again, He 'rues' that He has chosen Saul to be king and rejects him (1 S 15^{11}; cf. Jer 18^{10}). More commonly, however, the meaning is that God, having 'turned from his wrath' (and forgiven), 'repents of the evil' that He was about to inflict or had been inflicting. There is an early instance of this (Ex 32$^{12, 14}$ E), but otherwise it seems to occur first in Amos (7$^{3, 6}$). In both cases the LORD 'repents' on the plea of a prophet (cf. Jer 42^{9f}). In other passages He declares that He will *not* 'repent of the evil' (Jer 4^{28}; Ezk 24^{14}; cf. Zec 8^{14}). In yet others men yearn that He will 'turn and repent' (Jl 2^{14}; Ps 90^{13}), or declare that He has done so (Ps 106^{45}; Jon 3^{9}). When God 'rues' in this sense, penitents pass from sorrow into joy—that is,

God 'comforts' them. There is change of feeling on *both* sides. Consequently 'console' or 'comfort' is the uniform meaning when the verb is *not reflexive but active*.[1] Of this use Jeremiah has a first instance—'I will turn their mourning into joy, and will *comfort* them, and make them rejoice from their sorrow' (31^{13}; cf. Ezk 14^{22f}), but it is Deutero-Isaiah who is the great exponent of the Comfort of God. His opening word 'Comfort ye' (40^1) is the key to his message. Others of his famous phrases fall here—'Sing, O heavens; and be joyful O earth; and break forth into singing, O mountains; for the LORD hath comforted his people' (49^{13}), 'I, even I, am he that comforteth you' (51^{12}), 'The LORD hath comforted his people; he hath redeemed Jerusalem' (52^9). There are further examples in other late parts of the book—'Though thou wast angry with me, thine anger is turned away and thou comfortest me' (12^1), 'The LORD hath anointed me . . . to comfort all that mourn . . .' (61^{1f}), 'As one whom his mother comforteth, so will I comfort you' (66^{13}). The historical background explains the term. Israel had sinned and had been punished through exile (40^2); Israel (or the part of Israel that counted now) had repented there; God had forgiven her; He now turns to bless her. He comforts her, not by soothing her but by helping her. When God 'comforts' He acts. The word is parallel, not only to 'pity' (Is 49^{13}) and 'gladden' (Jer 31^{13}), but also to 'redeem' (Is 52^9) and 'help' (Ps 86^{17}; cf. 71^{21}). No doubt such 'comfort' *ipso facto* consoles and encourages, but the dominant concept is effective 'help'. This comes out very clearly in some passages in the Psalms, where God is not 'comforting' sinners but *helpless* saints. In the most famous Psalm it is the Shepherd's weapons against wolves and robbers, His 'club and staff', that 'comfort' in the darkest valley (23^4; cf. 86^{17}, $119^{76, 82}$). It is unfortunate that there is now no English word that combines the ideas of 'consolation' and 'help'. At one time 'comfort' sometimes meant 'help' in English—e.g. in the phrase 'to comfort the king's enemies'— as its Latin origin suggests, but this use is lost.

The doctrine of the 'Blessing of God' comes next. With it there goes the correlative doctrine of the Blessedness (and Happiness)

---

[1] The active Hebrew forms are *Piel*, and therefore should denote an *intense* change in God's feelings toward men, but this may be an instance where *Piel* has the causative force of *Hiphil*, the meaning being that God's change from anger to mercy leads to a change in men from sorrow to joy. Whatever the grammar may be, the psychology is clear.

of the man whom God blesses. Here there are two sets of terms. The first (from the root *brk*) has a variety of uses. For example, the righteous often 'bless the LORD'—that is, praise Him for His benefits, with a certain warmth of heart in the praise. It is God's blessing of men, however, that is relevant here. This is spoken of over a hundred times. The use is rare in the Prophets but common in the Psalms. Psalm 67 is a good example. Here 'God shall bless us' (v. 7) is a warmer phrase than 'God shall prosper us' would have been. While God's blessing, when complete, includes prosperity (e.g. Dt 15$^{4-18}$), prosperity is not a synonym for 'blessing', for the wicked may prosper, but it is *only* 'the righteous' that the LORD doth bless (e.g. Ps 5^{12}). Psalmists cry out against the prosperity of the wicked, and even admit that God 'fills their belly with (his) treasure' (17^{14}), but no Old Testament writer ever calls a wicked man 'blessed'. The second set of words are from the root *'shr*. Here 'happy' is the best rendering. The significant term (*40*) from this root is a word that amounts to an interjection—for instance, '*How happy* the man' whose 'delight is in the law of the LORD!' (Ps 1^{1f})—i.e. it is the righteous who are truly 'happy'. Even in the phrase 'How happy shall he be that taketh and dasheth thy (Babylon's) little ones against the rock' (Ps 137^9) the writer thinks that he is describing a righteous act, as verses 7 and 8 show. Prosperity is a factor in complete happiness as the first Psalm shows (v. 3), yet, while those who neglect God may 'count the proud happy' (Mal 3^{15}), no old Testament writer does so. There are passages where it is not prosperity that is happiness but such a thing as forgiveness— 'How happy he whose transgression is forgiven!' (Ps 32^1). In effect, the man is 'happy' who is 'blessed'.

Shālōm, the Hebrew word for 'peace', is common (*237*) and has a very wide meaning. Its root (*shlm*) denotes 'completeness', and for the Hebrew 'peace' (*shālōm*) meant, not just the absence of war, but everything that serves a man's weal. The word was used, alike in greeting and farewell (e.g. Jg 6^{23}; Ex 4^{18}), to wish a man every kind of good. It could be used of a city's unlimited prosperity (e.g. Jer 33^9), of quiet after a thunder-storm (Ps 29^{11}), of the right kind of sleep or death (e.g. Ps 4^8; Gn 15^{15}), of the return of exiles (Is 55^{12}), as a definition of 'life' (Mal 2^5), of a priest's invocation of universal good (Nu 6^{26}), and so on. Perhaps the English word that comes nearest its scope is 'welfare'. It is a true king's business to serve his people's universal welfare—that is, to be 'Prince of Peace' (Is 9^6; cf. Ps 72$^{3,\ 7}$; Is 60^{17f}). In God's 'covenant of peace' the LORD undertakes to give Israel every good thing (e.g. Jer 16^5; Ezk 34^{25}; Is 54^{10}; Mal 2^5). To pray 'Peace be upon Israel' (e.g. Ps 125^5) is to invoke a blessing as wide as life. But the Prophets taught that, when Israel sinned and so broke covenant it was no use to cry 'Peace, peace', for there was no 'peace' (Jer 6^{14}; Ezk 13^{10}; cf. Is 48^{18}). When Israel 'rebelled', God 'turned to be their enemy' (Is 63^{10}), as a king is the enemy of a criminal. 'There is no peace, saith the LORD, unto the wicked' (Is 48^{22}). On the other hand, the Prophets also insist again and again that when Israel turns to righteousness God will spend upon her His universal bounty of 'peace' (e.g. Is 32^{17}; Jer 16^5, 29^{11}; Ezk 37^{26}; Is 26^3, 54^{13}; Hag 2^9; cf. Mal 2^6). Similarly, the Wise Man declares that 'all (wisdom's) paths are peace' (Pr 3^{17}), and one Psalmist depicts a glad meeting of 'righteousness and peace' (85^{10}), and another exclaims, 'Great peace have they that love thy law' (119^{165}). Other texts might be added from the Psalter (37$^{11,\ 37}$, 72$^{3,\ 7}$, 122^6, 125^5, 147^{14}). While the benedictions of 'peace' were conceived largely in terms of outward prosperity, there can be no doubt that to a devout Jew the Peace of God brought an inward bliss. In English we might say that men like Jeremiah and Job and the writer of Psalm 51 were not 'at peace with themselves', but the word does not occur in this way in the Old Testament. There all true peace is fundamentally 'peace with God'.

Finally, there is the Old Testament doctrine of the *Love* of God. As with a good many other doctrines, it is implicit long before the term, *'ahabah*, occurs. For instance, it was because of His love that God gave Adam and Eve a paradise to live in. None the less, the date of the emergence of the *term* is significant. The Hebrew root (*'hb, 240*) is almost always rendered 'love'. It is in Hosea that it first occurs of *God's* love. With him this is primarily God's love to the whole nation, Israel—'And the LORD said unto me, Go yet, love a woman beloved of (her) friend and an adulteress, even as the LORD loveth the children of Israel, though they turn unto other gods' (Hos 3^1). Here God has *chosen* a wife—i.e. He *wills* to love and chooses whom He will love. It is true that in a later passage the love of God for Israel is compared to a father's love for his child—'When Israel was a child, then I loved him, and called my son out of Egypt (11^1)—and that ordinarily fathers love their children without any need to choose to do so, but in the text quoted the idea is that God chose to *adopt* Israel (cf. Ex 4^{22}). The modern idea that one 'falls in love' willy-nilly is quite irrelevant. The first of three ideas found in Hosea is that God loves whom He will. The second is that God continues to love Israel even though she has sinned and sinned. Whether or not Hosea already knew that Gomer was an adulteress when he chose her for his wife, he went on loving her in her sin. The word 'love', indeed, does not appear here, but the idea is what makes the Prophet's story so poignant. God goes on loving Israel though she sins and sins and sins. It is here that Hosea anticipates the New Testament. A third idea emerges in a passage where Hosea is speaking, not of the nation Israel as a whole, but of individual Israelites—'I will heal their backslidings; I will love them freely' (14^4). In the previous verse, the Hebrews, answering the plea, 'O Israel, return unto the LORD thy God', reply: 'Asshur shall not save us; neither will we ride upon horses: neither will we say any more to the works of our hands, Ye are our gods: for in thee the fatherless findeth mercy.' This verse describes repentance for the sins of the time (cf. v. 8). In other words, when the Israelites turn to righteousness, God will 'love them freely'. Of course this idea, that God will love only the righteous, is not consistent with the second idea, that God loves Israel even when she sins—but Hosea was a broken-hearted man and a broken-hearted man is not logical. He can say both that God loved Israel in her sin and that he 'hated' the Israelites whom He would 'love no more' (9^{15}). This is true to life. Did not Othello both love and hate Desdemona when Iago had done his fell work? But of the two ideas, it was not the idea that God loved Israel in her sin that prevailed later, but the idea that He would love her *on repentance*, as will appear below.

This does not mean, however, that the idea that God loves Israel even in her sin has no later instances. On the English translation it has an example when Jeremiah says, 'The LORD appeared of old unto me, saying, Yea, I have loved thee with an everlasting love' (31^3), though it is perhaps more likely that the Prophet here uses 'the prophetic perfect' and means 'the LORD appeared unto me from the far future (cf. 2 S 7^{19}), saying, I love thee with a love that shall never end'. The whole chapter deals with the righteous Israel that is to be. But it seems likely that the idea that God does love His sinful people occurs in a later verse,

'I am a father to Israel, and Ephraim is my first-born' (v. 9), even though this follows a description of Israel's repentance. Again, surely the idea that God loves sinners underlies the Servant Songs, especially the last, and the writer of Jonah implies that He loves even the Ninevites. But what may be called the normal idea appears if two Deuteronomic passages are taken together. One declares that 'God loved Israel for ever' (1 K 10⁹; cf. Dt 23⁵, etc.), but another declares that He 'will repay to his face' the man who breaks covenant, rewarding 'hate' with something very like hate (Dt 7⁷⁻¹¹)—that is, God loves Israel as a whole but not individual sinners. Other texts have the same burden (e.g. Ps 37²⁸, 146⁸; Pr 15⁹). But, while these texts are addressed to Hebrews, intrinsically they do not require that the 'righteous' were Jews. In the few passages where God is said to 'hate', while it is usually wickedness that He hates (e.g. Is 51⁸; Zec 8¹⁷), there are texts where He hates wicked men (e.g. Jer 12⁸; Ps 5⁵; Pr 6¹⁶, ¹⁹). The ruling concept in later Judaism comes out in the text, God 'loveth righteousness and hateth iniquity' (Ps 14⁷), and the corollary to this is 'I (wisdom) love them that love me and those that seek me diligently shall find me' (Pr 8¹⁷). Of Hosea's three ideas one, the belief that God passionately loves sinful Israel, seems to have almost died away. The other two remain—God *chooses* whom to love; He chooses those who are already *righteous, because they are righteous*. The Hebrew spoke relatively rarely of the 'love of God'. While the verb '*ahab* and its cognates occur about two hundred and fifty times in the Old Testament, only twenty-eight texts refer to God's love for men— twenty-two to His love for Israel, and six to His love for individual men (Dt 4³⁷; 2 S 12²⁴; Neh 13²⁶; Ps 146⁸; Pr 3¹², 15⁹). While the concept of the love of God is implied in the whole of this chapter, for the Hebrew the inclusive *word* was *chesed* rather than '*ahabah*.

CHAPTER THREE

FROM HEBREW INTO GREEK

IN EXAMINING the group of Greek words under the Hebrew root *chnn*, the noun *chen* will be taken first, and then its cognates. Under *chen* the dominant Greek rendering is *charis*. This word translates *chen* sixty times, seven other Greek words sharing a mere twelve texts among them. Out of the sixty uses of *charis* the term occurs fifty times in the phrases 'find favour' and 'show favour'. All the examples in the Books from Genesis to Second Chronicles (and Esther) come here. Suppliants to kings begin requests with the phrase: 'If now I have found favour in thy sight' (e.g. Gn 30^{27}; 1 S 16^{22}; 2 S 14^{22}; Pr 3^4, 18^{22}). Similar phrases are used in asking 'favours' from *God* (e.g. Gn 6^8; Ex 33^{10}; 2 S 15^{25}; Est 5^8.). He is said to 'show favour' in such passages as Ex 11^3; Ps 84^{11}; Pr 3^{24}. These phrases are best understood by thinking of the prostrate obeisance of a subject before an absolute king. Such a one pleads for a *personal* and *individual* 'favour'. There are a few texts where a *group* of individuals seek 'favour' for its members (e.g. Gn 47^{25}; 1 S 25^8). Even when God is said to 'give this *people* favour in the sight of the Egyptians' (Ex 3^{21}, 11^3), the context shows that an individual gift is in mind, for '*every* woman' is to 'ask jewels of her neighbour'. In three passages in Jeremiah, where the Prophet speaks of God's *chen* to the *nation* Israel, LXX does not render by *charis* ($16^{5, 13}$, 31^2), in one passage preferring another Hebrew text, in the second omitting a phrase, and in the third using *eleos*. First, therefore, *charis* denotes a *personal* 'favour'. Secondly, the phrase 'If I have found favour in thy sight' always implies that the suppliant is asking a 'favour' to which he has *no claim or right*. It denotes an appeal to generosity. Similarly, to 'show favour' is to be generous. Thirdly, usually it is the suppliant who takes the initiative, plea preceding 'favour'—that is, *charis* is rarely a spontaneous gift. Finally, the suppliant asks for an outward and not an inward benefit; for this reason 'favour' is a better rendering than 'grace' in the historical books.

To pass to other books of the Old Testament, *charis* occurs twelve times in Proverbs (six being additions to the Hebrew). Here the idea of 'beauty', which belongs to the secular use of the

Greek term, is sometimes found. For instance, the word is used both in the singular and plural to denote 'ornament' (e.g. 1^9, 3^{22}, 22^1). It is also used of the habit of a good life (25^{10}), of the temper of a good home (15^{17}), of a man's endearments of his wife (5^{19}), and even of a harlot's beguilements (7^5). It may also be used to mean a 'gift' considered as a 'favour' (17^8). In Proverbs there are only three texts that refer directly or indirectly to the 'favour' of *God* (4^9, 12^2, 30^7). In the first, Wisdom is said to 'give a chaplet of favour' (4^9)—that is she ornaments life. In this book also 'favour' is a better rendering than 'grace'.

Outside the historical books and Proverbs the use of *charis* is rare. Neither of the two texts where it occurs in Ecclesiastes (9^{11}, 10^{12}) refers to God's favour. Of the two in the Psalms one means 'Favour is poured out by (*en*) a king's lips' (45^2), and the other says 'The LORD will give' His worshippers 'favour and glory', apparently among men (84^{11}). In the Prophets Zechariah 6^{14} is a corrupt reading. In Ezekiel 12^2 *charis*, used of 'flattery', does not render *chen*. There is only one other passage (Zec 4^7). Apparently the Greek here means 'I will bring forth the (head-) stone of the inheritance, (and) the favour (of the inheritance) shall be equal to (its former) favour'. This is to interpret, not translate, the Hebrew. In Old Testament Apocalyptic *charis* only occurs twice—once of 'favour' with man (Dn 1^9 LXX—*eleos* in Theodotion) and once in the phrase 'a spirit (that brings) favour and compassion' (Zec 12^{10}). In this meagre list 'favour' is again a better rendering than 'grace'.

In the Apocrypha *charis* is found seventy-five times, of which thirty-nine belong to Sirach and nineteen to the Books of Maccabees. The phrases '*find favour*' and '*show favour*' occur of *men's* 'favour' (e.g. 1 Es 8^4; Bar 1^2; 1 Mac 10^{60}), Sirach using the phrases to denote such 'favours' as 'good turns' and 'pleasantries' (3^{31}, 20^{13}) and warning men against those who want to 'return a favour' (8^{19}). He sets 'shame' and 'favour' among men over against each other ($41^{17, 24}$; cf. 4^{21}). The two phrases are only used a few times of the 'favour of God' (To 7^{18}; Jth 10^8; Wis 8^{21}; Sir 3^{18}, 37^{21}; Ba 2^{14}; cf Jth 8^{23}). There are also two texts where God 'gives' men favour in the sight of 'other men' (To 1^{13}; Bar 2^{14}). The dominant idea is that God gives favour to the helpless and humble. On a review of the passages where 'find favour' and 'show favour' occur in the Apocrypha, it emerges that, as in the Greek Old Testament, God 'shows favour' personally to individuals (or groups of individuals); that for the most part He shows it, not spontaneously, but in answer to plea; and that it is a gift to which the suppliant lays no claim—that is, it is an appeal for generosity.

Apart from the phrases to 'show favour' and 'find favour' the word is used in Sirach in much the same way as in Proverbs—for instance, as a mark of the good life (e.g. 21^{16}, 32^{10}), or of the right kind of wife (7^{19}, $26^{13, 15}$), or of a true friend (30^6), or to denote 'gifts' or 'good offices' (e.g. 7^{23}, 17^{22}, 29^{15}), or to mean 'beauty' (40^{22}; cf. 2 Mac 15^{39}). It can also denote 'thanks' (e.g. Sir 12^1; 1 Mac 14^{25}), a use which recalls, though imperfectly, the mutual idea in *chesed*. The accusative, *charin*, is often used as a mere preposition to mean 'for the sake of' (e.g. Jth 8^{19}; Sir 20^{23}; Wis 18^2; 1 Mac 3^{29}). But the uses of *charis* for God's 'favour' are sparse. It is twice used of 'Wisdom' (Sir 24^{16f}; Wis 8^{21}) and therefore of God. The first text teaches that where Wisdom is, there are 'glory and favour' (among men), as also 'glory and riches'. There are four other texts, all in the Book of Wisdom. In three, God's 'favour' belongs to His 'elect' ($3^{9, 14}$, 4^{15}). The fourth speaks of heathen 'ingratitude for (the) benefits of (God's) favour' (4^{26}). This seems to refer to the blessings given to all men in creation and providence. *Charis* is not one of the great words of LXX. Its dominant meaning is outward 'favour'.

Four derivatives of *charis* occur. One of these, *charizesthai*, only appears once in the Old Testament and then to render the Hebrew word for 'give' and not for *chnn* (Est 8^7). The term literally means 'to show favour' but has narrowed to mean 'give'. It occurs once in Sirach (12^3) and five times in Second Maccabees (e.g. 1^{35}). The notion of 'gift' also attaches to the other three words, which, as they only occur once each—*charisma* (Sir 7^{33}, in the Sinaitic MS.), *charitousthai* (Sir 18^{17}), and *charistērion* (2 Mac 12^{45})—do not seem to have been in common use. The gift is *God's* gift in 2 Mac $3^{31, 33}$, 12^{45}. Since to 'show favour' is a *wider* idea than 'give', and as there were no commonly used derivatives of *charis* available to render this wider sense, the translators fell back upon two derivatives of *eleos—eleein*, and *eleēmōn*. The former occurs ninety-three times in the Greek Old Testament, rendering sixteen Hebrew terms, of which the commonest are *chanan* (*45*) and *racham* (*im*) (*27*). Of eighteen uses of *eleemon* twelve fall under *channun* and four under *chesed*. *Eleos* occurs twelve times for *chen* and its cognates (e.g. Gn 19^{19}; Jer 36^7). As *eleein* and *eleemon* render *chen* more often than any other word, they may be taken here.

The verb *eleein* is used for *chanan* fairly frequently in the books from Genesis to Kings; it is common in the Psalms, but rare in the Prophets. It is used both of God's 'mercy' and man's (e.g. Gn 33^{11}; Dt 7^2; Ps 6^2; Pr 14^{21}; Is 30^{19}). In the Apocrypha it generally refers to *God's* 'mercy', for out of twenty-seven texts only four relate to man's (Sir 12^{13f}; Bar 4^{15}; 2 Mac 3^{21}, 7^{27}). In Tobit the word occurs seven times of God's 'mercy' to faithful individual Jews (e.g. 8^4, $7^{11, 15, 17}$) as though righteousness were a condition of 'mercy'. The idea that God will 'show mercy' to the penitent, but not to the impenitent, occurs in Sir 18^4—'He hath mercy on them that accept chastening, And that diligently seek after his judgements'. Wisdom says paradoxically that because the Jews belong to God He will have mercy on them if they sin, yet that for the same reason they will not sin (15^{1-3}). There is a series of passages (To $13^{2, 5, 9}$, 14^5; Jth 6^{19}; Sir $36^{1, 12}$; Bar 3^2; 2 Mac 2^{18}) whose one burden is '(God) will scourge us for our iniquities and will again show mercy' (To 13^5). Here too there is a constant implication that Israel is God's covenant people. This becomes explicit in 'O Lord, have mercy upon the people that is called by thy name, And upon Israel, whom thou didst liken unto a firstborn' (Sir 36^{12}).

There is a passage in Wisdom (11^{21}–12^{11}) that brings out the full sense of *eleein*. Here the writer, beginning from the overwhelming 'might' of God's arm, declares that He 'shows mercy to all men' just because He 'has power to do all things'. Does He not 'love all things that are'? Does He not put His 'incorruptible spirit in all things'? Is He not the 'lover of souls'? Does He not for a long, long time 'overlook the sins of men to the end they may repent'—and 'admonish' them, and seek to 'convict them by little and little'? The passage is not limited to any Covenant People, but universal. Here, however, the fate of the Gentiles who persist in resisting mercy is emphasized, for all this is the prelude to an account of the deserved fate of the old inhabitants of God's 'holy land' (12^{3ff}).

For *eleemon* there are Old Testament examples in Exodus 34^6 and Psalm 86^{15}. It occurs nine times in the Apocrypha, always of God. In eight passages individual Jews, or Israel as a whole, or Judas Maccabæus and his band, plead with God because He is 'merciful' (To 6^{17}, 7^{12}; Sir 48^{20}, 1^{19}; 2 Mac 1^{24}, 8^{29}, 11^9, 13^{12}).

The remaining passage gives the key to all nine—'For the Lord is compassionate and merciful; And he forgiveth sins, and saveth in time of affliction' (Sir 2¹¹). The context refers to those who 'call upon (God)'.

This mention of prayer leads to the last of the cognates of *chen*, *techinnah* (*61*)—'supplication', a plea for 'mercy'. This term has nine renderings in LXX, of which the most frequent is *deēsis* (*30*—e.g. 1 K 8²⁸; Ps 6⁹), a word that refers rather to the need of the suppliant than the mercy of God. In the Apocrypha (*15*) it occurs once of supplication to a king (1 Mac 11⁴⁹), and once the Temple is called a 'house of supplication' (1 Mac 7³⁷). Sirach says that true work is supplication (38³⁴); and seven times forlorn Israel, or Zion, or some one forlorn Israelite, or Judas Maccabæus' desperate band, appeal to God for 'help in time of need' (Sir 36¹⁷; Bar 2¹⁴, 4²⁰; 2 Mac 1⁵, 9¹²; Ad. Est 4¹⁷; 1 Mac 10²⁷). Sirach repeatedly declares that the prayer of poor and helpless men avails with God (4⁶, 21⁵, 35¹³, ¹⁶, 51¹¹). The results of the examination of all the Greek renderings of Hebrew words of the root *chnn* harmonize with those reached under other terms— God is good to Israel, but the wicked foil His goodness; He is merciful to the righteous and the penitent; His mercy shows itself, not in the changing of the heart, but in the 'good things of this life'. The idea that the righteous *merit* mercy does not occur. On the contrary, it is God's *gift* to those who practise, or even seek to practise, righteousness.

For *chesed* the LXX has *eleos* in over a hundred and seventy texts, only using other terms forty-two times. Of these *hosios* and its verb (*29*) are the most frequent. Similarly there are only thirty-one texts where *eleos* stands for other Hebrew terms than *chesed*. Under the discussion of *chesed* it appeared that, while Covenant implies *chesed*, *chesed* does not necessarily imply Covenant. It is the same with *eleos*. The Old Testament passages need not be examined again. In the Apocrypha there are a number of passages where either the word 'covenant' or the idea of 'covenant' appears in the context (e.g. Jth 7³⁰; Sir 35¹⁹; Wis 3⁹; Three 12; 1 Mac 3⁴⁴; 2 Mac 2⁷), but, as this chapter abundantly shows, this phenomenon is not confined to *eleos*. Other terms too are used about Israel without the implication that *per se* they include the notion of 'covenant'. As to *eleos*, a text in Sirach is typical—'But the Lord will never forsake his mercy; And he will not destroy any of his work, Nor blot out the posterity of his elect' (47^{22}; cf. 50^{22-4}). In the great majority of the examples of *eleos* God shows 'mercy' to *righteous* Jews (e.g. To 7^{16}; Jth 13^{14}; Wis 3^9; Three 67f; 1 Mac 16^3). Here Sirach has illustrative passages of some length (2^{7-17}, 18^{1-14}, 35^{17-20}). Yet there are also some passages, as in the Old Testament, where God shows 'mercy' to *all* Jews. Indeed, this idea had become so common that Sirach has two passages where he warns the sinful Jew against presuming on the 'mercy' of God, threatening him instead with His 'wrath' (5^{4-7}, 16^{6-14}). God offers 'mercy' to a sinful Jew if he repents and sets himself to be righteous (e.g. Wis 11^9, 12^{22}; 1 Mac 13^{46}; 2 Mac $6^{1,\ 16}$). It may be added that the Old Testament class of 'poor' men, who are assumed to be righteous, hardly figures in the Apocrypha (cf. Sir 10^{22}, 26^4; Wis 2^{10}). There is a passage in Sirach about the Mercy of God (18^{1-14}) which develops the characteristic idea. It begins with a fine exposition of the incompetence of man's mind to take the measure of the Creator, but goes on to declare that God 'pours out his mercy' upon men just because they are so feeble. Since He foresees the miserable 'end' of their sin, He forgives them again and again, for His 'mercy is upon all flesh'. He keeps on chastening them in the hope that they will 'accept chastening' at last and let His 'mercy' have its way, for, like a shepherd, He delights in 'turning back' wandering sheep. This passage makes mercy as wide as beneficence, for it speaks, not of Israel, but of *all* men. On the other hand, it is assumed that men may prove so persistent in sin that at last they foil the mercy of God and come to an 'evil end', and it is not unlikely that Sirach would take it for granted that the Gentiles were persistent sinners of this kind.

There are no examples, of course, of man's 'showing mercy' to God. This means that the mutual concept whereby God and a righteous man are each other's liege, sometimes found under *chesed*, is not illustrated under *eleos*. At this important point it is an inadequate translation.

Three other points may also be noted. First, there are nine texts where *chesed* is rendered by *dikaiosunē*, 'righteousness', which shows that in the LXX, as in the Hebrew Old Testament, there is no contrast between righteousness and mercy (e.g. Gn 19^{19}, 21^{23}; Pr 20^{28}; Is 63^7). Second, the term for 'almsgiving' (*eleēmosunē*), a cognate of *eleos*, which is used eleven times for 'righteousness' (e.g. Dt 6^{25}; Ps 24^5), renders *chesed* eight times (seven in

Proverbs—e.g. 3⁸, 21²¹). It is found thirty-six times in the Apocrypha, of which eleven are in Sirach (e.g. 3³⁰, 7¹⁰) and twenty in Tobit, the Book of Alms (e.g. 4⁷⁻¹⁶). Third, of the two other cognates of *eleos*, *eleēmon* and *eleein*, the former only renders *chesed* four times (e.g. Pr 11¹⁷) and the latter only once (as a variant reading—Jer 3¹²). They fall under *chen* rather than under *chesed*.

One important cognate of *chesed*, *chasid* (*29*), is regularly rendered by *hosios*. Indeed, it has no other rendering (*24* times in Psalms). *Hosios* means 'pious' or 'devout', and, like *hagios*, in LXX it denotes an *ethical* piety. Occasionally, for instance, it is used to render *yashar*, 'upright' (Dt 32⁴), *tōm*, 'perfect' (Pr 10²⁹), and *tahor*, 'pure' (Pr 22¹¹). Similarly, in the Apocrypha (*14*) the context always requires that piety includes righteousness. God's 'ways are plain unto the devout' but 'stumbling-blocks unto the wicked' (Sir 39²⁴). While the ancient Israelites are unhistorically called 'devout' in Wisdom (18¹, ⁵, ⁹), the writer declares that Wisdom herself 'from generation to generation passeth into devout souls' (7²⁷; cf 6¹⁰, 10¹⁵, ¹⁷; Sir 39¹³), and Wisdom, of course, is the guide to righteousness. The 'righteous' are 'devout and humble of heart' (Three 64f). In the Maccabean struggle the Jews took the term *Chasidim* from the Psalms to denote those who 'offered (themselves) willingly for the law', refusing to commit the primary sin of apostasy (1 Mac 2⁴²). The martyrs among them are identified with 'the devout' (1 Mac 7¹³, ¹⁷). The man who is *hosios* is the man who is loyal to God. Under this term, though not under *eleos*, the original idea of *chesed*, mutual loyalty between God and men, survives. *Hosios* occurs seven times in Wisdom and derivatives six times. *Hosiotēs*, for instance, is called a good man's 'shield' and *dikaiosune* his 'breast-plate' (6¹⁸ᶠ). One text sums up the teaching: 'They that have kept piously the (things that are) pious shall be made pious' (6¹¹).

With *chesed* there go *rachamim* and its cognates. Here the verb is rendered variously: five times by *agapan* (e.g. Ps 18¹; Hos 2²³); twenty-six times by *eleein*, of which twenty-five are in the Prophets (e.g. Hos 1⁶; Is 13¹⁸; Jer 12¹⁵; Ezk 39²⁵); and eleven times by *oikteirein* (e.g. Ex 28¹⁹; Ps 103¹³; Mic 7¹⁹; Jer 11⁷). The adjective *oiktirmon*, in thirteen out of its sixteen occurrences, renders words of the root *rchm*, and the noun *oiktirmos* twenty-nine times out of its thirty-two. There are examples of *oiktirmon* in Ex 34⁶; Ps 103⁸, and of *oiktirmos* in 2 S 24¹⁴; Is 63¹⁵; Ps 40¹¹.

Perhaps the best English words are 'compassionate' and 'compassion'. The last two Greek words and their verb *oikteirein* are very rare in the Apocrypha—*oiktirmon* appearing once (Sir 2^{11}), and *oiktirmos* and *oikteirein* twice each (Sir 5^6, 36^{13}; 1 Mac 3^{44}; 2 Mac 8^2). Of the three passages in Sirach one encourages the penitent, the second warns the impenitent, and in the third a righteous man pleads for Zion on behalf of those who 'wait for' God (36^{16}). In other words the customary combination of ideas appears here too. Mercy is the sequel of righteousness.

Under the doctrine of the *Forgiveness* of God the first Hebrew term is *salach*. It has a number of Greek renderings, but of these three only occur in one text each (Ex 34^9; Is 33^8; Ps 86^5), and another only in a single passage (Nu $30^{6\cdot18}$). Yet another, *aphienai* (*9*), 'to dismiss', apart from one text (Is 55^7), is only used for *salach* in Leviticus and Numbers (e.g. Lv 4^{20}; Nu 15^{25}), and is taken below under *nasa'*. *Salach* is most commonly rendered by the cognates *hilaskesthai*, *hilasmos*, *hileōs*, and *euilatheuein* (*13*). Sometimes, therefore, the translators used these terms to denote spontaneous 'forgiveness' and not 'propitiation', for *salach* does not mean 'propitiate'. Twice, for instance, LXX uses *hilaskesthai* where Psalmists say that God forgives 'for his name's sake' (25^{11}, 130^4, LXX)—that is, because it is His nature to do so. This idea lies also behind such texts as 'O Lord GOD, forgive, I beseech thee' (Am 7^2), 'How can I pardon thee?' (Jer 5^7), 'To the LORD our God belong mercies and forgivenesses' (Dn 9^9), and 'Who forgiveth all thine iniquities' (Ps 103^3). In such passages the context shows also that God's 'forgiveness' means no mere remission of penalty, but the restoration of the fellowship of the Covenant. In the last passage the glad bells ring—'Who forgiveth', 'who healeth', 'who redeemeth', 'who crowneth', 'who satisfieth'! When this Psalmist is 'forgiven', he 'mews his mighty youth' 'like the eagle'! In all these passages the Greek word is *hilaskesthai* or one of the cognates named above. These are fully discussed under the renderings of *kpr* below.

Among the renderings of the Hebrew term, *nasa'*, in the relatively few instances where it means 'forgive', words of the root *hilaskesthai* only occur twice (Nu 14^{19}; Ps 99^8). Another rendering is *prosdechesthai*, 'receive' (Gn 32^{20}; Ex 10^{17}), and in one passage *luein*, 'loose', occurs—'(God) loosed sin for them for Job's sake' (Job 42^9)—but, as is shown later, Greek words from this root usually stand for *padah*, 'ransom', and *ga'al*, 'do a kinsman's part'. The commonest renderings of *nasa'* when it means 'forgive' or 'pardon' are *anienai* (*4*), 'send back' or 're-mit', and *aphienai* (*9*), 'send away' or 'dis-miss' (but not *aphesis*). The former occurs in 'He will not pardon your sins and lawlessnesses' (Jos 24¹⁹), 'I will not again pardon your sins' (Is 1¹⁴; cf. 2⁹), and '*I* will pardon' (Is 46⁴—a text where *ego*, 'I', occurs six times). *Aphienai* is found also in such passages as 'Yet now, if thou wilt forgive their sins' (Ex 32³²; cf. Gn 18²⁶); 'The people that dwell (in Zion) shall be forgiven their iniquity' (Is 33²⁴); ' . . . I said I will confess . . . and thou forgavest' (Ps 32⁵). There is the bliss of reconciliation in 'forgiveness'.

In the Apocrypha *anienai* and *anesis* never denote forgiveness, nor does *aphesis*, and *aphienai* only twice (Sir 2¹¹, 28²). The second text should be quoted since it anticipates the Lord's Prayer—'*Forgive* thy neighbour the hurt that he hath done, And then thy sins shall be pardoned' (*luein*). The idea that underlies the various uses of *aphienai* is 'release' (e.g. 1 Es 4⁷; 1 Mac 10²⁸⁻³⁴). When God 'forgives', He 'releases' like a king.

The question 'Does the Hebrew root *kpr* mean "forgive"?' was postponed until its Greek renderings fell for discussion. The first point to notice here is that *salach* and *nasa'*, though they are sometimes rendered by *hilaskesthai*, are never rendered by the compound verb *exilaskesthai* and its cognates, which, on the other hand, occur for the root *kpr* seventy-seven times. Did the Greek translators, then, make a distinction between *hilaskesthai* and *exilaskesthai*? The evidence suggests that they did. It lies almost altogether in those passages that do not directly describe the Temple ritual. Outside the Priestly documents in the Pentateuch, Chronicles and Ezekiel's description of the future Temple, *exilaskesthai* has only seven instances. While two of them would admit either the idea of 'propitiation' or of 'forgiveness' (Ezk 16⁶³; Dn 9²⁴), the term clearly describes 'placation' or 'propitiation' in five—Jacob hopes to 'appease' Esau, and David, the Gibeonites (Gn 32²⁰ E; 2 S 21³); a 'wise man will placate an angry king (Pr 16¹⁴); Samuel protests that he has never taken a 'bribe' to 'blind (the) eyes' of his anger against the wicked (1 S 12³); no rich man can 'buy off' God's anger against a sinner (Ps 49⁶ᶠ). On the other hand, of the six texts outside the ritualistic descriptions where the simple verb *hilaskesthai* and its cognates render the root *kpr*, five clearly speak of forgiveness. Three occur in the

Psalms. In one, 'As for our transgressions, thou shalt purge them away', God is praised because He forgives (65¹⁻³—LXX emphasizing '*Thou*'); in another, being 'full of compassion', God *Himself* 'turns away his anger' (78³⁸); similarly, 'Help', 'deliver', 'forgive' '*for thy name's sake*' is the plea of forlorn Israel (79⁹). In Deuteronomy Israel cries 'Be gracious!' and the 'Redeemer of Israel' 'forgives' a sin *for which no restitution is made* (21⁸). Only in one passage is there any doubt about the translation (1 S 3¹⁴). This series of texts at least suggests that in LXX *hilaskesthai* means 'forgive' and *exilaskesthai* 'placate' or 'propitiate', though both render *kpr*.

Some other LXX renderings suggest forgiveness rather than placation. In two passages (Job 33²⁴; Dn 9²⁴) 'wipe away' is used, and in six (Ex 29³⁷, 30¹⁰; Dt 32⁴³; Is 6⁷; Pr 16⁶, 21¹⁸) words derived from *katharos*, 'clean'—for instance, the 'live coal' 'cleanses' Isaiah's lips. Here and elsewhere 'cleanse' would be a better translation than 'purge'.[1] Words meaning 'Set aside' (Jer 18²³), 'sanctify' (Ex 29³³, ³⁶), and 'take away' (Is 27⁹, 28¹⁸), also occur. Once *kpr* is rendered outright by *aphienai*, 'forgive' (Is 24¹⁴). On the other side two terms may be quoted—*allagma*, 'price' (Am 5¹²; Is 53³), and *lutron*, 'ransom' (Ex 21³⁰, 30¹²; Nu 35³¹ᶠ; Pr 6³⁵, 13⁸—for these suggest that forgiveness is bought. These renderings, like the uses of *hilaskesthai* and *exilaskesthai*, suggest that, at least outside liturgical passages, the Greek translators sometimes took *kpr* to mean 'forgive' and sometimes 'propitiate'.

In the liturgical parts of the Old Testament there is no example of *hilaskesthai*, and *hilasmos* only occurs twice (Lv 25⁹; Nu 5⁸). In the second of these texts there is an alternative (and preferable) reading *exilasmos*. On the other hand, *exilaskesthai* and its cognates occur seventy-four times. As so often in descriptions of *forms* of ritual, the passages themselves give little or no guidance for the precise meaning of terms, but it seems plain that the Greek translators took sin-offerings to be propitiatory or placatory. On the other hand, *exilasmos* is only used once to describe the *kapporeth* or 'mercy-seat' and even here there is the alternative 'the house of the *hilasmos*' (1 Ch 28¹¹, ²⁰). Elsewhere—in Ex 25, 37; Lv 16, etc.—*kapporeth* is always rendered by *hilasterion* (*20*), never by *exilasterion*. This seems to mean that the Greek translators, while they thought of the blood of the *sin-offerings* as

---

[1] These two renderings perhaps suggest that the LXX translators took *kpr* to mean 'wipe away', not 'cover'.

propitiatory, thought of the *seat* of the Shekinah as the throne of forgiveness. On the Day of Atonement the High Priest made propitiation, indeed, but it was at the seat of forgiveness. For the Jews who made the Septuagint *both* ideas were present in the ritual. They seem to have associated placation with the blood and forgiveness with the *kapporeth*.[2]

Outside Sirach at any rate, the uses of these terms in the Apocrypha bear the same witness. Here, indeed, *hilaskesthai* and its cognates sometimes broaden, meaning 'mercy' at large and not only the kind called 'forgiveness'. In First Esdras *exilasmos* means 'propitiation' ($11^{13, 20}$), but *euilatos* means that God in His 'mercy' answered the prayer, *not* of sinners, but of the faithful (8^{53}). In Second Macabees a sacrifice on behalf of dead sinners is called an *exilasmos* ($12^{43, 45}$), but *hilasmos* is used for a prayer that God will '*show grace*' in the 'saving' of Heliodorus from imminent death (3^{31-3}). The only other instance of a term of the *exilaskesthai* group outside Sirach tells how Phineas, by the 'propitiation of incense', overcame the 'anger' of God in the very act of 'punishing' (Wis 18^{21f}). On the other hand, alike in Ad. Esther (13^{17}), in Judith (16^{15}), in First Maccabees (2^{21}), and in Second Maccabees ($2^{7, 22}$, 7^{37}, 10^{26}), some word of the *hilaskesthai* group is used to denote 'forgiveness' or 'mercy'—for instance, the passage from Judith reads: 'The rocks shall melt like wax at thy presence, But thou art yet merciful to them that fear thee.' This occurs in the thanksgiving, not of sinners to a placated God, but of righteous Judith to the God whose 'mercy' *saves* the righteous.

In the Apocrypha the verb *exilaskesthai* is confined to Sirach (*9*). *Exilasmos* (*7*) has *hilasmos* as a variant twice (18^{20}, 35^3), which suggests that in these texts, as in a third (3^3), either 'propitiation' or 'forgiveness' would suit the passage. But in the majority of texts

---

[2] This may underlie the description of the 'altar' (*mizbeach*, LXX *thusiasterion*) in Ezekiel's temple (43^{13-17}), for its structure is likely to be symbolic. Just above the base a channel ran round it. Into this the blood of the sacrifices (which were not slain *on* the altar) was poured. Above this channel there were two blocks, the lower and upper '*azarah*. The Revisers render this obscure word by 'settle', but LXX by *hilasterion*, as though '*azarah* were a synonym for *kapporeth*. As there seems to have been no Ark, and therefore no *kapporeth*, in Ezekiel's *Holy of Holies*, the Greek translators seem to be saying: 'Here, the great altar *outside* the shrine is the *kapporeth* now.' But this seems to require that they took '*azarah* to mean 'help'. This block (in its two parts) was an Ebenezer, a 'stone of help'—and *hilasterion* could be used to render this idea. Above the *hilasterion* there was 'the hearth of burning' itself. The channel, and block of stone, and the hearth, represent three stages in sacrifice—propitiation by blood (cf. v. 20), forgiveness (*hilasterion*), and offering (the hearth). It would be from the channel that the priest would take the blood to 'sprinkle' on the altar (v. 18; cf. 45^{19}). There is a diagram of this altar in *H.D.B.*, IV.709.

exilaskesthai and its noun either certainly or probably denote 'placation'. There are two references to the ritual (45$^{16, 23}$) and Sirach would know its terminology. Again, God was 'implacable' to the ancient giants in their 'strength' and the great 'Dynast' will not be 'placable' to a 'stiff-necked person' but 'pour out wrath upon him (46$^{7-11}$). As 'a wise man' will 'cultivate the great man' so as to placate his wrath by anticipation (20^{28}), so placatory alms may quench the fire of God's anger against sin (3^{30}; cf. To 4^{9f}). If a man 'nourish wrath' against his neighbour, who shall 'make propitiation for his sins' (28^5)? For a sinner who remains a sinner to multiply sacrifices does not 'propitiate' God (34^{19}, 5^{5f}). There are only two passages where 'forgiveness' would be a more natural translation if the texts were considered solitarily (17^{29}, 18^{12}) and the phrase 'to lessen offence' is used near one of these (17^{25}). When the evidence from all the rest of the Septuagint is remembered 'propitiatoriness' is more likely to be the meaning in these two texts than 'forgiveness'. At most they are the exceptions that prove the rule. Elsewhere the difference between words of the *exilaskesthai* and *hilaskesthai* groups is too nearly uniform to be ignored. The first group denotes 'propitiation' and the second 'forgiveness'.

Of the four Hebrew words denoting 'save', the rendering of the first, *yasha'*, is all but uniform. In 292 texts *sōzein* or one of its derivatives is used. The next commonest renderings are *boēthein*, 'help', and *ruesthai*, 'rescue', but each of these only occurs seven times (e.g. Dt 22^7; Is 49^{25f}). Apart from *sōzein* itself (*160*), *diasōzein* occurs (*5*), as do *sōtēr* (*23*), *sōtēria* (*58*), and *sōtērion* (*46*). While words of this Greek root render other Hebrew terms in earlier documents, their use for *yasha'* and its derivatives begins with the Deuteronomists and is specially frequent in the Psalms. A few examples will illustrate the variety of use—The LORD will 'save' Israel in battle (Dt 20^4); He promises to 'save' Jerusalem from Sennacherib (Is 37^{35}); He pledges Himself to 'save' Jeremiah from machinations (Jer 15^{20}); He will 'save' His faithful flock from false shepherds (Ezk 34^{22}); His 'hand is not shortened that it cannot save' His people (Is 59^1); one Psalmist, facing 'trouble', speaks of 'the saving strength of (God's) his right arm' (20$^{1, 6}$); another declares that God will 'save the afflicted people' (18^{27}); and a *chasid* speaks of 'the cup of salvation' (116^{13}).

For *padah*, 'ransom', the verb *lutroun*, 'to set loose', and its cognates occur fifty-five times. There are examples from various parts of the Old Testament in Ex 34[20]; Dt 7[8]; 2 S 4[9]; Jer 15[21]; Ps 25[22], 34[22]. The next commonest rendering, by *ruesthai*, 'rescue', has only five instances (e.g. Is 50[2]). *Ga'al*, 'to do a kinsman's part', is rendered literally by *agchisteuein* in the Book of Ruth and Numbers 35 and 36 (*43*), but elsewhere by far the commonest rendering is again by *lutroun* or a cognate (*58*). There are instances in Mic 4[10]; Is 43[1], 63[9]; Lv 25[25]; Ps 72[14], 77[15]. Here too *ruesthai* is the next commonest rendering (*12*). Where God is called 'Goel' in Deutero-Isaiah, *rusamenos* and *ruomenos*, participles from *ruesthai* (e.g. Is 44[6], 47[4], 48[17], 49[7, 26], 54[5, 8]) are used more often than *lutroumenos* (e.g. Is 41[14], 42[14], 44[24]). 'Rescue' seemed to suit the word even better than 'loose'. On the whole evidence it cannot be said that the Greek translators made any clear distinction between the meanings of *padah* and *ga'al*. For *natzal*, 'deliver', *ruesthai* and *exairein* (literally, 'take out'), each occur some ninety times, and *sozein* about twenty. In the Psalter *ruesthai* is far the favourite. There are passages where two of the three terms occur alternatively, which shows that the translators made no clear distinction between them. For example, both *ruesthai* and *exairein* occur in 2 K 18[29-35], both *exairein* and *sozein* in 2 Ch 32[11-17], and both *ruesthai* and *sozein* in Ezk 14[16-20]. For *ruesthai* there are instances in Ex 12[27]; Ps 18[17], 22[20], 40[13], 72[12]; Pr 2[12]—for *exairein* in Ex 3[8]; Dt 32[39]; 1 S 17[37]; Jer 1[8]; Ezk 34[10]—and for *sozein* in Is 19[20]; Ps 69[14].

In the Apocrypha—which, as shown in *The Bible Doctrine of Salvation*, makes no novel contribution to the doctrine of 'salvation—*sozein* occurs thirty-four times (e.g. To 6[17]; Sir 2[11]; Wis 9[18]; Ad. Est 22[1, 9]; Sus 62; 1 Mac 2[59]), *soter* seven times (e.g. Jth 9[11]; Sir 51[1]; Wis 16[7]; Bar 4[22]), *soteria* twenty-four times (e.g. Jth 8[17]; Sir 4[23], 46[1]; Wis 5[2], 6[24], 18[7]; Bar 4[22]; 1 Macc 3[6]; 2 Mac 3[29], 11[6], 13[3]) and *soterion* five times (e.g. Sir 35[1], 39[18]), of which four denote the so-called 'peace-offering'. These words usually refer to the saving of *righteous* Israel or righteous Israelites from *sufferings* of one kind or another, notably those of exile, but sometimes 'salvation' of this sort is offered to the sinful if they will repent and turn to righteousness (e.g. Bar 4 and 5). *Lutroun* only occurs seven times in the Apocrypha (e.g. Sir 48[20], 51[2f]; 1 Mac 4[11]), and of its derivatives only *apolutrōsis* (*1*), in a phrase added in LXX to the Aramaic, 'My time of redemption is come' (Dn 4[32]). Under *luein* there is a pertinent text in Sirach 38[2].

Luesthai has twenty-five examples, its meaning being like that of *sozein* (e.g. To 4¹⁰, 14¹¹; Sir 29¹⁷; Wis 2¹⁸, 10⁶, ⁹; 1 Mac 2⁶⁰, v. 17, 16²). The dominant concept, exhibited under other terms in this chapter, is that the righteous God must and will 'save' righteous Israel from suffering and woe. As normally in the Old Testament, a sinner can become righteous if he will. It is difficult to deny that this means that he can save himself from sin, though not from suffering. But, just as Jeremiah and Ezekiel and the writer of the Psalm 51 are exceptions in the Old Testament, so, in another way, is the writer of Second Esdras in the Apocrypha. He too knows that only God *can* save sinners. The two Prophets announce that one day He will; the Psalmist pleads desperately but hopefully with Him to save now; 'Ezra' asks and asks, 'Why wilt Thou not?'

For the Hebrew word *nacham* LXX has ten renderings. Several of these, however, only occur once. The most frequent are *eleein* (*5*—e.g. Is 12¹), *metanoein* (*14*—e.g. 1 S 15²⁹; Am 7³, ⁶; Jer 4²⁸), and *parakalein* (*58*). From its frequency it is plain that the last is the important word. Literally it means 'to call to one's side', but it is a chameleon term. In the Books of Maccabees, for instance, the Revisers use 'encourage', 'beseech', 'persuade', 'exhort', 'propose' and 'invite' (e.g. 1 Mac 5⁵³, 9³³; 2 Mac 4³⁴, 7⁵, 11¹⁵, 12³), 'exhort' being the commonest. Clearly the context colours the meaning of the term. In these passages, however, men call upon other *men* to do this or that. For the present purpose the pertinent passages are those that relate the word to *God*. There are seven passages where *parakaleisthai* (passive or middle) renders texts that speak of God's 'repentance' (e.g. Dt 32³⁶; 1 S 15¹¹; Ps 90¹³; 2 Mac 7⁶). This recalls the idea 'rue', expressed by *nacham*, and seems to be an instance where the Greek passive and middle 'voices' are not differentiated with any sharpness and where the sense is 'reflexive', *parakaleisthai* meaning 'to call upon oneself'.[3] 'Reconsider' is perhaps the nearest English, for it often implies a change of mind. For instance, in LXX God says to Samuel, 'I have reconsidered' Saul's appointment to the kingdom (1 S 15¹¹), just as He 'pondered' (*enthumeisthai*) over man's creation when He saw man's sin (Gn 6⁶). In these texts something of the stress of the Hebrew term on a change of *feeling* is lost, but it appears in the context when God, who is 'judge', 'reconsiders'

---

[3] J. H. Moulton, *Grammar of New Testament Greek*, I.162.

his sentence on His sinful people since He sees their helpless plight (Dt 32³⁶; cf. Jg 2¹⁸; 2 S 24¹⁶; Ps 135¹⁴). When the verb is used in the active voice in the Greek Old Testament, it always denotes some kind of *help*. When used of God it denotes that God 'calls men to His side' to help *them* in some way. Here as elsewhere, the term takes its colour from its context. It occurs six times in the first chapter of Lamentations, where '(Jerusalem) hath no comforter' means that her grief cannot be assuaged because there is none to *help* (La 1². ¹⁶ᶠ. ²¹). When Job's three friends come to 'comfort' him (2¹¹), it is not just to sympathize. It is to *help* him by persuading him that if he will only confess his sin, God will again bless him. This, for instance, is the theme of Eliphaz' first speech (Job 4 and 5). Similarly, the context of all the passages where the word is used in the latter part of Isaiah requires that God is now comforting Israel by the effective *help* He is giving her. There are three instances in one chapter (51³. ¹². ¹⁹). So too God's messengers 'speak to the heart' of His 'pardoned people' because they herald His invincible *help* (40¹⁻⁸). It is just the same with the use of *parakalein* in the Psalms. The Divine Shepherd's 'rod and club' are not for discipline but for defence (23⁴) as the context requires (cf. 71²¹. 86¹⁷, 119⁷⁶). The word only occurs twice in the Apocrypha of God's 'comfort' but both illustrate the same idea of 'consolation through help' (Sir 17²⁴, 35¹⁷). Where *parakaleisthai* is used of *men*, it does not mean 'repent' or 'reconsider', but 'be helped (if only by hope) and therefore comforted' (Is 66¹²ᶠ; Ps 119⁵²; cf. Is 54¹¹). It is the same with the noun *paraklēsis* (*8*), which all but once renders either *nacham* or a cognate. The 'help' of Egypt and therefore its 'comfort' is 'vain' (Is 30⁷ LXX), but God's 'comfort' is effective (Is 57¹⁸; Ps 94¹⁹; cf. Is 66¹¹). Job's friends are 'wearisome comforters' (*paraclētōr*, Job 16², where Aquila has *paracletos*) because their 'words' are 'words of wind', but 'God's comfortable words' (*paraklētikos*—Zec 1¹³⁻¹⁷) tell of the certainty of overflowing prosperity. Men's 'comfort' is often no more than helpless sympathy but it is never so with God's. His 'comfort' includes encouragement and hope as well as consolation, for when He 'comforts', He helps—as, indeed, the etymology of 'comfort' implies.

In the main the use of the terms in the Apocrypha follows that of the Old Testament, but there are a few texts where *parakalein* has a sense that is alien to *nacham*. In these it denotes that one man 'calls others to his side', not to offer them help, but *to ask them for help*, the meaning being 'beseech' or 'intreat'. There are instances in the Prologue to Sirach (v. 12), in First Maccabees (9^{35}), and in Second Maccabees (4^{34}, 6^{21}). In the last book the word occurs of petition to God in prayer (13^{12}; cf. 7^6).

In Second Maccabees the verb is also sometimes rendered 'exhort' (*8*). This English word denotes the *offer* of help by way of *advice*, but this rendering is inadequate in all the passages. In every case one man urges others to share in a common endeavour —that is, the notion is 'mutual help'. Unfortunately English has no word that quite expresses this idea. Perhaps 'appeal' comes nearest. When Epiphanes is stricken with his foul and fatal disease, he writes the Jews a letter, 'having the nature of a supplication', in which he 'exhorts and counts them worthy' to be loyal to his son because he has also written to his son to 'treat them with indulgence' ($9^{18,\ 25-7}$). It is an appeal for collaboration. In all the other passages one of 'the faithful' appeals to other faithful men to share in doing the will of God—as, for instance, Jeremiah had appealed to Nebuchadnezzar's captives to join him in loyalty to 'the law' (2^3). Judas Maccabæus 'appeals' to his comrades to share to the end in his desperate enterprise (8^{16}, 13^{14}, 15^8; cf. 12^{42}), and the Seven Brethren and their mother call upon each other 'to die nobly' ($7^{5,\ 21}$). The word does not denote advice from outside, but an appeal to share in the common enterprise or ordeal.

In the Old Testament it was found that there are three great passages where the belief that God will both forgive and help sinners culminates in the belief that He will make them into new men (Jer 31^{33f}; Ezk 36^{26f}; Ps 51). These passages, of course, are found in LXX, but they have no parallels in the Apocrypha. No doubt the Jews of the period relegated Jeremiah and Ezekiel's prophecies to a distant future. What use they made of Psalm 51 can only be surmised, but there is no writer that shows its temper. It is true that the author of Second Esdras believed, not in inward sinfulness, but in 'an evil impulse' which, while not conceived as itself sinful, yet made it practically inevitable that every man would sin, but, in face of this belief, he does not cry 'Create in us clean hearts' but 'Why didst Thou create us at all?'

In rendering the two Hebrew words relating to 'blessing' the LXX translators show an uncommon consistency. For the root *brk* the almost universal rendering is *eulogein* and its cognates. *Eulogein*, 'to bless' (literally 'to speak well of', 'to praise'), with its adjectives *eulogētos*, 'blessed', and its noun *eulogia*, 'blessing', occur four hundred and twelve times, and in all but seventeen of these the Hebrew root is *brk*. *Eulogein* is rare in the Prophetic books apart from Isaiah; *eulogetos* does not occur in them, nor, until after the Return from Exile, *eulogia*. There is a good instance of *eulogein* in the Deuteronomic list of 'blessings' (28^{3-12}; cf. Gn 1^{28}; 1 S 23^{21}; Ps 28^9; Is 19^{25}). For *eulogetos* one may quote Gn 14^{20}; 1 S 15^{13}; Dt 7^{14}; Ps 68^{19}; and for *eulogia* Gn 27^{38}; Jg 1^{15}; Ps 3^8; Mal 3^{10}. For words of the root *'shr*, LXX *always* uses *makarios*, 'happy', or a cognate (*56*). *Makarios* occurs twenty-five times in the Psalms, but in the Prophets it is confined to Isaiah (*4*). There are examples in Dt 33^{29}; Is 30^{18}; Ps 1^1; Pr 3^{18}. The superlative of this adjective, 'most happy', occurs three times in Proverbs (e.g. 16^{20}). The verb *makarizein* (*10*), to 'count happy', has examples in Ps 41^2; Is 3^{12}. As the two sets of Greek terms render different Hebrew roots in LXX, it is unfortunate that the English Versions, having at hand the two appropriate words 'blessed' and 'happy', sometimes use 'blessed' for both.

In the Apocrypha the difference between the two sets of terms comes out very clearly. *Eulogein* and its cognates occur one hundred and forty-nine times. *Eulogetos*, however, does not occur either in Sirach or Wisdom, and *eulogein* and *eulogia* only once each in Wisdom (14^7, 15^{19}). Sirach, on the other hand, uses the last two fairly frequently (*29*). Throughout the Apocrypha *eulogetos* (*19*) is always the term used in the phrase 'Blessed be the Lord' and its equivalents, except in Jth 13^{18} (and in three variants in the Sinaitic document in Tobit—e.g. 13^{18}). Some examples are given below. Similarly, *eulogein* is used chiefly of 'blessing God', and it is the same with *eulogia* (*21*). When men 'bless God' they thankfully praise Him for some boon. There is a good example in the *Benedicite*. Here Ananias, Azarias and Misael cry 'Blessed art thou' because in His might God has given them the boon of safety in the midst of the fire (Three 28-34); then (35-59) 'All (the) works of the Lord' are called to 'bless' Him because He has given them the boon of existence.[4] Finally, in culmination (60-8) all the 'children of men' are first summoned to 'bless the Lord', then the summons narrows to 'Israel', and at last to the 'spirits and souls' of such

---

[4] In the heat of his polemic against idols the writer of Wisdom, in a way quite unlike a Jew's, declares that there are ugly creatures that have 'escaped both the praise of God and His blessing' (15^{19})!

righteous men as the Three Children. Sirach puts the fundamental concept in a single phrase—'Bless ye the Lord for all his works' (39^{14}). The word is common in Tobit (*25*—e.g. 8^{15}; cf. 1 Es 4^{58}; Jth 13^{18}; Sus 60). 'The heaven blesseth truth' for 'in (truth) is no unrighteous thing', and her praises end with the cry 'Blessed be the God of truth' (1 Es 4^{35-40}). The very 'wood' of Noah's Ark is 'blessed' because it brought boon to the righteous (Wis 14^7). It is God who 'blesses' whether through 'truth' or 'wood'. Similarly, when Mattathias 'blesses' his sons (1 Mac 2^{69}), the phrase means that he appeals to God to bless them. Ultimately it is only God who 'blesses' men, and therefore it is for men to 'bless' God. The phrases are reciprocal and always refer to a divine boon, given and received. For *eulogetos* the phrase 'Blessed be the only Lord, the God of my fathers' is typical (1 Es 8^{25}), for this is Esdras' cry because God has 'put it into the heart of (Artaxerxes)' to grant the Jews a boon (cf. To 8^{15-17}; Jth 13^{17f}; 1 Mac 4^{30}; 2 Mac 1^{17}). For *eulogia* To 8^{17}; Sir 3^8; 1 Mac 3^7 are illustrations. 'The blessing of the Lord is in the reward of the godly' (Sir 11^{22}) expresses the idea of the passages where God 'blesses' men. In the minds of the Apocryphal writers 'blessing' is intrinsically religious. This basic idea re-echoes 'Bless the Lord, O my soul and forget not all his praises' (Ps 103^2 LXX). A glowing passage in Baruch describes the coming blessings of Jerusalem without the word (4^{36-59}).

It is otherwise with *makarios* and its verb *makarizein*. These are comparatively rare (*24*). God is never called 'happy', and the verb is only used of Him once—in a curious phrase that seems to mean '(God) counted (Aaron) happy in (his) goodly array' (Sir 45^7). The terms would be common in the Hellenistic world for it knew all about 'the pursuit of happiness' (cf. 2 Mac 7^{24}). All the texts in the Apocrypha imply that men are only truly happy if they 'love (God)' (To 3^{14}). Indeed in this passage Tobit declares that a man who knows how to 'sorrow' aright is 'happy'! (cf. Bar 4^{4ff}). Yet Sirach, for instance, sober writer as he is, admits that there are kinds of happiness that do not depend on righteousness. He has a sort of ladder of happinesses (25^{7-12}), which he says has ten rungs (though he seems to miss one). His lower rungs might be called 'secular', but the topmost happiness belongs to 'wisdom' and 'the fear of the Lord' (cf. 11^{28}, 14^{20}, 25^{23}, 26^1, 28^{19}, 34^{15f}). Sirach will not count a rich man really 'happy' unless he is 'righteous' (31^{8f}). In other words, happiness for Sirach is not ultimately a matter of outward success. Similarly, he confidently calls serious students of his own book 'happy', promising them 'the light of the Lord' ($40^{27\cdot9}$). So too a man with a clear conscience is 'happy' (14^{1f}). The difference between 'blessing' and 'happiness' comes out neatly in the text, 'A wise man shall be filled with the blessing (of God), And all (the men) that see him shall count him happy' (37^{24}). Of the three passages in the Book of Wisdom one declares that a suffering saint will be 'happy' at last (2^{16}), one that a barren woman is 'happy' if she is pure (3^{13}), and one that the Egyptians 'counted' it a 'happy thing' that the Plague of Darkness had, as they mistakenly supposed, fallen upon God's 'holy ones' as well as upon themselves (18^{1}). The last passage shows that this writer, like Sirach, could use 'happiness' in the current secular sense.

To sum up, in this realm the Apocryphal writers advance on Old Testament ideas. First, the connexion of happiness with earthly prosperity is loosened. Second, to use a modern term, 'happiness' has no absolute 'value'. Otherwise, these writers would have ascribed it to God. It is a small matter beside 'blessedness'. Third, the latter is now clearly distinguished from the former as the inevitable sequel of righteousness. There is therefore no longer a passionate insistence that God ought to give happiness to good men but does not, for happiness is no longer good *per se*. On the other hand, by His very nature He ought to give them blessedness—and He always does so. Fourth, happiness is not now something to be sought, for it is by its very nature an accompaniment. The Jew now knew, in effect, what modern psychology teaches—that happiness just 'comes' unsought to a man who is seeking and finding something else that he loves—money, for instance, or skill, or a wife. The distinction of the Jew is that for him the 'something else', the thing that is itself desirable because it is of ultimate 'worth' or 'value', is— God. He believed that 'happiness', if it comes, is a by-product of blessedness'.[5]

Shalom, the Hebrew word for 'peace', which compasses the whole gamut of 'blessings', is rendered by *soteria* or *soterion* eleven times

---

[5] It may be added that neither *eudaimonia*, the commonest Greek term for 'happiness', nor any of its cognates occurs in LXX—probably because they derive from *daimon*. For the Jew both *daimon*, as its one example shows (Is. 65^{11}, in one MS.), and its commoner synonym, *daimonion* (17), meant 'demon'. For instance, in Tobit, Asmodeus is a *daimonion* (3^8, etc.), and a Psalmist says 'All the gods of the nations are demons' (Ps 96^5). The Greeks used both terms for a 'divine being'.

(e.g. Gn 26³¹; Ps 50²³), with the meaning 'safety' rather than 'salvation', and ten times by a verb meaning 'to be in good health' (*hygiainein*), which is not used for any other term (e.g. Gn 29⁶, 43²⁷). But its regular rendering is *eirēnē*, which is used for it a hundred and eighty-eight times. This suggests that, for the translators, *eirene* had as wide a scope as *shalom*. The use of *eirene* in the Apocrypha (*50*) bears this out, for, while half its instances fall in the warlike Books of Maccabees and these naturally refer to peace as over against war (e.g. 1 Mac 5⁵⁴; cf. To 14⁴; Jth 7¹⁵; Sir 13¹⁸), the word has also the wider sense of 'welfare'. It is used in greeting and farewell (Jth 8³⁵; 2 Mac 1¹), of a physician's cures whereby 'there is peace upon the face of the earth' (Sir 38⁸), and of the prosperity of Solomon's reign (Sir 47¹³, ¹⁶). The writer of Wisdom speaks sarcastically of a 'multitude of evils that (the heathen) call peace' (14²²). For him the righteous who have died 'are in peace' (3³), which means much more than 'at rest'. Again, Sirach declares that it is one of the boons of forgotten saints that 'their bodies were buried in peace' (44⁴⁴)—that is, they were not left to the evil fate of the un-buried. The connexion with 'blessing' is explicit in Tobit's cry 'O blessed are they that love thee; They shall rejoice for thy peace' (13¹⁴), as is the connexion with 'health' in Sirach's sentence, 'The fear of the Lord is the crown of wisdom, Making peace and health of healing' (1¹⁸). There are other examples of the concept that 'peace', or 'welfare' at large, comes from God in Sirach's mention of God's 'covenant of peace' with zealous Phinehas (45²³ᶠ) and his prayer that God will grant Israel 'peace in our days ... for the days of eternity' (1²³). In Tobit Raphael says to Tobias and his wife, 'Ye shall have peace, but bless God for ever' (12¹⁷), and in Baruch true 'peace' epitomizes 'life' (3¹³ᶠ) for it is 'the peace of righteousness' (5⁴; cf. 2 Mac 1⁴).

In examining the teaching about the *love of God* for man the meanings of three Greek terms, *erōs, philia* and *agapē*, with their cognates, need to be noted. The first term, *eros*, only occurs once in the Old Testament (Pr 7¹⁸) and not at all in the Apocrypha. The verb *erasthai*, 'to love', (Es 2¹⁷) is found twice, and the noun *erastes*, 'lover', fourteen times (e.g. Hos 2⁷; Jer 22²⁰; Ezk 16²³). The former occurs once in the Apocrypha (1 Es 4²⁴) and the latter twice (Wis 8², 15⁶). Under all these terms the reference is always to sexual love, whether pure or impure—even when the words are used symbolically of the 'love' of 'Wisdom', for she may be loved like a wife (Pr 4⁶; cf. v. 8) or like a bride (Wis 8²)—or when idolaters are said to be 'lovers of evil things' (Wis 15⁶; cf. 14¹²). These Greek words are not used of God's love for man.

The next term, *philia*, with its cognates (*philein* and *philos*), is used twenty-six times to render words of the root *'hb*. For *philos* the English versions have 'friend' (e.g. Es 5¹⁰), but *philia* is rightly rendered 'love' (e.g. Gn 37⁴). While these words are not used of God's love for man, the text 'I (Wisdom) love (*agapan*) them that love (*philein*) me' (Pr 8¹⁷; cf. 8²¹, 29³) seems to equate *philein* with *agapan*. *Philein* and its cognates are used frequently in the Apocrypha (*117*)—occurring fifty times in Sirach and more than fifty in the Books of Maccabees—but apart from the possible implication of such texts as Wis 7¹⁴, ²⁷, 8¹⁸, it is only in rare compound words that they describe God's love. God is *philopsychos* 'lover of (the) *psyche* (of men)' (Wis 11²⁶) and Wisdom is *phil-agathos*, 'lover of good', and *phil-anthrōpos*, 'lover of man' (Wis 7²²ᶠ). The noun *philia* is not used of God's love.

The third term, *agape* (with *agapan* and *agapēsis*) is much the commonest rendering of *'hb*. The three terms occur two hundred and forty times in the Greek Old Testament and in more than two hundred they render words of this root. The range of use is very wide. *Agape* is used not only to describe the love of husband for wife (e.g. Gn 24⁶⁷) and of father for child (e.g. Gn 22⁷), but even of the love of a fornicator (2 S 13¹⁵). Again, it is used for the 'love' of friends and neighbours (e.g. 1 S 20¹⁷; Lv 19¹⁸), and it can be used of the 'love' of 'righteousness', 'iniquity', 'mercy', 'discipline' and so on (e.g. Ps 11⁶, ⁸; Mic 6⁸; Pr 12¹). There is a like wide range of reference in the Apocrypha (e.g. 1 Es 4²⁵; Sir 30¹, 7²¹, ³⁵; Wis 1¹, 6¹²). Along with all this the terms are used too of *men's love for God* (e.g. Dt 6⁵; Sir 2¹⁵ᶠ), and of *God's love for men* (e.g. Dt 4³⁷; Wis 16²⁶). *Agape* is just as wide in its reference as *'hb* in Hebrew and 'love' in English. It is a mistake, therefore, to attach any significance to the fact that God's 'love' is always denoted by *agape*. There is nothing that the other terms mean that it cannot mean. There are, of course, ways in which God does not love, but this is because it is *He* that loves. The term itself neither imposes limitations nor denotes any particular *kind* of 'love'. It is just the ordinary Greek word for all kinds.⁶ *Eros* refers to

---

⁶ Another Greek cognate, *agapētos*, 'beloved', occurs seventeen times in the Old Testament but never for *'hb*. It is found four (or perhaps five) times in the Apocrypha —To 3¹⁰(?), 10¹²; Sir 15¹³; Bar 4¹⁶; Sus 63.

sexual love, and *philia*, except in three rare compound words, is confined to human love, but *agape* may be used of *any* kind of love. It is the whole of which the other two are parts. The Hebrew idea that a man loves *from choice* recurs under *agapan*, for it is used in both the Great Commandments (Dt 6[5]; Lv 19[18]). 'Thou shalt love' means 'Thou shalt choose to love'. The idea of an involuntary love, as in the phrase 'to fall in love', is very rare, if indeed it occurs at all. The Hebrew was not given to isolating either thought or feeling or will.

To examine the passages where God is said to 'love' (*agapan*) in the Greek version of the Old Testament, would only be to repeat the examination of the Hebrew root *'ahab*. In the previous chapter it was found that the dominant idea is that God loves Israel, and, from the time of the Written Prophets, that He loves righteous Israel or righteous Israelites. In the Apocrypha there is a certain change. In these books the term *agapan* is used of *God's love* eight times. In one passage He is said to 'love all things that are ... because they are (his)' and to be the 'lover of men's souls' (Wis 11[24, 26]). The whole of this great description of the Beneficence of God might be quoted (vv. 23-26). The other seven texts all illustrate one idea. Tobit, praying that Israel may learn to be righteous, asks that God may 'love for ever those that are miserable in Israel, calling down a curse upon her enemies and a blessing upon her friends' (13[10, 12, 14]). Judith speaks of God's 'loved sons' who spoiled their enemies (9[4]). Sirach says that God 'loved' Moses and Samuel 45[1], 46[13]), and Wisdom that He 'loved' Enoch (4[10]). Sirach, describing a man who succours the fatherless and widow, declares: 'So shalt thou be as a son of the Most High, and he shall love thee more than thy mother doth' (4[10]). In a passage which tells how 'wisdom exalteth her sons' (4[11-19]), the same writer says that 'the Lord doth love them that love her' (v. 14). The Book of Wisdom speaks of 'Thy sons, whom thou lovest, O Lord' (16[26]). Finally, there are two texts that sum up the doctrine of all the seven passages. 'Nothing doth God love save him that dwelleth with wisdom' (Wis 7[28]); 'the faithful shall abide with him in love; Because grace and mercy are to his elect' (Wis 3[9]). While the second text does not say directly that God loves, and while the meaning may be 'The faithful through love shall abide with him', yet the sentence at heart *implies* the mutual love of God and the righteous. This is the constant idea. It is not so prominent in the Old Testament.

None the less, there are writers in the Apocrypha, as the evidence given elsewhere shows, that God does 'love His enemies' when they are Jews. But does He love His Gentile enemies? It has been shown that for the Apocryphists God is a beneficent creator and ruler who 'loves all things that are' and may be called 'the lover of men's souls' (Wis 11$^{24,\ 26}$), but in practice this belief was negatived by another which seemed so obvious that it could be taken for granted—the belief that the Gentiles were *incorrigible* sinners. If this were true, it was a right deduction that they were beyond forgiveness and that therefore God would sooner or later 'visit' them in 'wrath'. This repeats the dominant concept in the later Old Testament. The writer of Wisdom, to judge from the tone of his book (e.g. Wis. 14-19), is not sorry that the Gentiles are incorrigible. In his day this was the attitude that any Jew, living under Gentile domination, might very readily take. In the same situation men of another race would have felt just the same. None the less, even with Gentiles, the ground of the inevitable retribution that follows incorrigible sin is not that God is a sinner's 'enemy' but that *he* is God's. The incorrigible, *ipso facto*, baulk His forgiveness. The typical Jew did not trouble either to ask or answer abstract questions, and to ask 'Does God seek to forgive Gentiles?' would have seemed to him one of these.

CHAPTER FOUR

THE NEW TESTAMENT DOCTRINE OF GRACE

IT HAS already been noted that, while the Old Testament simply divides men into good and bad, the New Testament makes a crucial change. Normally it speaks, not of good men, but of believers in Christ. Any goodness that they have is derivative. There is also another significant change. It was seen that for the Hebrew, God's love, for instance, was predominately love for the good, and similarly with His goodness and grace and so on. The idea that He offers His love and grace to *all* men is quite in the background. In the New Testament, on the contrary, it is a dominant idea. The stress upon God's '*seeking* to save' *all* men is new. None the less, even in the New Testament such qualities as 'grace' are best studied where the Divine offer is not only made but accepted. Fundamentally Christianity is a fellowship between God and men. While this had been so with the Old Testament concept of Covenant after its beginnings—first with Abraham and again with Moses—it is rare to find the *offer* of Covenant emphasized. While some passages in the Wisdom Books urge men to be 'wise', and while some Prophets urge Israel to return unto God, this urgency does not pervade the whole *book*. A Hebrew child was born into the Covenant. It is true that for boys circumcision followed, but this did not so much make the boy an Israelite as show that he was one. Girls, who were not circumcised, were still 'daughters of Abraham'. In the New Testament the relation of children to the Church is so obscure that controversy about it continues to this day, but there, as in all Mission Fields, the Gospel is an *offer*—and an offer that is urgent indeed. Otherwise there would be no 'gospel'. But it is also true that God's active love or grace or mercy is only complete when it is accepted. It is consummated in fellowship. Consequently, when these terms are studied in the New Testament, the stress is upon qualities that are active in *those who accept them through Christ*. To quote one text among many, the perspective of the New Testament appears in the great summary, 'God so loved the world that he gave his only begotten Son, that *whosoever believeth* on him should not perish, but have eternal life' (Jn 3[16]). Here the activity of God's love has its unique and climacteric activity in the Incarnation—but it is not fully manifested except in 'believers'. 'The love of Jesus, what it is, None but His loved ones know.' While there is a revolutionary stress on God's *offer* to all, yet the idea that His love only consummates its activity in *believers* is also present. Indeed, it will appear below, under a number of terms, that it is this concept that is interpretative of them in the New Testament. This is just the other side of the doctrine that the refusal of grace is the Sin of Sins. Consequently, while the subject of this section might have been defined as 'God's Offer to All Men', it would be more accurately named 'The Ways of God with Believers'. It is not under 'seeking' but under 'saving' that His qualities are fully manifest in the Son of Man.

In the New Testament the Greek term for 'grace' is *charis* (*155— 101* in Paul), the usual LXX rendering of *chen*. *Charis* is common alike in secular Greek, in LXX, and in the New Testament. In the first two there is great variety in its use, but in the New Testament it gains a distinctively Christian meaning, which, beginning in Acts, culminates in Paul. It is a derivative of *chairein*, 'to rejoice', and it always expresses delight, whether in secular, Septuagintal, or Christian literature. It seems originally to have denoted the 'charm' of beautiful *things*, but outside this use it always refers to a *relation* of gladness between persons. The implied relation is that of giving and receiving, the word being used to denote both the good-will of the giver and the thanks of the receiver. It is a word that pre-supposes fellowship and is therefore apt for Christian use.[1]

In the Synoptic Gospels *charis* is only found in Luke (*8*), and its use there is like that in LXX. It is used of God's 'favour' to Mary (1^{30}), and of God and men's 'favour' to Jesus in the silent years ($2^{40, 52}$). Four times it means 'thanks' (6^{32-4}, 17^9). The remaining passage is 4^{22}, where the phrase 'the words of grace' probably means 'gracious' or 'winsome words'. Jesus Himself does not use the *word*, except to mean 'thanks', but the *idea* is, of course, constant in His message.

In the Acts (*17*) Luke uses *charis* to denote the 'favour' of 'the people', of the Jews, and of certain rulers (2^{47}, 7^{10}, 24^{27},

---

[1] *Charin*, the accusative of the noun, had been worn down into a preposition with the meaning 'because of'. It has examples (*9*) in the New Testament (e.g. Lk 7^{47}; Gal 3^{19}; 1 Jn 3^{12}), but may be omitted here.

EBDG

25$^{3, 9}$), and Stephen speaks of God's 'favour' to David (7^{46}). But there are also examples of its distinctively Christian use. It is the characteristic of the common life of the Church (4^{33}, 11^{23}, 13^{43}, 14^{26}, 15^{40}); it is the source of the power to work miracles (6^8, 14^3); it is correlative of 'faith' (15^{11}, 18^{27}); the gospel is 'the word of (the Lord's) grace' (14^3; cf. 20$^{24, 32}$). In Hebrews (*8*), while some texts illustrate common Christian ideas (12$^{15, 28}$, 13$^{9, 25}$), there are three peculiar texts—in one it is 'by the grace of God' that *Jesus* dies for every man (2^9); in another, apostates 'do despite to *the Spirit* of grace' (10^{29}); in the third, Christians draw near to 'the *throne* of grace' (4^{16}). For this writer 'grace' seems always to be 'the grace *of God*', even though this manifests itself through Christ in the Spirit. For James (*2*) 'grace' is certainly 'the grace *of God*', the connexion with Christianity being made by a reference to 'the Spirit which (God) made to dwell in us' (4^{5f}). In this text James, along with Peter (1 P 5^5), has the only quotation under this word from LXX (Pr 3^{34}). Peter uses the word more frequently than James (*10* in 1 Peter). For him too 'grace' is the 'grace *of God*', though he connects this closely with Christ (1$^{10f, 13}$, 5^{10}). The phrase 'the grace *of life*' (3^7) is his key phrase, for all the passages in this Epistle relate to the distinctively Christian way of life (e.g. 2^{19f}, 4^{10}, 5^{12}) rather than to a believer's initial conversion. This is so also with Jude in his one passage (v. 4), where, in a condemnation of antinomianism, he relates 'the grace of our God' to Jesus. In 2 Peter (*2*), the Apocalypse (*2*), and 2 John (*1*) *charis* occurs only in salutations and farewells (2 P 1^2, 3^{18}; Rev 1^{4f}, 22^{21}; 2 Jn 3; cf. 1 P 1^2; He 13^{25}), the word being related to God or to Christ or to both. This use shows that, in spite of the rarity of the word in these books, it was common in the churches. John does not use the word in his First Epistle, and in his Gospel (*3*) it is confined to the Prologue. Here, however, he sums up Christianity under *charis* (1$^{14-18}$)—'Of the fulness (of the Word) we all received, and grace after grace'. There remain Paul's passages (*101*). As two-thirds of the New Testament instances of the term occur in his Epistles, this word furnishes a good example for the claim that he provided the later Church with some of its distinctive terminology. The above evidence, however, taken together, shows that the Church as a whole gradually found that this word, like *agape*, was one of those that, being stamped with the image of Christ, best expressed its gospel, and that therefore its use, in a distinctive Christian sense, spread with Christianity. What Paul did, on this showing, was to select this familiar Christian term as his watch-word in the Judaistic controversy and make it thereafter his own permanent watch-word and that of his churches. This means that the Church owes, not the first use of the word, but its pre-eminence, to Paul. Still less, of course, does he monopolize its *idea*, for this is everywhere.

In examining Paul's use of *charis* a beginning may be made with the Salutations and Farewells of *all* his letters. He speaks of 'grace' in every instance. There is an interesting difference between the Salutations and Farewells. In the former the Apostle, in eleven Epistles, wishes his readers 'Grace and peace (with "mercy" added sometimes) *from God our Father and the Lord Jesus Christ*', and his two other Salutations are only exceptions in form (Col 1[2f]; 1 Th 1[1]); in the Farewells, except in 2 Corinthians, the phrase is sometimes 'The grace *of our Lord Jesus Christ* be with you' (or 'with your spirit'), and sometimes, in later letters, simply 'Grace be with you'. It looks as though the single word gradually became the customary Christian farewell. It was perhaps an intentionally Christian variant of the usual Greek farewell, '*chairete*', 'rejoice'. Paul uses the same Salutation and Farewell to the Churches that he had not founded or even visited as to others (Ro 1[7], 16[20]; Col 1[2], 4[18])—which once more suggests that it was a universal Christian word. The use of 'peace' and 'mercy' along with 'grace' shows that 'grace', like the other two, does not denote a thing, as much later theology has supposed under phrases like *quidam supernaturale*, but is parallel to such phrases at the end of English letters as 'With my love' or 'Give him my love'. It is true that Paul sometimes personalizes 'grace'—notably so in Ro 5[20f], where he treats 'sin' similarly—but he does the same with 'love' (e.g. 1 Co 13) and 'peace' (e.g. Ph 4[7]). When he ends a letter with the phrase 'The grace of our Lord Jesus Christ be with you', he means 'May Christ be with you exercising His grace'. There remains the so-called 'Apostolic Benediction' (2 Co 13[14]). This is a unique Farewell, but it epitomizes the Christian faith, and its three phrases, which are descriptions of different facets of the same experience, follow the historical order. Initially a believer experienced 'the grace of the Lord Jesus Christ'; from this, he learnt both 'the love of God' and 'the fellowship of the Holy Spirit'. The passage, of course, has Trinitarian implications—as have other passages discussed in the chapters on the New Testament—but this is beside the present subject.

In examining Paul's use of *charis outside* the Salutations and Farewells a beginning may be made with the phrase 'the grace of God' and the three synonyms 'the grace of our Lord Jesus Christ', 'the grace of the Lord Jesus Christ', and 'the grace of Christ'. The first occurs over twenty times, the other three only once each (2 Co 8^9, 13^{14}; Gal 1^6; cf. 2 Th 2^{16}). Even the first of these three —'Ye know the grace of our Lord Jesus Christ, that, though he was rich, yet for your sakes he became poor'—may mean 'the grace that God gave to Christ' (cf. Ph 2^9; He 2^9). It is clear that for Paul God is the ultimate fountain of grace. But in at least ten of the passages where he speaks of 'the grace of God' there is also some such phrase as 'through the redemption that is in Christ Jesus' or 'which was given you in Christ Jesus' (Ro 3^{24}; 1 Co 1^4; cf. Ro 5^{15}; Eph 1$^{5-7}$; 1 Ti 1^{14}). Indeed, some of these passages unite God and Christ under the term 'grace' in the same way as the Salutations (e.g. 2 Th 1^{12}, 2^{16}; 2 Ti 1^9). Further, even when the phrase 'the grace of God' occurs without explicit mention of Christ, the context shows that Paul was thinking of 'the grace of God that comes through and from and in Christ' (e.g. 1 Co 3^{10}; 2 Co 6^1; Gal 1^{15}; Eph 2^7; Col 1^6; Tit 2^{11}). Probably in all Paul's hundred uses of *charis* there is not a single instance where this idea is not present. Usually, indeed, it is expressed in some way in the context. It is the same with the two verbs, *charizesthai* and *charitoun* (e.g Ro 8^{32}; 1 Co 2^{12}; Eph 1^6; Ph 1^{29}; Col 2^{13}). The only possible summary of Paul's doctrine of 'grace' is 'the grace of God in Christ'.

There are no passages where grace is said to be given to all men. The three nearest are Ro 3$^{22-4}$; 5^{17f}; Tit 2^{11}, for the word 'all' is found in them. In the first, however, while 'all' occurs with the meaning 'all men' in a parenthesis about sinners, the phrase 'being justified freely by his grace' refers back to 'all them *that believe*'. There is, however, the implication that 'grace' *is offered* to all men. Similarly, in the second passage the 'abundance of grace' is offered 'unto all men to justification of life'. The preferable translation of the third is 'The grace of God hath appeared to all men, bringing salvation' (cf. 1 Ti 1^{15})—i.e. it is *offered* to all men. It is sometimes said that 'grace' is 'love at work'; rather, it is 'love successfully at work'. While God '*loves* the world' of 'perishing' sinners, His '*grace*' needs to be 'received' (Jn 3^{16}, 1^{16}). In other words, while God's 'love' is not perfected unless men respond, His 'grace', in Paul's use of the word, does not operate at all where there is no response. Paul emphasizes the truth that 'grace' is a 'gift' (e.g. Ro 3^{24}; 1 Co 1^4; Eph 4$^{7,\ 29}$), and exults in its 'riches' and 'abundance' (e.g. Ro 5^{20}; 2 Co 9^8; Eph 1^{18}, 2^7; 1 Ti 1^{14}), yet speaking accurately, there is a distinction between the offer of a gift and the gift itself. A gift is not a gift until it has been accepted. *Charis* is *agape* accepted and therefore operative. The connexion appears in the text 'God our Father which loved us and gave us eternal help and good hope through grace' (2 Th 2^{16}). The response is 'faith' (e.g. Ro 4^{16}, 5^2; Eph 2$^{5,\ 8}$). 'Grace' and 'faith' are as correlative as 'father' and 'child' or 'bridegroom' and 'bride'. Where there is one, *ipso facto* there is the other—but nowhere else.[2] While faith is the fundamental response to 'grace', there is also the derivative response of 'thanks'. Here *charis* occurs in a secondary sense. Paul uses it in this way once of 'thanks' to Christ (1 Ti 1^{12}), but seven times of 'thanks' to God (e.g. Ro 6^{17}; 1 Cor 15^{57}; 2 Co 2^{14}). Except perhaps in 2 Ti 1^3, wherever Paul says 'give thanks' to God, it is under one phrase or another thanks for 'his unspeakable gift' in Christ (2 Co 9^{15}).

Similar results follow if the use of *eucharistein* (*39—25* in Paul), 'to give thanks', and *eucharistia* (*15—12* in Paul), and *eucharistos* (*1*—Col 3^{15}), is examined. Except in Ac 24^3 and Ro 6^4, they always denote 'thanksgiving' *to God*. In the Synoptics the most notable instance is in the story of the Last Supper (e.g. Lk 22$^{17,\ 19}$). In Paul, apart from Romans 1^{21}, they are always used of *Christian* thanksgiving. Here, except in 1 Timothy 4^4, the full exegesis of every passage would show that the basis of thanksgiving is the 'unspeakable gift'. This is explicit in such texts as Ro 1^8; 1 Co 1^4; 2 Co 4^{14f}; Eph 5^{20}; Col 1^{12}, 3^{15}. The Pauline uses of *charis* and all its cognates pre-suppose and expound a factual fellowship between God and man 'in Christ'. It is 'by grace' that believers are 'justified' (Ro 3^{24}; Tit 3^7), 'through grace' that they are 'saved' (Eph 2$^{5,\ 8}$), and 'according to the riches of grace' that they have 'forgiveness of trespasses' (Eph 1^7). In the culminant passage (Ro 5$^{12-21}$) Paul, setting 'grace' over against its great antagonist 'sin', declares its omnipotence. 'Where sin abounded, grace did much more abound.'

---

[2] From this it follows that such a phrase as 'prevenient grace' does not use the term 'grace' in the New Testament way. It will be argued later that none the less the phrase does express a truth.

It does not belong to the present subject to discuss Paul's antithesis of 'faith' and 'works' except to note that it involves an antithesis of 'grace' and 'works' (Ro 4⁴, 6¹⁴; Gal 5⁴; 2 Ti 1⁹). Here the main point is that 'grace' is an *undeserved* gift. Strictly speaking, while 'works' may earn a payment, they cannot earn a gift (Ro 11⁶) for 'an earned gift' is a contradiction in terms. Another point to note is that *charis*, like *agape*, is used to describe the ground and realm of the *whole* of the Christian life. This comes out, for instance, in such phrases as 'the grace wherein we stand' (Ro 5²), 'grace rules through righteousness' (Ro 5²¹; cf. 6¹⁴), 'by the grace of God I am what I am' (1 Co 15¹⁰), 'my grace is sufficient for thee' (2 Co 12⁹). Similarly, every Salutation and Farewell implies that both for every Christian and every Church 'grace' is the breath of life.

Since the Holy Spirit might equally be called the Christian's 'breath of life' it is remarkable that, except at one point, Paul does not closely relate the *term charis* to the Spirit. Yet the phrase 'the Spirit of grace', found in Hebrews (10²⁹), does in *fact* correspond to Paul's teaching. For instance, while *charis* does not occur in his greatest passage about the Spirit (Ro 8), yet the chapter is just an exposition of 'grace'. In his one text about 'the love of the Spirit' he might as well have written 'the grace of the Spirit' (Ro 15³⁰; cf. 5⁵), but he prefers to keep the *word charis* for Christ and God-in-Christ. It was, however, 'according to the Spirit of holiness' in the Son of God that Jesus Christ gave him 'grace and apostleship' (Ro 1⁴) and there are passages that, however implicitly, require that the doctrines of 'the grace of the Lord Jesus Christ' and 'the fellowship of the Holy Spirit' are identifiable (e.g. 2 Co 13¹⁴; Eph 1⁶, ¹³, 4⁴, ⁷). One of Paul's Benedictions, 'the grace of our Lord Jesus Christ be with your spirit' (Gal 6¹⁸; Ph 4²³; 2 Ti 4²²; Philem 25), is, in fact, a kind of synopsis of what has been said in *The Christian Doctrine of Man* about the connexion between the Spirit of God and a believer's spirit. The verb *charizesthai* occurs in the middle of a passage that claims the gift of 'the Spirit of God' as the *differentia* of believers (1 Co 2¹⁰⁻¹³). The 'renewing of the Holy Spirit' accompanies justification by *grace* (Tit 3⁵⁻⁷) The unity of the two doctrines is like that of a geological *stratum* which is found everywhere if one digs, but only emerges once in a great outcrop. This is in 1 Co 12⁴⁻¹¹ (cf. Ro 12⁶ff), and the outcrop occurs, not under *charis*, but under its derivative *charisma* (*17*—Paul *16*). Peter expressly connects the two (1 P 4^{10}). The Pauline passage begins, 'Now concerning *spiritual* (things)', which means 'spiritual gifts', as is once stated (Ro 1^{11}) and implied more than once (e.g. 1 Co 9^{11}, 14^{1}; Gal 6^{1}). Paul goes on to insist that as all Christians have 'the one' and 'same Spirit', each of them has a *charisma*. This is better rendered 'grace-gift' than 'gift' for it denotes the product or resultant of the working of grace through the Spirit in every believer. While there are *charismata* that are common to all Christians (Ro 5^{15f}, 6^{23}), in 1 Corinthians 12 Paul is speaking of those that vary. Here each Christian's *charisma* is the outcome of the working of the one Spirit through each believer's idiosyncrasy, in the proper sense of that term. While these *charismata* are as various as human nature, the one Spirit, working through *agape*, which is greater than them all (12$^{13, 27-30}$, 13), unifies them all. In spite of the sporadic nature of the evidence Paul's doctrine of grace and the Spirit are two different expressions of one doctrine.

There is a sense in which Christians exercise grace to other men. *Charizesthai* is used about them, with the meaning 'freely forgive', Christians being exhorted to 'forgive' because 'God for Christ's sake' has forgiven them (Eph 4^{32}; Col 3^{13}; cf. 2 Co 2$^{7, 10}$). The noun *charis* itself is used to describe a gift of money to other Christians (1 Co 16^{3}), since it was given because of 'the grace of our Lord Jesus Christ' (2 Co 8^{9}). But the chief evidence here too is under *charisma*. Paul, in effect, expounds the meaning of the term when he speaks of 'the *charis* that was given' unto him for his Gentile ministry (e.g. Ro 1^{5}, 15^{15}; 1 Co 3^{10}; Gal 2^{9}; Eph 3^{8}). This was his outstanding *charisma*, though he does not use the word—and it typifies all Christian *charismata* because its origin is in the grace of Christ and its outcome is service to men. This, of course, leads again to 1 Corinthian 12 and so illustrates once more the unity of the doctrines of *charis* and the Spirit. Sometimes a *charisma* is mediated through one Christian to another, Paul being the chief instance (Ro 1^{11}; 2 Co 1^{11}; 1 Ti 4^{14}; 2 Ti 1^{6}; cf. 1 Co 1^{15}). It may be assumed that *every* Christian had the *charisma* that enables believers to witness for Christ to the outsider. Indeed, this follows from the duty of 'confessing' Christ. It is true that all the *charismata* that Paul enumerates in his two lists (Ro 12^{4ff}; 1 Co 12^{4ff}; cf. v. 28) are *charismata* that are exercised *within the Church*, but this is only because Paul's subject here requires this limitation, for he is speaking of the exercise of Christians' *charismata* to each other within the organic unity of 'the body of Christ'. In these passages Paul depicts the differentiation of the results of *charis* in the lives of different Christians as he does not under *agape*. The latter has indeed manifold manifestations (1 Co 8), but these ought to appear in *every* believer.

If now the use of *charis* in the New Testament is compared with that in LXX, it is plain that the meaning of the term was specialized and transfigured in Christian speech. The change can be seen *in process*. In the Synoptic Gospels and Acts the word is used in ways that have parallels in LXX, but in the other books there are many contrasts and only two likenesses. The chief contrasts may be summarized. First, outside historical books, *charis* is commonly used in LXX of the 'favour' of man, rarely of the 'favour' of God. In the New Testament this is reversed. Second, in LXX, the dominant reference is to outward boons, in the New Testament to an inward blessing. Third, in LXX, when men show *charis* to each other, it ranges in meaning from a king's boon to a harlot's beguilement. It is not rooted in God's *charis*. In the New Testament one Christian exercises *charis* to another Christian through a *charisma* of the Holy Spirit. Fourth, in LXX men usually ask the favour of God; in the New Testament He *offers* 'grace' to men through Christ. Fifth, in LXX God selects men for His favour; in the New Testament He offers it to all. The one text under *charis* that seems to contradict this (Ro. 11⁵) is considered under 'election'. Sixth, in LXX the *charis* of God is not related to 'salvation', even in the Old Testament meaning of that word; in the New Testament to speak of 'grace' is to say 'salvation'. The two points of likeness between the uses in LXX and in the Christian Church is that God *gives charis*, and that He gives it to men who cannot claim it. It was on these elements in the old meaning of the term that Paul and his fellow-Christians laid hold, alike in controversy and preaching. Even here, however, there is no small difference, for in the New Testament God gives grace, not merely to those who do not deserve it, but to those who deserve its opposite. The manifold contrasts and the two likenesses both root in the fact that in the New Testament the 'grace of God' is 'the grace of the Lord Jesus Christ'.

The next term is *eleos* (*27*), usually rendered 'mercy', though 'pity' is preferable, for this can be used also for the verb *eleein* (*31*), 'to pity' (where, under 'mercy' the unsatisfactory phrases 'to have mercy' and 'to obtain mercy' have to be used). The cognate adjectives are *eleemon* (*2*), 'pitiful', and *eleeinos* (*2*), 'pitiable'. It was shown that in LXX *eleos* is the usual rendering for *chesed*, but that *eleein* and *eleemon* generally stand for *chen* or one of its cognates. It was found too that *eleos* does not involve the mutual idea found under *chesed* but not under *chen*. So in the New Testament men do not reciprocate God or Christ's *eleos*. It is *agape*, not *eleos*, that is mutual. In the New Testament there is the usual novelty—the doctrine of God's 'pity' centres in Christ. This begins to appear in the *Magnificat* and *Benedictus*, which herald God's gift of the Messiah as a manifestation of His 'pity' to Israel or to 'those that fear him' within her (Lk 1[50, 54, 72, 78]). It continues in the story of Jesus' healing miracles, for they were manifestations of the 'pity' of God (Mk 5[19]; cf. Ph 2[27]). The cry 'Son of David, pity me' (e.g. Mk 10[47f]; Lk 13[38f]; Mt 9[27]; cf. Lk 17[13]) was an appeal to God's Messiah. For the later New Testament the typical text is 'God, being rich in pity, for his great love wherewith he loved us, even when we were dead through our trespasses, quickened us together with Christ (by grace have ye been saved)' (Eph 2[4f]; cf. Tit 3[5]; He 2[17], 4[16]; 1 P 1[3]; Jude 21). Here God's 'love' and 'pity' and 'grace' are linked in Christ. Similarly, 'grace' and 'pity' and 'peace' from God and Christ go together in salutations (1 Ti 1[2]; 2 Ti 1[2]; cf. 2 Jn 3; Jude 2; Gal 6[16]). In Paul none of the words occurs except in reference to Christ. The Apostle has sometimes an unexpected emphasis upon God's right to choose whom He will pity though the ultimate purpose of this election is that He 'might pity all' (Ro 9[15-18, 23], 11[30-2], 15[9]; cf. 1 P 2[10]). For instance, Paul believed that God had 'pitied' him in order that he might minister to others (1 Co 7[25]; 2 Co 4[1]; 1 Ti 1[13, 16]; cf. Ro 12[8]). Just as Jesus taught that God will forgive those that forgive, so He taught that God will pity those that pity (Mt 5[7], 18[33]), for He 'wills pity and not sacrifice' (Mt 9[13]; cf. 23[23]; Lk 10[37]; Ro 1[31]; Ja 2[13], 3[17]). In the New Testament, as in LXX, *eleemosune* (*13*), which always means 'alms', is not a merely humanitarian practice, but a duty to God (e.g. Mt 6[2-4]; Ac 10[4]), for 'pity' is a kind of sacrifice (Ac 10[31]). As with the doctrine of *agape*, the whole doctrine of *eleos* roots in the doctrine of God's 'pity'.

This becomes explicit in a text where the next word, *oiktirmōn* (*2*), 'compassionate', a synonym of *eleemon* (cf. Ro 9[15]), occurs— 'Be ye compassionate, even as your Father is compassionate' (Lk 6[36]; cf. Ja 5[11]). This term's cognates, *oiktirmos* (*5*) and *oikteirein* (*1*), are also used to denote the 'compassion' of God (Ro 12¹; 2 Co 1³; Ro 9¹⁵; cf. He 10²⁸ᶠ). From this there is a translation to the 'compassion' of Christ' (Ph 2¹) and hence to that of 'God's elect' (Col 3¹²). God's 'compassion' shows itself in Christ's and Christ's in the Christian's. Precisely the same three-fold idea obtains under the rare term *hosios* (*8*), which renders *chasid* in LXX, and its cognates *hosiōs* (*1*) and *hosiotēs* (*2*). Unfortunately in English it has to share the rendering 'holy' with *hagios*. In the Apocalypse one text says that 'only God' is *hosios* (Rev 15⁴; cf. 16⁵), but elsewhere Christ is His *chasid* and therefore is *hosios* too (Ac 2²⁷ and 13³⁴, quoting Ps 16¹⁰ and Is 55³). Again, through the Christ *men* are to practise *hosiotes* (Lk 1⁷⁵), as they do when they 'put on the new man which after God hath been created in righteousness and *holiness* of truth' (Eph 4²⁴). Similarly, in Hebrews only the truly 'holy High Priest' 'suits' the need of sinners (7²⁶). In most of the passages named *dikaios* or a cognate accompanies *hosios* (cf. 1 Th 2¹⁰; Tit 1⁸). As in LXX, when *hosios* is used of *men*, 'devout' is an alternative rendering, it being remembered that in Christianity true 'devotion' issues in righteousness. The believer is *hosios* through Christ, and Christ is *hosios* because He is the '*chasid* of God'.

Of the two Greek verbs rendered 'forgive' in the Revised Version the commoner is *aphienai*. This word (*145*) means literally 'send away' (e.g. 1 Cor 7¹¹), but it may also mean 'allow' (e.g. Mk 1³⁴) and 'leave' (e.g. Mk 1¹⁸). The great majority of its examples are in the Synoptic Gospels (*115*), but there it is only used explicitly of the 'dismissal' or 'forgiveness' of *sins* twenty-four times (e.g. Mk 2⁵⁻¹⁰, 3²⁸, 11²⁵; Lk 11⁴; Mt 12³¹). There are also a few implicit references to sin (e.g. Mk 4¹³). Outside the Synoptics among thirty instances only six refer to the forgiveness of sins (Ac 8²²; Ro 4⁷; Ja 5¹⁵; Jn 20²³; 1 Jn 1⁹, 2¹²). It is otherwise with the comparatively rare noun, *aphesis* (*17*), 'forgiveness' in the sense of 'remission'. This word is never used to mean 'forgiveness' in LXX, but in the New Testament, apart from a quotation from LXX (Lk 4¹⁸), it never means anything else (e.g. Mk 1⁴; Lk 1⁷⁷, 24⁴⁷; Mt 26²⁸; Ac 2³⁸; Eph 1⁷; He 9²²). The use both of the verb and noun for 'forgiveness' has three marks. First, the 'remission' of past sins is the Divine correlative of men's 'repentance'. This appears, for instance, in the Baptist's preaching (Mk 1⁴⁴; Lk 1⁷⁷; cf. Lk 24⁴⁷; Ac 2³⁸, 5³¹). So far the New

THE NEW TESTAMENT DOCTRINE OF GRACE 67

Testament only repeats the teaching of the Old Testament and of the Rabbis. But, secondly, Jesus insisted that God will only forgive men if they forgive each other (e.g. Lk 11⁴; Mt 6¹⁴ᶠ, 18³²ᶠ; cf. Eph 4³²ᶠ; Col 3¹³), and, thirdly, from the first He claims that 'the Son of Man hath authority on earth to forgive sins' (Mk 2¹⁰). Similarly the Apostles preached that 'remission' is *Christ's* gift (Ac 5³¹; cf. 2³⁸; Col 1¹⁴; He 10¹⁸, etc.). But why is the use of these terms for 'forgiveness' so comparatively rare in the New Testament? The answer seems to be that, as the majority of the passages show, they only refer to the *first stage* in the full Christian doctrine, the forgiveness of *past* sins. For this reason 'remission' is a better rendering than 'forgiveness'. If this were all that 'forgiveness' means, Christians, like the Jews (and Gentiles), could only look forward to a recurrent cycle of sinning, repenting, forgiveness—and then sinning again. It is true that since Constantine this cycle has been normal also with '*nominal* Christians' —except that, as the repentance is often 'nominal' too, there is no forgiveness. But, according to the Gospel, with true 'believers' the 'remission' of past sins is only the first item in a much wider experience—and it is the later and distinctive items in which the Apostles exult. They preached that through the Spirit Christians live in so close a fellowship with God in Christ that they are able to give up sinning. For them 'forgiveness' is more, far more, than mere 'remission', as this chapter shows under many terms.[3]

There is an example in the other term rendered 'forgive' in the English Versions—*charizesthai*, 'to exercise grace'. The term is rare in LXX (*8*), and there it never means 'forgive', but denotes God's 'boon' of life' (2 Mac 3³¹, ³³, 7²²), or a king's 'boon' of a 'house' (Est 8⁷), or a good man's 'boon' when he gives alms (Sir 12³). In the New Testament the word is confined to the Lucan books (*7*) and Paul (*14*). By Luke it is six times used, as in LXX, of someone's spontaneous and undeserved boon to another —e.g. of Jesus' gift of sight to the blind (Lk 7²¹), Pilate's gift of Barabbas to the people (Ac 3¹⁴), and God's gift of the lives of 'all them that sail with thee' to Paul (Ac 27²⁴). The passages nearly related to the present subject begin with the one Lucan passage where the verb is rendered 'forgive' (Lk 7⁴²ᶠ). When 'the woman, a sinner' anoints Jesus' feet, Simon the Pharisee silently protests—not to the 'remission' even of her sins if she were

---

[3] The rare terms *anienai* (*4*) and *anesis* (*5*), which occasionally denote 'forgiveness' in LXX, are not so used in the New Testament.

penitent, but to her intimate act. But Jesus adds 'boon' to 'remission' (vv. 42f, 47f). He does not just put away sins but welcomes penitents into His friendship. All the other relevant uses of *charizesthai* are in Paul (*10*). Sometimes the reference to sin is indirect or even remote, but the context always relates to the fellowship that the saved sinner shares with Christ through *charis*. In other words, here is 'forgiveness' in its *positive* content. The sweep of the context of one sentence, 'How shall not God with (Christ) give us the boon of all things?' (Ro 8^{31-9}) expounds its scope. It is the same in the two passages where *charizesthai* is directly used of God's 'forgiveness' of sins (Eph 4^{32}; Col 2^{13}). 'In Christ' and 'with Christ' are the key phrases (cf. Gal $3^{18, 22}$). Similarly, when Paul calls upon Christians to 'forgive one another' after the manner of God, he is speaking of the free and full restoration of fellowship and not to any meagre 'wiping of the slate' (Eph 4^{32}; cf. 2 Co $2^{7, 10}$). Or again, when Paul, in a passage that uses *charizesthai* in the LXX sense, says that God has 'given Jesus the name that is above every name' as a 'boon', he is describing the whole issue of the Incarnation in 'the fellowship of the Spirit' (Phil 2^{1-11}; cf. 1 Co 2^{12}; Ph 1^{29}). All this means that in the New Testament the meaning of *charizesthai* shares in the enlargement already traced for *charis* itself.[4]

Hilaskesthai and its cognates are rare in the New Testament—*hilaskesthai* (*2*), *hilasmos* (*2*), *hilasterion* (*2*), and *hileōs* (*2*). After the long discussion of their use in LXX they don't need a great deal of interpretation though this is not unimportant. It is very noteworthy that *exilaskesthai* and *exilasmos*, which denote 'placation' or 'propitiation' in LXX, do *not occur at all* in the New Testament. Of the two uses of *hilaskesthai* one clearly denotes 'forgiveness' (Lk 18^{13}), and the other 'atonement' in its literal sense of 'at-one-ment' (He 2^{17}). In a quotation from Jeremiah 31^{34} *hileōs*, similarly, means 'forgiving' (He 8^{12}), for it renders *salach*. Peter, addressing Jesus, uses the term in a current phrase that seems to mean what 'mercy on you' originally meant in English. It is an appeal to God's mercy (Mt 16^{22}; cf. 2 S 23^{17} LXX; 1 Mac 2^{21}). *Hilasterion* certainly means 'mercy-seat' (*kapporeth*) in one of its two instances (He 9^5), and probably in the other (Ro 3^{25}). Here Paul is saying that Christ is the *kapporeth* of believers. In the two examples of *hilasmos* (1 Jn 2^2, 4^{10}) Christ

---

[4] Under the verb *charitoun* (*2*), once used in LXX (Sir 18^{17}), Luke has the Jewish sense (1^{28}), but Paul Christianizes it (Eph 1^6)—as with *charizesthai*.

THE NEW TESTAMENT DOCTRINE OF GRACE 69

is the 'atonement' of Christians. In all the passages the main LXX use is followed. These terms do not denote the appeasement of anger, but the putting away of alienation and the restoration of fellowship.

Under 'salvation' four Hebrew terms were noted and in LXX it was found that, while there are four Greek renderings, each of these is used for more than one Hebrew term and that LXX translators seem to have been indifferent which Greek term they used. Two of these terms only need brief mention. *Ruesthai*, 'to draw out of harm's way', is used in the New Testament (*17*) to denote 'deliverance' from 'enemies' (Lk 1^{74}), from physical death (2 Co 1^{10}), from evil men (Ro 15^{31}; 2 Th 3^2), from 'trial' (2 P 2^7), from 'the body of this death' (Ro 7^{24}; cf. Col 1^{13}), and from 'the coming wrath' (1 Th 1^{10}). In the Synoptic Gospels, where the word is rare, it is God who delivers, but in other books Christ is the deliverer. Under *exairein* (*8*) the literal meaning appears in the 'taking out' of an eye (Mt 5^{29}) and, on one exposition, in God's choosing of Paul (Ac 26^{17}). Elsewhere in Acts it is used of God's delivering Joseph from 'afflictions', Israel from Egypt, and Peter from prison (Ac 7$^{10, 34}$, 12^{11}). In one Epistle Paul says that Christ delivers believers 'out of this present evil age' (Gal 1^4). The word is nowhere used of deliverance from sin.

In the New Testament the verb *lutroun*, which is so common in LXX, does not occur at all in the 'active voice' and only three times in the 'middle' ('save for oneself'). The cognates are *lutrōsis* (*3*), *apolutrōsis* (*10*), *lutrotēs* (*1*), *lutron* (*2*), and *antilutron* (*1*). The Christian use begins with our Lord's words at the Last Supper—'For verily the Son of Man came not to be ministered unto, but to minister, and to give his life a *ransom* (*lutron*) for many' (Mk 10^{45}). Jesus is teaching the Eleven that they are to be '*servants* of all' (v. 44) and it is generally agreed that here He declares that the 'Son of Man' is the Suffering *Servant* of Deutero-Isaiah. It is true that the noun *lutron* does not occur in Is 40-66, but the verb *lutroun* is found ten times. In the earlier part of these chapters LXX uses one of its forms six times for 'the redeemer of Israel' and in the later part another form four times for 'the redeemed' (cf. 35^9). In all the passages except 51^{11}, where *padah* occurs, the Hebrew term is *ga'al*, 'to do a kinsman's part'. God, 'the Holy One of Israel', 'created' her to be His 'servant', *not* Babylon's, and now because she is *His*, He will 'redeem' her (43$^{1.}$

14f, 44²¹f· ²⁴), but *not* with 'money' (52³). In four passages there is a reference in the context to God's redemption of Israel from Egypt under Moses (43¹⁴, ¹⁶, 51⁹, ¹¹, 52³f, 63⁹, ¹¹). In an intrusive oracle there is the phrase 'a year of redeeming is here' (63⁴). One text describes the ancient ways of the Great Goel at length— 'And he said, Are they not my people? They will in no wise set (me) aside. And he was a saviour (literally, for salvation) to them from all their affliction. No ambassador or angel but he himself saved them because he loved them and spared them. He himself redeemed them and undertook for them and exalted them all the days of old' (63⁸f LXX). It is true that none of these passages occur in the Servant Songs, but Jesus would not isolate the latter in the modern way, and the *idea* expressed in the word 'Goel' dominates them as well as the rest of Deutero-Isaiah. At the Supper Jesus is Goel. In accordance with this all the twenty examples of words of the *lutroun* group in the New Testament refer to Christ. In two the reference is indirect. Stephen suggests that, as the Israelites had rejected Moses, so his hearers were rejecting a greater Redeemer (Ac 7³⁵). It was because the writer to the Hebrews was addressing Christians who were tempted to apostatize (e.g. 6⁴ff) and who might soon need to 'resist unto blood' (12⁴), that he reminds them (11³⁵) of the Maccabean martyrs who did not accept 'the redemption' that comes by apostasy since they expected 'a better resurrection' than Elijah and Elisha wrought (2 Mac 7⁹ff; 1 K 17²²; 2 K 4³⁵). In all the other passages the writers speak directly of Christ, though in different ways. At the beginning of Luke's Gospel Zacharias and Anna see the fulfilment of the hope of the 'redemption' of Israel in the infant Jesus (1⁶⁸, 2³⁸); near its end Jesus speaks to His disciples of '*your* (final) redemption' and two disciples refer to *His* redemption of Israel (21²⁸, 24²¹). Both Peter and the writer to the Hebrews speak of 'redemption' through Christ's blood (1 P 1¹⁸f; He 9¹², ¹⁵). Outside the Pastorals, where *antilutron* and *lutrousthai* occur (1 Ti 2⁶; Tit 2¹⁴), Paul uses the emphatic word *apolutrosis* (7—cf. LXX in Ex 21⁸; Zeph 3¹; Dn 4³²). Christ *is* 'redemption' (1 Co 1³⁰); 'redemption' is 'in Christ Jesus' (Ro 3²⁴; Col 1¹⁴); in Him 'we have our redemption' (Eph 1⁷). These texts describe the experience of Christians now. Others relate to the future 'day of redemption' (Eph 4³⁰), when the 'body' will be 'redeemed' (Ro 8²³) and God will give 'his own' people their 'inheritance' (Eph 1¹⁴). The first Christians took the old gold of Deutero-Isaiah and stamped it with the image of Christ. They never use one of this group of words except when thinking of Him.

The phenomena relating to the much commoner word *sozein* (*103*), 'save', with its cognates *soter* (*24*), 'saviour', *soteria* (*24*) or *soterion* (*4*), 'salvation', and *soterios* (*1*), 'saving', are more complex. These terms were not only in common use among the Hellenistic Jews but in the whole Hellenistic world. The term *soter*, for instance, was applied to more than one of the Ptolemies as 'saviours' of Egypt. Again, the one purpose of the many mystery cults was to offer men *soteria*. A devotee of Isis, for instance, could have said of her: 'There is no other name whereby we must be saved.'[5] The continual political upheavals through two centuries after the death of Alexander and the failure of faith in the old gods of Greece and Rome combined to urge men to despair and to look almost anywhere for 'salvation'. Even Gentiles could speak of 'a way of salvation' or ask 'What must I do to be saved?' (Ac 16[17, 30]; cf. 11[14]). As for the Jews, in the Synoptic Gospels 'save' appears as a current term that needed no explanation. It could not be otherwise with heirs of the Old Testament. Probably the word was commonly used throughout Judaism of the expected 'salvation' of Israel from political servitude (cf. Lk 1[69]). This use, however, hardly appears in the New Testament. There the concept of the salvation *of the individual* is dominant. This begins to appear in the disciples' question, 'Then who can be saved?' (Mk 10[26]). Probably this means 'Who can be saved *at the end of the Age*?', as the saying 'Whosoever would save his life shall lose it; and whosoever shall lose his life for my sake and the gospels shall save it' seems to show, for it leads to a reference to the coming of the Son of Man (Mk 8[35-8]). This shows that, at least sometimes, the term was eschatological and Apocalyptic as well as individual. Was it always so? As will presently appear, the commonest Synoptic use is of *present* 'salvation' from sickness, and two other Synoptic passages speak of something *present* (Lk 13[23], 19[9f]), but these passages might be explained under the concept that with Jesus the Future Age had in essence begun, overlapping the Present Age. There were Gentile uses, however, such as those named above, which were not Apocalyptic, and it is remarkable that out of the

---

[5] See, for instance, *ERE*, XI.695-7; Kennedy, *St Paul and the Mystery Religions*, pp. 99-103, 107, 216f.

hundred and fifty-six instances of the New Testament use of the terms only fifteen are found in Apocalyptic, and of these ten belong to 2 Peter and Jude (Mk 13$^{13, 20}$; 2 P 1$^{1, 11}$, 2^{20}, 3$^{2, 15, 18}$; Jude 3, 5, 23, 25; Rev 7^{10}, 12^{10}, 19^{1}). Yet there are texts outside Apocalyptic that are clearly eschatological, as will appear later. Different people will give different answers to the question 'Is "save" always an Apocalyptic word in the New Testament?' according as they reply to the wider question 'Is Apocalyptic dominant in New Testament thought?'

In the Synoptic Gospels (*45*) the commonest use of 'save' describes Jesus' miracles of healing as 'saving'. Here the most striking fact is the connexion that Jesus made between 'faith' and 'save'. 'Thy faith hath saved thee' is His characteristic phrase (Mk 5^{34}, 10^{52}; Lk 17^{19}; cf. 8^{50}). Where men appeal to Him to 'save', faith in His power is implied (Mk 5^{25}; Mt 8^{25}, 14^{30}; cf. Mk 5^{28}, 6^{56}). Even where the term 'save' does not occur, the miracles of healing *are* 'saving'. While it is hazardous to claim that Jesus never healed out of mere compassion (cf. Lk 7$^{12\text{-}15}$, 8$^{28, 36}$), usually He made 'faith' (though not always the sick man's) the condition (and the only condition) of this kind of 'salvation'. It is regrettable that the English versions render the term by 'made whole' for this may suggest a merely physical cure, and it is unlikely that this is what is meant. While the Jews no longer believed that a man's suffering was *always* the result of his sin, for they had put the Book of Job into their Bible, it is all but certain that they still thought that this was *normally* so, though, as the story of the man 'born blind' shows, they added that in suffering God might be 'visiting the sins of the fathers upon the children' (Jn 9^{2}). In this story Jesus declares that the man's blindness was not the result of anyone's sin, and when He taught His disciples that they would be called to suffer for His sake, He implied that this would not be for *their own* sins. Again, they later learnt that in order to save others *He* must suffer for *others*' sin, and that it was for them to 'make up what was lacking' in this kind of suffering. Yet Jesus did not repudiate the doctrine that there was *sometimes* a connexion between a man's suffering and his sin. On the contrary, in what is probably meant to be a typical story, He claimed that when He cured a sick man this showed that his sins were forgiven (Mk 2$^{5\text{-}11}$). The Jews, unlike the modern man, did not habitually think of 'body' and 'soul' as separate but as one, and Jesus agreed. In the story just named He claimed that He had come to save the whole man and that He was doing so. It was a deliberate challenge to His enemies and a challenge under the word 'save' (Mk 3^{36}), and it began a controversy which culminated when they flung the word 'save' at Him on the Cross (Mk 15^{30f}; cf. Lk 23^{39}; Mt 27^{49}). Jesus claimed that if a sick man 'believed' in Him He could cure Him, and that when He had done so, this showed that any sin that went with the sickness was forgiven. It is a mistake to isolate 'miracle faith' and confine it to physical healing. They only occur together so frequently because Jesus' miracles were frequent and startling. In studying terms there may be a kind of 'fallacy of numbers'. In the Synoptics the Twelve are never said to 'believe' in Jesus or to 'love' Him, nor is it stated that they were 'saved' or that their sins were forgiven! Jesus challenged sick 'outsiders' to a faith that He took for granted with His disciples. This postulate emerged when He declared that a woman of many sins was 'forgiven' because 'she loved much' (Lk 7$^{47\text{-}50}$). *All* that is said in the Synoptics under the word 'save' is part and parcel of the one truth 'The Son of Man came to seek and to save that which was lost' (Lk 19^{9f}; cf. 8^{12}). When Matthew used the phrase 'It is he that shall save his people from their sins', he was too good a Jewish Christian to mean merely 'He shall save their souls', even though he would already know that to be saved from sin did not always mean salvation from sickness in this life. Yet it is possible that in Jesus' nearer circle no one was left to be sick (cf. Mk 1^{30f}; Jn 11^{3}). As soon as His ministry began He claimed to be Saviour of the whole man.

In the Acts of the Apostles the word 'save' (*13*) is twice used of miracles worked 'in the name' of Jesus (4^9, 14^9), but, as miracles grew rarer, the disciples still preached salvation from sin, even though they did not expect the full and universal 'redemption of the body' from all evils, even death itself, until 'the end' came (Ro 8^{23}; 1 Co 15$^{24, 26}$; Rev 21^4). In every passage in Acts— probably even in 27$^{20, 31}$—where 'save' occurs, the reference is to Jesus. It occurs five times about the salvation of Gentiles (11^{14}, 15$^{1, 11}$, 16^{30f}). Once it is eschatological (2^{21}), and twice it denotes a present salvation (2$^{40, 47}$). In a single text Peter sums up the whole Apostolic *kerugma*—'In none other is there salvation: for neither is there any other name under heaven, that is given among men, wherein we must be saved' (Ac 4^{12}). Here there are two leading words—'must' with its implication that this is God's will, and 'name' with its unique claim for Jesus.

In the Epistles of Paul *sozein* (*28*) is always used of salvation through Christ, though in one text the reference is indirect (Ro 9^{27}), and in three others Christian preachers are the organs of Christ's salvation (Ro 11^{14}; 1 Co 9^{22}; 1 Ti 4^{16}). Three passages speak of complete salvation at the Coming of Christ (1 Co 3^{15}, 5^{5}; 2 Ti 4^{18}), and others may also have this meaning (e.g. Ro 10$^{9, 13}$, 11^{26}; 1 Ti 2^{4}). Christians are saved 'by hope' and 'from the wrath' (Ro 8^{24}, 5^{9}). Other texts speak of a present salvation. Christians '*have been* saved' (Eph 2$^{5, 8}$; cf. 2 Ti 1^{9}; Tit 3^{5}) and 'are *being* saved' (1 Co 1^{18}, 15^{2}; 2 Co 2^{15}). The aorist tense is common, and, at least sometimes, it may be taken as a 'timeless' aorist, describing a Christian's distinctive state rather than a past event (e.g. Ro 8^{24}; 1 Co 10^{33}; 1 Th 2^{16}; 2 Th 2^{10}; 1 Ti 1^{15}; Tit 3^{5}). It goes without saying that Paul's exposition of such terms as 'justify' and 'sanctify' is an exposition of 'salvation', and that, while it is through Christ that men are 'saved', this is according to God's 'good pleasure' who 'willeth that all men should be saved' (1 Co 1^{21}; 1 Ti 2^{4}).

The writer of the Epistle to the Hebrews declares that God 'saved' *Christ* from death through death (5^{7}). In his one other use of the term he speaks of Christians' 'entire' salvation' (7^{25}). Of course, though the *word* is so rare, his whole Epistle is an exposition of salvation through Christ. The Seer of the Apocalypse never uses the term, but his book exults in the experience. In First Peter the term is used only twice, but in a way that assumes that it was one of *the* words of the Church (3^{21}, 4^{18}; cf. Jude 5). James ends his Epistle with a verse that calls every Christian to seek to 'save sinners' (5^{20}; cf. Jude 23). His four other texts all drew attention to some truth about the universal Christian experience—there is a useless 'faith' (2^{14}); but also 'a prayer of faith' that saves the sick (5^{15}); it is 'God' who saves through the 'implanted word' (4^{12}, 1^{21}). The term does not occur in the Epistles of John and it is only found six times in the Fourth Gospel. Once it is used of recovery from sickness (11^{12}). Twice Jesus claims that He brings the salvation for which the Jews hoped (5^{34}, 10^{9}). In Gethsemane He hesitates to ask that God will 'save' Him from His 'hour' (12^{27}), for how then could He save others? As usual, John has a short text that summarizes the whole New Testament teaching—'God sent . . . the Son into the world . . . that the *world* should be saved through him' (3^{17}).

The noun *soteria* (*46*) is used twice or perhaps thrice of physical 'safety' (Ac 27³⁴; He 11⁷; Ph 1¹⁹), but otherwise its uses are parallel to those of *sozein*, except that it never describes healing by miracle. The four Synoptic examples are all in Luke. It occurs three times in the *Benedictus*, celebrating the fulfilment of the Jewish hope in Jesus (Lk 1⁶⁹, ⁷¹, ⁷⁷), and Jesus Himself uses it in the story of Zacchæus (Lk 19⁹) as a current Jewish term. In the Acts it once describes the 'salvation' of Israel from Egypt (7²⁵), once a 'salvation' for which Gentiles looked (16¹⁷), and three times the Christian gospel alike for Jews and Gentiles (4¹², 13²⁶, ⁴⁷).

In Paul the *idea*, of course, is everywhere, though the *word* (*18*) does not occur in 1 Corinthians, Galatians, Colossians, or 1 Timothy. Three texts show both how the whole Trinity is at work in 'salvation' and how God's 'appointment' or 'election' and man's 'faith' are correlative (Ro 1¹⁶; 1 Th 5⁹; 2 Th 2¹³). 'Salvation' is for 'both Jews and Greeks' (Ro 1¹⁶, 10¹, 11¹¹). The Apostle mediates it (2 Co 1⁶; 2 Ti 2¹⁰). In its fullness it is a future salvation, through 'hope' from 'wrath' (Ro 13¹¹; 1 Th 5⁸ᶠ; 2 Ti 2¹⁰). Yet it is also present, for 'now is the day of salvation' (2 Co 6²). It involves repentance and confession (2 Co 7¹⁰; Ro 10¹⁰), and Christians need to 'work out their own salvation' for God Himself is their fellow-workman (Ph 2¹²). The 'sacred writings' will help them here (2 Ti 3¹⁵). Persecution is God's 'evident token' of their 'salvation' (Ph 1²⁸ᶠ), and the gift of 'the Holy Spirit' is its 'seal' (Eph 1¹³). For Paul everything in the Christian life is an ingredient of 'salvation'.

In the Epistle to the Hebrews (*7*) 'salvation' is everywhere a future goal. It is the final state of the world, a state that Christ will one day come to inaugurate (9²⁸). Christians are at once 'waiting for *him*' and journeying toward *it*, as though 'salvation' were His *rendezvous*. Their journey is through suffering in a world of sin and they make a long line of pilgrims. But Jesus has already come a first time, as His ear-witnesses have told (2³), and He Himself leads the line as *archēgos* (2¹⁰; cf. 12²). *The* Sufferer leads the sufferers. He Himself, 'learning obedience by the things that he suffered', was 'made perfect by suffering' on *His* pilgrimage. But He is not merely the first to reach the goal; He is the '*cause*' of eternal salvation to them that obey him' (5⁷⁻¹⁰), for He was 'once offered to bear the sins of many unto salvation' (9²⁸). Meanwhile, the 'heirs of salvation', whom angels 'serve', are to keep unbroken the line of those who have held by 'the better things that go with' it (1¹⁴, 6¹⁻¹²). In the Epistle to the Hebrews the doctrine of 'salvation' has to be integrated from scattered references, but it is just the doctrine of the Servant who 'succeeds' by 'bearing the sin of many' (9^{28}; cf. Is 52^{13}, 53^{12}).

Where 'salvation' is mentioned in First Peter it is future ($1^{5, 9f}$, 2^2). The writer of Second Peter refers to Paul for the singular idea that for imperfect Christians 'the long-suffering of God is salvation' (3^{15}), and Jude has the phrase 'our common 'salvation'. In the Apocalypse 'salvation' is shown in the 'casting down' of the Dragon of four names (12^{10}) and the judgement of the Great Harlot (19^{1f}). Its remaining text is *the* Christian doxology—'Salvation (belongeth) unto *our* God, which sitteth on the throne, and unto the Lamb' (7^{10}). A solitary instance in the Fourth Gospel (4^{22}) shows that *soteria* was one of the common words of the Christian (and Jewish) vocabulary. The adjective *soterios* is found once, of the 'saving grace of God', which is offered to all (Tit 2^{11}). Its neuter, *soterion* (*4*), used as a noun, occurs once to denote 'liberty' in its secular sense (Ac 28^{18}), but elsewhere it is used as a synonym for *soteria* to describe both 'the salvation of God' manifested in Jesus (Lk 2^{30}, 3^6) and the Christian's 'helmet' (Eph 6^{17}).

The term *soter* (*24*), 'saviour', is used four times in the Lucan writings—once by Mary after the Annunciation (Lk 1^{47}), and three times of Jesus as the promised 'saviour' of the Jews (Lk 2^{11}; Ac 5^{31}, 13^{23}). Elsewhere the distribution of the term is peculiar. To Jude, God is 'our Saviour through Jesus Christ our Lord' (v. 25). The writer of 2 Peter begins and ends his Epistle with the phrase '(the) Saviour Jesus Christ' (1^1, 3^{18}), and uses it or a synonym, three times in between (1^{11}, 2^{20}, 3^2). It looks as if in the early second century the phrase 'the Saviour' was on the way to become the treasured name for Jesus that it has remained ever since. Apart from the Pastorals (and Ac 13^{23}) Paul only uses the term twice and in both he is thinking of the salvation *of the body* (Eph 5^{28}; 3^{20f}). In the Pastoral Epistles the term occurs ten times. In 1 Timothy (*3*) it describes God, in 2 Timothy (*1*) Christ, and in Titus (*6*) it is used for both. In each of the three instances in 1 Timothy, however, God is, in effect, called 'Saviour' *through Christ*. Paul is 'an apostle of Christ Jesus according to the commandment of God our Saviour and Christ Jesus our hope' (1 Ti 1^1; cf. Tit 1^3). The second text, 'God our Saviour who willeth that all men should be saved', leads on to the mention of the 'one mediator' (1 Ti 2^{3-5}), and explains the third, where God is called 'the Saviour of all men, specially of them that believe' (1 Ti 4^{10}). In 2 Timothy God's eternal purpose 'to save' is manifested by the appearing of our Saviour Christ Jesus' (1^{9f}). In Titus the term 'Saviour' is three times used *both* of God *and* Christ in the *same* context (1^{3f}, $2^{10, 13}$, $3^{4, 6}$). It may be that the term came into common Christian use in reply to the claim of the mystery-cults, for they taught of 'Saviours' 'who abolished death and brought life and incorruption to light' (2 Ti 1^{10}). At any rate, in the Pastorals we are on the way to 2 Peter. There remain two Johannine texts (Jn 4^{42}; 1 Jn 4^{14}). In both there is a characteristic use of *kosmos*, and here again, John has the New Testament epitome—'We have beheld and bear witness that the Father hath sent the Son (to be) *the Saviour of the world*'. To be 'saved', when both the present and future uses of the word are considered, means that the believer is, or is to be, rid of every kind of ill and enjoy every kind of blessing.

In earlier chapters the next subject discussed fell under three Old Testament passages which teach that, if sinners are to be fully forgiven, God must and will re-create them, turning bad men into good men. The first of these passages is Jeremiah's prophecy of the New Covenant. In the texts where the New Testament writers speak of the Christian Covenant it is always *assumed* that their readers already knew what it meant. Even the writer to the Hebrews, when he quotes the passage from Jeremiah at length (8^{8-10}), does so, not to expound the New Covenant, but to show that 'the old covenant' was 'nigh unto vanishing away'. In Mark's account of the Last Supper the word 'covenant' is suddenly introduced in the phrase 'This is my blood of the covenant which is shed for many' (Mk 14^{24}). Of course the Eleven, being Jews, would know the word as the *palladium* of their race, as its uses alike in the Law, the Prophets and the Psalms show. If Jesus had never used the word before, it must have startled them indeed. The latter part of the phrase is probably a reference to Isaiah 53, with its teaching that sinners are to be redeemed, but Jesus leaves the reference to 'covenant' in the Old Testament altogether unexplained. One may wonder why He did not say more about it, but even as the words stand, the Disciples must have seen that Jesus was claiming that now '*the* Covenant' was beginning. In Paul's account of the Supper, which is probably the oldest, he uses the phrase 'The *new (kainos)* covenant in my blood' (1 Co 11^{25}). It is all but certain that the reference is to the passage in Jeremiah, where alone in the Old Testament the phrase 'new covenant' occurs. Here, as in Mark, Paul does not expound the word, but keeps to his immediate subject, the rebuking of the Corinthians for their 'divisions' at the Lord's Table itself. He assumes that they knew what 'new covenant' means. He uses the phrase a second time where he claims that he is 'minister of a new covenant' (2 Co 3^6). Here, while his immediate purpose is to vindicate himself, the context supplies indirect evidence of the Christian doctrine. The whole passage (2 Co 3$^{2-11}$) throbs with the word 'spirit', for this 'giveth life'. It is difficult to believe that, when Paul first expounded what was meant by *the new covenant* in his preaching in the churches, he did not relate it to the Spirit. At scattered points the writer to the Hebrews uses the adjectives 'better', 'new' (*neos*), and 'eternal' to describe the New Covenant (8^6, 12^{24}, 13^{20}), relating it in the last text to the 'perfecting' of Christians. In another passage he implies that it is 'the blood of the mediator of a new covenant' that '*cleanses* the conscience' of Christians (9^{14f}). Finally, when he quotes the passage from Jeremiah, he just takes it for granted that God had written His law 'on the hearts' of Christians and that so they are His people, every one of them 'knowing' Him *as one person knows another*. St Paul, of course, speaks of 'knowing' God or Christ in this way (Gal 4^{8f}; Ph 3^{10}; cf. 1 Cor 1^{21}, 13^{12}), and it is a key phrase in the First Epistle of John (2$^{3f. \ 13f}$). It is also pertinent to recall Jesus' words: 'No one *knoweth* . . . who the Father is, save the Son, and he to whomsoever the Son willeth to reveal him' (Lk 10^{22}). Was our Lord here referring to Jeremiah's oracle? The writer of the Fourth Gospel, in his account of the Upper Room, writes: 'This is life eternal, that they should *know* thee the only true God, and him whom thou didst send, Jesus Christ' (Jn 17^3). It does not seem too hazardous to suggest that, in the exposition of the Supper current before any of the New Testament books was written, there was reference, not only to the 'blood' that was shed when the Passover was instituted and when Moses made covenant with Israel (Ex 12^{22}, 24^8), but also to the passage in Jeremiah. The novelty in 'the new covenant' is that under it bad men are turned into good men.

It was seen above that in Ezekiel 36$^{25-7}$ the words 'spirit' and 'water' go together for the first time, and that the writer of Psalm 51, in effect, makes the same connexion. The latter, while he does not speak outright of a 'new birth', suggests the *idea* for he emphasizes his sinfulness *from birth*. Indeed, the Psalm might be epitomized either as a 'prayer for a new birth' or for 'a new creation'. In the New Testament the Baptist puts 'water' and 'spirit' together (Mk 1⁸; Jn 1²⁹⁻³⁴). Was he thinking of the promise in Ezekiel? In the Fourth Gospel there falls the most famous text that unites 'spirit' and 'water' (3^{3-7}). Under 'spirit' there is a possible reference to the re-birth of Israel as promised in Ezekiel 37 for there *ruach*, like *pneuma* in John 3^8, is both 'wind' and 'spirit'. There may also be a reference to Ezekiel 36^{26f}, the fourth Evangelist silently but pointedly using 'flesh', not in the Prophet's sense, but with the New Testament meaning. Paul also refers to the passage, but without this change (2 Co 3^3). There are other passages where 'the Spirit' is mentioned and 'water' is implied, 'sanctification' accompanying them as in Ezekiel. Paul says to the Corinthians 'But ye were washed, but ye were sanctified . . . in the Spirit of our God' (1 Co 6^{11}) and in Titus (3^5) there is the phrase 'According to his mercy he saved us through (the) washing of regeneration and (the) making anew of (the) Holy Spirit, which he poured out upon us richly through Jesus Christ'. Here 'poured out' is nearer to the Hebrew in Ezekiel 36^{25} than is the LXX rendering *rantizein*. These passages involve, of course, the whole New Testament doctrine of Baptism, as does John 3^{6-8}. To discuss it does not fall here, but, as the writer has tried to show elsewhere,[6] he holds that in the New Testament Baptism and the experience of the Spirit normally went so indissolubly together as to be a unit. This doctrine, again, enlarges into the doctrine of 'regeneration', which was discussed in *The Bible Doctrine of Man*. For the immediate purpose the next pertinent point is the use of the term *anakainōsis* (*2*)—'renewal', or rather 'making anew'— in Titus 3^5.

Paul uses this noun in the phrase 'the making anew of the mind' (Ro 12^2), where the context relates to the new *morphē* or 'form' of Christians. He has its verb *anakainein* (*2*) in two passages about the 'making anew' of the 'new' and 'inward man' (2 Co 4^{16}; Col 3^{10}).[7] In Hebrews the synonym *anakainizein* (*1*) occurs in close connexion with 'the Holy Spirit' ($6^{4,6}$). In Psalm 51, in rendering the Hebrew for 'make anew a right spirit within me' (v. 10), LXX has *enkainizein*, a synonym for *anakainizein*, as the use of

---

[6] In *The Sacramental Society*, Chap. 4.
[7] These phrases have been discussed in *The Bible Doctrine of Man*.

both in Hebrews shows (6⁶, 9¹⁸, 10²⁰). R.V. has 'dedicate' in the last two passages, but the meaning is 'making anew'. In the last passage the context speaks of 'the sprinkling of the hearts' of Christians 'from an evil conscience' and of 'the washing of (their) bodies with pure water'. Is not a reference to Psalm 51⁷ likely, as well as to some detail in the ritual? At any rate, when Paul says 'Wherefore, if any man is in Christ, there is a new creation' (*kainē ktisis*, 2 Co 5¹⁷) he is very nearly quoting 'Create (*ktizein* in LXX) in me a clean heart, O God, and make anew a stedfast spirit within me'. Here again he does not stay to interpret, but presently the context explains—'Him who knew no sin (God) made to be sin on our behalf that we might *become the righteousness of God in him*' (2 Co 5²¹). This is the 'new creation'. An examination of the use of *ktisis* (*18—11* in Paul) and its cognates *ktizein* (*14—10* in Paul), *ktisma* (*4*), and *ktistēs* (*1*) bears this out. Except once, where Peter uses *ktisis* in the secular sense of 'a human institution' (1 P 2¹³), these words always refer to *God's* act of creation, like *bara'* in Hebrew. The first two always refer either to 'the whole creation' of Genesis 1 or to the 'new creation' of Christians. Even under the first Paul has the figure of a 'new birth' (Ro 8²¹f), and the writer to the Hebrews implies that the world is to undergo a second creation (9¹¹). Reference to 'the whole creation' occur in most parts of the New Testament (e.g. Mk 10⁶; Ro 1²⁰; Col 1¹⁵; He 4¹³; 2 P 3⁴; Rev 3¹⁴; cf. Jn 1³), Christ being sometimes God's agent in creation. *Ktisis* never means 'creating', in spite of its form, but always 'something created'. Under the passages that refer to Christians as 'new creatures', Paul uses the phrase in Galatians (6¹⁵) with even less exposition than in 2 Corinthians 5¹⁷. He uses the verb 'create' three times in this way (Eph 2¹⁰, ¹⁵, 4²⁴) and at least by implication (along with *anakainoun*) in a fourth (Col 3¹⁰). In one of these texts he has *poiēma* (*2*) along with *ktizein*, perhaps following LXX, which renders *bara'* by *poiein* in Genesis 1¹ (Eph 2¹⁰; cf. Ro 1²⁰). Under the third term, *ktisma*, it is James who uses the word of the new creation of all things that begins with Christians (Ja 1¹⁸). Peter has the one example of *ktistēs* (1 P 4⁹), where the context suits the concept that God is the 'faithful creator' of every Christian rather than of every man. Whether the early believers found a proof of the doctrine in Psalm 51 or not, it seems plain that, when the New Testament books were written, a belief in a 'new creation' of men through Christ was already current among Christians. Christ had changed sinners into saints. 'Old things had passed away; behold! they had become new' (2 Co 5¹⁷). While the first Christians would base the belief primarily on their new experience, they do not seem to have been satisfied with any doctrine unless they could find Old Testament warrant for it. When all the evidence is taken together—however elusive it is, or rather just because it is elusive —it seems likely that their teachers had very early turned to the three passages here discussed for Old Testament evidence that God must needs turn bad men into good men if He were to carry out the full purpose of forgiveness. Now He has done so. A like result follows under the phrase 'my righteous servant shall make many righteous' (Is 53¹¹), named in Chapter 2, with the three passages just considered. It is not quoted directly in the New Testament, but it belongs to the last Servant Song and there is no doubt that this was often in the minds of New Testament writers. Probably Paul had the phrase itself in mind when he wrote Romans 5¹⁸ᶠ.

The next subject is 'comfort', the word being used with the implication of 'help'. Here the leading term is *parakalein* (*115*), with its cognates *paraklesis* (*29*) and *parakletos* (*5*). The New Testament use of the terms differs from that in LXX in two ways— *parakletos* does not occur in LXX (though it occurs once in Aquila's version—Job 16²), and in the New Testament *parakaleisthai* is never used of *God's* 'repentance' or 'reconsideration'. In considering the use of *parakalein* in the New Testament it is best to begin with the passages where it is used, as in the Apocrypha, to mean 'beseech', for this suits the many passages in the Synoptics where the diseased come to Jesus 'beseeching' His help (e.g. Mk 1⁴⁰, 6⁵⁶, 7³²). Even the demons ask His help when they beg Him to let them enter into swine, as do the Gadarenes when they 'beseech' Him to go away! (Mk 5¹⁰, ¹², ¹⁷). In the Synoptics *parakalein* (*25*) always means 'beseech' except in four texts (Lk 3¹⁸, 16²⁵; Mt 2¹⁸, 5⁴). It is also used with this sense in other New Testament books, as will appear below.

Of the English rendering 'exhort' there is one example in the Synoptics (Lk 3¹⁸), but, as in LXX, 'appeal' gives the sense better, for here the Baptist, 'appealing in many other ways', calls the people to take their stand *with him*. In the Acts of the Apostles *parakalein* (*23*) is used in four ways, all paralleled in LXX. It may mean either 'invite' (e.g. 16¹⁵, 28¹⁴), or 'encourage' (e.g.

18^{27}, 20^{12}), or 'beseech' (e.g. 8^{31}, 13^{42}, 16^{9}, 24^{4}), or 'appeal'—once to sinners (2^{40}), but elsewhere to fellow-disciples (e.g. 11^{23}, 14^{22}, 20^{1f}). In the last class of passages Christians do not so much 'exhort' one another as 'appeal' to one another, to 'cleave unto the Lord' and 'continue in the faith'—that is, as in 2 Maccabees, the concept is not the offer of advice, however good and urgent, from the outside, but a call to share fully in a common enterprise. This is always the meaning in Hebrews (*4*), and 1 Peter (*3*)—e.g. in 'appeal to one another day by day' (He 3^{13}), 'I, who am a fellow-elder, appeal to the elders' (1 P 5^{1}). Similarly, it is about 'our common salvation' that Jude (*1*) 'appeals' (v. 3).

Almost half of the uses of *parakalein* occur in the Pauline Epistles (*52*). The word is especially common in 2 Corinthians, which might be called 'the Epistle of *Paraklesis*'. Twenty of the twenty-nine uses of this noun are found in Paul. Of the verb the commonest English renderings are 'exhort' and 'comfort', but neither is satisfactory. For 'exhort', as already suggested, 'appeal' is nearer to the Greek meaning. Paul uses the phrase 'I appeal' or 'we appeal' some twenty times. When he does so, he is always calling upon other Christians as *sharers* in 'the life that (he) now lives'. There are instances in 'I appeal unto you, *brethren*, by the mercies of God, to present your bodies a living sacrifice' (Ro 12^{1}; cf. 1 Co 1^{10}, 16^{15}; 2 Co 9^{5}; 1 Th 4$^{1, 10}$, 5^{14}); 'I appeal unto you, therefore, be ye *imitators of me*' (1 Co 4^{16}); 'Wherefore I appeal unto you to confirm *love* toward him' (2 Co 2^{8}); 'I . . . appeal to you to walk worthily of the *calling* wherewith ye were called' (Eph 4^{1}; cf. 1 Th 2^{11f}); 'Rebuke not an elder, but appeal to him as a *father*' (1 Ti 5^{1}; cf. Philem, 9f).

Instead of 'comfort' it would probably be best to use 'help', leaving the context to define the kind of help. Here again Paul has about twenty examples, though some could be included under 'appeal'. It is true that usually the kind of help meant is consolation in affliction, though even here 'encouragement' would be a better rendering than 'comfort' (e.g. 2 Co 1^{3ff}, 2^{7}, 7^{13}; 1 Th 3^{7}, 4^{18}). But there seem to be a few passages that are best referred to other kinds of help (1 Co 14^{31}; 1 Th 5^{11}; 1 Ti 6^{2}; Tit 1^{9}). When Paul speaks of 'comforting the heart', for instance, the context suggests something wider than sympathetic consolation (Eph 6^{22}, Col 2^{2}, 4^{8}). In any case the fundamental idea is 'help'. *Parakalein*, whether it means 'appeal' or 'help', pre-supposes the sharing of a common life. While there were specialists in *paraclesis*

THE NEW TESTAMENT DOCTRINE OF GRACE 83

(Ro 12⁸), it was a universal function of Christians. The word could be used of an 'appeal' to God (Mt 26⁵³) or Christ (2 Co 12⁸), but this is rare.⁸

Like results appear from an examination of the uses of the noun *paraklesis* (*29*). Outside Paul (*20*) this word is only found in the Lucan books (*6*) and Hebrews (*3*). The usual renderings are 'exhortation' and 'consolation' (or 'comfort'), but in every case 'appeal' and 'help' (or possibly 'encouragement') are better. Israel, for instance, had long been 'looking' to God for a rescue that was more than 'consolation' (Lk 2²⁵), and in a passage where Luke uses *paraklesis* Matthew has 'reward' (Lk 6²⁴; Mt 6². ⁵. ¹⁶). In Acts 'exhortation' might suffice once (13¹⁵), but elsewhere the idea is 'encouragement through help' (4³⁶, 9³¹, 15³¹). This is the meaning in one of the three texts in Hebrews (6¹⁸); in the other two it is 'appeal' (12⁵, 13²²). Similarly, Paul's context requires that the *paraklēsis* of God, of Christ, and of the Scriptures, is more than 'consolation' (Ro 15⁴ᶠ; 2 Th 2¹⁶; Phil 2¹). Two-thirds of the Apostle's passages relate either to his 'appeal' to fellow-Christians (e.g. 2 Co 8¹⁷; 1 Th 2³ᶠ; cf. 1 Ti 4¹³) or to the mutual 'help' of Christians in the Church (e.g. 1 Co 14³; 2 Co 7⁴, 8⁴. ¹⁷).

In the great majority of the texts where the two words occur, it is Christians, and not God or Christ, who are said to 'help', but this does not mean that there is no reference to Divine action. There are a few texts where God or 'the Lord' 'help' (2 Co 1⁴, 7⁶; 2 Th 2⁷), and this is the implication of one or two others where the passive occurs—e.g. 'Blessed are they that mourn: for they shall be comforted (by help)' (Mt 5⁴; cf. Lk 16²⁵); 'Finally, brethren . . . be perfected, be encouraged' (2 Co 13¹¹). But the evidence is much wider than this. In the Synoptics men appeal to *Jesus* because they believe that through Him 'God hath visited his people' (Lk 7¹⁶), and in the rest of the New Testament Christians appeal to other men *in the name of the Son of God*. There are a few texts where the verb, being used in the way current in the world outside, has no reference to God (e.g. Lk 15²⁸; Ac 24⁴; 1 Co 16¹²), but these are the exceptions that prove the rule. One text sums up the distinctive 'entreaty' of the first

---

⁸ In LXX the usual Hebrew word for 'help' ('*azar*, *127*) has fourteen renderings, but in almost three cases out of four *boethein* or a cognate is used (*89*). These words are rare in the New Testament (*11*), and Paul's one example is in a quotation (2 Co 6²). In the Synoptics (*3*) the verb occurs, like *parakalein*, of appeals to Jesus (Mk 9²², ²⁴; Mat 15²⁵), and in Hebrews (*3*) the words are used of the 'help' of Jesus and God (2¹⁸, 4¹⁶, 13⁶; cf. Ac 16⁹). Under it Christians are not said to 'help' one another.

Christians to sinners—'The love of Christ constraineth us. . . . We are ambassadors therefore on behalf of Christ, as though God were appealing through us: we beg on behalf of Christ, Be ye reconciled to God' (2 Co $5^{14, 20}$). In Christ believers offer other men and each other the help of God. Texts under 'beseech' may be added—'I beseech you, brethren, by our Lord Jesus Christ, and by the love of the Spirit' (Ro 15^{30}); 'I beseech you, brethren, through the name of our Lord Jesus Christ' (1 Co 1^{10}); 'We beseech you that ye receive not the grace of God in vain' (2 Co 6^1); 'I beseech you by the meekness and gentleness of Christ' (2 Co 10^1); 'We ask and beseech you in the Lord Jesus' (1 Th 4^1); 'Beloved, I beseech you as sojourners and pilgrims' (1 P 2^{11}). In all the many passages the 'universe of discourse' is 'the Help of God'. A single passage exhibits the integration of the whole idea —'Blessed be the God and Father of our Lord Jesus Christ, the Father of all mercies, and God of all *help*; who *helpeth* us in all our tribulation, that we may be able to *help* them that are in any tribulation, through the *help* wherewith we ourselves are *helped* of God. For as the sufferings of Christ abound unto us, even also our *help* aboundeth through Christ. But whether we are in tribulation, it is for your *help* and salvation; or whether we be *helped*, it is for your *help*' (2 Co 1^{3-6}).

The last word, as so often, is with St John. In his books neither *parakalein* nor *paraklesis* occur, but he alone uses *parakletos* (5). As there is no adequate English rendering, it is best to transliterate the Greek term and use 'Paraclete'. When the word occurs for the first time Jesus speaks of 'another Paraclete' (14^{16}), implying that hitherto He Himself had been the disciples' Paraclete. He had helped them daily in far more ways than 'consolation' and now they were saying in their hearts, 'What shall we do without Him?' Again, in the First Epistle (2^1), the Ascended Christ is the Paraclete of a Christian who has sinned—i.e. He is Helper at the crucial point in a man's whole life, his reconciliation to God. The four passages in the Gospel use Paraclete to denote the manifold 'help' of the Spirit. God will give Him to the disciples, and while the gift will indeed console them for the loss of Jesus' earthly companionship, the Spirit's function is neither wholly 'comfort' in the modern sense of the term, nor even mainly 'comfort'. In the Acts of the Apostles the 'men of the Spirit' are not consoled mourners but glad and strong witnesses! In the Fourth Gospel the 'other Paraclete', who will never be missing, is *the* Helper of the

THE NEW TESTAMENT DOCTRINE OF GRACE 85

Church against 'the world' (14^{16f}), for He is to continue and complete the 'teaching' of Jesus (14²⁶), to lead the disciples in their one inclusive work of 'witness' (15²⁶), and to 'convict the world' of its capital sin, sin against Jesus (16^{7ff}). In other words, the Spirit, being 'the Spirit of truth' (in the New Testament sense of 'living and active truth'), is to 'help' the disciples in *every* way. In the first century the Jews had borrowed the Greek word *parakletos*, and to judge by its secular use in Greek it is possible, though there is no evidence on the point, that it was used in such a city as Alexandria for the Jew or Jews who represented and stood for the Jewish community before the government. It would be their duty to 'help' their fellow-Jews in *every* need and do their best to 'see them through' *every* difficulty. In any case, in the Johannine books 'Helper'—a rendering which could be used in the Epistle as well as the Gospel—is a far more nearly adequate rendering than 'Comforter'. Broadly speaking, the large doctrine of *paraklesis* is an application of the doctrine of Grace. A Paraclete was like a 'kinsman' (*go'ēl*) in the Old Testament, a friend on whom a man had a claim in every need.

In the New Testament *paramuthein* (*4*)—with its cognates *paramuthia* (*1*) and *paramuthion* (*1*)—is a synonym for *parakalein*. The verb occurs once in the Apocrypha, in parallel with *parakalein*, where Judas 'rouses the spirit' of his comrades (2 Mac 15⁸⁻¹⁰). The two nouns are used in the Apocrypha (*3*) of 'consolation' but it is a consolation that involves hope and help (Ad. Est 15¹⁶; Wis 3¹⁸, 19¹²). 'To cheer' is a good rendering. Paul 'cheers' his converts like a father and bids them 'cheer the faint-hearted' (1 Th 2¹¹, 5¹⁴; cf. 1 Co 14³; Phil 2¹). In all these four passages *parakalein* or *paraklesis* occurs in the context. In the Fourth Gospel the verb occurs where Jews come to *console* Martha and Mary concerning their brother (11^{19, 31}). Here the author seems to use a current phrase for a visit to a mourner. No doubt the Jews said to the two sisters, 'Your brother shall rise again at the last day'—that is, they consoled *by hope*—as, indeed, seems to be implied (vv. 23f). Jesus takes the current phrase and applies it to His coming miracle.

In the earlier parts of the book the next subject was, 'Does God long and seek to forgive Gentiles?', and it was found that, apart from a few great Old Testament passages, the question was not answered because it was not asked. For the great majority of

Jews it was not a practical question because they believed that the Gentiles, with all but negligible exceptions, were *incorrigible* sinners. It has already been seen that the New Testament challenged this postulate—and the spread of the Gospel among the Gentiles vindicated the challenge. Here, of course, *the differentia* of the New Testament emerges again. The evidence that God longs and seeks to forgive *all* men appears in many parts of this chapter and need not be recapitulated here.

The next term is 'blessing', *eulogia* (*15*), with its cognates *eulogein* (*41*), 'to bless', and *eulogētos* (*8*), 'blessed'. The last term is reserved for God (e.g. Mk 14[61]; Ro 1[25]), but in half its instances He is 'blessed' as the 'Father of our Lord Jesus Christ' (2 Co 1[3], 11[31]; Eph 1[3]; 1 P 1[3]). As in the Old Testament, it expresses an adoration that glows with love, and the Christian has his own reason for the glow. The verb has a participle, *eulogēmenos*, which is also rendered 'blessed'. Here the distinctive Christian use begins with the cry on Olivet: 'Blessed be he that cometh in the name of the Lord: Blessed be the coming kingdom of our father David' (Mk 11[9f]; cf. Jn 12[13]). In the other uses of *eulogein* and in those of *eulogia* there is the same implication of the mutual joy of God and His people as under *brk* in Hebrew. There are, on the one hand, passages where God blesses men (e.g. Lk 1[42]; Gal 3[9]; Eph 1[3]; He 6[14], 11[20f]), and, on the other, passages where men bless God (e.g. Lk 1[64], 24[53]; Ja 3[9]). The use of the words always pre-supposes fellowship between God and men. In Romans 16[18] Paul is not speaking merely of 'fair speech' but of a false claim to *this* fellowship. In many of the passages where *eulogein* and *eulogia* occur the Christian *differentia* appears. As with *eulogetos*, the first signs of this are in the Synoptics. It is possible that two or three of the texts where Jesus is said to 'bless' do no more than repeat Old Testament ideas (Mk 6[41], 8[7]; Lk 24[50f]), but in others the context requires a reference to Himself as well as God. For instance, when He blesses the babes (Mk 10[16]—*kateulogein*) He has just implied that those who belong to the Kingdom belong to *Him*; again, men who have served *Him* through His 'brethren' are 'blessed' of His Father (Mt 25[34]); and at the Supper the words 'This is *my* body' follow the 'blessing' of the loaf (Mk 14[22]; cf. Lk 24[30]; 1 Co 10[16]). Apart from Hebrews 6[7f], 11[20f], and perhaps James 3[9], 5[11], Peter's words 'God sent (his Servant) to bless you' (Ac 3[25f]) give the key to all the New Testament texts after Pentecost. Paul expects to come to Rome 'in all the fulness of the blessing of Christ' (Ro 15[29]; cf. Eph 1[3]). It is through Christ that the 'blessing of Abraham' comes even upon the Gentiles (Gal 3[9, 14]; He 6[14]), for Melchizedek, the antitype of Christ, 'blessed' Abraham himself (He 7[1, 6f]). To 'fall back from the grace of God' in Christ is to refuse, like Esau, to 'inherit the blessing' (He 12[17]; cf. 1 P 3[9]). It is when 'the Lamb' is seen to share God's throne that the Seer of the Apocalypse includes 'blessing' in the doxology of heaven (Rev 5[12f], 7[10-12]). 'To bless' is a characteristic of Christian worship (1 Co 14[16]). It is the glad duty of Christians, not only to 'bless' their fellow-Christians (2 Co 9[5f]), but to answer an unbeliever's 'curse' with a 'blessing' (Lk 6[28]; cf. Ro 12[14]; 1 Co 4[12]; 1 P 3[9]). The distinctively Christian doctrine of *eulogia*, like those of *agape* and *charis*, may be integrated under three phrases—first, blessing comes from God through Christ to man; then and therefore, from the Christian through Christ to God; and therefore, from the man who knows 'God in Christ' to *every* man he meets.

Unfortunately the other Septuagintal term, *makarios* (*50*), is usually also rendered 'blessed' in the English Versions, for its true meaning still is 'happy'. It has two cognates, the verb *makarizein* (*2*) and the noun *makarismos* (*3*). As has been seen, there is a distinction between 'blessedness' and 'happiness' in the Hebrew Old Testament, which continues in LXX, and culminates in the Apocrypha. The Vulgate reproduces it in the use of *benedictus* and *beatus*. *Makarios* is common in Luke (*15*; cf. Ac 10[35]) and Matthew (*13*). Its study begins with the Beatitudes. Here the rendering 'blessed' is peculiarly misleading, for it is an inherently religious word, while *marakios* was originally a word of 'the world'. In the Beatitudes, as elsewhere, Jesus is deliberately paradoxical, and to render *makarios* by 'blessed' blunts, and at least in one instance—'Blessed are the pure in heart for they shall see God'—destroys the paradox. 'Purity of heart' is obviously 'blessed' but to men of the world it lacks the spice of 'happiness'. In every Beatitude Jesus claims the word 'happy' for disciples. This is specially plain in Luke (6[20-6]; cf. 14[14f]) where Jesus catalogues under the *Woes* the chief items in the common concept of 'happiness'—wealth and fullness of bread and laughter and popularity. It is no accident that Matthew (5[3-12]) puts the eight Beatitudes at the head of his great summary of Jesus' teaching in the Sermon, nor that our Lord adds 'for my sake' to the last. All the eight say the same thing, or rather, present different facets of one truth. All the eight, again, imply that happiness is not to be sought directly, but is the sequel and outcome of a search for something else, the Kingdom, which alone is worth seeking (vv. 3, 10). The Evangelists never call Jesus Himself 'happy'—for they do not use adjectives to describe Him—but He was not promising them a 'happiness' that He Himself never experienced. Wherever He uses *makarios* outside the Beatitudes He is speaking of men's attitude to *Himself* (Lk 7^{23}, 10^{23}, 11^{27f}, 12$^{37-43}$, 14$^{15-24}$; cf. Jn 13^{17}, 20^{29}), and in the Beatitudes too He is challenging men to take the path that *He* takes. It is when Peter says 'Thou art the Christ' that Jesus declares 'Happy art thou, Simon, son of John' (Mt 16^{17}). As with other doctrines the doctrine of happiness involves alike what Jesus said, what Jesus did, and what Jesus was. A full exposition would, of course, include much else—for instance, an account of the relation between self-denial and happiness. Here the pertinent point is that Jesus is God's guarantee of happiness to His children. There can be little doubt that until Jesus set his face to 'go to Jerusalem' the disciples were happy because they *were* disciples. There is even less doubt that at Pentecost the converts were happy though the word is not used (cf. Ac 2^{46}), and that 'joy' always accompanied conversion. In Gal 4^{15} *makarismos* probably refers not to 'gratulation', but to the delight of the Galatians when they first believed and their consequent love for Paul. Yet happiness is rarely unintermittent and this is implied in a number of passages.

Outside the Gospels the uses of *makarios* are various. Once or twice it is used in the way of the world (Act 26^2, and perhaps 1 Co 7^{40}; cf. Lk 23^{29}). More than one of the score of other passages either directly or indirectly echoes Jesus' Synoptic sayings (Ja 1$^{12, 25}$, 5^{11}; 1 P 3^{14}; Rev 16^{15}). Other passages integrate happiness with the Gospel in significant ways—Paul in quoting a Psalm of happiness (Ro 4$^{5-9}$; cf. Rev 20^6, 22^{14}), and the writer of the Pastoral Epistles when, perhaps with deliberate singularity, he calls God Himself 'happy' because it is His 'glory' to save men through His Son (1 Ti 1^{11}, 6^{14f}; cf. Tit 2^{13}). There remain three passages where the connexion with Christ is more remote but still present (Ro 14^{22}; Rev 1^3, 22^7). While the use of the terms *makarios* and its cognates is sporadic in the New Testament, there is a single doctrine. Christ, in defiance of the world, claims the word for His own. Happiness is the heirloom of Christians. It is clouded for them in this 'age' by 'the humiliation of the body' and the pressure of sin, within and without, but the heaviest cloud does not quench the sun. In the coming 'age' there will be no cloud within *their* horizon. 'Happy are the dead which die in the Lord'. They find what they have never sought.[9]

As in LXX 'blessedness' issues in 'peace' (*eirene*, *91*). In the New Testament there are ten or a dozen instances of the secular use of the term, 'peace' meaning no more than the absence of strife (e.g. Lk 11^{21}; Ac 7^{26}, 12^{20}; 1 Th 5^3; He 11^{31}; Rev 6^4), but this is a meagre and elsewhere a misleading meaning. It has been seen that in Hebrew *shalom*, at its best, denotes the welfare of the whole man. In the New Testament the emphasis is on the fundamental welfare of the 'inner man'. In the Synoptics Jesus says 'Go into peace' quite in the Old Testament way to three of those whom He has healed (Mk 5^{34}; Lk 7^{50}, 8^{48}), but most passages have the Christian *differentia*. This begins to appear in Luke's Birth Stories (1^{79}, 2$^{14, 29}$). In all these three verses the context speaks of 'salvation' (1^{77}, 2$^{11, 30}$)—which is sometimes a translation of *shalom* in LXX—but of 'salvation' through Jesus. The most notable is in the Angels' Song, in the phrase 'On earth peace, God's good-pleasure among men'—a 'good pleasure' fully shown in Jesus (Lk 3^{22}). It is God's will to give men peace, but only in His own perfect way. At the end of Jesus' ministry the Jews had not learnt this, even though they rightly cried out about 'peace in heaven'—and so Jesus burst into tears (Lk 19$^{38, 42}$). This leads to the passage where His heart is torn because He has 'a baptism to be baptized with', which means that He must 'cast fire upon the earth', 'not peace but a sword' (Lk 12$^{49-53}$; Mt 10^{34f}). With this passage there goes another—where Jesus tells the Seventy that, where their Master's message is not welcome, their 'peace' is to 'return' to them, and they are to 'wipe the dust' of places like Capernaum from their feet for these out-sin Sodom. To reject Jesus' messengers is to reject Him and to reject Him is to reject God (Lk 10$^{5-16}$; cf. Mt 10$^{11-15}$). Where the Old Testament says 'There is no peace for the wicked', Jesus says 'There is no peace without me'. Here is, in effect, the sin against the Spirit once more. In Jesus' own life-time, as matter of fact, for a member of a Jewish home to become His disciple would often split the home in pieces (Lk 12^{52f}; Mt 10^{35ff}), as now, for instance, in India—and strife dogs the Gospel right through Acts—as it always does when

---

[9] As in LXX, *eudaimon* and *eudaimonia* do not occur in the New Testament.

Christian witness is robust and resolute. Jesus was a peace-maker *among His disciples* (Mk 9³⁴, ⁵⁰), but not immediately in the world, even though He showed the one way of making ultimate peace in a world of *sin*. The Synoptic testimony culminates in a Beatitude, 'Happy are the peace-makers: for they shall be called sons of God' (Mt 5⁹), but the cross is often the immediate way of the peace-maker. This word only occurs in this text. Its verb occurs once —'Having made peace *through the blood of his cross*' (Col 1²⁰; cf. Eph 2¹⁵). Here an Epistle, as so often, makes explicit what is implicit in the Synoptics. The word 'peace' occurs many times in salutations and farewells, both in Paul's Epistles (*21*) and others (*9*). 'Grace to you and peace from God our Father and the Lord Jesus Christ' (Ro 1⁷) is the typical salutation (cf. 1 Co 1³; Eph 1²; 1 Ti 1²; 1 P 1²; 2 Jn 3; Rev 1⁴ᶠ). The phrase combines and transfigures the customary Greek and Hebrew greetings, which respectively wished men 'grace' and 'peace'. The order of the words is significant. An experience that begins in 'grace' issues in 'peace'. A similar phrase is once found in a farewell (Eph 6²³), but here the type appears in 'The God of peace be with you all' (Ro 15³³; 1 Th 5²³; He 13²⁰; cf. Phil 4⁹). Once the phrase is 'The God of love and peace' (2 Co 13¹¹), and once 'The Lord of peace' (2 Th 3¹⁶). The phrase 'the God of peace' occurs also elsewhere (Ro 16²⁰; 1 Co 14³³), God being pitted against 'Satan' and 'confusion'. Once Paul personalizes 'the peace of God' as the invincible 'guard' of a Christian's 'heart and thoughts' (Ph 4⁷). 'The peace *of Christ*' breaks down the barriers between Jew and Gentile (Eph 2¹⁴) and 'arbitrates' in 'the hearts' of saints with the arbitrament of love (Col 3¹⁴ᶠ). Here too the Spirit has His share in the work and there is an implicit Trinitarianism—'The mind of the Spirit is life and peace' (Ro 8⁶); 'the fruit of the Spirit is love, joy, peace' (Gal 5²², cf. Ro 15¹³); 'the unity of the Spirit' is 'the bond of peace' (Eph 4³). God is the giver of peace through Christ in the Spirit, and for Christians 'peace' is primarily peace with God, not with men. 'Being therefore justified by faith, let us have peace with God through our Lord Jesus Christ' (Ro 5¹).

When men are at peace with God they will be at peace with one another. The 'saints', just so far as they are 'saints', will be at peace with one another because, loving God, they will love one another (e.g. Ro 14¹⁹; 1 Co 7¹⁵; 2 Co 13¹¹). Here the greatest example is Paul's Song of Love, for it is introduced to describe *the* way to settle church squabbles (1 Co 12-14)! 'Peace among men' is derivative. Its *fons et origo* is 'peace with God'. As history very abundantly shows, in a world of sinners there may be many an armistice, but never peace. 'The way of peace have they not known' (Ro 3^{17}), for they are not at peace with God.

But to all sinners—that is, to all men—God 'preaching good tidings of peace through Jesus Christ', 'sent the word' (Ac 10^{36}; cf. Eph 2^{17}). It is Christ who 'makes peace' among men (Eph 2^{15}), but this is upon terms, and the terms will not always be offered (1 Th 5^3). Paul, indeed, bids the Romans 'Be at peace with all men' (Ro 13^{18}; cf. He 12^{14}), but the behest is qualified—'if it be possible, as much as in you lieth'. Here his own life is the best commentary. He blames himself for setting the Sanhedrin by the ears on a false issue (Act 23^{6ff}, 24^{20f}), and he would not quarrel with the Jews about the circumcision of a half-Jew (Ac 16$^{1-3}$), but he fought the Judaizers to a finish because the issue of 'grace' was fundamental. For him the Christian is a soldier whose feet are 'shod with the preparation of the gospel of *peace*' but whose hand wields 'the *sword* of the Spirit'. Yet hand and foot are at one, for 'the sword' *is* 'the preparation'. Christianity is 'a war to end war'. For the Seer 'The Lamb' is a 'lion' (Rev 5^{5f})! As usual, the Fourth Gospel has the last word. In it Jesus speaks of 'peace' only to disciples. He gives '*His* peace' to *them* for He sends the Paraclete; this 'peace', unlike 'the world's', is a sure defence against all 'trouble' and 'fear' (Jn 14^{26f}); it is also proof against all the 'pressure' of their struggle with 'the world' for they know that this is a struggle with a beaten foe (Jn 16^{23}); 'Peace be with you' is and has always been the greeting of the Risen Christ to His disciples (Jn 20$^{19, 21, 26}$). In the New Testament there is no peace but the peace of God in Christ.

In discussing the Love of God in the last chapter, it was found that there are three terms for 'love' in LXX and that the first of these, the rare word *eros*, since it refers to sexual love, is never used of God's love. In the New Testament—while the writers sometimes speak of the abuse of sexual love under such terms as 'fornication'—they have no occasion to use *eros* itself. The same is true of its cognates *erasthai* and *erastes*. The second term is *philia*, 'friendship', with its cognates. Here the phenomena found in LXX reappear with little or no development. *Philia* itself only occurs once (Ja 4^4) in the phrase 'the friendship of the world', but *philos* (*29—15* in Luke) and *philein* (*25—13* in John) are fairly frequent.

The starting-point of thought is friendship between man and man, as in LXX. Though the New Testament does not happen to use *philia* to denote this ordinary kind of friendship, the use of *philein* to mean 'to kiss' and of *philema* to mean 'a kiss' (e.g. Mk 14⁴⁴; Lk 7⁴⁵; Ro 16¹⁶) illustrates it, for the kiss then, like the hand-shake now, was the ordinary token of friendship or, at least, of the absence of ill-will. It is likely that wherever either of the words is used the idea that there is friendship *on both sides* is present—except that Judas only pretended it. For instance, Jesus was 'the friend' of such 'publicans and sinners' (e.g. Lk 7³⁴) as were willing to be friends with Him. Similarly He calls His disciples His 'friends' (Lk 12⁴; Jn 15¹⁴f). *Philein* is used of their 'friendship' or 'love' for Him both before and after the Resurrection (Mt 10³⁷; 1 Co 16²²). Here *philein* rises into a synonym for *agapan* as the variation between the terms in Jn 21¹⁵⁻¹⁷ and Peter's phrase 'the *kiss* of *agape*' (1 P 5¹⁴; cf. Ro 16¹⁶) show. Abraham is called 'a friend of God' (Ja 2²³; cf. 2 Ti 3⁴). But *philein* is only once used to describe the Risen Christ's 'love' (Rev 3¹⁹), and it only occurs three times of God's love—of the Father's love for the Son (Jn 5²⁰), of the Father's love for the disciples (Jn 16²⁷), and, in a compound word, of His love toward man (Tit 3⁴). Among the early Christians as among all other men, friendship was a kind of love, but Christians rarely used the word to denote their characteristic kind.

On the other hand the next term, *agape* (*117*—Paul *75*, John's Gospel *7*, John's Epistles *21*), is one of the words that the first Christians borrowed from LXX, transfigured in meaning, and made Christian once for all. This transfiguration, however, took place gradually and something of the process can be traced in the documents. In the Synoptic Gospels, where the noun *agape* only occurs twice (Lk 11⁴²; Mt 24¹²) the main evidence falls under the verb *agapan* and the adjective *agapētos*. Where *agapan* (*134*—Synoptics *23*, Paul *32*, John's Gospel *34*, John's Epistles *30*) occurs in the Synoptists, the texts fall into three groups. First, the word may describe 'love' of various kinds (Mk 10²¹; Lk 7⁵, ⁴², ⁴⁷, 11⁴³, 16¹³; cf Jn 19²⁶; 2 Co 9⁷). The range is wide, though not as wide as in LXX. The passages show that the word was now in common use. Second, the term occurs in the passages about the two Great Commandments (Mk 12³⁰⁻³)—i.e. it describes the love of man for God and for other men. In Luke's Gospel Jesus quotes these Commandments in answer to a 'certain lawyer's' question (Lk 10$^{25\text{ff}}$; cf. 11^{42}), and the latter, lawyer-like, goes on to ask: 'And who is my neighbour?' Jesus, replying with the Parable of the Good Samaritan, says, in effect: 'Any man whom *you can help*, even though he is your enemy, is your neighbour.' Third, there are the passages where Jesus says 'Love your enemies' (Lk 6$^{27-36}$; Mt 5$^{44-6}$). Here He starts from the doctrine, found in the Apocrypha and current among the teachers of His time, that God is every *Jew's* 'father'. He says, in effect: 'You believe that God is your Father, but you do not apply the doctrine. A son ought to do what his father does. Why then do not you? To love your enemies would show that you are what you claim to be, the "sons of the Most High".' So far Jesus' argument convicts His hearers of not being true Jews, as the phrase '*Your* Father' shows. But, when Jesus appeals to the *universality* of the sunshine and the rain, He goes farther than the Apocrypha go. He says, in effect, that sun and rain show that God loves His enemies even when they are Gentiles. Any man with half an eye for the weather can see that! The final proof that God loves his enemies, for a New Testament Christian, of course, was that God sent His Son to die for sinners, but Jesus could not appeal to this, for He had not yet died. He turns, therefore, to an obvious piece of evidence—the rising of the sun and the falling of the rain.

The term *agapetos*, 'beloved' (*61*), common in Paul (*26*), is relatively rare in the Synoptics (*9*—e.g. Mk 12^6; Mt 12^{18}; Lk 20^{13}). There the phrase is used only of Jesus, '*The* Beloved' of God. His Father twice hails Him as 'My beloved Son'—once when the Servant undertakes His mission to *sinners*, and once when He is setting Himself to *die for them* (Mk 1^{11}; 9^7).

Christians learnt that 'God is love' through the death and resurrection of His Son—that is, they began with facts and the experience that sprang from the facts. It was only gradually that, selecting terms to express what their new experience involved, they gave them a distinctively Christian meaning. This comes out clearly if the distribution of the terms *agape* and *agapan* outside the Synoptic Gospels is noted. Neither noun nor verb occurs at all in the Acts of the Apostles and the adjective *agapetos* only once. Yet, of course, the *idea* is implicit everywhere. For instance, God gives His Spirit to men because He loves them; Christ would not have been called the 'Servant' of Is 53 (e.g. 4^{27}) unless He had so loved sinners as to die for their sins; Peter at Pentecost and Paul before Agrippa preached so urgently because they loved both Christ and their hearers; the Christians in all the churches loved each other, as the one use of *agapetos* shows (15²⁵). The *idea* of love dominates the book though the *words* are almost altogether lacking.

Again, in Hebrews and the Apocalypse, relatively to their length, *agape* and *agapan* are rare. In Hebrews there is only one incidental reference to God's love (12⁶); the love of Christians for God and for each other are each only mentioned once (6¹⁰, 10²⁴); and the Son is said to be the 'anointed' king because He 'loved righteousness and hated iniquity' (1⁹). But it would be quite misleading to argue from the paucity of the terms to the unimportance of the idea, for, as in Acts, the idea underlies the whole of this very different book. It will suffice to quote a phrase in which the writer himself sums up his theme—'Wherefore it behoved him in all things to be made like unto his brethren, that he might be a merciful and faithful high priest in things pertaining to God, to make atonement for the sins of the people' (2¹⁷). Unless God loves sinners there would be no Epistle to the Hebrews. It is the same with the Apocalypse. In it *agape* only occurs twice (2⁴, ¹⁹) and *agapan* four times (1⁵, 3⁹, 12¹¹, 20⁹), but is not the Slain Lamb the hero of the book? This writer too has a key text —'Unto him that *loveth* us, and loosed us from our sins by his blood; and he made us (to be) a kingdom, priests unto his God and Father; to him be the glory and the dominion for ever and ever Amen' (1⁵ᶠ). It is true, of course, that in all the other New Testament books too the *idea* of 'the love of God, which is in Christ Jesus our Lord' (Ro 8³⁹) is architectonic, but, as the *terms* are frequent in these, only passages where these occur are quoted below. They are most frequent in the writings of Paul and John, for the other books are comparatively brief. The whole Christian doctrine of love is at once complex and organic. As so often, John has a passage (1 Jn 4⁷–5³) from which the whole can be integrated. This is true even though his immediate purpose is to expound the plea 'Beloved, let us love one another', for the passage builds on what might be called the genealogy of *agape*. This may now be traced.

The fundamental concept is 'God is love' (1 Jn 4⁸, ¹⁶). The statement is only made in this passage, though Paul had come near it (2 Co 13¹¹). This is one of the instances where an architectonic idea, implicit all the time, only becomes explicit at the end of a process of thought. Astronomers had long pored over the heavens before Newton discovered gravitation, yet gravitation had all the time been the key to the universe. So the statement 'God is love' was the key to Christianity from the Incarnation onward—or, rather, one of the two keys, for John also says 'God is light' (1 Jn 1⁵)—that is, 'holiness'. It is not an accident that John finds the ground for both texts in the Atonement (1 Jn 1⁷, 4¹⁰). The Christian doctrine of God is not like a circle with one centre, but like an ellipse with two *foci*, Holiness and Love. In the Cross God says two things to men, 'Here is your sins' final affront to My holiness', 'Here is My love's way of meeting the affront'. In the first passage where John says 'God is love' he goes on to speak of the Incarnation; in the second he is thinking of 'the judgement' of the holy God (4¹⁷). Christians are 'bold in that 'day' because 'in Christ' they too are now 'holy' (cf. He 10¹⁹). This is to take the universal Christian ground. One text may stand for Paul—'God commendeth his own love toward us, in that, while we were yet sinners, Christ died for us' (Ro 5⁸; cf. Eph 2⁴ᶠ). In the Fourth Gospel too there is an epitomizing text— 'God so loved the world (of "perishing" men) that he gave his only begotten Son' (Jn 3¹⁶) or, to quote John's Epistle, 'Herein is love, not that we loved God, but that he loved us, and sent his Son to be the atonement for our sins' (1 Jn 4¹⁰). As the preceding verse and the passage from the Gospel both show, for this writer the Incarnation and the Crucifixion are parts of one whole. John works out a further idea which Paul had anticipated (Col 1¹³ᶠ), that the Father loves the incarnate Son *because* He 'lays down' His life for sinners and so fulfils the 'commandment' of 'the Father' (Jn 10¹⁴·¹⁸; cf. 14³¹, 17²⁴). Here is the *differentia* of the Christian doctrine of the Love of God. Whether other religions say much or little about it, none of them bases its teaching on Christ and the Cross. None of them can speak of 'the breadth and length and height and depth of the love of Christ' (Eph 3¹³), for they have no 'Christ crucified'.

If the Father loves sinners, it follows that the Son loves them too. This is implied in the phrase 'the Saviour of the world' (1 Jn 4¹⁴), but it is more explicit in Paul than in John—e.g. in the phrases 'who loved me, and gave himself up for me' (Gal 2²⁰), 'even as Christ loved you, and gave himself up for us' (Eph 5²). Again, the phrase 'because he hath given us of his Spirit' (1 Jn 4¹³) implies a connexion between the love of God and the Spirit which comes out more explicitly elsewhere—e.g. in the text, 'I beseech you, brethren, by our Lord Jesus Christ, and by the love of the Spirit' (Ro 15^{30}), 'the love of God hath been shed abroad in our hearts through the Holy Spirit' (Ro 5^5). It is because God loves men that He gives the Spirit of His Son to them that ask Him.

The interpretative passage in the First Epistle of John also illustrates God (and Christ's) love for *believers*. For instance, the recurrence of the word 'us' shows this—e.g. 'If God so loved us', 'the love which God hath in us', 'herein is love made perfect with us' (1 Jn 4$^{11, 16f}$; cf. 3^1). In John's Gospel, similarly, Jesus' discourse in the Upper Room tells again how He 'loved his own' and how God loved them (13$^{1, 34}$, 14$^{21, 23}$, 15$^{9f, 12f}$, 17^{23}). There are like passages in Paul—e.g. 'Who shall separate us from the love of Christ'—that is, of 'God'? (Ro 8$^{35, 39}$), 'through him that loved us' (Ro 8^{37}), 'God our Father which loved us' (2 Th 2^{16}), 'the love of Christ constraineth us' (2 Co 5^{14}). So in Hebrews it is God's loved sons that He 'chastens' (12^6). Indeed, Christians can be called 'those that have been (and are) loved of God' *hēgapēmenos*—(1 Th 1^4; 2 Th 2^{13}; Col 3^{12}; Jude 1)—that is, God's 'beloved' (*agapetos*—Ro 1^7). This emphasis on God's love for Christians in particular springs, in part, from the fact that the Epistles were written to churches and not unbelievers. Yet there is something else too. By its very nature love is incomplete unless it is mutual. It longs for reciprocity. God's love for a man is not satisfied until the man loves Him. The Son is 'the beloved' (*agapetos*) just because the Son loves the Father as the Father loves the Son (Eph 1^6; Jn 17$^{24, 26}$, etc.). But the Son and the creation go together (e.g. Col 1^{16f}), and there is a sense in which the Father's love is not consummated until 'the love wherewith thou lovedst me' is 'in (men) and I in them' (Jn 17^{26}), or, to revert to the integrating passage, 'God is love' and therefore craves that men should 'abide in love' and so 'in God' (1 Jn 4^{16}; cf. $^{12-15, 19}$). Only so is Christ 'all and in all' (Col 3^{10f}). God is love; He loves *all* men in their sin, and loves them so utterly that He 'spared not his own Son'; in believers His love begins to have free course. These are the first three steps in the Christian genealogy of love.

The remaining steps appear in the phrases '*We* love God', 'We love, because he first loved us', 'he that abideth in love abideth in God and God abideth in him', 'let us love one another' (1 Jn 5$^{1-3}$, 4$^{19, 16, 7}$). Taken together, they state or imply that the love of God in Christ is the source of Christians' love for God (cf. 2⁵ᶠ, 3²³, 4¹⁰)—that it is the source of a distinctively Christian kind of love—that *agape* is the ground and sphere of a Christian's constant and close fellowship with God (cf. 2¹⁵), and that this will inevitably and spontaneously issue in love to other Christians (cf. 2¹⁰ᶠ; 3¹⁶ᶠᶠ; Jn 13³⁴, 15¹²). It is true that the key passage in First John does not directly mention the Christian's love *for Christ*, but without this the genealogy would fall to pieces, and the Gospel supplies the link (Jn 14¹⁵, ²¹⁻⁴). Similarly, while the passage does not directly teach love for *unbelievers* (for John's immediate purpose is to urge his 'little children to love *one another*'), this is implied both in the phrase 'the Saviour of the world', and in the unlimitedness of the text 'We love, because he first loved us' (vv. 14, 19). Elsewhere John says that he who 'loves God' cannot 'love the world', as distinct from the men in it (1 Jn 2¹⁵⁻¹⁷, 3¹⁰). There are, of course, many passages in the Pauline and other Epistles that exemplify all these characteristics of *agape*. For instance, Christians are called 'they that love God' (Ro 8²⁸; 1 Co 2⁹; Ja 1¹², 2⁵; cf. He 6¹⁰) and 'they that love our Lord Jesus Christ' (Eph 6²⁴; cf. 2 Ti 4⁸; 1 P 1⁸). Paul has a magnificent passage about the Christian's love for Christ that 'roots and grounds' in Christ's inconceivable love for him (Ep 3¹⁷⁻¹⁹). The use of *agapetoi*, 'beloved', some fifty times to denote 'my fellow believers' suffices to show that Christians loved each other (e.g. Ro 12¹⁹; 1 Co 4⁴; 2 Co 7¹; Eph 5¹; Ph 2¹²; He 6⁹; Ja 1¹⁶; 1 P 2¹¹; 2 P 3¹; 1 Jn 2⁷; Jude 3). 'Love for all men' appears, as in the Synoptics, under the more precise form 'Thou shalt love thy neighbour as thyself' (Ro 3⁸⁻¹⁰; Gal 5¹⁴; Ja 2⁸), but it is usually a postulate, for the first Christians just took it for granted that they were sent to preach the Gospel of love, whatever happened. Paul was pre-eminent here, but not singular (e.g. 2 Co 6¹⁻¹⁰; cf. He 13¹³; 1 P 4¹²⁻¹⁴; Rev 13¹⁰ᶠ). In brief, as an indefinite number of passages show, it is *agape* that permeates and integrates the whole of a true Christian's life. The Thirteenth Chapter of 1 Corinthians, the classical exposition of *agape*, may be given as instance. There are a number of texts where exegetes ask whether the phrase 'the love of God' means 'God's love for Christians' or 'a Christian's love for God'. Probably it usually denotes their *mutual* love. There are similar passages under 'the love of Christ'.

The only adequate account of *agape* is Jesus Christ, 'the same yesterday and today and for ever' (He 13⁸). But since, short of anglicizing *agape*, the term has to be rendered 'love' and 'love' has so many different meanings in English, some of the marks of the distinctive meaning of the word when the Church had made it its own, may be recapitulated. They all exhibit the truth that the fount of the Christian doctrine is 'God is love'. There is no physical element, however innocent, in *agape* (though, for instance, in a Christian home it perfects physical love). *Agape* seeks nothing for itself. It longs for reciprocity but does not demand it. It is spontaneous, yet it calculates, for it has a clear purpose. That purpose is not primarily the happiness of the beloved, but his perfection; it seeks to help a man to be what God made him to be. Unlike much so-called 'love', it is wholly allergic to sin. It seeks the weal of any man, and therefore of every man. The cross of Christ is the immeasureable ground of the Christian's love for God. While other kinds of 'love' may at one point or another be more or less like it, in its integrity and purity it is unique.

Attempts have been made to distinguish *agape* from other kinds of 'love' through its etymology, but so far there are no agreed results about the latter. But, whatever the etymology, in LXX, as was shown above, *agape* can be used for any kind of love, from the best to the worst, including even illicit sexual love. There is no ground to suppose that this wide meaning had been lost among the Jews of the first century. Again, it has been argued that the '*will* to love' is emphasized under *agape*. This seeks to distinguish the term for *eros* (cf. the phrase 'falling in love'), but the truth is that *agape* is one of the large qualities that include both will and feeling and thought. The text 'Thou shalt love the Lord thy God with all thy *heart* and with all thy *soul* and with all thy *mind* and and with all thy *strength*' (Mk 12^{30}) illustrates this The peculiarity is not that the will is active under *agape*, but that it is in abeyance under *eros*. *Agape* involves the whole man. There are, of course, distinctions within the uses of *agape* as of 'love'. For instance, there are differences between the love of a father, the love of a mother, and the love of a brother. Indeed, every different kind of father has his own kind of love! But the distinctions depend, not upon any intrinsic meaning of the *term* itself, but upon the nature of the relationship between those who love one another and upon the character of those who love. It follows that Christian *agape* is distinct from other kinds because of the unique nature of the relation between God and men, and because of the character of God on the one hand, and of believers (who have been sinners) on the other. In this examination of the use of the term in the New Testament only a beginning has been made with an account of this distinction and *differentia*. To explore it fully would involve many Christian doctrines, particularly the whole doctrine of the Christ.

CHAPTER FIVE

TRIAL, TEMPTATION AND DISCIPLINE

An Eastern king, in order that he might judge his subjects aright, sometimes 'put them to the proof' and so 'tested' their loyalty. The Hebrews applied this idea to the King of Kings. Here there are three Hebrew terms. The usual renderings of all three, 'prove' and 'tempt', are both mis-leading, for today 'prove' generally means 'to show that a *thing* is true' and 'to tempt' is 'to seek to lead astray'. Here, for convenience, 'test' will be kept for the most frequent term, *nasah*, and 'try' will be used for the other two, *bachan* and *tzaraph*. They all mean 'to put to the proof'.

Under the first word, *nasah*, one may 'put' a sword or diet or a man's wisdom 'to the test' (1 S 17^{39}; Dn 1^{12}; 1 K 10^1). In its religious use (*23*) the term means 'to test loyalty'. Men may 'test' the loyalty of their god as Israel tested the Lord's at Massah (i.e. 'Testing'—Ex 17$^{1-7}$). As if the Lord who had done such wonders for her might fail her (Nu 14^{22})! A man might be allowed or challenged to put a particular promise of God to a 'test' (Jg 6^{39}; Is 7$^{10-12}$), but normally to 'test' God is to sin—'Ye shall not test the Lord your God, as ye tested him at the Place of Testing' (Dt 6^{16}; cf. Ps 78$^{18,\ 41,\ 54}$, 95^9, 106^{14}). God's testing of His servants' loyalty began when He 'tested' Abraham on 'Mount Moriah' (Gn 22^1 E). Here God said in effect, 'He that loveth his only son more than me is not worthy of Me'. There is a second instance in Exodus where disloyalty is described as 'sin' (20^{20} E; cf. 16^4 J). In Deuteronomy the Forty Years are one long 'test' (8$^{2,\ 16}$; cf. Jg 2^{22}), and, when a man shows the outward marks of a prophet but preaches apostasy, this tests Israel's loyalty (13^5). A Psalmist asks God to 'judge' him and 'test' his righteousness (26^{1f})—'Judge me, O Lord, for I have walked in my perfection; also in the Lord have I trusted, I slide not. *Try* me, O Lord, and *test* me; *examine* my reins and my heart'. Here all three Hebrew terms occur.

The second of the terms, *bachan* (*29*), is used of Joseph's 'trying' his brethren's good faith (Gn 42^{15f}), of the ear's 'trying' the wisdom of 'words' as the palate savours tastes (Job 12^{11}), and of a builder's 'trying' the stability of stones (Is 28^{16}). In the last text a 'tried stone' is truth as over against 'lies'. The word, while most frequent in Jeremiah (5) and Psalms (10), is used in many books. It occurs three times of man's 'trying' God. Twice this is counted sinful (Ps 95⁹; Mal 3¹⁵), but once God challenges men to put a particular promise of His to 'trial' (Mal 3¹⁰). God 'tries' the way of Israel through Jeremiah (6²⁷) and 'tries' the Prophet himself (12³). With Jeremiah, characteristically, there occurs first the statement that God 'tries the reins and the heart' (11²⁰, 17¹⁰; cf. Ps 7⁹; Pr 17³; 1 Ch 29¹⁷)—i.e., searches the *inward* man. Job marvels that God should take the trouble to 'try' mere man 'every moment' (7¹⁸). The notion that God 'tries' the righteous and they stand the 'trial' (Ps 11⁴ᶠ, 17³, 139²³ᶠ; Job 23¹⁰) implies that all suffering is not punishment, though this deduction is hardly drawn. In a psalm of praise, however, there seems to be the teaching that the 'trials' of the Jews from the Exile onward have punished as well as purified them (Ps 66¹⁰⁻¹²). Here, as elsewhere (Zec 13⁹; Pr 17³; Job 23¹⁰), 'trial' is compared to the assaying of silver, which leads to the third term, *tzaraph* (17).

The literal meaning of this word is 'smelt' and it is applied to the work of the 'silversmith' and 'goldsmith' (Jg 17⁴; Jer 10⁹, ¹⁴; Is 41⁷), who were not primarily sellers of the precious metals but workers in them. Sometimes they put them into a 'crucible' (Pr 27²¹) to discover whether there was dross in them (e.g. Is 1²⁵), sometimes to purge it away, and sometimes both. God's 'word' is said to be 'tried' or found reliable under this term (Ps 12⁶, 18³⁰, 119⁴⁰; Pr 30⁵). God puts individual men into His crucible and may find either that there is no 'dross' (Ps 26², 105¹⁹) or nothing but dross (Jer 6²⁸⁻³⁰, 9⁷) in them. More often, however, He 'smelts' the *people* Israel, and He does this in order to *purify* her—i.e. to separate dross from the genuine metal. This use begins with Isaiah (1²⁵), and is found once in an Exilic passage (Is 48¹⁰), but the other examples are all in post-Exilic books. Two Apocalyptic writers teach that even good men need to be purified (Zec 13⁹; Dn 11³⁵; cf. Mal 3²ᶠ), and the Exile may be compared to a crucible (Ps 66¹⁰⁻¹²). While this kind of 'purification' implies discipline, this idea is not explicit. Further, it is the nation and not individuals who are purified. Within the nation good men are the silver that survives, and bad men the dross that perishes.

In the Book of Job, while God is said to 'try' men (*bachan*—7¹⁸, 23¹⁰, 34²⁶), for this is the subject of the whole book, Job's trial is through 'the Satan', even though this person only appears in the prelude. Here, therefore, the question of the relation of the Satan to trial arises. The word itself means 'adversary', or, in modern English, 'opponent'. For instance, the 'princes of the Philistines' suspected that David, when he marched with Achish against Israel, would turn out to be 'a satan' (1 S 29⁴; cf. 2 S 19²²; 1 K 5⁴), and God 'raises up' more than one 'satan' against Solomon (1 K 11¹⁴, ²³, ²⁵), not so much to test him as to punish (cf. Ps 109⁶) and perhaps to discipline (cf. 2 S 7¹⁴). In these passages the 'satans' are *men*. Probably *satan* is used similarly of '*an* opponent' in a late passage (1 Ch 21¹), whether a man or a spirit is meant, for LXX, a witness from the same period, renders '*an* accuser'. The word, however, occurs of '*the* angel of the LORD' in the early story of Balaam (Nu 22²², 22 JE), but this angel tries to *keep* Balaam *from sinning* by opposing his journey. In Job 'the Opponent' is not this unique angel, but one among many 'sons of God' who wait upon Him to do His errands. Eastern kings often used what are now called 'informers' or 'spies' whose duty it was to 'go to and fro' among their subjects and report upon their loyalty—and still more upon any man's disloyalty. They might even practise *l'agence provocateuse*, for this practice is much older than its name and was reckoned legitimate. In Job 'the Satan' comes very near this, though it is Job's wife that directly urges him to treason (2⁹). We are not told outright that 'the Opponent' *wanted* to get Job to sin. In another passage, which may be earlier than Job (Zec 3¹⁻⁶), 'the angel of the LORD' is judging Joshua, the high priest, and 'the Satan' is urging the former 'iniquity' of the priesthood against him. The verdict is that this 'iniquity' is gone now, and the Opponent is 'rebuked'. He is a false accuser as in Job, but he is the Opponent of Job and of Joshua, not *of God*. In both passages 'the Satan' is something like the 'triers' of witchcraft in seventeenth-century Scotland. On God's behalf he sorts out the bad from the good. In 1 Ch 21¹, however, whether the rendering be 'an adversary' or 'Satan', there is the first hint that the Jews had begun to feel that God Himself would not suggest sin to a man, for the Chronicler here departs from the earlier version of the story which says that *God* 'moved David' to sin (2 S 24¹). This early concept, like that of 'an evil spirit from the LORD', disappeared as the Hebrew learnt what is meant by the righteousness of God. If the word denotes an evil spirit in 1 Ch 21¹, as it probably does, there is here the first unmistakable instance of the concept of an evil spirit who is *not* God's agent but His enemy, and who *wants* men to sin and tries to get them to do so. In other words, he *tempts* rather than tests. This means that, while God Himself does not tempt men to sin, He allows at least one evil spirit (as well as evil men) to do so.

So far the dominant notion in the terms examined is 'to test' or 'try', either in the sense of 'to find out whether a man (or nation) is good or bad', or 'to put a nation to test and trial in order to separate the good from the bad'. The concept of 'discipline'—i.e. an attempt to make a bad man good or to make a good man better —is not clearly found, though it is not far away. But it is quite explicit under two other terms, *yasar*, 'admonish' or 'chasten', and *shēbet*, 'rod'. The former is a frequent word (*43*), as is its noun *mūsar* (*51*). They have twelve renderings, of which 'chastise' and 'chastisement' (*17*), and 'chasten' and 'chastening' (*13*), are commonest. There is an extreme example in Rehoboam's threat to 'chasten (Israel) with scorpions' (1 K 12$^{11\text{ff}}$). The words are used nineteen times of God's 'chastening'. In some texts (e.g. Ps 38$^{1f, 18}$; Pr 6^{23}) *yasar* or its noun occurs along with *yakach*, 'to convict' and 'rebuke'. In a few passages they denote *merely* 'to exercise retribution' (1 K 12^{11}; Ps 94^{10}) on the one hand, or *merely* 'instruct' or 'admonish' (e.g. 1 Ch 15^{22}; Is 8^{11}) on the other, but usually under these terms both ideas are present, and the reference is to *disciplinary punishment*. The punishment is also retributive, but the emphasis under *yasar* is not on retribution but on discipline. Indeed, the noun *musar* may even mean 'instruction' or *verbal* 'correction', the notion of punishment being absent. This has examples in Proverbs, where the noun is very frequent. Both the Wise man and Wisdom discipline by instruction, but they do *not* punish (e.g. 1^{2f}, 4^{13}, 8$^{10, 33}$, 15^{33}). On the other hand, there are passages where *musar* perhaps denotes a more than verbal 'correction' (e.g. 5$^{12, 23}$, 16^{22}), and, as will presently appear, the Wise man believed in the 'correction' of the rod. Outside Proverbs the idea of punishment is present but it is discipline that is emphasized. For instance, a Deuteronomist writes, 'As a man chasteneth his son, so the LORD thy God chasteneth thee' (Dt 8^5), Jeremiah has the text 'Thou hast chastened me, and I was chastened. . . . Turn thou me and I shall be turned' (Jer 31^{18}), and a Psalmist cries 'Blessed is the man whom thou chastenest, O LORD, and teachest out of thy law' (Ps 94^{12}). In such passages God is teaching men not to disobey Him—i.e. the punishment is 'disciplinary'. The word 'rod' (*shēbet*) is used several times to denote a father's punishment of his son. Here the father, of course, both punishes a child and seeks thereby to lead him to be a good child. The commendations of 'the rod' in Proverbs illustrate the idea—e.g. in 'He that spareth his rod hateth his son, But he that loveth him chasteneth him betimes' and 'The rod of correction shall drive (foolishness) far from (a child)' (Pr 13^{24}, 22^{15}). God uses the 'rod' (*10*) like a good king. Sometimes, indeed, the word is rendered 'sceptre' and it may be that a king's 'sceptre' was originally a token that it was for him to punish, as with the Roman consul's *fasces* (cf. Ps 2^9, 45^6). In 2 Samuel (7^{14}; cf. Ps 89^{32}) God says that He will 'correct' wicked kings of David's line as human fathers correct their sons. The passages, however, where God is said to use 'the rod' with ordinary individuals are both late and few. There seem to be only four such passages at most (La 3^1; Job 9^{34}, 21^9, 37^{13}), and in two of these there is protest against the way in which God uses 'the rod'. On the other hand there are 'fools' who 'refuse correction' and there are young men who are wise enough to 'receive' it (e.g. Pr 8$^{10,\ 33}$, 13^{18}, 15^{32}, 24^{32})—that is, cure depends upon a man's own choice. Those who learn from discipline cure themselves. This, of course, is true whenever the phrase 'remedial punishment' is used, but it is not always remembered.

To pass to LXX and its answer to the first question in this chapter, 'How does God find out the facts about a man?', the first relevant Hebrew term, *nasah*, is always rendered by *peirazein* (or *ekpeirazein* or *peiran*), a term not used for any other Hebrew word (*37*). The root idea of the Greek word is 'to experiment'. As it never means 'to tempt' in the sense 'to try to lead astray', it is not used about the Satan's efforts against men. It can mean 'attempt' (Dt 4^{34}), but usually it means 'to test'. All the examples given under *nasah* illustrate it. The corresponding noun, *peirasmos* (*7*), is used for *massah*, 'trial' (e.g. Dt 7^{19}), and the place 'Massah' is called 'Trial' in Greek (e.g. Ps 95^{8f}).

In the Apocrypha *peirasmos* (*7*) is almost confined to Sirach (*6*). There are references to the classic instance of Abraham's 'trial' on Moriah (Sir 44^{20}; 1 Mac 2^{52}). Three texts give the general idea both of this noun and its verb—'Praise no man before thou hearest him reason, For this is the *test* of men' (Sir 27^7); 'There shall no evil happen unto him that feareth the LORD, But in *testing* once and again will he deliver him' (Sir 33¹); 'My son, if thou comest to serve the Lord, Prepare thy soul for *testing*' (Sir 2¹). While *peirazein* or *peiran* (*21*) may mean 'attempt' (e.g. 1 Mac 12¹⁰) or denote the 'experience' of a man who has 'put things to the test' (Sir 34⁹; cf. Wis 12²⁶), their regular use appears in the 'testing' of a road or of men or death or one's soul (Wis 19⁵, 2¹⁷, 2²⁴; Sir 37²⁷). The sin of 'putting God to the test' is the sin of mistrust (Wis 1²; cf. Jth 8¹²). Judith declares, on the other hand, that Israel should praise the God who from Abraham onwards has 'admonished' her by the 'scourge' of 'testing' (8²⁵⁻⁷). Here there is the suggestion that God's *peirasmos* may be a blessing. Sirach says more clearly that Wisdom 'tests' men by the 'torment' of her 'discipline' (4¹⁷), and for the writer of Wisdom God's 'testing' of Israel is 'chastening' (3⁵, 11⁹). Under these words in the Apocrypha it is God who 'tests', not the Devil who 'tempts'. In the last texts 'testing' is explicitly related to 'discipline'. This is discussed later under other terms, but it is pertinent here to recall that in the Old Testament the idea that 'testing' is 'discipline' is only *implicit*. The development in the Apocrypha is due to the growth of the idea that God, since He is *righteous*, will only 'test' men to make them better. The emphasis begins to be on discipline rather than test.

For the second Hebrew term, *bachan*, there are seven renderings in LXX. Some are expositions rather than translations—e.g. when a man 'tries' God he 'withstands' Him (Mal 3¹⁵), but when God 'tries' a man, He 'judges' him (Job 7¹⁸). Of the two commonest renderings one is *etazein* or *exetazein*, 'to examine a man or thing's genuineness'. All the passages where these words stand for *bachan* (*5*) occur in psalms. For instance, God '*searches the reins and the heart*' to discover the truth about a man (e.g. Ps 7⁹, 139²³). Under the second common rendering *dokimazein* (*15*), God puts a man to the test of ordeal so as to discover whether He can 'accept' him. This rendering is almost confined to the Psalter (*5*—e.g. 17³; cf. 95⁹) and Jeremiah (*8*—e.g. 6²⁷, 9⁷).¹ Under both these Greek terms 'tempt', in its modern sense, is quite misleading.

¹ In LXX, as it happens, the adjectives of the same Greek root as *dokimazein*—*dokimos* (*6*), 'found genuine', and *adokimos* (*2*), 'found spurious'—do not render any of the three Hebrew terms here in question. They always relate to the assaying of gold or silver by fire (e.g. Gn 23¹⁶; Ps 25⁴; cf. Zec 11¹³). They do not occur in the Apocrypha.

In the Apocrypha (*ex*) *etazein* (*15*) is sometimes well rendered 'examine' (e.g. Sir 18[20]; Sus 51). God 'searches out' the truth about a man (Wis 1[9], 4[6], 6[3]), or 'examines' him (Wis 6[5f], 11[10]), but though less clearly than with *peirazein*, there is perhaps some hint that the purpose is sometimes to better him. This change is clearer with *dokimazein* (*12*). This word may be rendered 'approved' (Sir 41[16], 42[8]; 2 Mac 4[3]), but generally, and perhaps always, it denotes *both* 'trial by ordeal' *and* a purpose to improve. For instance, a man under God's 'trial' is like gold or a potter's vessel in a furnace (Sir 2[5], 27[5], 31[26]; Wis 3[5f]). Again, wealth, like a crucible, 'tries' (and so improves) a man (Sir 31[10]). In one passage, while God 'searches out' (*etazein*) the wicked to punish them, in His 'trying' (*dokimazein*) of the righteous He seeks to 'chasten' and 'admonish' (Wis 11[9f]). Men, on the other hand, who set out to 'try the Power' are 'fools' (Wis 1[2f]). It is the 'ignorant' whose shoulders make haste to 'cast away' the burden of 'the mighty stone of trial' (*dokimasia*) called 'Wisdom' (Sir 6[21]). This weight is a test that is meant to be a blessing. The transition from the idea that God 'tries' a man to find out the truth about him to the idea that His use of 'trial' is altogether disciplinary is well on its way. In some of the passages God disciplines the good because they are not altogether good. The sharp distinction between good men and bad, which is normal in the Old Testament, breaks down as the doctrine of discipline in the Apocrypha develops. The word 'discipline' suggests the school-room, and a school-master assumes that in every boy there is something good and something bad, however much the good may predominate in some and the bad in others. This is the very temper of Sirach.

The third Hebrew word, *tzaraph* ('smelt'), has seven Greek renderings. Its noun, used literally, is rendered by 'worker in silver' (Jg 17[4]), 'brazier' (Is 41[7]), 'pourer out of gold' (Jer 10[9]), and so on. Jeremiah compares God to a 'worker in silver' (6[29]) as He attempts to 'smelt' Israel. By far the commonest rendering is *puroun* (*16*). This means 'burn'—but 'burn' in order to purify, as with metals. The participle 'burned' may even mean 'pure' (not 'purified'), as in 'The words of the LORD are *pure* words', as pure as 'silver purified seven times' (Ps 12[6]; cf. 119[40]). Half the instances of *puroun* are in the Psalms—e.g. 'Thou didst put me to the trial of fire. And foundest no iniquity in me' (17[3]); 'Thou hast tried us as silver is tried' (66[10]). In Isaiah God says of Israel 'I will

TRIAL, TEMPTATION AND DISCIPLINE   107

smelt (thee) pure' (1[25]), and in Jeremiah, 'Behold, I will smelt and try (*dokimazein*) them' (9[7]). Under this term too God's purpose is to do men good. Even the furnace is a blessing if men will have it so. In the Apocrypha, as it happens, *puroun* (5) is not used in this way.

To sum up, it is clear that where the translators render the three Hebrew terms by *peirazein*, *dokimazein* and *puroun*—that is, in the great majority of the relevant texts—they took them to mean, not just 'to find out the truth about a man', but 'to seek to make a man better'. This is the more significant because it was to *interpret* the Hebrew words rather than translate them. No doubt the change took place chiefly because the translators habitually thought of God as disciplining man. It was the period when He was often thought of as though He were a benevolent schoolmaster.

To pass to the passages where men are tested through an evil spirit, it may be noted that in one of the early Old Testament passages which speaks of 'an evil spirit from the LORD' 'evil' is rendered by *pseudēs*, 'false' (1 K 22[21ff]). This anticipates the idea that the Satan is a liar, and that it is by deceit, not force, that he influences men. The chief evidence falls under the passages where he is mentioned.

In these passages LXX uses more than one rendering for *satan*. In a passage that speaks of *human* adversaries some manuscripts transliterate the Hebrew word and some render by *antikeimenos*, the literal translation of *satan*, 'adversary' (1 K 11[14, 23, 25]). *Epiboulos*, 'plotter', also occurs for human adversaries (e.g. 1 S 29[4]; 1 K 5[4]; cf. 2 Mac 3[38], etc.). Where the adversary is a spirit, however, the rendering is *diabolos*, which literally means 'slanderer' or 'denigrator'. While the cognate verb, *diaballein*, does not always mean 'slander' (e.g. Nu 22[22, 32]), it sometimes implies it (Ps 38[20], 71[13], 109[4, 20, 29]). The term *diabolos* occurs in Est 7[4], 8[1], but not to render *satan*. In Ps 109[6] the phrase 'a *diabolos*' occurs, probably to denote a human 'adversary'. This is also possible in 1 Ch 21[1] though probably here, as in Job and Zechariah, the term refers to *the Devil*. In the last two books the phrase is '*the diabolos*'. For the translators the 'adversary' (*satan*) was a 'denigrator' (*diabolos*). In Zechariah (3[1]), where the verb *antikeisthai* occurs along with *diabolos*, the idea is clear. *The diabolos* is an 'adversary', not in battle, but in a law-court. He does not use force, but speech. He seeks to denigrate Joshua to God, the Judge. Similarly, in Job 1 and 2 *the diabolos* seeks to denigrate the Patriarch to God. Yet he is still a kind of *agent provocateur* and still an agent of God, for where the Hebrew puts him among 'the sons of God', LXX puts him among His 'angels' (Job 1[6]).

In the Apocrypha passages about Satan are rare. Both *antikeisthai* (*2*), 'withstand', and *epiboulos* (*4*), 'conspirator', occur, but not in ways pertinent here (e.g. 2 Mac 10[26], 14[26]). For the three terms *diaballein*, *diabolos* and *diabolē*, perhaps in one passage (Sir 38[17]) the renderings 'to slander', 'slanderer', and 'slander' are accurate. Under *diabole* (*7*—Sirach 6) the reference is regularly to an adversary's use of *the tongue* (Sir 19[15], 26[5], 28[9], 51[2, 6]; 2 Mac 14[27]). It is the same with the one instance of *diaballein* (2 Mac 3[11]). *Diabolos* only occurs twice. Once the Syrian citadel in Jerusalem is called 'a sore snare' and 'a wicked *diabolos*' to the Jews (1 Mac 1[35f]), perhaps because it deceived many Jews into the belief that Antiochus was stronger than God. Loyal Jews, on the other hand, counted the existence of a Gentile stronghold in the City of God a test of faith, for a 'snare' might be this (Ps 66[11]). In its other instance the phrase is '*the diabolos*' (Wis 2[24])—'By the envy of the devil death entered into the world'. Here *the diabolos* is *the* evil spirit. Taken along with the one text in the Apocrypha where *satan* is transliterated—'When the ungodly curseth the Satan, he curseth his own soul' (Sir 21[27])—it is enough to show that the belief in a Prince of Evil was now current. The 'ungodly' man curses Satan because he wants to foist the blame for his own sin on to the Devil. The Serpent in Eden is for the first time identified with the Devil in the passage quoted from Wisdom. Here for the first time too *the* Devil is unmistakably an *opponent* of God and not His agent. Probably he was a 'demon', though he is not called this. He is the Deceiver of men—as *diabolos* implies, for slander is meant to deceive—not their Destroyer. To name the 'wicked demon' who *kills* men Tobit does not use *diabolos* but 'Asmodæus', perhaps transliterating a Hebrew term for 'destroy' (*shamad*) (To 3[8], etc.). It is true that in Wisdom the Deceiver's lie *leads* to the death of men, but it is *God*, not the Devil, who inflicts death, and He sees to it that it does not harm the righteous (3[1]). The wicked, on the other hand, when they die, put death to the 'test' (2 [24]; cf. v. 17), and discover that for them it is God's instrument of doom. In this pregnant passage, while the Devil is now an arch-enemy both of God and man, and while the idea that the Devil 'tempts' men in the modern sense—i.e. *wants* to lead them into sin—is at last quite plain, the idea of Job and Zechariah that God uses the Satan to test men has not disappeared. It is involved in the wider concept, which dominates the whole of the first three Chapters of Wisdom, that God 'tests' men. As in the past He had *used* wicked nations as His tool (e.g. Jg 2^{22}; Is 10$^{5, 12}$), so He now *uses* a wicked and 'envious' Devil. None the less there is a very significant change. Since in Wisdom the Devil is no longer, as in Job, an 'angel' of God, but His enemy, the underlying concept is that the Almighty can and does *overrule* the Devil and use his temptations as His own tests. While the Devil 'tempts' men in the modern sense of the word, in this sense God 'tempts no man'. It was now finally plain that the Righteous One could not and would not do so. It was, no doubt, largely under the pressure of this idea that the writer of Wisdom transformed Satan from an 'angel' of God into His enemy. Even the contrary teaching in Job could not prevent this change. For the first time the idea appears that in one and the same experience *God* may be testing a man and *the Devil* tempting him.[2]

Under the renderings of the next Hebrew term, *yasar*, the development of the doctrine of discipline is even clearer. While this word is twice rendered by *nouthetein* (Job 4^3, 5^{17})—that is, 'admonish'—*paideuein*, *paideia* and their cognates are used for it seventy-eight times (e.g. Hos 5^2; 1 K 12^{11}; Jer 2^{30}; Ps 2^{10}, 94^{10}; Pr 1^2, 5^{23}, 19^{18}). *Paideuein* literally means 'to bring up a child'. It occurs twenty-three times in the Apocrypha, of which fifteen, as might be expected, are in Sirach. *Paideia* has forty-three instances, all but seven in Sirach. Examples of these two terms are given below. Of less frequent cognates *paideutes*, 'pedagogue', in its exact sense, has two examples, one in Hosea (5^2), and one in a satirical text in Sirach (37^{19}). He has also two negative words—*apaideusia* and *apaideutos*. As translating *musar* (with a negative) the latter has one Old Testament example (Pr 5^{23}), and it occurs once also in Wisdom (17^1). These words are sometimes translated by 'ignorance' and 'ignorant', but, wherever they are used there is an implication that it is a *culpable* ignorance. Sometimes the idea is that a man *is* blameworthy for his ignorance and sometimes that he *will be* blameworthy if he remains ignorant. Behind most of these texts there are vivid pictures, but

[2] In Jewish Apocalypses, from *Enoch* onwards, there are, of course, whole hierarchies of evil powers that throng the lower reaches of the 'heavenly places', but the idea that they proceed by temptation, which God uses for discipline, hardly occurs. They do not tempt individual men but fight for the control of mankind.

there is no room here to illustrate this (e.g. Sir 4^{25}, 6^{20}, 8^4, 21^{24}, 22^3).

The education of the home still included the discipline of the 'rod' or 'whip'—*shebet*, when referring to discipline, being usually rendered by the former (*rabdos*, 27—e.g. Ex 21^{19f}; Pr 22^{15}), but once by the latter (*mastix*, Job 21^9). In the Apocrypha, however, while 'rod' only occurs once in this sense (Sir 33^{24}) and then of the beating of *asses*, 'whip' is found twelve times (e.g. To 13^{14}; Sir 22^6). It looks as if *men* were treated to the whip rather than the rod in the Hellenistic world, for criminals as well as children were whipped (e.g. 2 Mac 7^1). In the home perhaps sons as well as fathers preferred it to the rod! The stick for an *ass*, says Sirach, and *paideia* for a servant (33^{24}), and, speaking of sons and daughters, he says 'Whips and *paideia* belong to wisdom at every season' (22^6; cf. 7^{23})! Tobit speaks of the 'blessings' of the 'whips' of God (13^{14}). To punish a child with the whip was, no doubt, meant to be at once retributive and deterrent and disciplinary, though, while God 'disciplines' His 'sons', He has 'ten thousand' merely retributive 'whips' for their (and His) 'enemies' (Wis 12^{21f}; cf. 3^{4f}; 11^9, 12^2). The idea that God was disciplining or 'chastening' *Israel* by punishing her, both for her fathers' sins and her own, occurs under the term *paideia* in books of different dates (To 4^{14}; Bar 4^{13}; 2 Mac $6^{12, 16}$, 7^{33}, 10^4; cf. 1 Es 8^{73-90}), the underlying idea being that the Jewish people *deserved* its sufferings. No doubt it was partly because of the prevalence of this belief that in the Apocrypha there is no Job-like girding at *undeserved* suffering. Even the writer of Second Esdras does not cry 'We do not deserve our woes!', but 'Why didst Thou make men at all when Thou knewest that all but a handful of their millions would sin?'

While the passages about the 'whip' show that there are a few texts in the two Wisdom Books that require the idea that *paideia* is at once retributive, deterrent and remedial punishment, this is not their characteristic use of the term. Under this it means 'discipline' in the original sense of that word—that is, 'teaching' or 'instruction' without any idea of punishment at all. It is frequently used in close connexion with the word 'wisdom'—so closely, indeed, as to be almost synonymous with it. For instance, Sirach declares that 'the fear of the Lord is wisdom and *instruction*' (1^{26}; cf. 6^{18}) and says of himself, 'I bowed down mine ear a little, and received (wisdom), And found for myself much *instruction*' (51¹⁶). Similarly he has it that 'a wise judge will instruct his people', but 'an uninstructed king will destroy his people' (10¹, ³). Sirach's fellow Wise Man writes that Wisdom's 'truest beginning is the desire of instruction; And care for instruction is love of her' (Wis 6¹⁷; cf. 7¹⁴). These two books might, indeed, be called 'Instruction Books' just as properly as 'Wisdom Books'. Here *paideia* is not punishment but altogether a boon. The writer of Sirach says as much in the epilogue of his book (51²³⁻³⁰), and his grandson echoes him in the Prologue (vv. 3, 10, 21). The tool of *paideia* under this concept is not suffering or the whip but 'speech' (Sir 4²⁴, 8⁸, 16²⁴ᶠ; Wis 6¹¹, ²⁵). Young men of the right kind listen and obey, but any man may be 'fool' enough to refuse 'instruction' if he likes (Sir 21¹¹⁻²¹; cf. Wis 1⁵ᶠ). But why are there so many 'fools'? Because, says Sirach, 'at the first (Wisdom) walketh with (a man) in crooked ways', 'torments him with her instruction', and 'tries him by her judgements' (4¹⁷; cf. 6²⁰); because, adds Wisdom, it 'pays' better in this life to sin against 'instruction' (2¹²) and to refuse to be 'tried' like gold (3⁵ᶠ; cf. 17¹). Here the 'discipline' of Wisdom involves the rigours of self-discipline but there is no question of punishment. A man has to *learn* to be righteous and at first it is hard to learn, but discipline brings its reward later on. The burden of these two books is 'Keep the Law and all is well'—and it is assumed that any man *can* keep it if he will. *Paideia* is now discipline in righteousness rather than rebuke for sin. Just as the concept underlying *peirazein*, *dokimazein* and *puroun*, passes from 'test' to 'discipline', so the idea expressed by *paideuein*, ceasing to include punishment, is confined to 'discipline'—i.e. the ruling notion under all four words now is that God sets Himself to make men better. The doctrine of grace is not far away.

To pass to the New Testament doctrines of 'Trial, Temptation, and Discipline', the first terms that fall for examination are *peirazein* (*37*), its synonym, *ekpeirazein* (*4*), and the nouns *peirasmos* (*20*) and *peira* (*2*, He 11²⁹, ³⁶). The first three of these words sometimes occur of *man's* trial of God. As in the Old Testament this is forbidden (Lk 4¹²; Ac 15¹⁰; 1 Co 10⁹; He 3⁹; cf. Acts 5⁹). To 'test' God is to 'provoke' Him to anger (He 3⁸⁻¹¹). In the New Testament, under this group of words, God is never said to 'test' or 'try' men in order to discover whether they are good or bad. As has been shown, in Old Testament times this concept does occur, but in the Apocrypha it tended to die away because God, being omniscient, does not need to find out anything. In the New Testament the idea disappears altogether, unless it be in the phrase 'Abraham, being tried' (He 11¹⁷) and 'the hour of trial' (Rev 3¹⁰). Next, it was shown that, while in the Old Testament, the idea of 'discipline' was at most *implicit* under *nasah*, in the Apocrypha it became *explicit* in the use of *peirazein* and *peirasmos*. In the New Testament there is a further development. There God is never *directly* said even to *discipline* men through *peirasmos*. This is because *peirazein* in the New Testament (except in one or two texts, e.g. Jn 6⁶) means 'to try to get a man to sin'—that is, to 'tempt' him in the modern sense of the word—and, of course, God, being righteous, never does this (cf. Ja 1¹³). It is evil men or the Evil Spirit that 'tempt'. None the less, God is *related* to 'temptation' and even acts in it, for He *uses* the 'temptations' of evil men or the Evil Spirit' to 'discipline' both Jesus and disciples. This means, as already began to appear under the Apocrypha, that in a single experience evil men or the Evil Spirit may be trying to get a man to sin but that God may be seeking to make him into a better man. This experience is *both* 'temptation' *and* 'trial' in the sense of 'discipline'. The classical example is in the Lord's Prayer: 'Lead us not into *peirasmos*, but deliver us from the Evil One' (Mt 6¹³)—i.e. 'Do not let the Devil tempt us to sin even by way of discipline'—a prayer that it is fitting that frail man should offer, but that God does not always literally answer. Paul explains why in his own case (2 Co 12⁷⁻⁹).

The Synoptic Gospels use the noun *peirasmos* of the 'temptations' both of Jesus (Lk 22²⁸) and the disciples (Mk 14³⁸; Lk 11⁴), but the verb *peirazein* is only used when evil men or the Devil 'tempt' Jesus. When the Pharisees, Scribes and Sadducees 'hunt' Him 'in his talk', as one 'lays wait' for a wild beast, they 'tempt' Him (Mk 12¹³⁻¹⁵; cf. Lk 11⁵⁴). There are other passages where the term occurs in this way (Mk 8¹¹, 10²; Lk 10²⁵, 11¹⁶). Jesus' answers, alike to the Devil and human tempters, show both the clarity and depth of His mind. It is likely that the Gospel writers believed that He was tempted to *intellectual* dishonesty by men, just as in the Wilderness Satan tried to mislead His *mind* and through it His actions. The word *peirasmos* is not applied to His *physical* sufferings in the Synoptics unless these are implied in Lk 22²⁸. So far as we know, Jesus' own *physical* sufferings were not intense until He came to die. The temptation to intellectual dishonesty is not sufficiently recognized today, even though it has a climacteric example in the excuses of many who refuse to be Christians.

Outside the Synoptics, omitting the passages that refer to Satan, which are taken later, a sentence in James is exceptional because it refers a man's temptation to the man himself—'Each man is tempted when he is drawn away by his own *desire* and enticed' (1^{14}). Such inward desires, however, may be roused by outward opportunity, as when the Galatians were 'tempted' to 'scoff' at Paul (Gal 4^{14}; cf. 1 Ti 6^9; 2 P 2^9). There are also passages where the noun is used of the 'trials' of persecution,[3] and this, of course, comes from without. Except perhaps in Ja 1^{14}, the source of temptation lies outside a man.

This synopsis requires that even though God does not Himself directly 'tempt' men, He is related to temptation in three ways. First, He *allows* Satan and men—e.g. the opponents of Jesus and the persecutors of Christians—to 'tempt' a man. This, indeed, is required by the belief that He has given men freedom. Second, God 'with the temptation *makes the way of escape*' (1 Co 10^{13}; cf. 2 Co 13^{5-7}; He 11^{17-19}; 2 P 2^9), and through Christ 'keeps' a church 'in the hour of temptation' (Rev. 3^{10}; cf. 2^9). Third, if a man resists temptation, God *turns it into a blessing* (Ja 1^{2f}; 1 P 1^{6f}, 4^{12-14}). The ultimate blessing is three times called 'the crown of life' (Ja 1^{12}; Rev 2^{10}, 3^{10f}).

The next term discussed under LXX, *etazein*, does not occur in the New Testament, but the compound verb *exetazein* is found three times (Mt 2^8, 10^{11}; Jn 21^{12}). In none of these texts, however, is *God* said to 'examine' or 'try to find out the truth about' a man. There is not even an implication, as there is under *peirazein*, that God is in some way related to the 'examination'.

The next term, *dokimazein*, literally means 'to put to the proof in order to find out whether a man or a thing is good'. In the twenty-two uses of the word in the New Testament sixteen describe man's 'testing' of a man or a thing. The word is not used of the Devil's 'testing', for, when he 'tempts' men, it is not to discover whether they are good or bad, but to lead them into sin. On the other hand, while there is only one text where *dokimazein* is directly used of *God's* testing (1 Th 2^4), there is a frequent *implication* that God does 'test' men, but, as under *dokimazein* in the

---

[3] Here the implication is that the Christian is not so much tempted to apostasy as to complaint (Ja $1^{2, 12}$; 1 P 1^6, 4^{12}; cf. Ac 20^{19}; He 11^{36}).

Apocrypha, this is in order to *improve* them. In other words, the idea of 'discipline' appears here as under *peirazein*.

The terms to be examined are the verbs *dokimazein* (*22—17* in Paul) and *apodokimazein* (*9*), the noun *dokimē* 'proof' (*7*, all in Paul), with its synonyms *dokimion* (*2*) and *dokimasia* (*1*), and the adjective *dokimos*, 'approved' (*7—6* in Paul), with its opposite *adokimos*, 'disapproved' (*8—7* in Paul). The one use of the noun *dokimasia* shows that it is wrong for men to 'tempt' God by 'testing' His goodness (He 3⁹). On the other hand, it is for a Christian to 'put the will of God to the test', believing that it will prove itself good (Ro 12²; Eph 5¹⁰; cf. Ro 1²⁸). Again, it is for Christians to put *themselves* or their 'work' to the test (1 Co 11²⁸; 2 Co 13⁵; Gal 6⁴), and to do this by 'testing' the worth of actions (Ro 2¹⁸; Ph 1¹⁰; 1 Th 5²¹). In one text, and perhaps elsewhere, *dokimazein* means 'to test and to count genuine' and so to 'approve' (Ro 14²²). In two texts there are references to the testing of precious metals by fire (1 Co 3¹³; 1 P 1⁷; cf. *peirazein* in 1 P 4¹²). *Dokimos* and *adokimos* are only found once each outside Paul's Epistles (Ja 1¹²; He 6⁸). In both passages it is implied, though not stated, that it is *God* who finally 'approves' or 'disapproves' of men. This phenomenon recurs in all the Pauline texts. There are typical instances, in 'Give diligence to present thyself approved unto God' (2 Ti 2¹⁵; cf. 2 Co 10¹⁸), and 'Lest by any means, after that I have preached to others I myself should be disapproved' (1 Co 9²⁷; cf. 2 Ti 3⁸; Tit 1¹⁶), and 'There must be factions among you, that they which are approved may be made manifest among you' (1 Co 11¹⁹). In the last text Paul will not say 'God proves you by factions' lest God be held responsible for the factions. Similarly, it is when sinners 'do not approve God' that He 'gives (them) over to a dis-approved mind' (Ro 1²⁸). In another passage, where Paul uses *adokimos* with some irony, he makes it clear that if 'Jesus Christ is in' a man, the man is sure to be *dokimos* with God (2 Co 13⁵⁻⁷; cf. Ro 16¹⁰). *Dokimē* generally means a 'proof' offered *to men* (e.g. 2 Co 2⁹, 13³; Ph 2²²), but in a list of the Christian virtues that, springing *from* 'tribulations' are achieved *through* the Holy Spirit' (Ro 5³⁻⁵), it seems to denote God's approval. Where Paul says 'tribulations' (*thlipsis*) James and Peter say 'trials' (*peirasmos*—James 1²ᶠ; 1 P 1⁶ᶠ). In the one relevant passage where *apodokimazein* occurs, it is implied that God 'rejected' Esau (He 12¹⁷) because he was a 'profane person'. The refusal of the New Testament writers to say that God 'tries

TRIAL, TEMPTATION AND DISCIPLINE 115

to get a man to sin (*peirazein*)' is easy to understand, but they even hesitate to say outright that He 'tests a man to see whether he is good' (*dokimazein*). No doubt this is in part because the Omniscient does not need to do this, but probably also because even this kind of test involves the temptation to sin. If these writers avoided the phrase subconsciously rather than deliberately, the phenomenon is the more significant. But when 'factions' and 'tribulations' arise because Christians or their persecutors abuse their freedom, God silently uses them to put Christians to the proof, and the final judgement, 'approved' or 'disapproved', is His.

The next term, *puroun*, does not occur in the New Testament, but its noun *purōsis* is found three times (1 P 4[12]; Rev 18[9, 18]). Only the first of these passages is relevant here. In it Peter describes a present *peirasmos*. In Paul there is a passage where he half uses the idea of 'smelt', but names 'wood, hay, stubble' instead of 'dross'. Here, speaking of the 'testing' of a man's '*work*' at the last, he uses *dokimazein* about it, but 'saved' of the man himself (1 Co 3[13, 15]). A man's works may be destroyed by 'fire', but the good metal in *the man* survives. For him the 'fire' is the final discipline. He is 'saved so as by fire'. In a parallel passage Peter, using the metaphor of smelting, has both *peirasmos* and *dokimazein* in the context (1 P 1[6f]). It follows that the Petrine and Pauline passages that refer to the *purosis* of men fall under 'discipline' for they equate it with *peirazein* and *dokimazein*. All this means that the writers of the New Testament perfect two concepts already found in the Apocrypha—(*a*) God does not need to find out what a man is, but (*b*) disciplines to bless.

In the New Testament, as in the Apocrypha, there is an evil being called 'the Satan' or 'Satan' who is active against men, nothing being said of his origin. There is a compendious description of him in the Apocalypse—'The great dragon, the ancient serpent, he that is called Devil and the Satan, he that deceiveth the whole world of men' (Rev 12[9]). Paul too mentions 'the serpent' who 'deceived Eve in his craftiness' (2 Co 11[3]), but the other passages about Satan (*34*) or the Devil (*37*), with one or two exceptions (e.g. Jude 9; Rev 12[9]), relate, not to his past or future activities, but to his present attacks on men. Passages of this sort are found in all parts of the New Testament. There Satan's present habitat is not 'hell', as in Milton—though he and his angels will one day pass into 'the fire of the age to come' (Mt 25^{41}; Rev 20^{10})—but 'the air' (Eph 2^2), for which 'heaven' is sometimes a synonym (Mk 4^4). Scattered references in Paul show that the first Christians accepted the cosmogony of their time, and divided 'heaven' into ascending parts (2 Co 12^2), which could be called 'the heavenlies'. The highest of these were the abode of God, of the Ascended Christ, and of the (good) angels (e.g. Eph 1^3, ^{20}; Phil 2^{10}; Lk 15^7). Next below them there apparently came the habitat of 'the prince of the power of the air' and of 'the principalities, the powers, the world-rulers of this darkness, the spiritual (beings) of wickedness in the heavenlies' (Eph 2^2, 6^{12}). From these lower 'heavenlies' downwards Satan has power, for he is 'the prince' of 'the demons' (Mk 3$^{22-6}$)—which haunt the *surface* of the earth, like flies (including, no doubt, mosquitoes), as 'Beelzebub', Satan's name in this realm, perhaps shows (2 K 1$^{2-6}$). A modern might paraphrase by saying that the very atmosphere reeks with evil. It is true that 'demons' cause physical rather than moral evil, but almost always their master, the Devil, busies himself with sin, not disease. The Greek translation of 'Satan', *antikeimenos* ('adversary'), occurs twice (2 Th 2$^{4, 9}$; 1 Ti 5^{14}; cf. *antidikos* in 1 P 5^8). In the second of these texts 'the adversary' of God, as well as of man, is Satan himself, and in the first he is 'the Man of Sin' who is a tool of Satan. Satan may be called *'the* enemy' (*echthros*—Lk 10^{18f}; cf. Mt 13^{39}), and *'the* tempter' (1 Th 3^5). But the commonest synonym, is 'the Devil' (*diabolos, 37*), as the story of Jesus' Temptation, for instance, shows (Mt 4$^{8, 10}$). While the Greek term originally meant 'a slanderer' and still seems to have this restricted sense in the New Testament when it is used of men and women (1 Ti 3^{11}; 2 Ti 3^3), it is not possible to find this sense in all the passages that describe *the Diabolos*. Similarly, the derived meaning 'deceiver' does not cover all the texts in the New Testament, as it does in the Apocrypha. The Greek phrase, like the English 'the Devil', denotes Satan in the *whole range* of his activities. He may slander God (e.g. Lk 4^{9f}), and deceive men (e.g. Eph 6^{11}; Rev 12^9), but he has more 'devices' than these two (2 Co 2^{11})! He inflicts physical evils, as 'demons' do, for one of his names is Beelzebub, 'the prince of the demons' (Mk 3^{22f}; cf. Lk 13^{16}). He also uses persecution (Rev 2^{10}) as well as spiritual pressure, and may be like a 'roaring lion' as well as an 'angel of light' (1 P 5^8; 2 Co 11^4). The whole realm of evil is his realm, but his chief purpose is to urge men to *sin*, for in the New Testament sin is worse than sickness.

In the Old Testament the Satan is the tool of God; in the Apocrypha he is the enemy of God; in the New Testament he is both. There is perhaps some hint of this in the Book of Wisdom, but in the New Testament it is quite clear. Indeed, it is taken for granted that this dual concept was accepted by the Jews of the first century. Jesus could say to Peter that Satan had 'asked to have' the Twelve—i.e. that he has asked God's permission to 'test' them as he had asked it to 'test' Job (Lk 22[31]). Jesus implies that under Peter's leadership they would not only pass the dire ordeal but be the better for it. They will be like 'sifted' wheat. Similarly, the Lord permits Satan to send one of *his* 'messengers' or 'angels' to 'buffet' Paul through the 'thorn in the flesh' in order that 'strength may be made perfect in weakness' (2 Co 12[7]), and Paul himself, as Christ's agent, can 'deliver' a sinful Christian to Satan for 'the destruction of the flesh' and the saving of 'the spirit' (1 Co 5[5]; cf. 1 Ti 1[20]). This means that, as in the Apocrypha, both God and Satan may be active in one human experience, God seeking to bless a man through trial and Satan to curse him. Under the same Greek verb Satan 'tempts', for he hopes the tempted man will sin, but God 'tests' that He may thereby bless. This duality in the meaning of *peirazein* comes out starkly in the story of Jesus' temptation—He is 'led', or 'driven', '*of the Spirit* into the wilderness to be tempted *of the Devil*' (Mt 4[1]; Mk 1[12f]). Satan is called 'the Evil One', or rather 'the wicked One' (*ponēros*), about a dozen times, and in the words 'Lead us not into trial (*peirasmos*) but (if Thou dost,) deliver us from the Wicked One' (Mt 6[13])—which is not two petitions but one—both God and Satan are again related to 'trial'. It is clear that Satan, like man, has his sphere of freedom, though it is limited—that is, here too there is the antinomy involved in all doctrines that combine a belief in the sovereignty of God with a belief in any other being's freedom. One might say that God, like a master at chess, allows his opponent to make moves as he will, but 'has the game in hand' all the time (the 'pieces' here, however, are not men but 'devices'—2 Co 2[11]). While Satan can be compared to a warrior or a 'lion' (Eph 6[16]; 1 P 5[8]; cf. Rev 2[10]) generally he is a 'deceiver', as the word *diabolos* means, and uses 'wiles' and 'snares' and 'lies' (Eph 6[11]; 1 Ti 3[7]; Jn 8[44]; cf. 2 Co 11[14]). A man may 'withstand' him (Ja 4[7]). When Jesus sent out the Seventy 'two by two', He sent them into 'temptation', for they could not turn to Him for help, but in casting out demons they dragged Satan from his seat (Lk 10¹, 17f).⁴ As with Eve, so with all others, Satan is only the 'origin of evil' in the sense that he tries to get them to sin. None the less, the pressure of Satan's kingdom in 'the air' around and above men is a chief factor in the universalizing of sin, and John can say 'The whole world (*kosmos*) lieth in the Wicked One' (1 Jn 5¹⁹). A sinner may be called a 'son' or 'child' of the devil, or even a 'devil' (Ac 13¹⁰; Jn 6⁷⁰; 1 Jn 3¹⁰; cf. Mt 16²³). When a man consents with Satan, the latter 'enters into' the man (Lk 22³; Jn 13², ²⁷), and the man is in his 'power' (Act 26¹⁸)—or, as Paul puts it, the 'prince of the power of the air' is 'the spirit that worketh in the sons of disobedience' (Eph 2²). He therefore has 'the power of death', for it is through sin that men die the real death. Thereby he holds men in the slavery of a life-long terror (He 2¹⁴f). This idea does not occur in the Apocrypha because there Satan does not 'enter into' a man. There can be no doubt that the early Christians believed that there is a 'personal devil' and that he sets himself to spread sin. This idea is not congenial to the 'modern mind', but, whatever terms are used, after two World Wars who can deny that the very atmosphere of human life stinks of sin? Modern thought may not talk of 'the flesh' and Satan, but it does establish the truths that these terms denote. Until these truths once more permeate the minds of men, they cannot understand the joy that runs through the New Testament as its writers cry, in one phrase or another, 'To this end was the Son of God manifested that he might destroy the works of the devil' (1 Jn 3⁸; cf. Mk 3²⁷; Ro 16²⁰: 2 Th 3³; 1 Jn 2¹³f, 5¹⁸; Rev 20¹⁰). As 'the spirit of the world' Satan stands over against the Holy Spirit (1 Co 2¹²; cf. Mk 3²³, ²⁹; Ac 5³), the inveterate 'enemy' of God and man (Lk 10¹⁹; Mt 13³⁹). There are the same three assumptions about him as about man, but on a wider scale—God has given him freedom, and he sins; since he is free, he has power, and so he can harm others, especially by 'tempting' them to sin; yet his power is neither absolute nor permanent. As already seen, God 'provides' men with 'a way of escape' and He has doomed the devil to Gehenna.

As would be expected, the chief *differentia* of the New Testament

⁴ It is possible, however, that Jesus here used the Aramaic word for 'fall' in the sense of 'alight' (cf. the Hebrew in Gn 24⁶⁴; 2 K 5²¹), and the meaning is that Satan, seeing the disciples separated from Jesus, seized his opportunity and sped to attack them.

teaching about Satan appears in relation to Jesus. 'The unclean spirits' know that *He* is 'the holy one of God' who has come to 'destroy' them (Mk 1²⁴), but there is more than this. It is when the devil offers 'the Beloved Son' a kingdom of 'this world', tacitly offering it as an alternative to *the Cross*, that Jesus cries 'Get thee hence, Satan' (Mt 4⁹ᶠ). Again, it is when Peter 'rebukes' Jesus for declaring that the 'Son of Man' *must* die, that his Master replies 'Get thee behind me, Satan' (Mk 8³²ᶠ). Again, it is on the eve of Calvary, when the disciples share the last of Jesus' 'temptations', that He says 'Satan hath obtained you by asking that he may sift you as wheat' (Lk 22²⁸, ³¹). 'John', as usual, elucidates the Synoptists—'He that loveth his life loseth it, . . . Now is the crisis of this world; now shall the prince of this world be cast out' (Jn 12²⁵⁻³¹). In the Apocalypse it is 'the Lamb *as it had been alain*' that overcomes the Brute. So Jesus' faithful followers, 'wrestling' with the Devil and all his myrmidons, but being 'enabled in the Lord and in the might of his strength', can 'withstand in the evil day and, having beaten down all, *stand*' (Eph 6¹⁰⁻¹²; cf. Ja 4⁷). To the Devil's hosts in 'the air' are to be added his 'children' among men (1 Jn 3¹⁰; cf. Jn 8⁴⁴; Ac 13¹⁰). 'The children of God' out-match the 'world' for 'the Son of God' 'destroys the works of the devil' (1 Jn 3¹, ⁸). It is by the Cross that the Incarnate Son 'brings the devil to naught' (He 2¹⁴). Everywhere in the New Testament the Cross is set over against Satan.

The remaining words are the Hebrew *yasar* with its noun *musar*, and *shebet*. In LXX the first two terms are rendered by *paideuein* (with its cognates and *nouthetein*), while for *shebet* there are *mastix* and *rabdos*. In the New Testament we have the terms *paideuein* (*13*), *paideia* (*6*), *paideutes* (*2*), *paidagogos* (*3*—all in Paul), and *apaideutos* (*1*); with them go *nouthetein* (*8*—all in Paul), and *nouthesia* (*3*—all in Paul); then there are *mastix* (*6*), *mastigoun* (*7*), and *mastizein* (*1*), with *rabdos* (*11*), *rabdizein* (*2*) and *rabdoukos* (*2*). For the use of *mastix* and *rabdos*, in particular, the historical background is illuminating. The Romans had reintroduced the more severe punishment of the 'rod'. In a Roman colony like Philippi, for instance, there were 'men having the rods' or 'lictors' (Ac 16³⁵, ³⁸), and it was there that Paul and Silas were 'beaten with rods' (Ac 16²²). Paul suffered this punishment elsewhere too (2 Co 11²⁵). The Romans also used the less severe punishment of the whip, sometimes to force the

120   TRIAL, TEMPTATION AND DISCIPLINE

truth out of a man (Ac 22^{24}). It was also used in the Synogogues (Mt 10^{17}, 23^{34}). It is possible that the Romans had sanctioned this, but it is more likely that a loyal Jew submitted himself to the discipline of the Jewish society even in this extreme form. In the days before the Christians separated from the Synagogue they endured 'the scourge' there, however undeservedly, for Christ's sake, as the Matthæan texts just quoted show. Paul suffered by the scourge five times (2 Co 11^{24}). Jesus Himself had been 'scourged' without cause, though by the Romans, not the Jews (Mk 10^{34}; Jn 19^{1}). Under these terms the references to Christian discipline are few. In the Apocalypse the phrase in the second Psalm, 'He shall rule them with a rod of iron', which describes the ways of a king in his wrath, is applied three times to the rule of Christ and His saints at the *end* of the Age (Rev 2^{27}, 12^{5}, 19^{15}). Under this figure mere punishment seems to be meant, and not discipline in its true sense. There is no idea of making men better. There is one text where God uses the 'scourge' with His 'sons' (He 12^{6}), and one where Paul speaks of using the 'rod' with his converts (1 Co 4^{21}). The first text is taken later. Under the second, Paul, using 'rod' and not 'scourge', is warning the Corinthians that, if need be, he will use the most extreme kind of discipline. This seems to have been excommunication, for the Apostle, remembering Job, speaks presently of 'delivering' an extreme sinner to Satan (1 Co 5^{5}). No doubt, unless the sinner repented, the excommunication would be permanent. There is, however, an implication that, as Jews voluntarily submitted to the discipline of the Synagogue, so Christians submitted voluntarily to the discipline of the Church. In this instance 'rod' undoubtedly implied punishment, but, as Paul expressly says, it is punishment that is meant to benefit—that is, it is discipline.

The Pauline words *nouthetein* and *nouthesia* may be taken next. It has appeared earlier that in talking of discipline the writers of Proverbs and Sirach, in particular, refer to the discipline of the home and the school. In these there is a 'discipline' that has nothing to do with punishment. It aims at the ordering and development of a true kind of life. It is used with the good as well as with the bad, the purpose being to make both better. Under this kind of discipline the children in a good home or the scholars in a good school teach each other. While a parent or a schoolmaster sometimes himself exercises such discipline, it is part of his business unobtrusively to secure that the children and scholars exercise, not only self-discipline, but mutual discipline. *Nouthetein* and *nouthesia* are used both of the way in which Paul or some other leader in the Church exercised this kind of discipline (Ac 20[31]; Col 1[28]; 1 Th 5[12, 14]; Tit 3[10]), and also of the way in which the members of a church ought to 'discipline each other' (Ro 15[14]; 2 Th 3[15]). The latter may do this through 'psalms and hymns and spiritual songs' (Col 3[16])! This perhaps refers rather to the sudden outburst of individual song than to 'congregational singing'. It may have gradually superseded the 'speaking with tongues'. Unlike this, it was 'unto edification', and is said to 'teach' as well as to 'admonish'. This last word, however, is hardly a happy rendering of *nouthetein*, for 'admonish' usually suggests rebuke for a fault, and the Greek verb does not imply this. Literally this term means, not to 'put in mind' in the sense of 'remind', but 'to put something into another's mind'—in the New Testament always with a good purpose. In other words, it is a form of teaching, and very much of the New Testament might be put under the term. In this sense, indeed, the whole book might be called a 'book of discipline'. In one text Paul uses the word of parts of the Old Testament that were pertinent to the problems at Corinth (1 Cor 10[11]), and in another he puts *nouthesia* alongside 'chastening' (*paideia*), for both are to be used in the home (Eph 6[4]). There is only one text where *nouthetein* may imply punishment and one where *nouthesia* may do so (1 Cor 4[14]; Tit 3[10]). In the latter the writer probably means 'Use *nouthesia* with factious men, but if that fails, reject them', the idea of punishment, if it is present at all, falling under 'reject' and not under *nouthesia*. In the other passage (1 Cor 4[14]) Paul probably uses just *this* word in order to suggest that he is not yet punishing, even though he is rebuking the Corinthians for their faults (cf. vv. 19-21). Behind all this, of course, there lies the idea that, whether sin is in question or not, a man may learn to be better. There is a discipline that is not punishment. 'Instruct' would today be a better rendering of *nouthetein* than 'admonish'. While 'whip' and 'rod' denote discipline through punishment, *nouthetein* denotes discipline through teaching.

For *paideuein* 'train' is the best rendering. Training by punishment occurs both when Paul delivers two extreme sinners 'to Satan' (1 Ti 1[20]) and in a passage in Hebrews considered below. It is under this term *paideuein* that Pilate proposes to scourge Jesus 'and let him go' (Lk 23[16, 22]), meaning, 'I will teach him not to do the things that you Jews so much dislike'. This, of course, is the last perversion of discipline. On the other hand, *paideuein* or a cognate may be used to denote 'training' by *speech* —either for a fault (2 Ti 2^{25}; Rev 3^{19}), or with no idea of fault at all (Ac 7^{22}, 22^3). In the passage from 2 Timothy 'the Lord's servant' is told 'gently' to teach people who have brought him the 'questionings' of 'untrained' minds (2 Ti 2^{23}). Paul has an ironic text about the way in which Jews set themselves up to teach other people how to live (Ro 2^{20}). In the two passages where he speaks of a *paidagogos* he is describing a tutor's teaching without punishing (1 Co 4^{15}; Gal 3^{24f}). It is not only that he may be cured of faults that a child is sent to school. When 'grace' and 'scripture' train, they do not punish (Tit 2^{12}; 2 Ti 3^{16}). God 'judges' imperfect Christians *now* in the sense that He declares that they have done wrong, just in order that they may escape the *future* 'condemnation' and punishment of 'the world' (1 Co 11^{32}). Under *paideuein* and its cognates punishment is occasional, but discipline constant; the former, when it occurs, is no more than ancillary to the latter. God trains every Christian, whether he has done wrong or not. It is noteworthy that in the New Testament, under all the words that denote discipline, it is *Christians*, and not sinners, who are disciplined.

There is a passage of some length in the Epistle to the Hebrews which both deals with a particular kind of 'discipline' and, by implication, recapitulates not a few of the ideas in this chapter. We may begin with its later part (12^{4-13}). The 'Hebrews' are suffering a particular kind of persecution, though none of them has yet been called to the supreme test of martyrdom. The concept of *'test'* is present. Some of them, unlike Paul (2 Co 6^9), have failed under this test, and their 'hands hang down' and their 'knees' are 'palsied' (cf. Is 35^3). The writer calls upon the others to exercise the *mutual discipline* that belongs to the members of a church (vv. 12f). But the burden of the passage is that God 'trains' Christians through the persecutions of men. This implies that, in one and the same experience, men *tempt* others in the fashion of the Devil, but God *disciplines* them through test. The writer compares God at some length to earthly 'fathers', but adds that, unlike them, He trains His children for the supreme 'profit' of sharing in His 'holiness'. Discipline may be 'grievous' now but its 'fruit' is the peace of righteousness (v. 11). The writer quotes a passage from Proverbs (3^{11f}) to enforce what he is saying, and, since this includes the word 'scourge', he is quietly suggesting that their persecutions do contain an element of punishment for sin, but it is punishment that is meant to be remedial. The New Testament knows nothing of the modern idea that God is indiscriminating love 'on tap'. In the first three verses of the passage, however, the writer has something to say of the *undeserved* part of their persecutions, for he points them to *Christ's* sufferings. He had been leading up to this through the whole of his Eleventh Chapter. There he has called a kind of roll of those who, though their faith in God, were disciplined by one or another kind of test and passed the test, even though they had no knowledge of Christ. Some of these had 'resisted unto blood' (11^{37}). The last of the roll in point of time and the greatest is Jesus. On the Cross He was both 'pioneer' and 'perfecter' of faith in God— leading the long file of unjustly persecuted Christians and setting the example of perfect discipline. In one and the same experience this 'Pioneer' had 'brought to naught the Devil' and passed the ultimate test of 'obedience' to God (He 2$^{10, 15}$, 5^{8f}). God disciplined even His sinless Son! When He died for others He learnt a higher kind of perfection than when He 'walked and talked' in Galilee. Christians, in so far as their sufferings are undeserved, are called to 'make up what is lacking of the sufferings of the Christ' (Col 1^{24}), and are *thereby* themselves the better, as even their Lord had been. Christ leaves some things for the 'members' of His 'body' to do, and He does so in order that they be like Him. Willingly to suffer for others is the finest discipline of all. It is triumphant in the Cross. He that loseth his life for Christ's sake, the same shall find it. God's discipline is a tool of grace.

CHAPTER SIX

THE CO-EXISTENCE OF GRACE AND SIN

U̲N̲D̲E̲R̲ this subject there are three questions—'Does grace co-exist with sin in *sinners*?', 'Does sin co-exist with grace *at the moment* when a sinner is saved by grace?', and 'Do the two co-exist in the Christian *in his subsequent life*?' The customary answers today are—'Whenever a sinner does a good deed or even thinks a good thought, grace is at work in him, and this may be described as "general" or "pre-venient" grace'; 'When a sinner becomes a Christian, something sinful survives in him'; 'Every Christian sins over and over again throughout his Christian life'. This chapter examines the question, 'Are these the New Testament answers?' While its answer to the third question, 'Do Christians sin?', is explicit, this is not so with the two others, and there is something like a *lacuna* in New Testament teaching at this point. As the writer thinks, however, there is an implicit answer in certain passages to both questions, which can be drawn out fully. He thinks that, under one of the questions, 'Is there grace in sinners?', the New Testament answer is the same as the modern answer, but that under the other, 'Does something sinful remain in Christians at the moment of conversion?', it contradicts it.

While the New Testament teaches that all men are sinners, there is no doubt that its writers believed that sinners sometimes do good things. In the Acts of the Apostles, for instance, Luke uses the words *sebomenos*, *eusebēs*, and *eulabēs*, 'devout', of a number of people who are not (or not yet) Christians (2^7, 10^2, $13^{48, 50}$, 16^{14}, $17^{4, 17}$, 18^{17}). Among these is Cornelius, described as 'a devout man, and one that feared God with all his house, who gave much alms to the people, and prayed to God always' (10^{1f}). When Peter reached Cornelius' house, he drew a general conclusion—'Of a truth I perceive that God is no respecter of persons: but in every nation he that feareth him, and worketh righteousness, is acceptable to him' (10^{34f}). There is no doubt that this quickly became the common opinion of Christians. It is at least possible, however, that the three words rendered 'devout' denote Gentiles who worshipped the God of the Jews, attending the

Synagogues. If so, Peter's principle would not apply to *all* good Gentiles but only to those who 'feared' the true God. Paul went farther. It is true that, when speaking of all men apart from Christ, he used such phrases as 'dead in trespasses and sins' and 'he that is in the flesh cannot please God'. These have been examined at length in *The Bible Doctrine of Sin*. It will suffice to say here that the Apostle cannot have meant, for instance, that among the many honest Pharisees in the days before Christ there was not one who never did one good thing. Indeed, had not he himself done many a good thing in the days before Stephen roused his conscience? The Pharisees, of course, were Jews, but Paul has also left his own evidence that he believed that there were good Gentiles who did 'by nature the things of the law . . . written in their hearts' and who would abide 'the day when God shall judge the secrets of men according to my gospel, by Jesus Christ' (Ro 2$^{14\text{-}16}$). Paul did not share Tertullian's opinion that the virtues of the heathen were *splendida vitia*. Believing that all men are 'the offspring of God' and that He made them to 'feel after him and find him' (Ac 17$^{26\text{-}9}$), he believed that there were Gentiles who did not altogether fail to do so. But what was the relation, if any, between these men's goodness and grace?

There is at least the beginning of an answer to the question in the attitude of the first Christians to the heroes of the Old Testament. They believed, of course, that these heroes were sinners, for when men are measured by the measure of God, set forth in the Sermon on the Mount, 'there is none righteous, no, not one' (Ro 3^{9f}). But when the New Testament writers speak of the Hebrew heroes, they do not mention this. For them the long line that begins with 'Abel the righteous' (Mt 23^{35}) is a line of men that 'wrought righteousness' (He 11^{33}). How did they do this? In the long chapter in which the writer to the Hebrews calls their roll until 'the time fails' him (11^{32}), he gives an answer. His whole purpose is to show that 'the elders' were righteous because they had 'faith' in God, living by faith in the God who 'made the ages' of history 'by His word' and who rewards them that 'seek after him' (vv. 3, 6). There can be no doubt that this writer believed too that God helped these men to live the right kind of life. Had he not read, for instance, in story after Old Testament story, the words 'Surely I will be with thee'? May not this help be called 'grace'? It might be said that behind the great Chapter there lies the creed, 'By grace were they saved by faith', so long as it is remembered that the 'grace' is the grace of *God* and the 'faith' is faith in *God*. These might even be called 'prevenient', or better 'pre-Incarnational', grace and faith, for the whole chapter leads up to 'Jesus, the author and perfecter of faith' (He 12[2]). But there is more than this. The writer says that Moses 'accounted the reproach of *the Christ* greater riches than the treasures of Egypt' (v. 26). This is almost certainly a reference to the deeds of the pre-Incarnate Son through whom God 'made the ages' (He 1[2]; cf. Col 1[16f]; Jn 1[3f], etc.). Similarly Peter ascribes 'the Spirit of *Christ*' to the Old Testament prophets (1 P 1[10-12]), and Paul declares that 'a spiritual rock' followed the Israelites in the Wilderness and that 'this rock was *the Christ*' (1 Co 10[4]). Here the Apostle does not mean that the 'rock' was a 'symbol' of Christ in the modern sense of the term, but, speaking in a Philonic way, that the word 'rock' may be taken in two senses, both of them *factual*. These passages seem clearly to imply that the first Christians had a doctrine of the 'prevenient Christ', and it may be deduced, so long as it is remembered that it *is* a deduction, that this included the belief that the righteous men of old time were saved, all unknowingly, by the 'grace of our Lord Jesus Christ'.

If this be granted, two other deductions may be made. First, it may be claimed that the Gentiles who obey their conscience are also, though they do not know it, actuated by the grace of Christ. Second, to carry deductions to their utmost limit, it may be said that when even bad men do good deeds, as they all sometimes do, it is through the grace of the Christ whom, consciously or unconsciously, they otherwise reject. In this way a doctrine of 'general grace' may be reached. It may be added that, as usual, a parallel doctrine of the 'prevenient' Holy Spirit may be formulated. Probably the first Christians would believe that, before the Incarnation as after it, Christ worked through the Spirit, Pentecost being fulfilment as well as origin. This would mean that, outside Christendom as well as within it, the Spirit of God in Christ is always appealing to every man, and that every man, however sinful, does sometimes yield to the appeal. The conclusion is that, though sin and grace are deadly enemies, they do co-exist in every sinner.

The second *lacuna* in Apostolic teaching falls under 'sin in believers'. So far as the evidence goes, indeed, there seems to be a contradiction rather than a *lacuna*, but this may be because no account of the full Apostolic teaching on this subject has survived. The milder word '*lacuna*' is therefore preferred. The first thing to note is the obvious one—the first Christian believers did sin. The several writers of Epistles, for instance, when they warn their readers against this and that and that sin, imply that these sins were committed, or why mention them? Was there any Christian who was sinless from the moment of his conversion to the end of his life? If the answer is 'no', this means, not only that some Christians sinned, but that every Christian did. Paul himself refers, all but incidentally, to a sin of his own (Ac 24^{20f}). Again the universality of sin is implied in the Lord's Prayer. This was part of the Christian tradition, and there can be no doubt that all the early Christians used to say 'Forgive us our trespasses' (cf. 1 Jn 1$^{8, 10}$). It is true that our Lord taught His disciples this prayer before they received the Spirit, but they continued to use it after this. As with 'goodness in unbelievers', so with 'sin in believers', the problem is not about the fact, but about its *origin*.

Today the usual explanation of the universality of sin in believers is that, whether a Christian grows gradually into Christianity through the influence of a Christian environment or is more or less suddenly 'converted', there still remains something sinful in his nature and that this, along with temptations from without, accounts for his later sins. This doctrine, indeed, is not so much argued as taken for granted. Today we believe that the work of grace is incomplete in every Christian even though Christ's 'grace is sufficient' for him—i.e. that grace is sufficient but faith is insufficient from the beginning of the Christian life onwards. Many would even say that every Christian *must* sin.

To the present writer it appears that in the New Testament there is a series of passages where the writers contradict this account. In these texts the Apostolic writers seem to teach that at conversion believers are not only forgiven for all past sin, but that they are altogether cleansed from sin—that is, at the moment of conversion they become sinless and there is nothing left in them to lead to future sin. Here the historical situation must be remembered. The word 'conversion' is deliberately used because the characteristic phenomenon in the New Testament is that, at a given moment, a man ceases to be a Jew or a heathen and becomes a Christian—that is, that the later phenomenon under which a child in a Christian home, for instance, may gradually grow up into Christianity is not contemplated. The modern parallel is on the Mission Field. In this situation to become a Christian means the joining of a small, unpopular and sometimes persecuted community. A man does not do this except from deep conviction. The 'outward and visible sign' of the conviction is (adult) baptism. As in all healthy societies, but especially in this one, the experience and its sign went as closely together as a man and his skin. To be converted and to be baptized were two parts of one thing. To use another simile, conversion and baptism were like the concave and convex of the curve of a circle. It is not surprising, therefore, that some of the passages relevant here fall under texts about baptism. Some of the chief of them run—'For I say unto you that as many as were baptized into Christ did put on Christ' (Gal 3^{27}); 'But ye washed yourselves, but ye were sanctified, but ye were justified' (1 Co 6^{11}); 'Or are ye ignorant that all we who were baptized into Jesus Christ were baptized into his death? We were buried therefore with him through baptism into death' (Ro 6^{3f}); 'Having been buried with him in baptism' (Col 2^{12}). There can be no doubt that, especially if these texts are taken together, their *natural* meaning is, 'At baptism there was a clean cut between your past and future and there was a new life for the old'—because sin was gone.

Some other texts, where baptism is not mentioned, have a bearing on the subject. For instance, there are passages linked by the term 'crucified'. In two Paul says that he was 'crucified with Christ' (Gal 2^{20}, 6^{14}), in one that Christians 'have crucified the flesh with the passions and the desires thereof' (Gal 5^{24}), and in another that their 'old man was crucified with (Christ) that the body of sin might be done away' and that so they 'died with Christ' (Ro $6^{6, 8}$). These texts also suggest that on conversion believers were entirely rid of sin.

Attempts have been made to explain some of these texts under the rubric, 'Be what you are'—i.e. 'Become what you potentially are'. This is perhaps possible in 1 Corinthians 6^{11}, but not in the whole series of texts. It does not suit such words as 'crucified' and 'buried'. Again, there is the text, 'If any man is in Christ, there is *a new creation*: the ancient things are passed away; behold, they are become new!' (2 Co 5^{17}). Can 'creation' here mean 'a new, yet partly sinful creation'? An attempt has been made to interpret it of a *process* of gradual 'creating', but, as already seen, this requires that *ktisis* should have a meaning without parallel

THE CO-EXISTENCE OF GRACE AND SIN 129

in the Bible, and the Apostle ought to have gone on to say 'Ancient things *are passing* away: behold, they *are becoming* new'—and he does not say this. It might be suggested that, when Paul says 'If any man is in Christ', he means that this state is yet to come, but he uses this phrase or a parallel to describe Christians as they *are* (e.g. Ro 16$^{7\cdot 11}$), and does this even when he is addressing those who are by no means sinless (Col 1^2, 1 Thess 1^1; cf. Col 3$^{5\cdot 11}$; 1 Thess 4$^{1\cdot 8}$). What the phrase means is: 'If any man is in Christ (as you *are*).' Again, Paul, in the texts relating to baptism, does not say 'Be what you *are*' but 'Be what you *were*', —at baptism. For him at baptism there was not only the forgiveness of past sins but the 'death' of sinfulness in the sinner. At Pentecost the converts would for a while feel as if this were so. In sudden conversions this feeling has often recurred. At baptisms of converts on the Mission Field the sense of 'the clean cut' is normal. Paul's readers would not think that his doctrine contradicted their initial experience. Indeed, he argues *from it*. On a common interpretation of a phrase in the context of one of the passages, 'Even so *reckon (logizesthai)* ye also yourselves to be dead unto sin, but alive unto God in Christ Jesus' (Ro 6^{11}), this means: 'Behave as if you were what you aren't in yourselves but are potentially "In Christ Jesus".' This would sound artificial if we were not accustomed to it, and it has been argued in *The Bible Doctrine of Sin* that *logizesthai* does not bear this meaning either in LXX or the New Testament, but, on the contrary, means 'Take account of what you *are*'. Paul is denouncing antinomians and what he means is, 'Sin as they do? God forbid! take account of the *fact* that you are dead to sin, but alive unto God in Christ Jesus—and then you will not sin'. When he uses the phrases '*If* we have become united with him' and '*If* we died with Christ' (vv. 5, 8), he means 'as in fact, we were united with him and died with him'. The Apostle believed that in baptism believers 'died with Christ to sin' (Ro 6^2; Col 2^{20}).

While this teaching is found chiefly in Paul, it is not peculiar to him. When writing to the Roman Church *which he had not yet visited*, he asks, 'Or are ye ignorant that all we who were baptized into Christ Jesus were baptized into his death?' (Ro 6^3). Under the phrase 'Are ye ignorant?', as under 'Know ye not?', the Apostle appeals to some well-known Christian truth—in this case, already well-known in Rome. As to other New Testament writers, it may be noted that the natural connotation of the expression 'begotten again of God', which Peter prefers to Paul's 'adoption' and 'new creation' (1 P 1³, ²³; cf. 2²), is that there is a quite new beginning. Does God beget a partly sinful man? John too, when he uses the phrase 'having been begotten of God' (1 Jn 2²⁹, 3⁹, 4⁷, 5¹, ⁴, ¹⁸), uses the perfect participle (of *gennan*), and while, as has been argued in *The Bible Doctrine of Man*, he *is* here saying to his readers 'Become what you are', this does not preclude that he means 'Be what you potentially are—*and once were*'. It is not to be expected that New Testament writers, with their practical purposes, would discuss at length the problem of the origin of sin in believers, but so far the evidence suggests that in the experience whose inward part was the consciousness of the gift of the Spirit and whose outward part was (normally) baptism, they believed that both sins *and sinfulness* were gone. There is corroborative evidence in two passages in the Fourth Gospel under the word 'clean' (*katharos*). When Jesus had washed the feet of the Twelve, He said to the Eleven, '*You* are clean *every whit*' (*holos*) (Jn 13¹⁰). The text implies that Jesus was completing a process of 'washing'. He had been cleansing the Eleven for long, and now, though they did not yet understand how (v. 7), they were 'clean'. As in the Synoptics (e.g. Mk 14²²⁻⁴), Jesus' death availed for the Eleven before He died. At a later point, when speaking of the Vine, He says '*Already* ye are clean... Abide in me' (Jn 15³ᶠ). The latter phrase suggests that while the Eleven are 'already clean', they will sin again *unless* they 'abide in Christ' and so 'keep (His) commandments' (v. 10). Presently Peter did sin. In these texts the word 'grace' does not occur, but the idea is fundamental to them all.

There is therefore very considerable evidence that the first Christians believed that they began their new life sinless. Behind this belief there seems to be the sense of release and liberty that came to a man when he took the step that decisively cut him away from his old way-of-life. It is likely enough indeed that for a little while a newly founded *church* too had the same sense of freedom. The little community throbbed with the feeling, 'We are free! We are free!': Luke has described the first halcyon days of the church at Jerusalem. Their practice of voluntary communism was singular, but otherwise, *mutatis mutandis*, their first days were probably typical of the first days of the other churches. For a little while there would be the exhilaration of freedom. If then Paul believed that at baptism there was a 'clean cut' between the

THE CO-EXISTENCE OF GRACE AND SIN

old life and the new, how did he account for the origin of sin in believers?

It might be supposed that the complete answer is given by the study of 'temptation' found in the last chapter. Here it was seen that temptation comes from *without* the Christian, the attack being led by the Devil. As the temptations are so manifold and continuous, it might be argued that every Christian, even though sinless at first, will sin at one time or another, because, amid multitudes of temptations, a fall will sooner or later come by the laws of probability. It would follow that the origin of sin in believers is wholly outside them. Yet, for those who, unlike the writer, believe that in Ro 7 Paul is describing his state *after* conversion, this one passage is sufficient refutation of this idea. But there are certain other passages that *seem* to contradict the belief in a 'clean cut' at conversion-baptism, and to require that something sinful does remain even after the 'new creation' or 'new birth'. It will be argued here that this is not so. Most of the passages fall under three terms—'body', 'flesh', and 'desire' or, better, 'craving' (*epithumia*). The New Testament teaching about them was examined in *The Bible Doctrine of Man*. It is only relevant here in so far as it seems to relate to the origin of sin in believers.

It will be convenient to prelude the discussion with an examination of an instance where a believer is tempted, but does *not* sin— Paul's passage about the 'spike in the flesh' (2 Co 12[7-9]). Here there is temptation from without for the 'spike' is a 'messenger of Satan' (though God turns the 'temptation' into the discipline of 'buffeting'). But the 'spike' is also some physical malady—that is, Satan uses something within Paul as a point of attack (*aphormē*— Rom 8[8, 11]). This malady is not sinful, but one of Paul's 'weaknesses' (v. 9). He has three times 'besought the Lord' to take this weakness away, but the Lord has answered: 'My grace is sufficient for thee, for (my) power is made perfect in weakness.' One recalls the prayer of Jesus Himself in Gethsemane, for it was through the weakness even of *His* 'flesh' that He shrank from the Cross. Under the temptation through the 'spike' Paul is 'saved by grace through faith' (Eph 2[8]), and 'glories' in his 'weaknesses' because through them Christ is able to manifest His strength in him. It is likely enough that Paul's malady antedated his conversion. If so, it would follow that, while, as the texts quoted above suggest, his sinfulness did not survive conversion, his 'weakness' did. It is suggested that, with a Christian who was 'weak in faith', it was the conjunction of temptation from without and *weakness* within (whether physical or not), that led him to sin again—and not through a surviving *sinfulness* within. Of course, when a believer had committed one sin, there would again be sinfulness within him and it would be easier to commit others.

How does this account of 'sin in believers' apply to the 'body' (*sōma*)? In the Bible the 'body' is not sinful *per se*, yet in Paul's lists of the sins that 'easily beset' converts several denote sins of the body (Gal 5$^{19\text{-}21}$; Col 3^5). This is because the body is weak, so weak as to be 'dead because of (the) sin (committed before conversion)' (Ro 8^{10}). Here 'dead' is equivalent to 'mortal', for the phrase 'your mortal body' occurs in the next verse. The body, then, is weak indeed, and its weakness persists through conversion. Through it sin from without seeks to gain entrance again. When it once gains entrance, as it regularly does, it spreads and spreads, and the sinful 'practices (*praxis*) of the body' ensue (Ro 8^{13}).

Under the term *sarx* ('flesh') four meanings were distinguished in *The Bible Doctrine of Man*, it being admitted that there are texts of doubtful assignment. Under the first three meanings 'the flesh' is not sinful. Here there are (*a*) passages where *sarx* has a wholly physical meaning (e.g. Lk 24^{39}; He 2^{14}; Rev 19^8, and probably Ro 1^3); (*b*) passages where 'flesh' denotes the whole man, attention being called to his weakness, or frailty, or troubles, or death (e.g. Mt 16^{18}; Gal 2^{20}; and the phrase 'all flesh'—e.g. Mk 13^{20}; Ac 2^{17}; 1 Co 1^{28}; Jn 17^2); (*c*) passages where the emphasis is on weakness against temptation to sin (e.g. Mk 14^{38}; 2 Co 4^{11}, 12^7; Ph 1$^{22,\ 24}$). Under the fourth meaning, illustrated again and again in Ro 8$^{1\text{-}9}$, 'the flesh' *is sinful*. This use is particularly frequent in Paul. The passages that require a 'clean cut' at conversion imply that 'the flesh' in the fourth sense perished then. This is not so with 'the flesh' in any of the first three senses. They survived conversion. The way is open to the suggestion that it was through 'the flesh' in the third sense—i.e. with the connotation 'weak against temptation to sin'—that sin from without again found its way within a believer when his faith failed, and that, once within, it spread and spread in his life. Perhaps the most difficult text under this suggestion is the first sentence in 1 Corinthians 3$^{1\text{-}3}$—'And I, brethren, could not speak unto you (immediately after conversion) as unto spiritual, but as unto fleshly (*sarkinos*), as

THE CO-EXISTENCE OF GRACE AND SIN 133

unto babes in Christ'. In this passage the two adjectives from *sarx, sarkinos* and *sarkikos*, both occur. It is difficult to make any distinction between them, but, as other passages show, both might be used either in an innocent or in a sinful sense. There is an innocent example for *sarkinos* in 2 Corinthians 3[3], and for *sarkikos* in Romans 15[27]. On the other hand, *sarkinos* is used in a sinful sense in Romans 7[14] and *sarkikos* in 2 Corinthians 1[12]. As there is this variation, it is better to render by 'fleshly' than 'carnal', for the latter word has usually, if not always, a sinful connotation. Again, there are texts under both where they describe something weak (He 7[16]; 2 Co 10[4]). So far as the words go, therefore, there is no reason why the meaning in 1 Corinthians 3[1-3] should not be 'weak against sin' and not 'sinful'. Among other things the phrase 'babes in Christ' (v. 1) denotes 'weakness'. The sentence quoted above may therefore mean: 'At your conversion, brethren, I could not speak unto you as spiritual (strong against sin through the Spirit), but as still weak against sin.' This would bring the sentence into line with the suggestion made above. Similarly, verse 3 may mean: 'You are yet weak against sin: your quarrels show that you are, for they show that you have yielded to sin and are again walking after the manner of (sinful) men?'

It is under the examination of the use of *epithumia* and *epithumein* that an attempt may be made to show more fully how the suggested doctrine may be found in Apostolic teaching. As shown in *The Bible Doctrine of Man*, both in LXX and the New Testament the words may be used either in an innocent or a guilty sense. In the New Testament, where the two words occur fifty-three times, they are used fifteen times with an innocent meaning. An English word is needed that reflects this phenomenon. In the Authorized Version 'lust' is commonly used. In the days of James I it appears that this word could be used in an innocent sense as well as in a guilty one (as indeed it is today in the adjectives 'lusty' and 'lustful' respectively), but this is not so now. The word 'desire', of course, offers itself, but it is too pale a word. The nearest literal rendering of *epithumein* is 'to set the heart upon', and a word is needed that denotes 'a *strong* desire'. The words 'crave' and 'craving' may be used because they denote this. They have the further advantage that, like *epithumia*, while they are more often used in a guilty sense, they may also be used in an innocent one. For instance, while a drunkard craves for over-much beer guiltily, a traveller just out of a desert craves for water quite innocently; or again, a man may healthily crave to excel at his work, though he ought not to crave to push others out of his way; or again, while there is an evil craving for women, now called 'lust', it is possible, though not usual, to say that a young fellow innocently craves to marry the girl that he loves. There is no need to say that, when a man is converted, innocent cravings survive within him. In the New Testament this duality of meaning may be illustrated from two paragraphs in the Sermon on the Mount. In one (Mt $5^{27\text{-}32}$) Jesus, speaking about adultery, says, 'I say unto you that every one that looketh on a (married) woman to crave after her hath committed adultery with her already in his heart'. Here a man sees another man's desirable wife—i.e. there is a temptation from outside—and lets his sexual impulse, which is innocent *per se*, fasten guiltily on the other man's wife. Jesus declares that, though he never goes on to *act* on this motive, he is already a sinner—that is, that sin begins *within* a man. Yet, while this is so, it does not follow that the man was already sinful. It might be that, for the first time in his life, the man directed an innocent impulse to a wrong end. (Of course, many modern psychologists would say that this is impossible, for they deny that there is any such thing as 'free choice', but freedom to choose between good and bad is a Bible postulate.) The second illustration from the Sermon belongs to the paragraph about property (Mt $6^{19\text{-}34}$). Here Jesus says (v. 25), 'I say unto you, Be not anxious (or, over-careful) for your life, what ye shall eat, or what ye shall drink, nor yet for your body, what ye shall put on'. He Himself says, in effect, though he does not use the word *epithumia*, that here He is speaking of *innocent* desires, for He adds, 'Your heavenly Father knoweth that ye have need of all these things' (v. 32). It is not wrong to desire food and clothing, or even to 'crave' for them in the sense 'do your best to secure them'. The principle, of course, may be extended to such other kinds of property as furnish the means for the good life. What Jesus is warning His disciples against is *pleonexia*, the unhealthy 'itch for more' (Lk 12^{15}). This word, of course, describes an evil *inward* quality, but it is the outcome of the exaggeration of innocent desires. A Hebrew would believe that sin may begin in an innocent heart, as with Eve.

It is probable that James, in one of the relevant passages, was thinking of the story of Eve. At any rate this story may illustrate the current ideas of the time, it being remembered that both Jews and Christians would believe that the story was literal history. The passage runs: 'Each man is tempted when he is drawn away by his own craving and enticed. Then the craving, when it hath conceived, beareth sin: and the sin, when it is full-grown, bringeth forth death' (Ja 1¹⁴ᶠ). The term for 'tempt' is *peirazein*, 'tempt to sin', not *dokimazein*, 'put to the test' (cf. *dokimos* in v. 12). The word rendered 'enticed' (*deleazein*) means 'entice by a bait', and James is thinking of a fisherman who 'draws', or 'drags out (*exelkein*)' a fish that he has 'enticed' by a bait. Here the bait is temptation from outside, but it is not effective unless there is also craving within. James, however, is not bound by the metaphor, for, perhaps with intentional paradox, he says that it is the craving *within* that is the bait. In the story of Eve there is, similarly, outward temptation and inward consent. Under the latter, an inward craving for something 'good for food', innocent in itself, becomes guilty when it fastens on the 'forbidden thing'. Here James introduces the metaphor of conception. In it the male element from without unites with the female element from within. James, transferring this to the origin of sin, declares that it is in the union of temptation from without and craving from within (innocent hitherto) that sin begins to be. In due time it is born—that is, issues in outward act. If it is then allowed to become mature (*apotelein*) the result is death. The passage does not require that there is a sinful craving in a man's heart which is a survival of the sinfulness that was his before conversion. Of course this analysis only applies to the *beginning* of sin after conversion. If the convert had already sinned, there would remain—unless he 'confessed his sins' and so gained renewed 'forgiveness' and 'cleansing' (1 Jn 1⁹)—a sinful craving within him that would make him more likely to go on sinning. It may be said that the text in James covers all a believer's sins, both the first and every other. This is so, but it did not belong to James' immediate purpose—to repudiate the suggestion that *God* tempts men to sin—to make any distinction between the first sin and others. In both cases the believer's sin had its origin in *his own* cravings. What is urged here is that, when the passage is applied to the *beginning* of sin in a believer, it does not require that this arises because at conversion sin was not completely done away. In other words, it is at this point consonant with the passages quoted from the Sermon on the Mount.

It will now be clear that an attempt is being made to draw out a doctrine that is only implicit in the New Testament. The fact is that the Apostolic writers, being set on practice and not on theory, only drew out doctrines when practical needs required it —and this was not so with the one now in question. In practice the Apostles were facing churches whose members had already sinned many times and it is to this situation that they speak. For instance, James as much as says this when he writes: 'Ye crave and have not: ye kill and are jealous and cannot obtain: ye fight and war:' and so on (Ja 4^{2f}). The present writer does not think that here 'kill' is to be taken literally (cf. 1 Jn 3^{15}), but it is no wonder that some expositors cannot believe that James is here speaking to Christians at all. Yet there is something similar implied when Peter urges his readers not to 'fashion themselves according to the cravings' that were theirs before conversion and which still mark the lives of men in general (1 P 1^{14}, 4^2; cf. 2^{11}). There are other texts that speak specially of the sinful 'cravings' of false teachers (2 Tim 4^3; 2 P 3^3; Jude 16). While all these texts speak of inward cravings that issue in outward behaviour, none of them requires that the source of the sin that now infests the cravings is to be found in a sinfulness that is a 'carry over' from pre-conversion sin. Similarly, when John says 'If we say that we have no sin, we deceive ourselves' (1 Jn 1^8), he is speaking of believers (including himself) as they *now* are.

For Paul the earliest of the principal passages under the word 'craving' is Gal 5$^{13-26}$. Here the pivotal sentences are, 'But I say, Walk by the Spirit, and ye shall not fulfil the cravings of the flesh. For the flesh craveth against the Spirit, and the Spirit against the flesh; for these are contrary the one to the other; that ye may not do those things that ye will' (Gal 5^{16f}). The last phrase may be taken to imply that the purpose of 'the flesh' (semi-personified) is to get unwilling men to sin. Here 'the flesh' is clearly sinful. But it does not necessarily follow that this is so because the sinful flesh of their earlier days had survived in the Galatians after conversion. On the contrary, as already noted, Paul says that 'they that are of Christ Jesus crucified the flesh with the passions and cravings thereof' (v. 24). In the passage one thing is assumed and two asserted—before conversion the Galatians had been the slaves of the sinful flesh; at conversion they had been set free from this slavery (v. 13); now they are again falling into it, for the church is infested with sin once more. It is here suggested that this had happened, not because the *sinful* flesh survived conversion, but because the innocent or *amoral* flesh did so, and that the believers, allowing its cravings once more to fasten on sinful objects, had once more fallen into sin. As Paul puts it elsewhere (Ro 8^{12f}), these Christians are once again beginning to 'live after the flesh' and to practise 'the (evil) practices of the body'—and their only hope is, as at conversion, to 'put to death' these practices 'by the Spirit'. On this showing the origin of sin in believers is the same as the origin of sin in the human race, as typified by the story of Adam and Eve. After conversion, as at creation, there are amoral cravings in human nature; after conversion, as 'at the beginning', these have innocent objects; after conversion, again as 'at the beginning', a man is tempted to direct them to guilty objects; the converted Galatian, like 'Adam', has yielded to the temptation, and the Christian is again a sinner. If Paul's terrible list of 'the works of the flesh' is examined, it will be found to fall into three categories and the origin of all three may be traced to the misdirection of innocent cravings. The first group of words describes the abuses of the innocent physical cravings of sex and hunger and thirst—'fornication, uncleanness, lasciviousness, . . . drunkenness, revellings'. The second group, 'idolatries' and 'sorceries', describe the misuse of art and (according to the ideas of the time) of power over nature. The third and longest group—'enmities, strife, jealousies, wraths, factions, divisions, parties, envyings'—is a list of the misdirections of a less noticed but not less important endowment of men, the right to differ. A few minutes' thought will show that, rightly used, this is a prolific source of progress, and, what is even more pertinent, to learn how to use it is the very school of love.

In Romans 6, Paul's polemic against the antinomians, there is another mention of 'cravings'—this time 'the cravings of your mortal body' (v. 12). Here again three stages in the life of the believers may be distinguished—before conversion they had been 'bondmen of sin' (v. 20); at conversion their 'old man' was 'crucified with (Christ)' (v. 6), they had 'died with Christ' (v. 8), were 'alive from the dead' (v. 13), and 'made free from sin' (vv. 18, 22); now there were those among them who were deliberately 'continuing to sin'—i.e. giving themselves again to a life of sin—and were urging their fellow-Christians to do the same, claiming that sin gave Christ the more opportunities to exercise grace (vv. 1, 15). This is the situation that the Apostle faces right through the passionate passage. The phrase 'Reckon ye also yourselves to be dead unto sin' (v. 11) does not contradict the assertion that at conversion believers 'died to sin', but enforces it, for, as already noted, the Greek word rendered 'reckon', *logizesthais* both in LXX and the New Testament, means, not 'count yourselves to be what you are not (but will one day be)', but 'take account of what you are'—in this case, 'dead unto sin'. It is perhaps worth noting that when Paul mentions 'the flesh' in this passage, he does not speak of its sinfulness but of its 'weakness' (v. 19). It is possible that this means that it was because the 'weak flesh' survived conversion that the appeal of the antinomians was so strong. At any rate there is nothing in the passage that demands that at conversion something sinful survived conversion. In particular, it should be noted that the phrase 'Shall we continue in sin?', with which Paul begins the passage (v. 1), does not mean 'Shall we continue in the state of sin because at conversion sin continued in us?', but, as the next *ten* verses show, 'Shall we go on sinning when, at conversion, sin ceased to continue in us?' In the phrase, 'Let not sin be king in your mortal body, to obey its cravings' (as the antinomians did) Paul probably includes the adjective 'mortal' because mortality is the final evidence of the *weakness* that lays a believer open to temptation through his bodily cravings. Elsewhere he epitomizes his argument under a particular sin—'Know ye not that your bodies are members of Christ? Shall I then take away the members of Christ and make them members of a harlot? Never!' (1 Co 6^{15}).

The same situation and teaching recur in Colossians 2^{16}–3^{17}, with a difference in terminology. Here Paul again gives a long list of the sins that were invading the churches (3$^{5-9}$). To meet this danger there were those who practised and preached an excessive asceticism (2$^{20-3}$). Paul declares that the right way to meet it is to 'hold fast the Head' (2^{19})—that is, to betake oneself to the grace of our Lord Jesus Christ. He says that before conversion the Colossians had 'walked' and 'lived' in sins (3^{7}), but declares that at conversion they had 'put off (*ekduesthai*) the old man with his practices and put on (*enduesthai*) the new man who is being renewed unto knowledge after the image of him that created him' (2^{9f}; cf. Gal 3^{27}). Now that they have again begun to commit a whole series of sins, they are again to 'put to death (*nekroun*) their members that are upon the earth', to put away (*apotithenai*—cf. Eph 4^{22}; Ja 1^{21}; 1 P. 2^{1}) 'anger, wrath, malice' and so on, and 'to put on (*enduesthai*)' virtues whose basis and culmination is 'love' (3⁵, ⁸, ¹²; cf. Eph. 4²⁴). The phrase 'your members which are upon the earth' is to be interpreted by 'your mortal body' in Romans 6¹², for this is followed at once by a mention of 'your members' (cf. Ja 4¹ᶠ). These 'members', while not sinful *per se*, are especially prone to sin and have now become sinful—and they are therefore to be 'put to death'. This use of 'members' goes back to the Hebrew use under which each of the principal parts of the body sometimes acts for itself, while at other times the whole man has one will. In the New Testament the members may fight each other (Ja 4¹ᶠ; cf. 1 Co 12¹⁵ᶠ), or may make war on the mind (Ro 7²³). The phrases 'the old man' and 'the new man' are a well-known *crux interpretum*. They probably mean something more objective than 'the old manhood' and 'the new manhood', but for the present purpose these phrases will serve. At conversion the believers 'put off the old manhood' and 'put on the new'. Now that they are again sinning, they must repeat this process. 'The new manhood' is the 'manhood' of the 'image of God' which was man's at the creation (Gn 1²⁷). The best exposition of the passage is a verse from another Epistle—'Put ye on the Lord Jesus Christ, and make no provision for the flesh, to (fulfil) its cravings' (Ro 13¹⁴). While there is no account of the *source* of the new sinfulness, for this is an academic question, the Apostle giving himself to the practical question 'What is now to be done?', it is very difficult to suppose that the 'putting off of the old manhood' at conversion was a proleptic divestment.

Two notes may be added. The first is that this doctrine harmonizes with two others that were drawn out in *The Bible Doctrine of Sin*—that the Bible does not teach 'original sin' but racial weakness, and that *dikaioun*, 'justify', does not mean 'to treat a man as being righteous because this is what "in Christ" he is to be', but 'to treat a man as righteous because, through Christ at conversion, he *is* righteous'. The second note relates to what are called 'sins of ignorance'. As shown in the same volume, the Bible deals with known sin, and a 'sin of ignorance' is not counted a sin unless the 'ignorance' is itself culpable and therefore sinful. 'Sin is not charged to a man's account where there is no (known) law' (Ro 5¹³; cf. Ac 17³⁰). As a Christian 'grew in knowledge', he might easily discover that some old habit that he had previously not known to be sinful, was sinful. If, on this discovery, he again followed it, he would then, but not till then, begin to sin under it in the full New Testament sense of the word. Innocent ignorance goes with weakness, if indeed it is not a part of it. It is the *will* that is purged in the conversion-baptism of the New Testament, and *there* that there 'is a new creation', for, as shown in the earlier volume, the Bible account of sin roots in the will.

It will be clear that, even more than under 'Righteousness in Sinners', the doctrine here described is not explicit in the New Testament, but is deduced from the implications of a number of passages. Of course, if it be accepted, some theological questions emerge. The purpose here, however, is only to describe Apostolic doctrine, not to discuss resultant problems.

CHAPTER SEVEN

THE DOCTRINE OF ELECTION

THE WHOLE discussion of Old Testament teaching above presupposes and illustrates the Hebrew belief, at least in its monotheistic period, that there is nothing arbitrary in the ways of God with men, but that He treats the righteous in one way and the wicked in another according to the principle of righteousness. Of course, in the experience of life this did not always seem to be so, especially in the Exile and after. So the one problem that vexed the Jewish mind appeared,—'Why do the wicked so often prosper and the righteous so often suffer?' This problem has already been examined in some of its aspects. For the rest it belongs rather to the doctrine of God than to that of man, and the answers that the Jew attempted are not fully examined here. Broadly speaking there were four,—the answer of some Psalmists, 'In the end God will do justice both to the good and the bad'; the answer of the Book of Job, 'There is something in God's ways past human understanding, as the wonders of nature show, but, though He is sometimes inscrutable, He is always righteous'; the answer of Koheleth, at least in some of his moods, 'God makes no difference between the righteous and the wicked'; and the answer of the 'Servant Songs', 'The righteous suffer in order that the wicked may be saved'. Apart, at any rate, from Koheleth's solitary voice, all these answers accept the axiom 'God is righteous'. In other words, the Hebrew still held, even though there were problems that he could not solve, that, at least in the end, God does treat the good in one way and the bad in another. There is, of course, nothing remarkable in the holding of a creed in spite of unsolved questions. These attend *all* creeds—whether religious, scientific, political, or any other—yet men still hold creeds firmly and even passionately.

As has already been claimed, the Hebrew thought of the relation of God to men principally under the analogy of a king and his subjects, and this allows or even demands the concept that while the King is sovereign, yet each of His subjects, within limits, is free to do as he chooses. There is, however, a passage in Jeremiah (ch. 18) which uses another analogy—that of the potter and the vessels or utensils that he makes. Taken in its full orbit, this analogy would teach, not that God's ways are sometimes puzzling, but that they are clearly arbitrary, for a potter, no doubt, did sometimes choose one lump of clay for one kind of vessel and another lump for a second kind arbitrarily. Jeremiah, however, says nothing of this. What he says is that a vessel may be '*marred* in the hand of the potter'. This might happen for either of two reasons. The first is that the potter's skill might fail him. This, of course, is not the reason why Israel was 'marred' in God's hand. The second reason may be called 'the recalcitrance of the clay'. Like all other parables, this one fails to match the situation at all points. Men, unlike clay, have wills of their own. The context shows that Israel was marred in the hands of God because Israel chose to sin (vv. 5ff). Here Jeremiah, in effect, admits that there is a point where his analogy fails. He does, indeed, teach God's sovereignty under the figure, for he states that the potter can take marred clay and 'make it again another vessel', and elsewhere, without using the parable again, he teaches that God will do this with Israel (e.g. ch. 31). But in the parable itself the concept that God is arbitrary would require that this Potter did what no potter ever did, mar clay on purpose! If the limitations of the Prophet's use of the analogy are examined, it follows that this passage does not contradict the composite doctrine that God is sovereign, yet man is free.

Two other Prophets use the Parable of the Potter. Isaiah has an oracle against Jerusalem in which he charges its inhabitants with evil plotting and planning in secret even though all the while they assiduously practise the cult of the LORD in the Temple (Is 29). Do they suppose that they hood-wink and 'manage' God? As well might clay think that it controls the potter (v. 16)! They will presently find out who is master! Here Isaiah teaches God's sovereignty, but he implies that men sin, not because God makes them sin, but because they choose to do so. Here there is nothing arbitrary in the concept of sovereignty. In the later chapters of Isaiah there are two references to the great Potter (45[9], 64[8]). The first relates to the sovereignty of the Creator. God has been pleased to 'anoint' Cyrus in order to vindicate His righteousness in the salvation of the faithful among the exiles (45[1ff]). It is implied that some of the Hebrews protest. They are compared to 'potsherds' who strive with the potter (v. 9)—which means, of course, not that these human 'potsherds' have no will of their own, but that God acts without asking men's leave, a truth irrelevant here. In the other passage the *penitent* exiles appeal to their 'father', who has been moulding their clay in punishment, to mould it now in deliverance. The pre-supposition again is that God deals righteously. None of the Old Testament passages about the Potter teaches that God arbitrarily makes some men good and others bad—some therefore to be blessed and some to be cursed.

This, of course, has brought us to the Old Testament doctrine of 'election'. There is no need to say that it deals wholly with this life and that it has nothing to do with 'election to heaven' and 'election to hell'. Of course, since the Hebrew, from first to last, believed in what we call 'a personal god', he believed that God, like all other persons, was always 'choosing'. Like human kings, again, He chose some to be His 'servants', or, as we say, in our politics, 'ministers'—and *ipso facto*, therefore, rejected others. The classical example of an Eastern king's right to select his 'servants' is Rehoboam's choice of young fools as over against Solomon's choice of old and wise men. We should call the former, but not the latter, 'favourites'. With a like freedom the great King chose both David and his line (e.g. 1 S 16^{8-10}; 2 S 6^{21}; Dt 17^5; Ps 78^{70}; cf. Hag 2^{23}) and Aaron and his line to be His ministers (e.g. Dt 18^5; Jer 33^{24}; Ps 105^{26}). In all such passages the Hebrew term is *bachar*. It is used of God's choice some fifty times. The leading case is the choice of Abraham and his 'seed' to be a 'chosen people'. While God is not *said* to have 'chosen' Abraham till Nehemiah (9^7), the *idea* is found from Genesis 12 onwards. Presently we read that when Abraham trusted God's promise, this fidelity was 'counted unto him for righteousness' (Gn 15^6). While neither 'righteous' nor 'righteousness' is used elsewhere in Genesis about any of the three Patriarchs, there is no doubt that the Hebrews thought of them all as 'perfect' (Gn 17^1).[1] The Deuteronomist implies this when, calling upon Israel to 'walk in the ways' of the LORD, he declares that God 'had a delight in their fathers to love them' (10^{12-22}; cf. 4^{37}), for a Deuteronomist was as unlikely as a Prophet to believe that the LORD could 'take delight' in sinners. It is true that in the early documents no moral reason is given for God's choice of Abel rather than Cain, or Isaac rather than Ishmael, or Jacob rather

---

[1] Cf. *The Bible Doctrine of Society*, ch. 1.

than Esau, and this choice might therefore be called 'arbitrary' or even 'capricious' in the sense that men do not know the 'reason why'—though the rejected Cain is not left without protection, or Ishmael and Esau without a 'blessing'—but with the Written Prophets there is a change. Amos, in effect, declares that as Israel, the chosen people, has proved unrighteous, it will be rejected (3^2). The dominant idea now is that God chose Israel *in order that she might learn to be righteous*—though not to *force* her to be righteous, as her refusal showed. This idea is drawn out, for instance, by the Deuteronomist, by Jeremiah, and by Ezekiel. From among the passages in Deuteronomy that explain the nature and reasons of this 'election' one may be taken as typical (7^{6-11})— Israel is to be 'a *holy* people unto the LORD', and by this time the idea of 'holiness' included 'righteousness'. Among 'all the peoples' she is to be the LORD's '*segullah*' ('peculiar people')—that is a king's 'private' (or 'personal') property as over against his 'public property', which was the whole kingdom. He 'loves' her and has delivered her from Egypt because of 'the oath which he sware' when He made covenant with her 'fathers'. He is a God who keeps covenant—that is, He *both* 'shows mercy' to those who 'love' Him and keep his commandments, *and* 'destroys' them that 'hate' Him. '*Therefore*' Israel is to be faithful. In brief, she is chosen in order that she may be righteous (cf. 4^{31-40}, 10^{12-22}, 29^2-30^{20}) but on her side she must consent. Similarly, Jeremiah has an oracle (ch. 30) concerning 'the two families (i.e. the two Hebrew kingdoms) which the LORD did choose' (v. 24). They have failed to be righteous, but now, if they will 'call unto' God, He will 'answer'—if they will forsake 'their iniquity', He will be their 'righteousness' (v. 16), as certainly as day follows night (v. 25). There is a purpose in God's election; the people can either foil or further it as they will. This is the only passage in Jeremiah where the *word* 'choose' is relevant, but he has the same company of ideas, of course, elsewhere without the word. There is also one oracle of Ezekiel (ch. 20) where the word is pertinent (v. 5). Here the main idea is that God 'chose Israel' in Egypt in order that she might 'forsake' the 'abomination' of 'idols'. Though she has consistently 'rebelled' against Him, He has again and again appealed to her through 'wonders' to 'walk in His statutes'—but all in vain. So He will now 'purge out' the 'transgressors' and they 'shall know that I am the LORD' (vv. 38, 42, 44). The dominant concept is of a 'chosen' people who have long thwarted

THE DOCTRINE OF ELECTION

the choice of God. Ezekiel implies that there was a penitent 'remnant' who accepted God's choice (vv. 40-4). Therefore, to turn to Isaiah, the LORD will 'yet choose Israel' (Is 14¹). The idea without the word is summed up in the later part of Isaiah's initial vision (6⁹⁻¹³). The great majority of the Chosen People have eyes but will not look and have ears but will not listen. Hence, under the law that we call atrophy, they will lose the power to see and hear. Yet there is a 'holy seed' who accept God's ancient choice. They consent to be righteous, and their very consent implies that they have already begun to be righteous. God chooses those who are willing to be chosen *for His purposes*. The dual idea is expressed in a Psalm—'Blessed is the nation whose God is the LORD. The people whom he hath chosen for his inheritance' (Ps 30¹²), for 'a nation whose God is the LORD' is one that chooses and 'rejoices' to be righteous (v. 1). The verb is rarely used of an individual saint, but a proverb says outright that God 'chooses' the righteous (Pr 21³), and a psalm exclaims 'Blessed is the man whom thou choosest', meaning a man who is glad to be 'purged' from 'transgressions' and so to 'dwell in the courts' of God (Ps 65¹⁻⁴). Again, *bachar* is found nine times in Deutero-Isaiah (e.g. 41⁸, 49⁷) to describe the faithful in the Exile.

This leads to the noun *bachir* (*13*), 'a chosen one'. If the present Hebrew text is not corrupt, this term is first used of Saul (2 S 21⁶), who *refused* the terms of his election. Elsewhere it is only used in Psalms and the later part of Isaiah. In the Psalms it describes *faithful* Israel (15⁷,³², 106⁵; 1 Ch 16¹³), or Moses (106²³), or David (89⁴). In Isaiah God speaks five times of 'my people, my chosen ones' (43²⁰, 45⁴, 65⁹, ¹⁵, ²²). This, of course, does not mean *all* the exiles but the *faithful* exiles. Finally, the first 'Servant Song' begins, 'Behold my servant, whom I uphold; my *chosen* one, in whom my soul delighteth'—and goes on at once to describe his mission to men. In other words, like Aaron and David of old, the Servant is 'chosen' *to serve others in God's behalf*. All the Servant Songs describe this mission. It does not end with Jews but spreads to the Gentiles. The Servant accepts election unmurmuringly, though it brings the smiting of the cheek and the pouring out of the soul unto death for sinners' sakes. This is the climax of the Old Testament doctrine of 'election'. Its final doctrine is that to fulfil His purposes in history, God chooses those who consent utterly to 'serve' Him. 'Choose' and 'serve' are correlative terms, as when a king chooses a loyal subject for some mission.

The same result follows if the use of another term *ratzah* (*58*) and its noun *ratzōn* (*56*) is examined. Both are rare before the Exile. Among many English renderings the commonest are 'accept' (*17*), 'acceptable' (*13*), and 'favour' (*15*). The last comes nearest to the meaning of the complex Hebrew idea, 'the spontaneous choice of a man to receive goodwill and boon'. The emphasis seems to be on 'unfettered choice', for the words occur in a phrase meaning 'to do as one likes (whether for good or ill)'. A master of empire, for instance, does as he likes (Dn 11[3, 16, 36]; cf. Gn 49[6]; Neh 9[14]), as does a 'hireling' when his master is not watching him (Job 14[6]; cf. Est 1[8]). Men may spontaneously choose to 'draw near unto God' (Is 58[2]). While one man may seek another's 'goodwill' by gifts or service, these do not constitute a *claim* as of right (Gn 33[10] J; 1 S 29[4]). The words are naturally used of a king or other ruler's 'good pleasure' (e.g. 2 Ch 10[7]; Pr 16[13, 15]; Mal 1[8]), but they occur more often of God's 'good pleasure' than of man's. This use is especially frequent in the Psalms. When used of God the terms always denote His selection of a 'people' (Is 60[10]; Ps 44[3]), or of a 'land' (Ps 85[1]), or, much more often, of individuals, for the gift of a boon. God elects the penitent (Ps 19[14], 30[5], 143[10]), the 'meek' (Ps 149[4]), 'them that fear him' (Ps 147[11]; cf. Job 33[26]), and the 'righteous' (Ps 5[13], 51[19]; Pr 12[2, 22], 16[7], etc.). Similarly He shows His 'good pleasure' to a penitent or righteous 'people' (Ezr 10[11]; Ps 89[17], 106[4]) and He 'accepts' a righteous man's offerings (1 Ch 29[17]; Ps 119[108]). His choice is unfettered, of course, but He chooses a certain kind of man. There is a passage in an early song (Dt 33[11, 16, 23]) where God's 'goodwill' might be called 'arbitrary', but when once the Prophets had established the creed that God is righteous, the idea disappears. Koheleth, indeed, in one of his several moods, waxes sarcastic over the notion that prosperity and a good wife are proof, as his contemporaries held, of God's 'good pleasure' (Ec 9[7-10]), but this was only to raise the problem, 'Why do bad men sometimes flourish?', and it has been seen that Israel believed in the righteousness of God's dealings with men even though this problem remained unsolved. The Wise Man, declaring that it is 'wisdom' that brings God's 'good pleasure', represents the prevalent doctrine (Pr 8[35]). When a man offered a particular kind of sacrifice because it was 'acceptable' to God (e.g. Lev 1[3]; cf. 7[18]), it could be said that God's choice of one *sacrifice* rather than another was arbitrary, but the Prophets, of course, denounced the idea that God would 'accept' a *man* because he offered the proper sacrifices (e.g. Am 5^{22}; Hos 8^{13}; Mic 6^7; Jer 5^{20}; Mal 2^{13}). Ezekiel has a passionate passage in which he declares that it is only the right kind of Israelite who will be chosen to return to Palestine, there to offer 'acceptable' sacrifices (Ezk $20^{39\text{-}41}$). There are several texts in Isaiah 40–66. Deutero-Isaiah declares, in an unusual phrase, that Israel's 'punishment' in Exile is 'accepted' as more than enough (40^2). Trito-Isaiah extends Ezekiel's idea to the 'strangers' of 'all peoples' who 'love the name of the LORD' (though he specially mentions the Sabbath) ($56^{1\text{-}8}$; cf. 50^7). 'The time of good pleasure' or 'day of salvation' is the LORD's answer to the 'Servant's' prayers for his people ($49^{5\text{-}13}$), and it is at least possible that it is 'the Servant' who heralds both 'the day of retribution' for God's enemies and 'the year of good pleasure' to 'broken-hearted' Israel ($61^{1\text{n}}$). A culminant text unites five ideas—'Behold my *servant*, whom I uphold; my *chosen*, in whom my soul *takes pleasure*: I have put *my spirit* upon him; he shall bring forth judgement to *the Gentiles*' (42^1). The 'Servant' is so called just because he is willing both to do and, still more, to suffer all God's will. The text that declares that God 'formed (him) from the womb' to be Servant (44^2) does not mean that he was Servant without his own consent, any more than the phrase 'born to be an evangelist', if used, for instance, of Wesley or Moody, means that they were involuntarily evangelists. The alternative phrase, 'called from the womb' (49^1) requires the opposite, for 'call' here implies 'answer'. Under *ratzah*, as under *bachar*, God's choice of a man and the man's consent to be chosen are not contradictory but complementary, as when a king selects a loyal servant for a task.

While God 'chooses' some He 'rejects' (*ma'as*) others. The Hebrew word is also rendered 'cast out', 'refuse', and 'despise'. A man may 'refuse' food (Is 7^{17}) or 'despise' other men (Jg 9^{38}) or 'reject' land (Nu 14^{31} J) or 'cast away' idols (Is 31^7). The term is used about twenty times each of men's 'rejecting' God (or His 'word', 'law', 'statutes', and so on) and of God's 'rejecting' man. These uses begin in the story of Saul and the Amalekites. Saul had been 'chosen' (1 S 10^{24}), but now Samuel says 'Because thou hast rejected the word of the LORD, he hath also rejected thee from being king' (1 S $15^{23,\ 26}$). Here the sequence of thought is—God chose Saul; Saul rejected God; God rejected Saul. This is the regular sequence. The phrases are rare before the Written Prophets. Here, of course, the concept is clearly ethicized. For instance, Hosea, addressing Israel, says, 'Because thou hast rejected knowledge, I will also reject thee' (Hos 4^6; cf. 9^{17}; Am 2^4); Isaiah teaches that to sin is to 'despise the Holy One of Israel' (5^{24}; cf. 30^{12}); Jeremiah, speaking of Israel's 'rejection' of God (6^{19}, 8^9), speaks also of God's 'rejection' of Israel—'Rejected silver shall men call them, because the LORD hath rejected them' (6^{30}; cf. 7^{29})—yet declares that God will not 'reject' the Israel of the New Covenant (31^{37}; cf. 33$^{24, 26}$); Ezekiel has just the same message—since Israel has 'rejected' God's judgements, 'Behold, I, even I, am against thee' (5^6; cf. 20$^{13, 16}$). The phrases are found also in the Deuteronomists (2 K 17$^{15, 20}$), and the Code of Holiness (Lev 26$^{15, 43f}$), but are more frequent in the Poetical Books—for instance, in Job 5^{17}, 8^{20}; Psalm 89^{38}. Some Psalms teach that 'rejection' follows sin (e.g. 53^5, 78$^{59, 67}$). A man who does not 'fear the LORD' is 'reprobate', or rather 'rejected', both by God and 'him that worketh righteousness' (15$^{2, 4}$). Under *ma'as* it is clear that God's decision is not arbitrary but depends on man's choice.

Four other terms may be taken next. Three of them occur both in earlier and later documents and go together. Their use before the Prophets' clear enunciation of the doctrine of Righteousness may be taken first. One of the words means to 'make heavy' or 'dull' (*kabēd*). Pharaoh is three times said to have 'dulled his (own) heart' (Ex 8$^{15, 32}$, 9^{34}; cf. 3^{19}—all J), and once God is said to have 'dulled' it—that is, since the heart was counted the seat of the will, to have made Pharaoh obstinate (Ex 10^1 J). The second term, *qasheh*, means 'hard'. It does not occur in J and E of God's hardening of men, but there is the text 'the hand of the LORD was hard on the men of Ashdod' (1 S 5^7). Under the phrase 'hard of neck', or 'stiff-necked' (e.g. Ex 32^9 JE, 33^3 E, 34^9 J) men harden themselves. Under the third word, *chazēq*, which means 'firm', it is said that God 'made firm Pharaoh's heart (Ex 4^{21} E), and that Pharaoh 'made firm' his own (Ex 9^{35} J). Just as one might 'make firm' or 'strengthen' the watch (Jer 51^{12}), so one might 'make firm the heart'—that is, 'strengthen the will'. It will be noticed that where these terms are used of God in early documents, He is acting against the enemies of Israel and therefore of Israel's god. From Abraham (Gn 14) to Ahab the LORD fights for Israel—the question whether their enemy is morally good or bad being quite irrelevant. In these conflicts He is able, when He likes, to use even an enemy as His tool. God is strengthening Pharaoh's will when he strengthens it himself! An Englishman approximates to the idea when he says 'Give him enough rope and he will hang himself'. Already there is an implicit antinomy—God is sovereign though man is free. But so far there is no question of the ethics of God. He does not doom Pharaoh to be a bad man but to be His unwitting tool. At this stage no Hebrew even asked the question, 'Was this fair to Pharaoh?', for the early Hebrew believed that an enemy had no rights.[2]

It is otherwise with these terms in the documents from Amos onwards. He is the first clearly to declare that God will punish *all* nations, Israel included, for their *sin* (Am 1 and 2). Tyre, for instance, which was *not* Israel's enemy, is to be punished because of its cruelty to Edom, which *was*. Isaiah teaches that God 'dulls' Judah's ears because she has refused to hear (6[10]). God punishes her because, as Zechariah says, she has herself 'dulled' her own ears and 'made (her) heart like an adamant 'stone' (7[8-14]). Israel, of course, is still 'hard of neck' (e.g. 2 K 17[4]; Jer 7[26]). The older idea may linger in one Deuteronomist's mind when he says that God 'hardened the spirit (of Og) and made stout his heart' (Dt 2[30]), but hardly in another's when he writes 'It was of the LORD to strengthen (the Canaanites') hearts . . . that he might death-devote them' (Jos 11[20]), for to the Deuteronomists idolatry was the first of sins and it was the Canaanites who taught it to Israel. Trito-Isaiah, acknowledging that Israel's 'rebellions' had turned its God into its 'enemy', pleads with Him no longer to 'make (His people) err' and 'harden their heart' against Him (Is 63[10, 17]). The Priestly writer, for whom all the heathen were sinners, would reckon Pharaoh a sinner, and finds it easy, therefore, to echo J and E and say that God 'strengthened' Pharaoh's will (Ex 9[12], 14[8]; cf. 1 S 6[6]), but this is now God's response to Pharaoh's sin. Finally, there is the fourth term, 'make fat' (*shāmēn*—5). It occurs first in Isaiah's Vision—'Make the heart of this people fat' (Is 6[10]). In its literal meaning, to be 'fat' was to prosper (e.g. Nu 13[20]). When a bull grew fat it was more likely to 'kick against the goad'. This is what Israel did when she prospered (Dt 32[15]; cf. 6 [10ff]). 'In the year when king Uzziah died' Judah had grown prosperous, and God tells Isaiah both that he is to preach repentance (e.g. ch. 1) and that Judah will reject

[2] See *The Bible Doctrine of Society*, pp. 84ff.

the message more and more, as a bull that begins to kick will develop a habit of kicking. God foresees all this and He has a dread way of dealing with it. To use modern terms, God has a law of hypertrophy as well as of atrophy. Under the second a man who refuses to look loses the power to see; under the first a man who rebels and rebels becomes a habitual rebel. Because he chooses to be bad, he grows worse. God has decreed that an evil appetite strengthens with use. The laws of atrophy and hypertrophy are laws of God's sovereignty, but they describe the way in which His sovereignty deals with man's abuse of his freedom. As under other terms, sovereignty and freedom are not contradictory but complementary.

There is a text about Pharaoh that introduces another term (Ex 9[16f] J). He has been 'exalting himself' against God, and God says to him, 'For this cause have I made thee to stand (*'amad*)— or 'set thee up'—'for to show thee my power'. The Hebrew word cannot mean 'raise up' in the sense of 'create'. Here God is not creator, but king. It was kings who set up one subject and cast down another, as Ahasuerus did, for instance, with Haman and Mordecai. God is a king who 'sets others up' in the stead of 'mighty men' (Job 34[24]), and 'sets' His anointed's feet in 'high places' (Ps 18[33]). There are parallels to the text about Pharaoh under another term, *qūm* ('stand up', 'rise'). Under its 'causative' form God may 'raise up a king' to rule Israel (Jer 30[9]), or 'raise up' an evil 'shepherd' over His people (Zec 11[16]), or 'raise up the poor out of the dust . . . to set him with princes' (Ps 113[7f]). Is He not sovereign of all men, even though they know it not? Here, as often, in order to understand Hebrew thought one must turn to history, not philosophy. Such a statesman as Bismarck, for instance, is said first to have *used* the German Liberals and then the German Socialists to further absolutism. At the time they did not know it—and they were given considerable freedom in the process. Similarly, in Garibaldi's anti-monarchist days Cavour *used* him to establish a monarchy. It is government, not creation, that is in question—sovereignty, not determinism. Pharaoh was doing as he liked—yet he was God's tool. An able and good king 'chooses' the loyal and 'rejects' the rebel; his subjects can be neither loyal nor rebellious unless they are free; yet, if he is great enough, he uses rebellion as well as loyalty to serve his own ends. 'Thine own wickedness shall correct thee', saith the LORD, for, by His decree, sinners do evil unto themselves (Jer 2[19]; Is 3[9]).

THE DOCTRINE OF ELECTION

Another term may be included here so far as it illustrates the concept of God's sovereignty. Under one of its very many uses the verb 'give' (*nathan*) is translated 'give up'. In the earliest documents the LORD is said to 'give up' the Canaanites and Amorites 'into the hand' of Israel in battle (Nu 21³, ³⁴) and the Deuteronomist has the phrase several times (e.g. Dt 2²⁴, 7²), extending its meaning to cover all Israel's 'enemies' (Dt 23¹⁴). So far, while it is assumed that the LORD decides the issues of war, the question 'Which of the combatants has right on its side?' is not raised. But this question emerges in the great chapter of Blessings and Curses (Dt 28). Here, if Israel 'observes' the LORD's commandments, He will 'give up' her assailants to be 'smitten' before her; but, if she refuses to 'hearken' unto the LORD, He will 'give her up' to be 'smitten' by her enemies (vv. 1, 7, 15, 25). God, that is, deals with His own people ethically. The ethical issue is not raised for other peoples, for it is not pertinent to the great sermon, but there is no doubt that they were idolaters and that the Deuteronomist thought all idolaters wicked (e.g. 12²⁹ᶠ, 13⁶⁻¹¹). The same word 'give up' had already been used of God's rejection of Northern Israel because of its sin (Hos 11⁸; cf. 1K 14¹⁶). From Hosea onwards God's sovereign act, under this term too, corresponds to His people's use of freedom.

On turning to the subject of Election in the Apocrypha, we find that while Sirach uses the Parable of the Potter (33⁷⁻¹⁵), he does not use it in quite the same way as Jeremiah. He does not speak of the 'marring' of the clay, but only of a potter's power to make what he will of it. As God, according to His 'knowledge' of what is best, makes one day 'holy' and others profane, so in 'the abundance of his knowledge', He 'makes (men's) ways various'. At first sight it seems as if Sirach means that God makes some men good and some bad but presently he says that God '*rewards* men according to his judgement' (*krisis*). This phrase, on Hebrew analogy, means that God judges men by their deeds and rewards them accordingly. Sirach himself, as we have seen, often says this. The fact is that at this point the analogy between God's 'separating' of days and of men has broken down. He does not 'judge' days. Sirach's purpose here, as elsewhere, is to warn sinners that God is Almighty and that He does 'discriminate' between the good and the bad. Knowing beforehand by 'the abundance of his knowledge' whether a man will be good or bad, He appoints him a 'blessing' or a 'curse'. As Judith says, God's *'krisis* is with fore-knowledge' (9^6). This interpretation of the passage is at least possible and it suits the rest of Sirach. On the other hand, to take the passage in a fatalistic way contradicts the whole purpose of this writer. What would be the good of telling men to be 'wise' through fifty chapters when a young fellow might reply, 'But you yourself say that I can't'?

For the Hebrew word *bachar* ('choose') and its cognates LXX has seventeen renderings. All but three are very rare, but some of these show that the translators thought both of God's choice and man's, not as arbitrary, but as reasonable. Things or men are 'chosen' because of what they *are* and because they are therefore suited to the chooser's *purpose*. For instance, a translator renders 'choice silver' by *'purified* silver', assuming that the choice has a reason (Pr 8^{10}), and 'chosen' men are *'able (dunatos)* men' (2 Ch $13^{3, 17}$). This appears also in one of the three commoner renderings, for the phrase 'chosen men' is rendered over forty times by *'young* men' (e.g. 2 S 6^1; Am 2^{11}; Is 9^{16}, 62^5; Jer 6^{11}; Ps 78^{63}). The 'young' were 'chosen' because they were 'fit for war'. Such renderings show that the translators, assuming that choice or election is not arbitrary, subconsciously supplied the reason for the choice. Once, indeed, they even render *tōb* ('good') by 'elect' (Ezk 31^{16}). The instances of one of the two *literal* renderings of *bachar*, *hairein* and its cognates (*19*), do not happen to bear upon the subject of God's election. The other term, *eklegein*, occurs a hundred and eight times. In modern English its best rendering is 'select'. To examine its use in the Greek Old Testament would lead to the same conclusions as the examination of the use of *bachar* in Hebrew. There is no need to go through these passages again. God chooses men because of what they are. *Bachir*, 'chosen one', is *always* (*36*) rendered by *eklektos*, and it has been shown that *bachir* means 'selected because of faithfulness'.

In the Apocrypha the verb *eklegein* is used of God's choice five times. He 'chose' Jerusalem for His chosen people's sake, and its fate depends upon their sin or righteousness (2 Mac 5^{18-20}; cf. To 1^4; 1 Mac 7^{37}). He would not 'choose' the ancient giants, giving them no 'wisdom' because of their own 'foolishness' (Bar 3^{27f})—a characteristically Hebrew combination of the ideas of election and freedom. He 'chose' Moses and equipped him for his high mission, and through Moses 'chose' Aaron, for it was God who 'exalted' him (Sir 45⁴, ⁶, ¹⁶)—as a king selects loyal servants for his services. Such things as myrrh and soldiers are 'elect' (Sir 24¹⁵; Jdth 2¹⁵; 1 Mac 4¹, 9⁵) when they excel. The verbal noun *eklektos* is used nine times of God's 'elect'—once apparently of angels (To 8¹⁵), once of Jerusalem, 'the elect city' (Sir 49⁶), and seven times of men. Sirach speaks of David's 'elect posterity' (47²²)—'elect' because David had been righteous (vv. 2ff). A righteous eunuch will receive 'an elect favour' from God (Wis 3¹⁴). In the other five passages the phrase is 'his (God's) elect'. Three writers speak of the ancient Israelites under this phrase (Sir 46¹; Wis 4¹⁵; 2 Mac 1²⁵). As already noted, the writer of Wisdom counted them righteous, and this was probably the prevalent idea. In two texts the manuscripts vary between *eklektos* and *hosios* (Wis 3⁹, 4¹⁵)—i.e. the elect are the same as the 'devout'. Finally, in a famous passage Wisdom uses the word 'elect' to describe sufferers who cling to righteousness unto death (3⁹). They are to be immortal, not by any arbitrary fiat at birth, but because they are righteous (v. 1). This is the burden of the whole passage (chh. 2 and 3). God chooses those who choose Him. It is a mutual choice, as in friendship, each choosing the other because of what he is. There is nothing arbitrary in the concept of God's 'election' of men in the Apocrypha.

The same results emerge from an examination of the renderings of *ratzah* and *ratzon*. Here there are four terms derived from the same root—*prosdechesthai* (*13*), *dektos* (*25*), *eudokein* (*22*), and *eudokia* (*8*). There is no need to discuss again the texts found in the Hebrew books. In most of the passages in the Apocrypha where the words are used to describe God's choice, the question 'Who is pleasing to Him?' is present, either explicitly or implicitly, and the answer is always 'The righteous'. *Prosdechesthai*, 'accept', is so used four times, always in relation to sacrifice. 'As a burnt offering (God) accepted (the righteous)' is typical (Wis 3⁶; cf. Sir 7⁹; 35¹²; 2 Mac 1²⁶). The second term *dektos*, which means both 'acceptable' and 'accepted', has its three examples in Sirach, where it is once used *simpliciter* to mean a man whom God 'accepts' (3¹⁷; cf. 2⁵, 35⁷). *Eudokein* ('approve'), and *eudokia*, 'approval', are much more frequent (*32*), especially in Sirach (*20*), but the texts that use the terms of *God's* 'good pleasure' are not numerous. While He has absolute power and 'at his command is all his good pleasure done' (Sir 39¹⁸; cf. 41⁴), it is the man that 'serveth (God) according to his good pleasure' who is 'accepted'

(Sir 36^{16}; cf. 2^{16}, 11^{17}, 32^{14}, 35$^{3, 16}$, 45^{19}; Jdth 15^{10}). God is absolute but not arbitrary. His 'good pleasure' rests on the righteous because they please Him.

Of the Hebrew terms under 'reject' the first, *ma'as*, has twenty-four Greek renderings. Some of the least frequent show that the translators interpreted the word in varying ways to suit the context. For instance, a 'rejected' wife is a *'hated'* (*misein*) wife (Is 55^6), Israel *'overlooks'* (*hyperoran*) or 'neglects' the judgements of God (Lev 26^{43}), and Job *'slights himself'* (*phaulesthai*) after the great theophany (Job 42^6). These texts show that the use of many Greek renderings does not obscure the unity of the meaning of *ma'as*. One of the three commonest renderings is *apōthein*, 'to thrust away' (*20*). A text in Hosea, for instance, runs—'Because *thou* hast thrust away knowledge, *I* also will thrust thee away' (4^6; cf. Am 2^4; Jer 3^{37}; Ezk 5^{11}). The second commonest rendering is *exoudenein* (and its cognates). This means 'to set at naught' (*16*). When Israel 'provoked' God to anger, for instance, He 'set her at naught' (Ps 78^{59}; cf. 1 S 16$^{1, 7}$; Ps 53^5). The third term, *apodokimazein* (*8*), 'to discard (after test)', belongs to Jeremiah— e.g. in 'Hast thou utterly discarded Judah? ... We acknowledge, O LORD, our wickedness' (14^{19f}; cf. 6^{30}, 7^{29}). Under all these three renderings Israel rejects God before He rejects her (e.g. Jer 6^{19}; 1 S 8^7; Jer 8^9). Jeremiah and other Prophets taught that a certain *race* had been chosen, had proved false, and had *then* been discarded. The adjective *adokimos* renders a Hebrew word (*sīg*) that means 'dross'. In one of its two uses a king 'rejects' evil men as refiners reject dross (Pr 25 ^{4ff}), and in the other the 'silver' of the once 'faithful' Jerusalem has failed to pass the great Refiner's test (Is 1^{22} LXX; cf. Jer 6^{30}; Mal 3^3). He rejects her because she deserves to be rejected.

While the Greek terms now in question occur in the Apocrypha, they are not used of God's 'rejection' of *Israel*, for after the Exile the Jews believed that they were not a discarded race but a chosen race under discipline. This is the *motif* of such books as Esther, Tobit, Judith, Susanna, and Maccabees. But three of the terms are used in a way that, in effect, applies the idea of rejection to *individual men*. 'Give me wisdom ...', says 'Solomon', 'And discard (*apodokimazein*) me not' (Wis 9^4); 'Who did ever ... call upon (God), and he neglected (*hyperoran*) him?' says Sirach (2^{10}; cf. Wis 19^{22}); 'He that setteth at naught (*exoudenein*) wisdom and discipline is miserable', declares the writer of Wisdom (3^{11}; cf.

THE DOCTRINE OF ELECTION 155

4¹⁸; Sir 31²²). The implication is that *if* a man rejects God, God will reject him.

Three of the next group of Hebrew roots are rendered literally —*kbd*, 'heavy', by *barunein* or a cognate (e.g. Ex 7¹⁴, 8¹⁵, ³²); *qshh*, 'hard' by *skleros* Pr 28¹⁴; and *shmn*, 'fat', either by *lipainein* (e.g. Dt 32¹⁵) or *pachunein* (Is 6¹⁰), though the last term means 'stout' rather than 'fat'. The fourth root *chzq* has many meanings and therefore many translations but it is rendered by *stereoun*, 'solidify' in Jer 5³. The 'stiff-necked' is also rendered literally by *sklerotrachelos* (e.g. Ex 33³, ⁵; Dt 9⁶, ¹³). The LXX rendering, or rather interpretation, of the capital passage, Isaiah 6⁹ᶠ, is significant. Its literal meaning is 'And (God) said, Go and tell this people, Verily *ye shall hear* and in no wise understand, And verily *ye shall look* and in no wise see. For the heart of this people *grew stout*, And with their ears *they heard* heavily. And their eyes *they shut*, lest they should see at all with their eyes, and hear with their ears, and understand with their heart, and should turn— and I will heal them.' This variation from the Hebrew makes it plain that the Greek translators took the passage to mean three things: 'This people has sinned in the past and therefore finds it harder now to see and hear; it will still refuse Isaiah's reiterated message in spite of his warning of punishment after punishment (cf. vv. 11–13); by the law of atrophy, therefore, it will grow deafer and deafer and blinder and blinder.' The literal translation of two other LXX passages of the last century of the Kingdom of Judah are the best comment—'And Jacob ate and was filled, And he that had been loved (of God) kicked, grew fat, grew stout, grew broad, And forsook the God who made him, And revolted from God, his saviour. . . . And the LORD saw and was jealous and was provoked on account of anger (against) his sons and daughters' (Dt 34¹⁵, ¹⁹); 'They were unwilling to receive discipline; they made their faces more solid than rock, And were unwilling to turn' (Jer 5³). These two passages use parables similar to those in Is 6⁹ᶠ, and the fact that the makers of the Greek version interpreted rather than translated the last text show unmistakably that they took it to be a parallel.

Under the terms now in question there are hardly any relevant passages in the Apocrypha. A text in Baruch echoes the old phrase, 'for they are a stiff-necked people' (2³⁰), and Sirach has it that 'a heart that is *hard* (where there is a variant "*made heavy*") shall fare ill at the last, And he that loveth danger shall perish therein. A *hard* heart shall be laden with troubles, And the sinner shall add sin upon sins' (3²⁶ᶠ). Similarly, he writes 'Even if there be one *hard-necked* person, it is a marvel if he shall be unpunished' (16¹¹). There is no passage that even seems to teach predestination to evil. The Jew in the Dispersion kept the Law or not, as he liked, for there was no one to make him do so. Such an environment encourages the sense of *individual* freedom, not of fate. As for the *race*, the current Jewish belief was that it was being disciplined because it had resolutely chosen to sin.

Under the next two words, '*amad* and *qum*, the LXX renderings of the Hebrew passages quoted above are uniform except in Exodus 9¹⁶, where the Greek means 'For this cause thou (Pharaoh) wast carefully kept' (*diatērein*), a term used in Wisdom of the sway of God's 'mighty arm' in the universe (11²¹, ²⁵). Elsewhere *histanai*, 'set up', is used for '*amad*, and either *histanai* or *egeirein*, 'rouse', or a compound of one of these, for *qum*. The relevant Old Testament passages have been examined under the Hebrew terms. In the Apocrypha the Lord is said to 'rouse the spirit' of Cyrus and of the faithful Jews to rebuild the Temple (1 Es 2²ᶠ, ⁸ᶠ). The context shows that, for this writer, Cyrus was both consciously and willingly the vicegerent of God. Sirach asserts that because the '*authority* of the earth' is 'in the hand of the Lord', He is sure to 'set up over it the serviceable one' (10⁴; cf. 36¹⁵). Perhaps with an eye to the earlier Ptolemies, he here says that a wise king will choose to do the will of the King of Kings. Under the passages where '*amad* and *qum* occur in the Hebrew, LXX rightly uses renderings that envisage God, not as creator, but as king. An Eastern king, however despotic, knew that all his subjects had wills of their own, even though he might sometimes *use* some of them for a purpose beyond their ken. For God's way with Pharaoh, who was unconsciously His subject, the right word is a word of kingship, 'over-*rule*'. As LXX suggests, God had been 'carefully keeping' him against the time when He would use him, as a huntsman, for instance, being king of a kennel, carefully keeps dogs—yet even a dog, within limits, does as it likes!

In the passages quoted from the Old Testament where *nathan* means 'to give up', the regular LXX rendering is either by *didonai* or, more often, *paradidonai*. There is one exception (Hos 11⁸), where 'How shall I give thee up, Ephraim?' is mitigated to 'How am I to treat thee (*diatithenai*)?' In the Apocrypha there are passages which show that the Deuteronomic warning to

Israel, 'If thou keep not my commandments, I will give thee up into the hands of thine enemies', had burnt itself into the hearts of faithful individual Jews (1 Esd 6^{15}, 8^{77}; Est 14^6; Three 9, 11; cf. 2 Mac 1^{17}, 10^4), and Sirach applies the word directly to *the individual*—'If (a man) go astray (wisdom) will forsake him, And give him up to the hands of his fall' (4^{19}; cf. 23^6). Here to 'give up' is a synonym for 'forsake'. The uniform evidences of the whole series of relevant terms, both in the Greek Old Testament and the Apocrypha, is that God uses the sovereignty of a king to match His subjects' use or abuse of freedom. 'Sovereignty' is not 'arbitrary fate'. It has often been pointed out that Josephus[3] states that the Pharisees held the same doctrine. Like all practical theists, they accepted the antinomy, 'God is sovereign, yet man is free'.

Before considering the New Testament use of the terms 'elect' and 'reprobate' in detail some general comments may be made. First, as already shown, the Jews believed both in the Sovereignty of God and in a limited but real Freedom of Man. As just noted, it was the teaching of the Pharisees. In his Pharisaic days, therefore, Paul would hold both these beliefs. Second, as under the Old Testament and Apocrypha, it is better to speak of God's 'sovereignty' rather than His 'omnipotence', for throughout the Bible He is king and not a personified 'fate'. Strictly speaking, human kings are never 'absolute', for the mightiest of them cannot control every act and word and thought of every one of his subjects. No doubt God, the only absolute king, could do so, but, just *because* He is absolute, He can safely allow His subjects some degree of liberty if He will. He does allow it, or there could be no sin or guilt. This is particularly true if 'to sin', as with the Hebrews, is primarily 'to disobey God'. Third, it can hardly be disputed that, apart from certain Pauline passages, the presupposition of the whole New Testament is that every man who hears the Gospel *can* either accept or reject it as he will—that 'Whosoever will, may come'. There is no need to quote the particular passages in which this axiom becomes explicit. Fourth, there are references below to God's Law of Opportunity—with its two parts, the Laws of Development and of Atrophy—without further exposition than has already been given. It is, of course, a law about the use and misuse of freedom—and also an account of the reaction of the Sovereign to His subjects' use of freedom.

[3] *Jewish War*, II.viii.14; cf. *HDB*, III.826.

In LXX it was found that a certain group of terms go together with the word 'elect' (*eklektos*). This is so too in the New Testament. Among the Greek terms some are verbal adjectives ending in *-tos*. J. H. Moulton[4] points out that in Greek, as in the corresponding English words, these terms are sometimes equivalent to past participles and sometimes bear one or other of the senses of the Greek 'gerundive'—and that the context must decide which is meant. He does not say, though he might be held to imply, that a word may have *both* senses at once. Is not this the reason why there seems to be ambiguity in the meaning of these terms in both the Greek and English languages (and others)? Sometimes, indeed, the context requires that one meaning must be taken and the other left, but at other times both ideas are implied in one way or another. There is an example in *parakletos*, which means both 'one called in to help' and 'one able to help'. Similarly *eulogētos* ('blessed'), used so often of God, means both that He is 'worthy to be blessed' and is 'blessed'. The word is almost confined to Him because, in the absolute sense, He alone is worthy to be blessed. In the one passage where the opposite term *epikataratos* occurs, Paul means first that all who fail to keep the law *are* 'accursed' because they *ought* to be and second that Christ 'became a curse for us' because a true Saviour *must* do so (Gal $3^{10, \cdot 13}$). *Agapētos* (*61*), 'beloved', is another example. In by far the most frequent use of the word the phrase 'beloved brethren' is typical. Christians love one another because fellow-believers are *ipso facto* 'love-able' (e.g. Ac 15^{25}; Ro 16 $^{5 \cdot 12}$; 2 Co 7^1; Heb 6^9; Ja 1^{16}; 1 P 2^{11}; 1 Jn 2^7). On the other hand, Christians are only twice called *God's agapetoi* (Ro 1^7; Eph 5^1), perhaps because the term might seem to suggest that they were worthy of *His* love (cf. Ro 11^{28}). In the Synoptics Jesus only is called God's 'beloved', for it is *He* who is worthy of God's love. Except once (Mk 12^6) the phrase is peculiar to the stories of His baptism and transfiguration (e.g. Mk 1^{11}, 9^7; cf. 2 P 1^{17}). At the baptism the full text is, 'Thou art my beloved Son, in thee I am well-pleased'. In the latter phrase the verb is *eudokein*, which is discussed below. It has no verbal adjective, and it is hard to resist the impression that Paul (*8*) and the writer to the Hebrews (*1*) use *euarestos*, the verbal adjective of *euareskein*, in place of this, for this verb too means 'to be well-pleasing', or, better, 'to well-please'. In the Greek Old Testament (*14*) it is used ten times for *hithhallēk*

[4] *Grammar of New Testament Greek*, I.221f.

('to walk with' or 'walk before'). Of these texts nine speak of a man's 'walk with (or before) *God*'. They all occur either in Genesis or Psalms (26³, 56¹³, 116⁹), and in the former describe the life of Enoch, Noah, Abraham, and Isaac (Gn 5²², ²⁴, 6⁹, 24⁴⁰, 48⁵). According to LXX, to 'walk before God' is to be 'well-pleasing' to Him. The adjective *euarestos* does not occur till the Book of Wisdom (4¹⁹, 9¹⁰), but then it means that God *is* pleased with a man who *deserves* His pleasure. *Euarestos* and its verb seem to have been in common use to describe Enoch (Sir 44¹⁶; Wis 4¹⁰; He 11⁵ᶠ). The writer of Wisdom says that because he was 'well-pleasing to God', he was 'loved' and 'translated'. God, if the phrase is permissible, was 'delighted' with him because he was 'delightsome'—i.e., the verbal adjective combines two senses. In the New Testament, *euarestein* (*3*) is peculiar to Hebrews (11⁵ᶠ, 12¹⁶), but it always refers to *God's* 'good pleasure', as does *euarestos* in at least six of its ten instances. Paul (*9*) declares in one sentence that the 'holy sacrifice' of a true Christian life is 'delightsome' to God, and that the 'will of God', when 'put to the proof', is 'delightsome' to Christians—but he also implies that, in *fact*, God 'delights' in the one and Christians 'delight' in the other (Rom 12¹ᶠ; cf. 14¹⁸; Eph 5¹⁰; Phil 4¹⁸). Again, when he says 'we are ambitious to be well-pleasing to (God)', he implies that God *is* sometimes 'well-pleased' with Christians. Here the one text in Hebrews is complementary (He 13²¹)—God Himself, 'through Jesus Christ', seeks to 'perfect' Christians 'in every good thing to do his will', that is, 'works in (them) that which is well-pleasing in his sight'. It will be noticed that all the verbal adjectives here examined *imply* that God chooses or selects or 'elects' a certain kind of man. The conclusion seems to be clear— that usually the adjectives combine one of the senses of the 'gerundive' with the sense of the past participle—that is, that God chooses men because they are for some reason 'choose-able'— that is, His choice is not arbitrary. Is this the same with *eklektos* ('elect')? And, if so, for what reason are the elect 'choose-able'? These are the next questions. It will be convenient to leave five passages in Paul (Ro 1¹⁸⁻³², 8²⁶⁻³⁰, 9–11; 1 Co 1 ¹⁰⁻¹⁷; Ephs 1³⁻¹⁴) till the end of the discussion, and to take first the other passages where either 'elect' or 'predestinate' and their allied terms occur.

In the New Testament the verb 'choose' or 'elect' (*eklegesthai*, *22*) has two uses. Under the first it means 'to choose for some particular purpose'. For instance, Jesus 'chose twelve whom also he named apostles' (Lk 6¹³; cf. Ac 1²; Jn 15¹⁶)—that is, He chose them in order to 'send' them on His errand. It was not an arbitrary choice, but a choice of those who best suited His purpose. Perhaps their chief qualification was their willingness to do all His will, for they never refused outright to obey Him. They were 'not of the world' (Jn 15¹⁹). Judas, however, proved faithless. This shows that our Lord's choice did not override a disciple's own will. In the Fourth Gospel it is implied both that Judas ceased to be 'chosen', and that God foresaw and used his treachery (Jn 6⁷⁰, 13¹⁸). Similarly, when Matthias and Stephen and Barsabbas and Silas were 'chosen' for particular pieces of service, it is assumed that they were willing to undertake them (Ac 1²⁴, 6⁵, 15²², ²⁵). In one passage Paul repeats the Old Testament doctrine that God 'chose' Israel, but goes on to argue that 'they that dwell in Jerusalem' have refused to fulfil His purpose in that choice (Ac 13¹⁷, ²⁷). Peter, on the other hand, obeyed when God surprised him by 'choosing' him to evangelize Gentiles (Ac 15⁷). Most of all, when God said at the Transfiguration, 'This is my son, my chosen' (Lk 9³⁵), surely Jesus was willing to do God's will even unto death (cf. vv. 21ff). Under the first use of the verb the New Testament teaches, as the Jews had long believed, that, while it is for God to choose, it is for man to consent to be chosen. So far the Divine choice is neither arbitrary nor coercive, and it does not mean 'select to be saved hereafter' but 'select for a particular service now'.

Under the second use of *eklegesthai*, God 'chooses' men, not for a particular task, but to be saved. The few instances of this use of the verb may be taken with the verbal adjective *eklektos* ('select' or 'elect', *24*) and the noun *eklogē* ('choice' or 'election', *7*). The New Testament use of these terms cannot be understood unless it is remembered that the phrase 'the elect' was already current among the Jews. The controversy between Jesus and the Pharisees grew into a controversy between Christians and Jews. This lasted throughout the New Testament period. In its course, in spite of an initial success at and after Pentecost, it became ever clearer that the Jews, taken as a whole, were rejecting their own Messiah—so much so that the writer of the Fourth Gospel often calls Jesus' opponents, not 'the Pharisees' or 'the rulers', but 'the Jews'. The continuous controversy between Jews and Christians arising from the question 'Who is Messiah?', drew with it the question 'Who are God's elect?' The Jews replied: 'We, or at least, those among us who keep God's law, are His elect.' The Christians declared: 'Jesus is God's elect *par excellence*, and therefore those who believe in Him are His elect too.' It has been shown from the Apocrypha (and the later Old Testament) that, when the Jews used the word 'elect', they did not mean that God's choice was either arbitrary or coercive. The presumption is that when the Christians used the phrase they used it in the same sense. No doubt some of them knew of the Stoic doctrine that God is a kind of inscrutable Fate, but this would not attract believers in a personal God and a living Christ.

The use of *eklektos* is not common in the Synoptic Gospels (*10*). In Luke 'the rulers' used it when they scoffed at the Cross (23^{35}). Here 'save' and 'the Christ of God' and 'his elect' appear, probably correctly, as if they were in current use about Jesus before He died. Later on Matthew applied to Him the prophecy, 'Behold, my servant whom I have chosen; My beloved, in whom my soul is well-pleased' (Mt 12^{18}; Is 42^1). Again, Peter, quoting a Psalm under which Jesus had compared Himself to a 'stone rejected' of men (Mt 21^{42}), interprets the phrase 'which was made the head of the corner' to mean 'elect' (1 P 2^{4-7}). Clearly for the early Church it was primarily Christ who was 'elect'. The complementary truth is that He always willed what God willed (Mk 14^{36}; Jn 10^{17f}). In the Synoptics, when 'the elect' is used of others, the phrase seems to denote His followers (cf. 1 P 2^5). The phrase occurs three times in Mark's 'Little Apocalypse' ($13^{20, 22, 27}$), as though it were already a well-known Christian term. It is the same in Luke's phrase, 'Shall not God vindicate his own elect, which cry to him day and night?' (18^7). These texts presuppose the later persecutions, which were more severe than the reproach and slander that befell the disciples while Jesus was on earth (Mt 5^{10f}; cf. Jn 16^2; Rev 6^{9f}). They imply that it is the loyal disciples who are 'elect'. Finally, there is Matthew's phrase 'For many are called but few elect' (22^{14}). At first sight it does not seem to suit the parable in the context at all. While those who had first been 'called' or 'invited' to the wedding were probably 'many', they had *all* refused the invitation. They *chose* to refuse, and the implied deduction would be '*Many* are called, but (because of their refusal) *none* of them is any longer chosen', for they had shown themselves unworthy (v. 8). Next, when the bondservants have 'called' all and sundry and 'constrained' or urged them to come, the wedding is 'filled with guests' (vv. 9f). Surely it took more than 'few' to fill the chamber. The implied conclusion, under the second part of the parable, would be '*Many* are called, and *all* (except the one man without a wedding-garment) are chosen!' The phrase '*many* are called but *few* chosen' seems quite inept to *either* part of the parable. But, since it is agreed that the first Gospel was written or compiled for a church where there were a number of Jewish converts, may not the whole passage be their teacher's answer to a question that their Jewish neighbours would be continually pressing upon them—'Since the Jews are the elect people, why do so few *Jews* believe?' The Matthaean teacher begins his answer by using a parable found also in Luke (14$^{16-24}$—where 'constrain' in verse 23 is to be interpreted as 'urge'—cf. Mk 6^{45}; Ac 28^{19}, etc.)—that is, he appeals to our Lord's own account of the *Jews*' refusal of Him. Then he adds a warning of its dire consequences (Mt 22^7). Next, he points to the *many* Gentiles who are flocking into the Church, adding a warning to *them* that they need a wedding-garment. Finally, he sums up his answer to the question from which he started—'Many (of the Jews) are called but few (of them) are elect'. On this interpretation this is not Jesus' phrase but the teacher's. Yet, while it is a deduction that he makes, it is a justifiable deduction. The First Gospel has another word about 'the few'—'Few there be that find (the narrow gate)' (Mt 7^{14}). Here the Third Gospel, which supplies the context (Lk 13$^{23-30}$), shows that Jesus is answering the question, 'Lord, are they few that *are being saved*?', and He answers, in effect, 'Few Jews but many Gentiles', for, while the children of Abraham are 'cast forth without' the Kingdom, crowds from all the ends of the earth 'sit down' in it. On this showing the phrase 'Many are called but few elect' is not a universal principle, but the application of the universal Law of Opportunity to the particular case of the Jews. Most of *them* refused the invitation of Jesus and the Law of Atrophy began to work; a few of them accept it, and *therefore* God in His sovereignty chose them 'to sit down in His Kingdom' (cf. Lk 13^{29}). All the passages where the word 'elect' occurs in the Synoptic Gospels probably *imply* the early Christians' answer to the controversial question, 'Who are God's elect?' The answer is 'Not you Jews, for you reject your own Messiah—but first Jesus, and then those who obey God's call through Him'. Here, though in a way that suited new circumstances, they said what their Master had said. Today

THE DOCTRINE OF ELECTION 163

some Christians seem to think that He received all who came, but this is not so. He made conditions (e.g. Mk 8^{34}; Lk 9$^{57-62}$)—that is, He selected. The doctrine of Election in the Synoptic Gospels always presupposes the consent of the selected.

For the use of the word 'elect' outside the Synoptics a beginning may be made from a kind of 'study in election' which Peter puts in the middle of an exhortation to Christian godliness (1 P 2$^{4-10}$). It is a study of 'a stone', and centres in the fact that the *same* stone might either serve in the building of a house or be a 'stumbling-block' on a road. The Greek word for 'stumbling-block' is *skandalon* (*15*). The fundamental idea of this word is the *misuse* of a *good* thing. In the First Gospel Jesus, in one story, calls Peter himself first a 'stone' and then a 'stumbling-block' (Mt 16$^{18, 23}$). In a few moments the good had turned itself to misuse. But Jesus, quoting Psalm 118^{22}, had also called *Himself* a 'rejected stone' that was to become 'head of the corner' (which perhaps should rather be rendered '*chief* corner stone', meaning the stone set to mark the first corner in laying out the *foundations* of a house). Peter, quoting the same passage, adds two quotations from Isaiah (28^{16}, 8$^{13-15}$). In one the Lord lays a stone in Zion; in the other He Himself is the stone. Peter applies both to Christ. In Isaiah 28^{16}, he adds 'elect' to the Hebrew, as does LXX.[5] Here the phrase 'He that *believeth* shall not be ashamed' (LXX) was very apt for Christian use. In Isaiah 8$^{13-15}$ there is a contrast between the use and misuse of 'the stone'. To some 'the LORD' is a (stone of) 'sanctuary'[6]; to others He is 'a stone of stumbling' and 'a rock of offence'. For the last word Peter (but not LXX) rightly uses *skandalon*. Isaiah means that God is either a help or hindrance to a man *as the man chooses*. Similarly, Peter sets 'the believer' over against 'the disbeliever' (*apistos*). To the latter God had said 'If you reject my Chosen, He will be a *skandalon* to you'—or, as Peter, being a true Hebrew, puts it, 'To this doom the disobedient are also *appointed* by God, because they *are* disobedient'. 'Appointed' is a king's word, not a creator's (cf. Lk 12^{46}). Probably Peter is referring to the *skandalon* of the Cross (cf. 1 Co 1^{23}; Mt 16$^{21-3}$). A man became either better or worse as he answered God's appeal in the crucified Christ with a 'Yes' or 'No', and it was God's will that this should be so. The oftener he said 'No', the

---

[5] There is a passage in John where on very early authority Jesus is called 'the elect of God' (1^{34}, Syr. ver.).

[6] This seems to be the sense of the Hebrew (cf. 1 K 2^{28}).

harder it would be to say 'Yes'. His spiritual capacity would atrophy. What we call 'inevitable atrophy' a Jew called 'appointed doom', for the Law of Atrophy is a law of God. At the end of Peter's 'study' he returns to his starting-point. Christians are themselves 'stones' in 'a spiritual house' built on Christ, and it is now no longer the old Israel but the Church that is 'an elect race, a royal priesthood, a holy nation, a people for (the King's) personal possession' (cf. 1 Ch 29³; Mal 3¹⁷). These synonymous phrases, borrowed from the Old Covenant (Ex 19⁶; Dt 10¹⁵), are now claimed under the New, an apposite quotation being added from Hosea (1⁹ᶠ, 2²³). For Peter, who had already addressed the new 'Dispersion' as 'elect' (1 P 1¹), it is believers and the Church that are *ipso facto* 'elect'—yet they must still see to their 'way of life' (v. 12). If they had been 'elect' *nolentes volentes*, the whole passage (2¹⁻¹²), would be pointless. Peter was a 'practical man' and, like all 'practical men', he took human freedom for granted. The burden of the passage is 'If a man elects to believe in Christ, God will elect him; if he rejects Christ, God will reject him'. As James, another 'practical man', says, 'God *chose* the poor . . . to be rich in faith' *because* they 'love him' (Ja 2⁵). Similarly, John the Seer speaks of the Lamb's companions as 'called and elect and *faithful*' (Rev. 17¹⁴). Here the last word, at least, has both an adjectival and gerundive sense, for *pistos* means both 'believing' and 'trust-worthy'. God chooses to trust those who choose to trust Him. It is on the ground of *their* choice that they are *His* 'elect'.

The quotation from the Apocalypse includes another relevant term *klētos*, 'called'. This is not very common in LXX (*17*), but there it has two clearly defined senses. In one it means 'guests'—that is, people who have been invited to a feast *and* have accepted the invitation (Jg 14¹¹; 2 S 15¹¹; 1 K 1⁴¹, ²⁹). In these the Hebrew word (*qara'*) is rendered both by the perfect participle *keklēmenos* and *kletos*. In another passage *xenos*, the ordinary Greek term for 'guest', is used (1 S 9¹³). In one text *kletoi* is used for *God's* 'guests' at a grim festival (Zeph 1⁷). When they arrive He 'hallows' them (*hagiazein*)! This brings together the ideas of 'call' (invitation) and 'holiness', and leads to the second use of *klētos* in LXX. Under this it occurs twelve times in combination with *hagios* to describe 'a day of holy festival' (ten times in Lev 23), *kletē hagia* rendering a Hebrew phrase that means 'a convocation of holiness' (*miqra qōdesh*). The idea of a 'guest' also occurs in the two texts

THE DOCTRINE OF ELECTION

where *klēsis*, literally 'calling', is found. In one manuscript it describes Holofernes' 'banquet' (Jth 12^{10} A); in a text in Jeremiah it is used of 'a day of (God's) invitation' to Ephraim (31^6). It will be seen that in *both* uses of *kletos* in LXX the underlying idea is that an invitation has been given and accepted. No doubt every host 'sanctified his guests', as we 'ask a blessing', but when *God* sanctified His, they were indeed *kletoi hagioi*, though this phrase does not occur. Among Hellenistic Jews the 'compound noun' '*klete hagia*', 'a holy convocation', would be almost in as common use as 'Sunday' is today. Under it God calls men to worship and they choose to come.

In the New Testament *kletos* (*11*) is used of Paul's call to apostleship (Ro 1^1; 1 Co 1^1)—i.e. like *eklektos*, for a Christian who is chosen for a particular enterprise—but it occurs more often in the plural to denote 'Christians'. They are 'Jesus Christ's beloved and holy guests' (Rom 1^{6f}; 1 Co 1$^{2, 24}$; cf. Jude 1), for they have accepted His invitation. When Paul greets them as *kletoi hagioi*, he is thinking of a church as a holy convocation of 'God's beloved', who in turn 'call upon' the name of our Lord Jesus Christ (Ro 1^7; 1 Co 1^2). Similarly, the idea of 'invitation' is probably not absent in most of the texts where *klesis* (*11*) occurs in the New Testament. It too may be used of a particular 'vocation', the vocation of marriage (1 Co 7^{20}), but it is elsewhere used either of 'the calling of God' to Christians or of 'the calling' of Christians by God. In a majority of passages the meaning of this 'vocation' *for the future* is in the writer's mind. There is, for instance, 'a prize of God's high calling' and 'a hope' (Ph 3^{14}; Eph 1^{18}, 4$^{1, 4}$), for it is 'heavenly' (He 3^1). Christians are therefore urged to 'walk worthily' of it (Eph 4^1; cf. 2 Th 1^{11}) and to 'make their calling and election sure' (2 P 1^{10}). It seems clear, both under *kletos* and *klesis*, that the concepts of God's call and of man's willing response are both present.[7]

Next there is the noun *eklogē* ('election', *7*), a term not found in LXX. Here three passages exhibit the same phenomena as *kletos*. In one 'the Lord' tells Ananias that Paul is 'a vessel of election unto me' for a *particular* purpose (Ac 9^{15}). Under the 'goad' of Christ Saul had at last consented to do Christ's will. In the other two texts there are significant parallel terms. The Thessalonians, being '*beloved*' (*ēgapēmenos*) of God, are to 'know'

[7] The solitary use of *kletos* in Mt 22^{14} to mean 'the called' who do *not* respond, already discussed, is perhaps intentionally unusual.

their 'election' (1 Th 1⁴), and the readers of Second Peter are to 'make their *calling* and election sure' (1¹⁰). In the first passage Paul refers to the Thessalonians' '*work* of faith' and the second is a direct appeal to Christians' own '*diligence*', a word characteristic of 2 Peter. In both cases believers had 'accepted the word' that they had 'received' (cf. 1 Th 2¹³). The whole discussion more than suggests that the renderings 'chosen' and 'called' do not exhaust the meaning of *eklektos* and *kletos*, but that these two verbal adjectives, like *pistos*, have both an adjectival and a gerundial sense. They denote 'choose-able' and 'call-able', as well as 'chosen' and 'called'. It is God who takes the initiative—but it is the men who through faith show themselves 'choose-able' and 'call-able' that are 'the elect' and 'the called'.

A like result follows if the uses of *dektos* (*5*) are examined. In Nazareth Jesus was not 'accepted' by his fellow-villagers because He was not 'acceptable' to them (Lk 4²⁴). In one passage men, and in another sacrifices, are both 'acceptable' to God and 'accepted' by Him (Ac 10³⁵; Ph 4¹⁸). The other two passages, following Deutero-Isaiah (Is 49⁸, 61²), speak of a 'year' or 'season' that is 'acceptable', because 'now is . . . the day of salvation'— i.e. now is the time when men are 'accepted' (Lk 4¹⁹; 2 Co 6²). The verb *prosdechesthai* (*14*), sometimes relevant in LXX, is only once so in the New Testament. Here Jesus' critics 'murmur' because He 'accepts sinners' (Lk 15²), but of course He did not 'accept' all sinners but only such as were ready to repent and 'follow' Him. The notions 'acceptable' and 'accepted' are both present.

The other term relevant to 'election' is *eudokia* (*9*), with its verb *eudokein* (*21*). As in LXX the ideas of 'good pleasure', 'approval', and 'good will' are all present, but they are inadequate in the New Testament, for there *eudokia* has a warmer and more active meaning. Paul, for instance, uses it of his 'yearning' for the salvation of the Jews (Ro 10¹). It has already been argued that *euarestos* is used as verbal adjective for these terms since there was no word *eudoktos*. Its use is consonant with theirs. In the Synoptic Gospels, in a passage from Is 42¹, describing 'the Servant of the Lord', *eudokein* is applied to Jesus at His baptism (Mk 1¹¹). Matthew quotes the passage itself and uses it also at the Transfiguration (12¹⁸, 17⁵). *The* man whom God 'approves' is His 'beloved' whom He has 'chosen'. Here, as in LXX, God approves the Righteous because He is righteous. But in Luke the two terms are also used of the disciples. They are the 'babes' who are Jesus' 'little flock' (10²¹, 12³²)—just because they are *His*. They have heard and answered His call. As with 'election', so with *eudokia*—other men's blessing is mediated through Jesus. No doubt Luke would apply the angels' phrase, 'peace to men of (God's) good pleasure' (2¹⁴), to Jesus' disciples for he is telling of the birth of 'a Saviour' (v. 11). God's ardent 'good pleasure' goes out to those who welcome His Beloved Son. Response is implied.

In the Epistles, *eudokia* and *eudokein* are used of Christians' active, though derivative, good-will (Ro 10¹, 15²⁶ᶠ; 2 Co 5⁸; Ph 1¹⁵), but more often of God's good-will. In two quotations the writer to the Hebrews draws contrasts. In one he sets Christ who has 'come to do (God's) will' over against the old sacrifices; in the other he warns Christians who 'shrink back' because of persecution that they will lose God's *eudokia* (He 10⁵⁻⁷, ³⁸). It is Christ and Christians who are the 'men of good-pleasure', and in both passages willing obedience is its condition. The other passages are Pauline. The Apostle, finding anticipations of both Sacraments in the Exodus, points out that 'our fathers' did not secure God's permanent 'good pleasure' (1 Co 10¹⁻⁶) because of disobedience. In another text the Apostle declares that it is God's 'good pleasure' to 'save them *that believe*' (1 Co 1²¹). In a third (Ph 2¹³), where Paul is urging Christians to persist in obedience to 'the word of life', there falls a famous antinomy— 'Work out your own salvation', 'It is God that worketh in you'. In a fourth, Paul prays that God will 'fulfil every good-pleasure of goodness and work of faith' (2 Th 1¹¹). Finally, in a passage that articulates the whole New Testament concept of *eudokia*, Paul declares that 'it was the good-pleasure (of God) that in (Christ) should all the fulness dwell' so that God 'might reconcile all things unto Himself', beginning with Christians who '*continue in the faith*' (Col 1¹⁹ᶠ, ²³). In all these passages Paul makes the Christian application of the Pharisaic belief both in the sovereignty of God and the freedom of man. It is those who have consented to believe in whom God is well-pleased.

The opposite of Election is Rejection. It was found that three terms commonly render *ma'as* in LXX. One, *puroun*, has no relevant examples in the New Testament, for there it means 'purify', not 'reject'. Of the other two one is *apothein*, 'thrust away'. In the New Testament (*6*) it is once used literally (Ac 7^{27}), and in three texts *men* 'thrust away' God's 'angel' or 'the word of God' or 'a good conscience' (Ac 7^{39}, 13^{46}; 1 Ti 1^{19}). The word is only once used of *God*—under the question 'Did God thrust away his people?' (Ro 11^{1f}), the answer being 'Never!' The second term is *exouthenein*, 'to treat as nothing'—and its variants (*12*). It may be rendered 'set at naught'. It is used of mockers (Lk 23^{11}), of the contemptuous (2 Co 10^{10}; Gal 4^{14}), and of 'superior persons' (Lk 18^{9}). Men 'set at naught the Son of Man' (Mk 9^{12})— that is, 'the Stone' (Ac 4^{11}). *Exouthenein* too is only once used of God. He 'sets at naught' or counts as nothing what men prize (1 Co 1^{28}). The discussion of the third term *apodokimazein* (*9*) has been partly anticipated under *dokimazein*. It is not used by Paul. It means as in LXX, 'to discard' or 'reject *after test*'. The 'Son of Man' and 'the Stone' did not pass the test of 'the elders' and 'builders' (Mk 8^{31}, 12^{10}; cf. Lk 17^{25}; 1 P 2$^{4, 7}$). Once more there is only one passage where this term denotes *God's* 'rejection'. God 'discarded' Esau *because* that 'profane person' 'sold his birthright'—as Christians are tempted to do (He 12^{16f}). On the other hand *all* the texts under *adokimos* (*8*), a term that Paul prefers (*7*), relate to *God's* 'rejection' of men. 'Reprobation', however, is a more accurate word, for *adokimos* too always means 'rejected *after test*'. It is used, for instance, to denote the fate of apostates (2 Ti 3^{8}; Tit 1^{16}; He 6^{8}). Paul, in a half-ironical passage, says to the Corinthians, in effect, 'Are you not failing to pass the test of the faith?' (2 Co 13$^{5-7}$). The Apostle himself had to 'box' hard lest he should 'become *adokimos*' (1 Co 9^{26f}). The remaining text is discussed later (Ro 1^{28}). Two phenomena are notable—the passages under the terms for 'rejection' are scanty in comparison with those under 'election'; so far all the evidence requires that God rejects those who have been faithless to Him.

Of the LXX renderings of the next group of Hebrew words one, *pachunein*, only occurs in Matthew and Paul's quotations of Isaiah 6^{9f} (Mt 13^{5}; Ac 28^{17}), which is discussed elsewhere, and two others, *barunein* and *lipainein*, are not found in the New Testament. Another verb, *stereoun*, which occurs once in an apposite sense, and its cognate adjective and noun are found in passages that imply the happy side of the Law of Opportunity—'To him that hath (faith) shall be given' (Ac 16^{5}; 2 Ti 2^{19}; 1 P 5^{9f}; Col 2^{5f}). *Sklēros*, 'hard', only occurs in the compound *sklērotrachēlos* (*1*), 'hard-necked', Stephen using it of those who refused the

Opportunity of Christ (Ac 7⁵¹). Except in one text, discussed later (Ro 9¹⁸), the cognate verb (6) and noun (1) are used of *man's* share in the 'hardening'. The writer to the Hebrews, quoting Psalm 95⁸, uses the verb to describe the Hebrew people's reaction to the opportunity of the Promised Land (He 3⁸, ¹³, ¹⁵, 4⁷), and Luke puts it with 'disobedient' in describing the reaction of Jews to Paul's preaching (Ac 19⁹). Paul uses the noun, along with 'impenitent heart', to describe the man who 'despises' God's 'goodness' and so brings God's 'righteous wrath' upon himself (Ro 2⁵). John's quotation (12⁴⁰ᶠ) of Isaiah 6¹⁰ shows that right to the end of the first century Christians found in this text their very pertinent reply to the Jews' claim: 'The Book says that *we* are God's elect.' But John's quotation is paraphrastic and introduces two new terms, *tuphloun* (*3*—to 'blind') and *pōroun* (*5*—to 'petrify' and so to 'harden'). He probably borrowed *tuphloun* from Isaiah 42¹⁸⁻²⁰, where *man's* part in his own 'blinding' is just the burden of the passage. The synonym *apotuphloun* occurs in LXX of the way in which bribes 'blind' a judge (Dt 16¹⁹; Sir 20²⁹) and 'malice' a dishonest disputant (Wis 2²¹). Similarly in the New Testament 'the god of this age' blinds unbelievers to the 'illumination of the gospel of the glory of Christ' (2 Co 4⁴) and 'darkness' blinds the eyes of a man who 'hates his brother' (1 Jn 2¹¹). The other verb, *poroun*, only occurs once in LXX, of the 'hardening' of the eye by cataract (Job 17⁷). Here 'hardening' means 'blinding', and it is likely that this is the meaning in the New Testament passages. In Job the man cannot help the 'hardening' or 'blinding', but Jesus, in a passage that recalls Isaiah 41¹⁸⁻²⁰, uses the word in expostulating with the disciples for a fault that they *could* help (Mk 8¹⁷), and Mark has both the verb and the cognate noun in texts that describe a wrong reaction to the miracles of Jesus (6⁵², 3⁵). Paul, declaring that, unlike Moses, he does not veil his message, intrudes a parenthesis to show that there was a 'hardening', or 'blinding' of 'thoughts' in the Wilderness as well as a 'veil' (2 Co 3¹⁴), which issued in Israel's continual ignorance, and he repeats the same set of ideas about the Gentiles (Eph 4¹⁷⁻¹⁹). So far, in the use of this series of words too the emphasis is on *man's* part under the Law of Opportunity, *God's* being implied. When Matthew and Paul quote Isaiah 6⁹ᶠ (Mt 13¹⁴ᶠ; Ac 28¹⁷), they follow LXX, which, as shown above, brings out man's side more explicitly than the Hebrew does.

Of the next two terms under LXX, *diaterein* and *egeirein* (with *exegeirein*), the use of the first (*2*) is not pertinent in the New Testament, though in some passages the use of the corresponding simple verb, *terein*, could be quoted to show, on the one hand, that God 'keeps' the faithful because through His help they 'keep themselves' by 'keeping his word' (e.g. Jn 17^6, ^{11f}; 1 Jn 2$^{3-5}$, 5^{18})—and, on the other hand, that God 'keeps' the 'unrighteous' for 'judgement' because they *are* 'unrighteous' (2 P 2^9). Once more 'he that hath' is set over against 'he that refuseth to have'. The terms *egeirein* and *exegeirein* are best taken later. Under the next word, *paradidonai*, 'deliver up', there is *the* instance where *the* King used and *over-ruled* rebels. On the one hand, it was men, and Judas in particular, who 'delivered up' the Son of Man (e.g. Mk 9^{31}, 14$^{10f, 16}$), yet it was God who 'delivered him up for us all' (Ro 4^{25}, 8^{32}; Gal 2^{20}). This is the culminant example of the antinomy, 'God is sovereign yet man is free'. *Paradidonai* also occurs of God's 'giving up' or 'delivering up' sinners to the results of their sin. Stephen uses the word in quite the Old Testament way (Ac 7^{42}; cf. 2 P 2^4), and Paul has a passage that might be called 'a study in God's giving up of sinners' (Ro 1$^{24, 26, 28}$), which will be taken presently. The greater part of the New Testament evidence about Election and Rejection has now been discussed. Under it God's choice and man's freedom go together.

We now pass to the reserved Pauline passages—the passages to which appeal is usually made when it is argued that Paul taught that God chooses men for salvation apart from their own choice, or even in spite of their own choice. Only cursory reference has so far been made to them. The long discussion of other passages, just concluded, has been undertaken in part because there is an antecedent likelihood that in the remaining passages the terms are used in the same sense as elsewhere—i.e. that they admit the doctrine that the 'elect' man is a free man. It follows that if in these passages there are texts that allow of more than one interpretation, it is the one that is consonant with the results just reached that should be preferred, and not one that contradicts them. The passages are five in number. The first is Romans 1$^{18-32}$, which has just been called 'a study in God's giving up of sinners'. While it formally deals with 'all ungodliness and unrighteousness of men' (Ro 1^{18}), it is actually Paul's arraignment of the *Gentiles*. He depicts them at their worst, perhaps because the Judaizers had accused him of palliating their sinfulness. He follows the same line of thought as the writer of the Book of Wisdom—Men began with *some* knowledge of the true God; they 'sinned against' this light and therefore their 'un-understanding heart was darkened' (i.e. there is a wilful ignorance and it begins an atrophy of mind); the first outcome of this sin was the iniquity of idolatry; this led (as in fact it had done in the Hellenistic world as well as elsewhere) to the vilest immoralities (1^{18-27}). All this, says Paul, 'reveals God's wrath' against sin in the world *now*. The remainder of the passage (vv. 28–32) not only catalogues other items in 'the fulness of unrighteousness', but introduces the word 'reprobate' (v. 28), and this is the word that gives the key to Paul's purpose in writing the whole passage. His immediate subject is not so much the wider doctrine of 'wrath' as the narrower one of 'reprobation'. Here he uses *dokimazein* and *adokimos*, 'test' and 'reprobate', in the same sentence. Under the verb he implies that, God having offered men 'full knowledge' (*epignōsis*) of Himself, they put *Him* to the test and rejected *Him*. 'In accordance with this' (*kathōs*) God, having put *them* to the test, 'gave them up unto a reprobate mind'. They therefore went on and on with their sinning and are 'worthy of death' (v. 32). There is the implication that, if a man who has begun to choose to sin, continues so to choose until it is more and more habitual, at last he loses his freedom to do anything else. This introduces the Law of Habit, which is wider than the Law of Atrophy. The latter is merely negative, declaring that a man loses a power which he refuses to use. The former is positive as well as negative. Under it a man finds it easier and easier to do what he has long chosen to do and harder and harder to do what he has refused to do. With the habitual sinner this would ultimately mean that he finds it is so easy to sin and so hard to do right that he cannot help sinning —just as, with a man who has made a habit of doing right, it is at last happily though paradoxically true that, as St John says, he 'cannot sin'. For the Jew, and surely for all serious theists, the Law of Habit, like the narrower Law of Atrophy, is God's law. At last He 'gives up' inveterate sinners to 'a reprobate mind'. Here Paul draws out what is implicit in Isaiah 6^{9f}, and is dealing, like the Prophet, not with the fate of habitual sinners *hereafter*, but with their *present* condition. The Gentiles, he says, are 'worthy of death', but it was his glory to tell them that, none the less, they need not 'die' in his sense of 'die', for the Law of Habit had not yet reached its ultimate term. It was only for a while that God had 'given them up'. Through the grace of Christ the fell consequence of habit for the sinful may now be turned into its happy consequence for the 'believer'. Neither Gentile nor Jew need any longer sin. Paul gives the Christians' triumphant answer to 2 Esdras.

This passage illustrates a phenomenon that recurs in the others. In no one of them does Paul draw out his *whole* doctrine of Election and Reprobation. He is always dealing with another subject, and he only introduces this doctrine as far as it is pertinent to that subject. This means that he treats it, in a sense, incidentally. To reach his whole doctrine of Election and Reprobation all the passages need to be taken together—and, indeed, his use of the relevant terms outside these particular passages as well. Yet, though no one passage exhibits Paul's complete doctrine, it is possible to discern its outlines if all the passages are taken together, and it is convenient to summarize it at this point. Like his contemporaries Paul believed in the Two Ages. The first was so long that it might be divided into several. At least sometimes, there were three—the first stretching from Adam to Noah, the second from Noah to Abraham, and the third from Abraham to the catastrophe and consummation with which the Present Age (or series of Ages) will end. Possibly Paul would have divided the last period at the time of Elijah, for he has references that emphasize the 'remnant' that emerged then (1 K 19[18]; Ro 9[27], 11[2-5]). The Christian *differentia* did not fall under the scheme of the Two Ages for this was current doctrine—but to the place that Christians gave to Christ in the scheme. The *differentia* was, of course, all-important, as this book illustrates at many points. One of its results was that Christians already 'tasted the powers of the coming Age' (He 6[5]), though this was only by anticipation. While the *fons et origo* of the Future Age lay in their experience of Christ, He had yet to consummate 'the Present Age' and so open the next in its 'glory'. Paul saw that the controversy under 'Who are the elect?' raised the whole problem 'What is God doing *in the Present Age*?', and, being Paul, he must needs grapple with it. Where he said 'the Present Age' we say 'history'. Paul had a doctrine of history.

The Apostle's name for his doctrine is 'A purpose (or design, *prothesis*) according to election'. In LXX *prothesis* (*12*) is only used in *this* sense in one passage, where it describes a *king's* 'plan'

THE DOCTRINE OF ELECTION   173

(2 Mac 3⁸). In the New Testament the word, as in LXX, is sometimes a technical name for the 'shew-bread' (Mk 2²⁶; He 9²). Apart from this it is used three times to denote *men's* 'purposes' (Ac 11²³, 27¹³; 2 Ti 3¹⁰). Paul uses it four times of *God's* 'purpose' and always of His 'design' in history (Ro 8²⁸, 9¹¹; Eph 1¹¹, 3¹¹), and a Pauline writer follows suit (2 Ti 1⁹). The Old Testament was, of course, the source of the doctrine. God first chose Abel, rejecting Cain; then He chose Seth (and his 'seed'); next He chose Noah and rejected all others; then Shem, rejecting his brothers; then Abraham, rejecting Nahor; then Isaac, rejecting Ishmael; then Jacob, rejecting Esau; and, much later, two Tribes, rejecting Ten; finally, the Remnant, rejecting other Jews. Under this series the 'elect' are sometimes called 'righteous' or 'faithful' or 'godly'. Probably the Jews of Paul's day believed that, from Abel onwards, they were *all* righteous. Did not the lines of Sethites and Shemites, for instance, *all* flourish (Gn 5 and 11), and was not prosperity God's reward for righteousness? There was one point, however, where the doctrine that Election and Righteousness are correlatives seemed to break down. Both Isaac and Jacob—and after them Jeremiah and Deutero-Isaiah and the Baptist and Paul—were 'elect' *before birth* (Gn 17¹⁹, 25²³; Is 49¹, ⁵; Jer 1⁵; Lk 1¹⁵ff; Gal 1¹⁵). Here God is Creator rather than King, and it is under the doctrine of Creation that the antinomy of sovereignty and freedom is starkest. Yet even here there are other considerations. It can, of course, be said that when God created, He foreknew, and *therefore* foreordained. It can also be said that in the stories of all the six who were elected before birth there would come a point where each man himself heard and freely accepted God's call. For instance, for Jacob this was at Bethel (Gn 28¹¹⁻²²). It may be added that all these six were 'chosen', not to be saved hereafter, but to serve God's design in history. A further suggestion may be made—all six men were created, not only to serve God in the present Age, but to serve a *good* purpose in it; it might be argued from these instances that God creates *every* man for a good purpose, to be fulfilled in the present Age, *and* that bad men, by their abuse of freedom, foil that purpose. The great mass of men did this; *could* not the six have foiled it? There is no instance where God is said to *create* men to do evil; not even Pharaoh, as already shown.

It is likely enough that some Jews (and Paul) believed that from Abel onward all the 'elect' rejected the primary sin of idolatry and that the law 'to him that hath shall be given' therefore applied to them. In particular, believing that, in spite of all apostasies, there were always Israelites who answered God's 'call', they may have believed that it was *therefore* to Israel that the knowledge of the true God had been given. This would imply that if any other race had responded aright, it too would have been 'elect'. This is perhaps too hypothetical a theory, but it is noteworthy that Paul taught that the first sin of the Gentiles was that they sinned against 'the *unseen* things of (God)' and turned to idolatry (Ro 1^{20-3}). What if some of them had not shut their eyes to 'the unseen things that are clearly seen'? At any rate the Apostle believed that ever 'since the creation of the world' God had given all nations the opportunity of a primary revelation, and that, apart from the godly in Israel, they had all chosen to reject it.

Paul's Jewish opponents would agree with his doctrine of the Reprobation or Rejection of the Gentiles as set out in Romans 1^{18-32}. Three of the ways in which it illustrates Paul's treatment of the doctrine of God's Design, of which it is a part, may be mentioned. First, Paul is speaking of a *class*—though a very large class—and not of every individual within it. Presently he himself says that there are exceptions (Ro 2^{14-16}). Second, as already shown, he is speaking of God's way with that class in the *Present* Age and not in the Future Age. In the New Testament it is never classes but always individuals who are 'judged' at the End, as the passage just named shows (Ro 2^{16}). All class distinctions belong to this Age and this Age only. Third, as already suggested, Paul is only dealing with *part* of his larger doctrine, the part pertinent to his immediate subject, *and keeps to that part*. He believed, of course, that the period of the Rejection of the huge class called 'the Gentiles' was now over; indeed, to say this was no small part of his purpose in writing to the Romans; but in this passage he gives no hint of it. These three phenomena recur.

In the second reserved passage (Ro 8^{28-30}), Paul is not speaking of the 'reprobate' of the past but of 'God's elect' in the present (v. 33), whom he also describes as 'them that love God' and 'the called (and call-able) according to design'. It is part of a longer passage of encouragement that mounts to exultation (vv. 26–38), and it tells Christians of the triumphant progress destined for those that 'love God'. Here there are two terms that have not so far been considered, 'foreknew' and 'foreordained'. Paul clearly makes God's foreknowledge the prelude and condition of His foreordination. Under the phrase 'Whom he foreknew' the question 'What did He foreknow *about them*?' emerges. The answer appears if the passages where 'foreknow' (*proginōskein*, 5) and its noun 'foreknowledge' (*prognōsis*, 2) are considered. Apart from two texts about men's foreknowledge (Ac 26[5]; 2 P 3[17]), and one about God's 'foreknowledge' of Israel (Ro 11[2]), the passages fall into two small groups. In one it is Christ whom God 'foreknows' (Ac 2[23]; 1 P 1[20]), and in the other it is Christians (1 P 1[2]; Ro 8[29]). As usual, Christ and His people go together. And, just as it is Christ's *salvation* of men through His death and resurrection that God is said to have 'foreknown', so He foreknew which men would *believe* in Christ and thereby be *saved*. The verb 'foreordain' (*pro-orizein*, 'to mark out beforehand', 6), which is not found in LXX, has the same dual reference as *proginoskein*. It is used of God's 'foreordaining' of Christ's Crucifixion and Resurrection (Ac 4[28]; cf. 1 Co 2[7]), and of God's 'foreordaining' of Christians (Ro 8[29f]; Eph 1[5]). Christ's 'predestination' and His people's go together. The latter are 'foreordained (to be) conformed to the image of (God's) Son, that he may be the first-born among many brethren.' To say that God's foreordination of the death of Christ robbed Jesus of his freedom is to contradict Gethsemane. 'Not my will, but thine be done.' However incomprehensibly, here God's foreordination and man's freedom co-exist. Is it not so with Christians as well as Christ? Do not He and they go together under freedom as well as under foreknowledge and foreordination? Are not they the men who, in answer to Christ's challenge, *choose* to say, 'Not my will, but thine be done'? When Peter says to the 'men of Israel' at Pentecost, 'Him, being delivered up by the determinate (*horizein*) counsel and foreknowledge of God, ye by the hand of lawless men did crucify and slay' (Ac 2[23]), he is asserting that in the Crucifixion there was both the foreordination of God and the freedom of men. When he later excuses the Jews for 'delivering up' Jesus, it is on the ground of 'ignorance', not of impotence (Ac 3[12f, 17]). A text that uses another verb, *tassein*, 'to appoint', may be quoted here, for, considered alone, it might be taken to deny human freedom. It runs, 'As many as were *appointed* to eternal life believed' (Ac 13[48]) —but the context furnishes a corrective phrase, 'Seeing ... ye judge yourselves unworthy of eternal life' (v. 46). This implies the wrong use of freedom. To return to Romans 8[29f], this examination of the use of the words 'foreknow' and 'foreordain' confirms the exposition 'God, foreknowing which men would *freely* believe in Christ, foreordained *those men* to salvation'. Paul adds three other terms—'called', 'justified', 'glorified'. When his use of the terms elsewhere is examined, it appears that they all presuppose man's freedom. This has been argued earlier for 'called'; justification has its grounds in God's good-pleasure *and* man's free faith; the Christian's 'glory' is the accompaniment and completion of the continuous practice of such faith. In this passage there is nothing about reprobation for this is not pertinent to the immediate theme.

The third reserved passage (Eph 1³⁻¹⁴) describes at magnificent length the destiny of Christians briefly summarized in Romans 8²⁹ᶠ. It only expands, however, the same ideas. Some points may be noted. It is the passage of the Blessing of Christians (v. 3). But this Blessing is all theirs because they are '*in Christ*'. This phrase peals through the verses. 'In him' God 'chose' Christians 'before the foundation of the world' (v. 4). They are 'foreordained *unto adoption*' (v. 5). There are three phrases about the *will* of God—'the good-pleasure of his will', 'the mystery of his will', 'the counsel of his will' (vv. 5, 9, 11)—but Paul is speaking here of God's invincible will for those 'who have believed in (Christ)' (v. 13) and have 'faith in the Lord Jesus' (v. 15), and he goes on to strain at the leash of speech as he tells *believers* of the 'fulness' of the church in Christ (vv. 15–23). He uses another term, *pro-tithenai* ('to settle beforehand', *3*), which is only pertinent to the present subject in this passage (v. 9). It describes God's 'purpose in (Christ)'. The writer to the Hebrews has a parallel passage under the simple verb *tithenai* (He 1²). In Eph 1³⁻¹⁴ Paul keeps himself to the pertinent part of his large doctrine of God's Design. This is the inflexibility of God's 'will' for those who are and remain 'in Christ' through their free exercise of faith.

The Apostle uses the same parsimony of reference in the fourth reserved passage (1 Co 1²⁶⁻³¹). He is telling the Corinthians that their only fit kind of 'glorying' is to 'glory in the Lord' (v. 31). They can do this because they belong to God 'in Christ Jesus' (v. 30). This should be obvious to them if only because, before their 'calling', most of them (as in other churches) had been 'foolish' and 'weak' and 'base' and 'despised' and 'nobodies' (vv. 26–8). Such are the people whom God 'chose out' (*eklegesthai*) for Himself (cf. Eph 1⁴). Taken alone the passage might either mean that God chose out foolish and weak men to believe because

THE DOCTRINE OF ELECTION 177

they were foolish and weak, or that God, having foreseen that most of the future believers would be foolish and weak, used this fact for His own purposes. When other passages where Paul speaks of God's Design are considered, and when the other passages where the New Testament writers use *eklegesthai* (already examined) are added, it appears that the second is Paul's meaning. Indeed, his immediately preceding paragraph (vv. 18–25) teaches that those who reject 'Christ crucified' are 'perishing' and those that accept Him are 'being saved'. This implies freedom to reject or accept. Of course it might be maintained that, wherever Paul says or implies that men are free, it is only because he, like all determinists, *must* needs speak in this inconsistent way, but so far it seems more likely that this former Pharisee did not abandon the Pharisaic belief both in the Sovereignty of God and the freedom of man. This, of course, involved an antinomy that the human mind cannot resolve, but Paul had no belief in the unlimited competence of the human mind. It does not 'know all mysteries and all knowledge' (1 Co 13^2).

The fifth and last reserved passage is Ro 9–11. Historically this has been the stronghold of Christian determinists. Here it will not be discussed altogether in Paul's order, for even in this passage it is not his purpose to integrate his whole doctrine of Election and Rejection, but to use such parts of it as illustrate at various points the subjects of God's *Design* in the present Age— i.e. in history. He only refers incidentally to the future Age.

More exactly, the Apostle's subject is God's 'Design, according to election, in history *since Abraham*'. There were two reasons for the limitation. First, it was about the period from Abraham onwards that the Christian and the Jew differed. Second, it was part of Paul's teaching that God's method is a mystery that has only gradually become clear. While it has only become fully 'manifest' in Christ, it had begun to work itself clear in Abraham.

Again, while Paul is dealing with history, he is not dealing with it in what is now called an 'objective' way. He is engaged in controversy, and, like all great controversialists, while he tries to be fair to his opponents' case, he is setting himself to establish his own. This means that, though he refers when need be to other subjects, they are not fully treated. He had already dealt with some of them in earlier parts of his letter to the Romans, and he just takes it for granted that there were still others which were part of the common Christian tradition. Here, as elsewhere, he

178   THE DOCTRINE OF ELECTION

keeps as close as may be to his immediate subject. He had his eye on one thing.

As in some other passages about Election the Apostle is dealing mainly with *classes*, not with individuals. Even when he names individuals (Jacob and Esau and Pharaoh), they are societary men—that is, they stand for nations even more than for themselves. As elsewhere when Paul is dealing with classes, he is describing the way in which God uses them within the Present Age and not in the next. Where there are implications about the Coming Age, on the other hand, the implied reference is not to classes but to individuals.

The occasion of the passage was a charge against Paul himself. Because of his attitude to the Law and the Gentiles, he had been called a traitor to his race. This had cut him to the quick, and at the beginning of each of the three chapters he cries out in protest (Ro 9^{1-5}, 10^{1f}, 11^1). He claims that he is loyal to his race just *because* he is loyal to Christ—for it is through Christ, and only through Him, that his race will be saved. This is to happen at the end of the Present Age—'and so all Israel shall be saved' (11^{26}). Meanwhile, however, there is a temporary Rejection of Israel. While this doctrine is part of a larger whole, the Apostle's immediate object is to establish the truth that the great Sovereign is using Israel's *present* rejection of its own Messiah for His own ends.

Paul's subject might also be called a Study in Covenant. Quite early he enumerates the nine chief items in the Old Covenant (9^{4f}),[8] carefully closing the list with 'the Christ according to flesh'. The controversy between Jews and Christians grew hot over the meaning of every one of the nine items—and Paul is claiming that he is loyal to every one. This appears, for instance, under the word 'promises'. In LXX this term, *epangelia* (*5*), and its verb *epangelein* (*9*) are rare, and they only occur three times there of *God's* promise (Am 9^6; Ps 46^8; 2 Mac 2^{18}), but it is clear from the way in which *epangelia* is used in the New Testament (*52*) that it was current among the Hellenistic Jews of Paul's day to describe the ground of 'the hope of Israel'. It was a part of the concept of Covenant (e.g. Gal 3^{14-22}, $4^{23, 28}$). The Christians had made it their own, claiming that the 'promise' made to Abraham and 'the fathers' was fulfilled in Christ through the

---

[8] This is so even though the word 'covenants' appears as an item in the list, the reference there being to the series of covenants made first with Abraham, then with Isaac and with Jacob, and then with Israel through Moses. It may even include, as a separate item, the New Covenant made 'with the house of Israel' (Jer 31^{31}).

THE DOCTRINE OF ELECTION 179

Spirit (e.g. Ro 4[13-20]; Gal 3[14-22]; He 11[13, 39f]). It included eternal life for the individual (e.g. 1 Ti 4[8]; He 9[15]; Ja 1[12]; 1 Jn 2[25]). Ro 9–11 is as much a study in Covenant and in Promise as in Election. But in Covenant there were always *both* God's choice *and* man's consent. Even if a man were born a Hebrew and he had been circumcised, the Covenant did not hold for him if he rejected it. Paul's opponents, with the Old Testament in their hands, would not dispute this. Similarly, the Promise only held for the man who accepted it in faith and lived accordingly. The writer to the Hebrews, between two exhortations to Christians (10[35-9], 12[1f]), illustrates this for the Old Testament in a famous chapter of Faith and Promise (ch. 11). There is no doubt that under Covenant and Promise a belief in freedom goes with the belief in Sovereignty. This, along with the passages already examined under Election and other terms, suggests that, if any passage in Romans 9–11 is of doubtful interpretation, the exegesis that admits human freedom should be preferred.

Paul's doctrine of God's Design was simple, though its exposition required elaborate argument. He divided the part of the Present Age that fell between Abraham and the End of the Age into three periods. In the first period, from Abraham to Jesus, God has used for His 'purpose' the Election of the class called 'Hebrews' and the Rejection of the class called 'Gentiles'—in the second period, which was now in progress, He used the Election of the Gentiles and the Rejection of the Jews—and in the third, which was still to come, but is within this Age, He will elect both classes, rejecting neither. Paul believed that in all three periods there were individuals that were exceptions. In the first period there were both Hebrews who rebelled against God and Gentiles who were faithful to 'the law written in the heart'; in the second and current period there were some Jews who did accept their own Messiah and Gentiles who refused to hear and obey the Gospel; in the third there would be individual men (no doubt both Jew and Gentile) who would refuse Christ. Some of the evidence for the first two periods has already been given. Every text about the judgement that is to *end* the Age is evidence for the third. *Then* every man will be treated alone and there will be no more question of the classes 'Jews' and 'Gentiles'. How far a class or race may be said to exercise freedom need not be discussed here. The admission of individual exceptions within both classes during this Age, as well as the Judgement on men one by one at its close, suggests that God always respects the freedom of individuals. This is in accordance with the findings of the examination above of the use of 'elect' outside the reserved passages.

At first sight it seems as if Paul directly contradicts this in the passage where he says that God chose Isaac and Jacob, and rejected Ishmael and Esau, *before birth* (9⁸⁻¹³). It is true, as Paul's quotation from Malachi shows (v. 13), that he is thinking of Esau and Jacob, on whom he concentrates, as societary men, and that the phrase 'Jacob I loved, but Esau I hated' means 'I chose the Israelite *race* and rejected the Edomite'. Yet Paul is also treating Esau and Jacob as individuals. But his Jewish adversaries would agree with him that the one brother was rejected and the other chosen before birth because God 'foresaw' what they would do in the future. They would agree with Paul that God knew beforehand that Esau would one day sell the birthright of Covenant (cf. He 12¹⁶) and that at Bethel Jacob would accept it. 'Whom he foresaw, him did he predestinate.' There was no need for Paul to refer to God's foresight at this point for it did not concern the challenge that he was meeting. The Jews said 'Your doctrine that God is rejecting Israel means that the word of God has come to naught' (v. 6). 'No,' replies Paul, 'I believe that this rejection is only temporary and that, as I hope to show presently, God's election of Israel finally holds. Meanwhile, as a first point, I want you to notice that even in the days of the Patriarchs God did reject some of Abraham's seed and elect others. In that part of the present Age He did proceed by a Design according to Election (and Rejection)'. So far Paul's opponents could not contest his argument. The question of the freedom of Esau and Jacob (about which, as just seen, Paul and his opponents were agreed) is not raised because it was not pertinent.

But already there is a phrase in which Paul has raised a very pertinent point. The phrase is 'not of works (which unborn children could not have done) but of him that calleth (i.e. chooseth)' (9¹¹). To this the Jews would reply, 'That is to make God arbitrary and therefore unrighteous'. While Paul at once repudiates this with a *mē genoito* or 'Never!!' (v. 14), he does not give his *full* answer to the challenge *here*, but earlier he had argued it at length (ch. 3), and it emerges again later in this passage (10³ᶠᶠ). It concerned 'the righteousness of God'. Paul's opponents claimed that God 'shewed' His righteousness by choosing the righteous Jews—or rather the righteous among them (cf. 2 Es)—

and rejecting the unrighteous Gentiles. Paul's reply is twofold. First, he claimed that if God chose by this standard He could choose *none* at all, for 'there is none that doeth good, no, not so much as one' (3^{12}). Second, he claimed that God is now choosing those who through faith in Christ 'believe unto *righteousness*' (10^{9f}). In a world where 'all have sinned' this is precisely *the* manifestation of 'the righteousness of God' (3^{22f}). There is nothing arbitrary in God's choosing to save those who through faith became righteous rather than those who are righteous by 'works' (of whom there are none). In 9$^{14-18}$ Paul does not work all this out, but contents himself with applying a famous word to Moses, 'I will have mercy on whom I have mercy' (Ex 33^{19}) to the contemporary situation. *God* decides that His mercy shall fall on those who 'believe' and not on those who in their ignorance think that they are righteous (10^3). If Paul had been asked 'How does your argument about Jacob's being chosen before birth agree with this, for at that point Jacob had not believed?', he would have replied that God foresaw that at Bethel Jacob would enter into the Covenant and that he so entered because, like Abraham at Hebron, he 'believed God and it was counted unto him for righteousness'. His choice of God conditioned God's choice of him.

In this paragraph (9$^{14-18}$) there is also the phrase, 'The scripture saith unto Pharaoh, For this very purpose did I raise thee up' (Ex 9^{16}). This leads on to the next point. As already seen, in Exodus, 'raise thee up' means 'give thee power', not 'create thee'. It is true that here, while LXX renders by *diaterein*, 'keep', Paul uses *exegeirein*, 'raise', but LXX has the latter in parallel texts (Jer 1^{41}; Hab 1^6; Zec 11^{16}). In the New Testament *exegeirein* only occurs in one other passage (1 Cor 6^{14}), where it means 'rouse from the dead', but *egeirein* is very frequent and it never means 'create' *ex nihilo*. In Matthew 3^8, for instance, the Baptist uses it to say that if God will, He can turn stones into 'children of Abraham'—that is, turn one thing into another, or 'create' in the secondary sense in which artists and artificers are said to 'create'.[9] A potter is such an artificer. This leads to Paul's Parable of the Potter (9$^{19-24}$). Its immediate purpose is to show that God can 'have mercy' or refuse to have mercy on whom He will, for Paul returns to this point at its close, applying it now, under quotations

---

[9] In LXX the phrase 'raise up (*qum*) children' is not rendered by *egeirein* but *anistanai* (Gn 38^8; cf. Dt 25^7; Mt 22^{24}; Mk 12^{19}).

from Hosea and Isaiah, both to the Gentiles and Jews (9^{24-33}), and asserting that God's rule is not arbitrary but according to 'righteousness', for He rejects the Jews who do not attain righteousness and accepts Gentiles who do (vv. 30f). The Parable, however, applies to more than this one point. It describes Paul's whole account of God's Design in history, but it describes it as bound up with the Law of Opportuntiy, which Paul takes for granted all the time. This law was a Christian commonplace, as already shown, but before Paul finishes his argument he needs to refer to it at some length (10^{16-21}). Before examining the Parable of the Potter further this passage needs consideration.

In the earlier part of the tenth chapter Paul argues that the text 'Whosoever shall call upon the name of the Lord shall be saved' (10^{13}) applies to *all*, Jews and Gentiles. He goes on to defend his Gentile mission, pointing out that men cannot call upon God in the name of a Christ of whom they have not 'heard'. Then he says, 'But they (both Jews and Gentiles) did not all hearken', significantly using *hypakouein* now instead of *akouein*, for the former verb means 'hearken' and to 'hearken' is to *consent* to 'hear'. Next he quotes Isaiah 53^1, apparently believing that this referred to the *Gentiles* (cf. Is 52^{15}), for he goes on to quote the Psalm (19^1) that speaks of the *universal* witness of the 'heavens' and the 'firmament' (cf. Ro 1^{20}). Their speech was for Paul Christ's speech (*rhēma*) (cf. Col 1^{15-17}, etc.). Even the Gentiles had always had 'ears to hear' *it*, but did not 'hearken'. This had led to an 'ignorance' that God for a time 'overlooked' (*hyperoran*—Ac 17^{30}). The Jews, of course, had heard more from God than the witness of 'the heavens', but most of them had not 'hearkened' to the fuller witness, as both Moses and Isaiah testified (10^{19-21}). *Now* in Christ both are being given a new opportunity—and for the time being Israel is refusing the opportunity and the Gentiles taking it. In the next chapter Paul goes on to say that in the days of Elijah all but a 'remnant' of Hebrews had forsaken God and that therefore God, applying His law of atrophy to them, had given them 'a spirit of stupor, eyes that they should not see, and ears that they should not hear' ($11^{4, 8}$). There is hardly need to add that, as in the Old Testament and the Synoptic Gospels, so in the Epistles, both God and man play a part in the 'hardening' of heart under the law of atrophy (Ro 9^{18}, 11^7; He 3^8, 4^7; cf. Ac 19^9). This is not all that Paul says in the passages quoted, but it is an integral element in them. The Apostle presupposes the Law

THE DOCTRINE OF ELECTION 183

of Opportunity (of which the law of atrophy is part), and this, as already shown, exhibits both man's freedom and the reaction of God's sovereignty to man's use of freedom. Indeed, as has often been urged, the whole of Romans 10 presupposes the freedom of man.

To return to the Parable of the Potter, in it Paul three times uses the term *skeuos* (Ro 9$^{21\text{-}3}$). This is rendered 'vessel', but both the Hebrew *keli*, by which it is regularly rendered in LXX, and *skeuos* itself mean 'utensil' rather than 'vessel'. There are examples for the Old Testament in Hos 8^8; Jer 1^{25}; Zec 11^{15}; Ps 7^{13}; Ec 9^{18}, the English rendering sometimes being 'instrument'. In the Apocrypha the Greek term is used for the various 'utensils' that a carpenter or smith or potter makes (Sir 27^5, 38^{28}; Wis 13^{11}) (though in the potter's case the 'utensils' are, in fact, vessels as well as utensils). A passage in Wisdom (15^7) develops the same idea as Paul's—that a potter himself decides whether he will make a utensil for high or ignoble use—and this passage may have been in the Apostle's mind. In the New Testament the term *skeuos* (*23*), when used literally, similarly describes *anything* that men use (e.g. Mk 3^{27}, 11^{16}; Ac 10^{11}, 27^{17}). The idea of 'use' is probably never absent even when the term is metaphorical. The body is a 'vessel' for a given *use* (2 Co 4^7) and so is sex (1 Th 4^4; 1 P 3^7). Paul is a 'vessel chosen' by God for a particular service (Ac 9^{15}). Here it is implied that he *consented* to be such a 'utensil' and in 2 Ti 2$^{19\text{-}21}$ it is virtually asserted that if a man *chooses* to 'name the name of the Lord' and therefore 'departs from unrighteousness', the Lord will *thereby* 'know that he is his' and *therefore* make him a 'sanctified utensil unto honour, meet for the master's use, prepared unto every good work'. In other words, the Law of Opportunity will operate on its good side. It will be noted that (even when the term refers to the body or sex) the writer is speaking of individuals and not of classes. It is the same when *skeuos* is used in the Parable of the Potter. To say that God, being able to do what He chooses, 'fits' resolute sinners for ultimate 'destruction' and 'prepares beforehand' believers for ultimate 'glory', is only a stark assertion of the Jewish belief that God is the master of the Law of Opportunity. Paul, of course, is referring to Jeremiah's parable (Jer 18) and here, as there, it is assumed, as also in some other parables (e.g. Jg 9$^{8\text{ff}}$; Mk 4$^{15\text{ff}}$), that, even when men are compared to *things*, they still have freedom. This was so with Pharaoh (9^{17}). He shut his eyes to 'sign' after 'sign' after 'sign' (e.g. Ex 7^3). He misused his freedom, and in response God, using His law of atrophy, 'hardened' his heart.

While, in 9^{17f}, Paul speaks, not of Pharaoh's ultimate fate, but of the use God made of him at a given point in his life, there follows a paragraph where the Apostle turns to the doctrine of the Potter as applied to the *ultimate* fate of individuals ($9^{19\text{-}29}$). It is this passage that, taken *alone*, seems most of all to teach that some individuals are fore-ordained to eternal life and some to eternal destruction. In order to show that it *need* not teach this, some parallel verses near the end of Paul's whole argument ($11^{30\text{-}2}$) may be considered. Here the Apostle includes the words 'obedience' and 'disobedience', *terms that imply freedom*, yet he says that God 'hath shut up all unto disobedience that he might have mercy upon all' as though *men had no freedom*! Behind the passage there is a series of doctrines—first, the doctrine that God has made men free to obey or disobey; second, that, as a man's temptations to sin are multitudinous it is certain in fact, though not logically necessary, that every man has sinned (e.g. that every man has at some time told a lie); third, that, since God made men in this way, there is a sense in which He is responsible for the inevitability and universality of sin, even though man only sins by his own choice; fourth, God is not baffled by this inevitability and universality, for He offers every sinner mercy in Christ.[10] This passage suggests that behind the parallel passage in $9^{19\text{-}29}$ there lies the doctrine that it is the obedient who are the 'vessels of mercy' and the disobedient who are 'vessels of wrath', as, indeed, the quotations from Isaiah in $9^{27\text{-}9}$ imply. 'The remnant' in Isaiah are the faithful Israelites and these are 'saved'; the others, the great majority, are sinners and perish. A like result follows if Paul's use elsewhere of the term 'wrath' (v. 22) is noted. It is the 'sons of *disobedience*' who are 'children of wrath' (Eph 2^{2f}, 5^6; Col 3^6). In two of these texts Paul *appeals* to his readers not to sin as the other Gentiles sin and as they themselves once sinned, and it is only to *free* men that anyone can appeal to do this or that. The 'wrath' of God is His *ultimate* reply to the disobedience of *free* men. Here, again, this is implied in Ro 9-11 itself, for it contains the verses: 'What if God, willing to show his wrath, and to make his power known, endured with much *long-suffering* vessels of wrath fitted unto destruction. And that he might make known

---

[10] In *The Bible Doctrine of Sin*, under the phrase 'historical inevitability' there is a full discussion of the subject here laid out summarily.

the riches of his glory upon vessels of mercy, which he afore prepared unto glory' (9²²f). The last phrase, 'afore prepared unto glory', may be interpreted as implying that God acted, not by foreordination, but with foreknowledge (cf. 11²⁻⁴). For the rest Paul is pursuing his parable of the Potter under which God is not creating but moulding vessels. Here, as in Jeremiah, the parallel between clay and men fails at one point. Each 'lump' of clay, being a man, has a will of its own and can be either obedient or disobedient. The great Moulder treats each 'lump' in accordance with its series of responses. He 'endures' rebellious responses with 'much long-suffering'—a phrase that has no meaning unless the 'lumps' can resist. It implies that God gives them opportunity after opportunity to 'obey'. But if they persist and persist in disobedience His 'anger'—which always limits itself to 'retribution'—'fits them unto destruction'—just as, on the other hand, he 'makes known the riches of his glory' upon the vessels that, as He foresaw, would respond to His 'mercy'. In other words, in the parable of the Potter Paul is asserting, so far as this parable allows, the Law of Opportunity. Through it God moulds men according as they respond to His treatment. To leave the parable and take Paul's other teaching into account—in answer to the question 'Can not God do what He will?' (cf. 9¹⁹f) Paul says, 'Yes, of course He can, but what has He willed? He has, indeed, so made men that it is, in fact, inevitable that every man would sometimes disobey; this is in order that He may offer every man salvation, not by works, but by faith (vv. 30–2); He gives every man the opportunity to believe, or rather, in Christ *pleads* with every man to believe; He has determined to decide every man's ultimate destiny by the way in which he reacts to this offer; had He not the right to proceed in this way if He would?' It is only by insisting that the Parable of the Potter applies at *every* point, in spite of the warning of the word 'longsuffering', that the passage can be taken to teach that God has made an absolute decree about the ultimate fate of every man. It is now a commonplace, however, that *no* parable applies at every point. Of course, the question arises, 'But what about the multitudes who never heard of Christ? What indeed of those who had not even Abraham's opportunity to believe? How does the Potter treat *them*?', but, as seen above, it is possible to answer this question under a wider application of the Law of Opportunity.

Paul's chief subject, however, as already noted, is God's

Design according to the Election of two *classes*, the Jews and Gentiles. He does not apply the parable of the Potter to *them*. With these, in this passage, God is neither potter nor creator but king—and a king who over-rules even rebellions for His own ends. He is a king who is a matchless statesman. He sees to it that even 'the wrath of man shall praise him' (Ps 76[10]). Paul could see before his eyes the evidence that God was using the Jews' refusal of Christ to secure the obedience of the Gentiles (cf. Ac 18[6], etc.) —that is, he discerns God's method in the current part of the present Age. Looking back upon a longer part, from Abraham to Jesus, he claims that in it the King had used the same method in the opposite way—He had used the disobedience of the Gentiles to secure the obedience of Israel. But Paul is not content with this. He speaks of a third period (Ro 11[25-36]), the end of the Age, indeed, but still *within* it—when those 'beloved enemies' (v. 28) the Jews shall no longer reject their own Christ but accept Him and so 'all Israel shall be saved'. At the end of the Age, therefore, God will 'have mercy upon *all*'. It is at this point that Paul breaks out into a final paean of wonder. If any deduction about *individuals* could be drawn from this conclusion it would be that *all* are to be saved, but in this passage itself, under the Parable of the Olive, he implies that every 'branch' has a will of its own, and that if the branch abuse its freedom it will be 'cut off' (11[22]; cf. Jn 15[4]). This is further evidence that even in Ro 9-11, especially when it is compared with Paul's teaching elsewhere, there is nothing which *requires* that the doctrine, found throughout the rest of the Bible, that God is sovereign yet man is free, should be abandoned.

CHAPTER EIGHT

THE FELLOWSHIP OF GOD WITH MAN IN CHRIST

THE MANY different definitions of religion agree in this—that God (or the gods) and man have something to do with each other. When God and men are conceived as *persons*, the 'something' is fellowship, for this is the characteristic relation of persons. The religion of the Bible is the chief example of this kind of religion. It is true that the *concept* of personality is not reached until long after the phenomenon that it describes occurs in *practice*, but this is the usual story of abstract ideas. It is true, again, that for long the dominant idea in the Bible was that God chose a *people* and not ordinary men, for fellowship with Himself. But it is also true that He did so through individual leaders. From Abraham onwards the Old Testament story is of leaders of Israel, or of the faithful part of Israel, and in some way or other the leaders are all 'men of God'—i.e. men who live in fellowship with Him. This, indeed, is their mark. When, at last, the idea that every single man is a person clearly emerged at the time of Jeremiah, its chief token was that that Prophet declared that in due time *every* man would 'know God' as one person knows another—i.e. live in fellowship with Him. There were already Psalmists that did so. Indeed, the fellowship between God and man is the overriding subject of the whole Bible. The crown of the doctrine is in the Incarnation and Atonement. These, which go together, are the climax of the concept that God seeks and finds fellowship with men. The three books of which this is the last, of course, all illustrate the idea. In *The Bible Doctrine of Man* an attempt was made to show that man was created to be like God so that he might 'know God'; in *The Bible Doctrine of Sin* man's refusal of fellowship with God was examined and God's ways of seeking to restore it; in this book all the terms discussed, beginning with 'grace' and 'love', exemplify the fellowship of God with men. Fully to expound the idea would be to rewrite most of the book. None the less, the concept is so fundamental and embracing that it needs a chapter to itself. A beginning will be made by examining the pertinent uses of the words 'fellowship' and 'friendship', with their cognates, in the Bible. Next an attempt will be made to exhibit the use of the word 'know' in such phrases as 'to know

God', for under them this word, which, when used of 'knowing' persons, usually expresses fellowship at its minimum, has a deepening meaning which culminates in the Fourth Gospel. Finally, there is a unique group of phrases, of which 'in Christ' is the commonest, that brings the whole doctrine of fellowship with God to its distinctive Christian climax.

The New Testament word for 'fellowship' is *koinōnia*. With it there go two cognates, *koinōnos* and *koinōnein*. The nearest English words of one root seem to be 'partnership', 'partner', and 'to partner'. When 'fellowship' with God is meant, the words hardly have a pedigree. *Koinonia* is very rare in LXX (*2*), and *koinonos* (*8*) and *koinonein* (*11*) are infrequent. In the Old Testament they most commonly render a Hebrew root *chbr* (*13*), which means 'unite with' or 'join'. The LXX renderings involve some change of emphasis for the Greek words denote the 'sharing' that accompanies the 'union' of persons rather than the union itself. In LXX *koinonos* denotes a human 'companion' (e.g. Is 1²³; Mal 2¹⁴; Pr 28²⁴) and *koinonein* human 'companionship' (e.g. Job 34⁸; Pr 1¹¹). These meanings recur in the Apocrypha (e.g. Est 16³, Sir 6¹⁰, 13¹ᶠ, 41¹⁸; 2 Mac 4²⁵), but here, under the word 'wisdom', there are two far-away suggestions of the idea of fellowship *with God*. Both are in the Book of Wisdom. In one the writer says that envy 'shall have no fellowship (*koinonein*) with wisdom', and in the other that there is 'renown in the fellowship of her words' (Wis 6²³, 8¹⁸), *philia* 'friendship', and *homilia*, 'intercourse', being parallels with *koinonia* in the second passage. In the one text where *koinonia* occurs in LXX it does not render *chbr* and seems to mean a business 'contract' (Lv 6²). While, of course, all the Old Testament heroes had some experience of fellowship with God, for He spoke to them all, there is as yet no abstract term for this 'fellowship'. Further, there is little suggestion of *continuous* fellowship with God (e.g. Is 41⁸; Ps 51¹¹).

Under *koinonein* (*8*), *koinonos* (*10*) and *koinonia* (*18*), the last is relatively frequent in the New Testament. Only one of the three words, *koinonos*, occurs in the Synoptic Gospels and then in texts not relevant here (Mt 23³⁰; Lk 5¹⁰). For the rest, all three words, apart from two passages (1 Ti 5²²; 2 Jn 11), are used only in relation to Christians, and, significantly, they all occur after the birth of the church at Pentecost. Sometimes they refer to the 'fellowship' of believers with Christ or God or the Spirit, and sometimes to their fellowship with each other. As far as possible, these will be taken separately, though the first always implies the second.

In their Epistles Paul, Peter and John all speak of 'fellowship with *Christ*'. Paul describes Christians as the men whom God 'has called into the fellowship of his Son Jesus Christ our Lord' (1 Co 1⁹) and he uses *koinonia* to describe the Sacrament of the Lord's Supper (1 Co 10¹⁶⁻²¹). Here, under the alternative rendering 'communion', the church has followed his lead. Whatever other convictions they hold, all Christians agree that at the Lord's Supper there is fellowship, a common meal, its ancient symbol and means, being hereby hallowed once for all. Twice there are references to 'the fellowship of (Christ's) sufferings' (Ph 3¹⁰; 1 P 4¹³), and once to the fellowship of His future 'glory' (1 P 5¹). The writer to the Hebrews, on the other hand, speaks of *Christ's* 'sharing' (*koinonein*) with men in 'blood and flesh' (He 2¹⁴). Paul speaks twice of the 'fellowship of *the Spirit*' (2 Co 13¹⁴; Ph 2¹; cf. Ro 8¹⁶). The passage about the Lord's Supper introduces the idea of the fellowship of Christians with each other through Christ. In 1 John the two ideas are integrated (1³, ⁶ᶠ). 'Our fellowship' with each other grounds in our common 'fellowship with *the Father*'. This, in turn, results from fellowship 'with his Son Jesus Christ' (cf. v. 7), 'and', as elsewhere in John, being epexegetic. Apart from a phrase in Second Peter, 'sharers of divine nature' (2 P 1⁴), this is the only direct mention in the New Testament of believers' 'fellowship' with God Himself, but it draws out the inevitable meaning of fellowship with Christ. It is the ground of the fullness of joy (1 Jn 1⁴). It will be seen that, if all the passages are taken together, the doctrine of 'fellowship' is Trinitarian. None of the three words occurs in the Fourth Gospel, but the chapters of the Supper (Jn 13–17) are the culminant example of the *idea*, for they are Jesus' last words to 'his own' beloved ones (13¹).

Under the 'fellowship' of Christians with each other one of the three words occurs in the Acts of the Apostles (2⁴²). It may refer either to 'the fellowship' of other Christians with the Apostles or 'the fellowship' of Christians with each other. This book has little to say directly of the internal life of the churches, but the *continuity* of Christian *koinonia* is always implied. The Epistles, with accurate psychology, say nothing of 'fellowship' *per se*, but always speak of 'fellowship' *in something*. As already implied, the words denote 'sharing'. The fundamental passage here is the Sacramental sharing in Christ, which has already been named (1 Co 10$^{16-20}$). Derivatively Christians share with each other in 'spiritual things' and therefore 'in carnal things' (Ro 15^{26f}; cf. 12^{13}; Gal 6^6; Ph 4^{15}). In this passage, as elsewhere (2 Co 8^4, 9^{13}), Paul calls the 'contribution' to the needs of the poor saints at Jerusalem *koinonia*. It was not almsgiving, but fellowship. Alms are given to those outside the church. For the Christian gift is not humanitarianism but 'sacrifice' (He 13^{16}). Christians have fellowship in each other's 'sufferings' even when they are parted (2 Co 1^{6f}). They also 'share' in the Christian enterprise (2 Co 8^{23}; Ph 1^5; cf. Philem 5f, 17). There is a signal instance of this when the leaders at Jerusalem give 'the right hands of fellowship' to Paul and Barnabas (Gal 2^9). Christians are to be 'one' as Father and Son are 'one' in order that 'the world may believe' (Jn 17$^{21-3}$). When Christians forget that they share an enterprise, their distinctive kind of fellowship withers away. Again, since 'light has no fellowship with darkness', Paul lays it down that a Christian should not marry an 'unbeliever' (2 Co 6^{14f}). John uses the contrast between 'light' and 'darkness' in a more far-reaching way when he epitomizes the whole doctrine of Christian *koinonia* (1 Jn 1$^{5-7}$). Two people cannot have fellowship when one is 'walking in the light' and the other 'in the darkness'! But those that 'come to the light' (Jn 3^{21}) find themselves one there. The secret of the church is the fellowship of Christians with God in Christ and with each other. Here, as elsewhere, the individual and societary uses of a word are indissoluble.

The term 'friendship' is much commoner today than 'fellowship', but under it there are fewer pertinent texts. Ordinarily there is a suggestion of equality about it, however different the status of the friends may be, but this, of course, is not so when the Bible speaks of 'friendship' with God. There are only three relevant Old Testament texts. In two Abraham is called 'the friend of God' (Is 41^8; 2 Ch 20^7). Here the Hebrew term denotes 'love' (*'ahab*), and LXX renders by *agapan*. As James explains, however, when he quotes the phrase, using *philos* (Ja 2^{23}), Abraham was God's 'friend' because he was ready to do all that God bade him, even to the sacrificing of his son. In the third text it is said that 'the LORD spake unto Moses face to face, as a man speaketh unto his

THE FELLOWSHIP OF GOD WITH MAN IN CHRIST 191

friend' (Ex 33:11 E). Here a Hebrew term (*rec'*; *philos* in LXX) is used that varies in meaning from 'friend' to 'acquaintance'; it is often rendered 'neighbour'. Far more frequently Moses is called 'the *servant* of the LORD'. To judge by the sequel of the text, indeed, the Hebrew compilers seem to have felt that it needed qualification (Ex 33:20-3 J). In the Apocrypha the use of *philos* and its noun *philia*, 'friendship', is only relevant, as with some other terms, in the Book of Wisdom, and falls under *sophia*. Once 'friendship with (*pros*) God' is a 'treasure' won by the 'discipline' of 'wisdom' (Wis 7:14); once the 'delight' of '(wisdom's) friendship' follows from the 'exercise of intercourse' with her, 'fellowship' being used as a parallel word (8:18); and once '(wisdom), passing into holy souls maketh (them) friends of God and prophets'—the last word meaning 'able to speak for Him' (7:27). This might be called a 'one-way friendship'. In the New Testament *philia* only occurs once in the phrase 'the friendship of the world' (Ja 4:4). *Philos* (*29*) is particularly frequent in Luke. The examples of the ordinary meaning of the words illustrate the variety in the closeness of the bond (e.g. Lk 11:5-8, 23:12, Jn 11:11, 19:12; Ac 19:31). The Baptist compares himself to 'the friend of the bridegroom' (Jn 3:29). In one passage 'friends' seems to mean 'fellow-Christians' (3 Jn 14). But there are only three closely relevant texts. In one the Pharisees scoff at Jesus because He is 'a friend of publicans and sinners' (Lk 7:34), yet He was no 'friend' of any publican or sinner who, like the Pharisees, refused to listen to Him, preferring to continue to sin. It was at people like Zacchaeus and Mary Magdalene that the Pharisees pointed. Jesus tried to be a friend of every man, but there is no coercive friendship. In the second text Jesus says, 'I say unto you, my friends, Be not afraid of them which kill the body' (Lk 12:4). 'I say unto you', as always, is authoritative. In the whole passage Jesus is not giving friendly counsel but prescribing a way-of-life. The third passage is Johannine and, as usual, explains the others (Jn 15:13-15). Jesus is His disciples' 'Master and Lord' (Jn 13:13) and they have been His 'servants', but now He will 'call them friends' for He is able to explain His ways to them as He had not so far been able (cf. Jn 16:12f). Yet 'Ye are my friends *if* ye do the things which I command you'. It is a strange and unique condition of friendship. Jesus is Lord as well as friend. It is noteworthy that, while the first Christians habitually call Christ 'Lord' and speak of themselves as His 'servants', none of them ever calls Christ his 'friend'.

It was *He* who called *them* 'friends', just as it was *He* who called *them* 'brothers' (Mt 25^{40}, 28^{10}; Jn 20^{17}; He 2^{11}). The New Testament Christian used a certain reticence in speaking of his Lord.

Of all the New Testament words that describe fellowship 'know' is the commonest. Here a distinction needs to be made. Clearly there is a difference between the meanings of 'know' in the statements 'I know that Mr Robinson lives in London' and 'I know Robinson'—i.e. between knowing *something* and knowing *someone*. Students of epistemology tend to emphasize the difference more and more. Indeed, some of them insist that the two concepts are not only widely different but intrinsically so, and that epistemology should be studied in two disparate parts. If a man says 'I know Robinson', it is no doubt implied that he knows some *facts* about Robinson, but, it is claimed, this is only the periphery of the matter. Similarly a man may know many things about God without 'knowing God'. To 'know God' is to have fellowship with Him.

In the Old Testament the word 'know' (*yada'*), of course, is very frequent (about *740* times). For our present purpose the important texts are almost confined to the Prophets. There is, however, a passage where God is said to 'know' Moses and Moses is said to 'know' God (Ex 33$^{12-23}$ J), which involves a full account of the doctrine. It will be named once and again below. The other early passages only furnish a background for the Prophetic teaching. It is more often said that men 'know' God than that God 'knows' men. In Deuteronomy it is several times said that Israel 'knows *not* other gods' (e.g. Dt 11^{28}). On the other hand the heathen 'know *not* the LORD' (e.g. Ps 79^6; cf. Ex 5^2; Job 18^{21}). A people was said to 'know' the god or gods that it worshipped. Hophni and Phineas are individuals who 'knew not the Lord' (1 S 2^{12}, 3^7; cf. Jg 2^{10}). Job asks why those who 'know' the Almighty do not 'see his days' of prosperity (Job 24^1). A prophet could be called a man who 'knew the LORD' (1 S 3^7). In some of the rare texts where God is said to 'know' a man it means no more than that God knows what sort of a man he is (2 S 7^{20}; Ps 139^1; Job 1^{11}). God 'knows' Abraham, however, in the ways of fellowship (Gn 18^{19} J), as He does Moses. In the Prophets, apart from the texts where 'to know not God' occurs, men are said 'to know God' (or 'to know me') sixteen times, most frequently in Hosea

(4) and Jeremiah (9). On the other hand, in the Prophets God is only said to 'know' men (or a people) four times, and in two all that is meant is that He knows what they are (Hos 5³; Nah 1⁷). Of the other two one is discussed later (Jer 1⁵). The second is in Amos, 'You only *have I known* of all the families of the earth; therefore I will visit upon you all your iniquities' (Am 3²). Yet it must not be assumed that, because God is rarely *said* 'to know' Israel, the *idea* is rare. For instance, God offers Covenant to Israel, and Covenant is a form of fellowship. For a particular purpose Amos asserts what is everywhere else assumed. He says that it was Israel's unique privilege that God chose to 'know' her, and therefore, as she has refused the fellowship of God, her punishment too will be unique. Here there are three important points for our present purpose. The first is that it is God who *offers* fellowship. This idea is permanent, and it will usually be assumed below. The second important point is that in the fellowship that God offers to man, God is to have all His own way. Amos goes on to ask, 'Shall two walk together except they have agreed?' (Am 3³). Here 'to walk together' is a Hebrew synonym for 'to be in fellowship'. The context implies that it is God who chooses the way in which the two shall walk. This comes out too, for example, in the Greek rendering of the Hebrew word for 'covenant' (*berith*), when made between God and men. *Diathēkē* is preferred to *synthēkē*, for the latter implies equality. There is even a passage where *berith* is rendered by 'commands' (*entolē*— 1 K 11¹¹)! In ordinary speech, of course, when we speak of 'fellowship' between two men, there is a tacit assumption that there is a 'give and take', the two sometimes going one man's way and sometimes the other's. It is not so in the fellowship of God with men. In this fellowship God always has His own way—to the benefit and delight of His friend. 'To know God' is to do His will and to love to do it. The third permanent truth follows. If a man 'knows God', it makes all the difference in his life. Here the chief difference between 'knowing something' and 'knowing someone' appears. A man may know that Mr Robinson lives in London without its making any difference at all to his life. If, on the other hand, he 'knows Robinson' it makes some difference, however slight, both to him and Robinson. But, if he knows him with any intimacy, it makes a greater difference. In other words, the knowledge implied in fellowship is not *mere* knowledge. It implies and involves feeling and action as well as knowledge. In

the fellowship of God with man, the fellowship does not indeed make any difference to the *character* of God, but it does make a difference in His feeling and action. God delights in the man who accepts His offer of fellowship as He cannot delight in the man who refuses it. Similarly, He acts toward the former in a way in which the latter will not allow Him to act. *To the man* fellowship with God makes all the difference in the world, alike in his feelings, his actions, and his *character*. In Amos three permanent ideas in the concept of the fellowship of God with man appear—it is God who calls men to fellowship; in the fellowship the man wholeheartedly agrees that God shall have all His way; the fellowship makes all the difference, not only to the man's knowledge, but to his whole life. The passage about Moses (Ex $33^{12\text{-}28}$) illustrates all three ideas.

In Hosea the Prophet declares in one passage that Ephraim, having 'the spirit of whoredom', 'knows not the LORD', and in another the sinful people say uselessly to God, 'We Israel know thee' (Hos 5^4, 8^2). It is in two other passages that this Prophet's *differentia* appears. In both he connects God's knowledge of Israel with the Wilderness. In one the LORD claims that Israel shall 'know no other god' because 'I did know thee in the wilderness' (Hos 13^{4f}). In the other God declares that the days of the Wilderness shall return—'Behold, I will allure her, and bring her into the wilderness, and speak to her heart. . . . And I will betroth thee unto me in faithfulness: and thou shalt know the LORD' (Hos $2^{14,\ 20}$). God's knowledge of Israel and Israel's of God is like courtship and marriage. This shows that for the Hebrew the word for 'know' sometimes glowed with a warmth that is absent in the English word, for, when we say 'I know him', we imply a *minimum* of fellowship, adding some such phrase as 'he is a friend of mine' if we wish to express something more than the cold minimum. But a 'cold courtship' would not be a courtship.[1]

Similarly in the passage in Exodus ($33^{12,\ 13,\ 16,\ 17}$) the key phrase is 'find mercy'. Moses enters into the fellowship that God offers him through 'mercy' (*chen*). 'Cold mercy' is a contradiction in terms. When God offers men His fellowship, He offers them His love. Hosea brings this out. For him God woos Israel.

Apart from Jeremiah the evidence from other Prophets is

---

[1] From first to last a Hebrew could use the phrase 'to know' one's wife or husband (e.g. Gn 4^1; Lk 1^{34}) as a euphemism for sexual intercourse. This use has never been assimilated in English, for it doesn't suit our word 'know'.

unimportant. When Isaiah says 'The ox knoweth his owner, and the ass his master's crib, (but) Israel doth not know' (Is 1³), probably he means 'doth not know *me*'. When Deutero-Isaiah says 'Ye are my witnesses . . . that ye may know and believe me, and understand that I am he' (Is 43¹⁰), he probably means that Israel is both to know something and someone. On the other hand when Ezekiel declares that the LORD will punish Israel by the invasions of Gog in order that 'the nations may know me', he probably means no more than that they will learn that He is master of the world (Ez 38¹⁶). There is a happier prophecy in the Book of Isaiah— 'The LORD shall make himself known to Egypt, and the Egyptians shall know the LORD in that day' (Is 19²¹). Here, as usual, the initiative is with God. The Egyptians are 'to worship (Him) with sacrifice', as Israel did. While 'worship' may degenerate into formalism, where there is true worship, as in this text, there is fellowship with God.

In Jeremiah some texts repeat what is said elsewhere. The phrase 'know not (the LORD)' (Jer 10²⁵) describes the heathen, and, as in Deuteronomy, Israel, 'knows no other gods' (e.g. Jer 7⁹) if she is what she ought to be. But in fact God declares 'My people know me not . . . they are wise to do evil, but to do good they have no understanding' (Jer 4²², cf. 9³⁶). Even the priests, whose duty it is to teach others, 'know' not the LORD (Jer 2⁸). On the other hand Josiah, who judged 'the cause of the poor and needy', did 'know' Him (Jer 22¹⁵). Here Jeremiah speaks of an individual and this introduces his distinctive contribution to the doctrine. 'Before I formed thee in the belly I knew thee', said the LORD to the young prophet (Jer 1⁵). This recalls God's word to Moses 'I know thee by name' (Ex 33¹², ¹⁷). It is significant that the phrase should occur in Jeremiah—and that he should himself say 'Thou, O LORD, knowest me' (Jer 12³) —for he is the Prophet of the Individual, and, in the last resort when persons know persons, it is always an individual experience on both sides. Jeremiah uses the phrase to 'know God' three times in other texts—'Let him that glorieth glory in this, that he understandeth and knoweth me' (Jer 9²⁴); 'I will give (the captives in Babylon) an heart to know me' (Jer 24⁷); 'They shall all know me, from the least of them unto the greatest of them, saith the LORD' (Jer 31³⁴). In all three passages the context describes the righteousness that is the will of God for men. Men who 'know' God both know and do His will. As elsewhere, the

English word 'know' is far too pale and limited a term. The comparison of Jeremiah with Moses is close. We hear them both sometimes in conversation with God, and even expostulating with Him—but with both there is always the axiom that, if He insists, they will do His will. They are the best Old Testament examples of the fellowship between God and man expressed by the Hebrew word for 'know'. With them fellowship with God is intimate. There is intimacy without equality, a phenomenon common between parents and children, but rare elsewhere. Just because both Moses and Jeremiah knew God in this way, they both suffered for forty years with a people who refused to 'know' Him. God had spoken with Moses 'as a friend' (Ex 33^{11} J). For centuries this was Moses' unique privilege. With Jeremiah, and with some Psalmists, God speaks with the same individual intimacy though the word 'friend' is not used. Among phrases that *imply* that a man 'knows' God, to 'walk with God' is notable (Gn 5^{22}, 6^9; Mic 1^8; Mal 2^6). A few passages under the phrase 'the knowledge of God' might be added (e.g. Hos 6^6; Jer 22^{16}; Pr 9^{10}).

In LXX the Hebrew word for 'know' is rendered by *ginōskein* about five hundred and forty times, by *epiginōskein* over fifty, and by *eidenai* about two hundred. In the texts relevant here LXX has *ginōskein* nine times, *epiginōskein* twice, and *eidenai* four times (all in Jeremiah), with *epistasthai* once. In a single passage it has *ginōskein* and *eidenai* as alternatives (Jer 9$^{3, 6}$). The translators do not habitually make any distinction between the words, though in Jeremiah 31^{34} it may be that they purposely passed from *ginōskein* to *eidenai*, implying that 'in the last days' men would not need to '*get* to know' God, as *ginōskein* suggests. There is very little to be said under the Apocrypha. Under *eidenai* one manuscript speaks of the men who 'knew' God in the past (Sir 48^{11}), and there is a passage where, *eidenai* and *epiginoskein* both occurring, idolaters are said to have 'refused to know' the true God for even the heathen might have known that there is a 'first author' of things (Wis 12^{27}, 13^3). Under *epiginoskein* Judith twice says that the Jews 'know' God (5^8, 8^{20}), and Sirach has two relevant texts under the same word (36^5, 44^{23}). The writer of Wisdom, using *ginōskein*, says that it is through 'wisdom' and God's 'holy spirit' that men 'know his counsel' (9$^{13, 17}$). Strictly speaking, the last passage should not be quoted, for it declares that men know *about* God rather than that they know Him. In all periods the ordinary Hebrew, like multitudes who are counted Christians today, knew about God but did not personally know Him. It should perhaps be added that *gnōsis* renders *yada'* or words of the same root over thirty times and *epignōsis* five. Under *gnōsis* men's 'knowledge of God' is twice mentioned (Wis 2^{13}, 14^{22}), but there is no other relevant text. Some may think that the whole doctrine of 'Wisdom' should fall here, but to the present writer 'Wisdom' seems to teach men to 'know about God', and in particular to know His will, rather than to know Him personally. In any case neither the Hebrew nor the Greek term for 'Wisdom' derives from the words now under discussion. In the Old Testament three stages may be traced in the connotation of the word 'know'—even 'the *nations*' might have known God the Creator; through the Covenant one *nation*, Israel, knows Him far better than the rest; in Jeremiah's prophecy of the New Covenant *individuals* are to know God with an intimacy like the Prophet's own. Here, for the individual the axioms hold that are found in Amos for the nation —it is God who begins the deeper fellowship by 'writing his law' in the heart; this fellowship is only with those who are willing that in it God should have all His way; the fellowship makes all the difference in the character of the man.

In the New Testament, in contrast with LXX, *eidenai* (about *300* times) occurs more often than *ginoskein* (about *220*) and *epiginoskein* (about *40* times) taken together. With these there go *gnosis* (*29*) and *epignosis* (*20*). Except in the Gospel and First Epistle of John, however, the number of texts here relevant is again small, the writers expressing fellowship by such terms as *agape* and *charis*, whose intrinsic connotation denotes a closer fellowship. 'Know' may be as warm but need not be. Paul, for instance, speaks of 'knowing the *love* of Christ which passeth knowledge' (Eph 3^{19}). It is not always easy to determine which texts to include—for instance, should 2 Co 6^9 be included or Jn 8^{32} (cf. v. 36)?—but on the present writer's reckoning there are forty-five passages where *ginoskein* is relevant (of which thirty are Johannine), three where *epiginoskein* is relevant (none being Johannine), and twenty where *eidenai* is relevant (ten being Johannine). There are also five relevant examples of *gnosis* and eight of *epignosis*, all thirteen occurring either in Paul or Second Peter.

It is usual, to borrow phrases from Abbott-Smith's *Lexicon*, to distinguish *ginoskein*, as meaning 'to know by observation and experience', from *eidenai* as denoting 'a mental process, based on intuition or information', and to define *epiginoskein* as the 'directive' of *ginoskein*, but it is more than doubtful whether these distinctions are *maintained* in the New Testament. It is, of course, quite common for specialists to discriminate between words with an exactness that is lost in common speech. In English the difference between 'understand' and 'comprehend' is an example. The New Testament was not written for scholars. However, the reader may decide the point for himself under the discussion below, where texts that use *eidenai* have the letter *e* appended.

For the understanding of the whole New Testament doctrine of the knowledge of God one passage, whatever its origin, is fundamental—'All things have been delivered unto me of my Father: and no one knoweth the Son save the Father; neither doth any know the Father save the Son, and he to whomsoever the Son willeth to reveal him' (Mt 11^{27}). It is true that Luke gives part of the saying in a different form, 'No one knoweth who the Son is save the Father; and who the Father is save the Son' (10^{22}), the meaning being that only the Father 'knows' the *nature* of the Son and only the Son the *nature* of the Father, but a son and a father know each other's nature by knowing each other. Indeed it is a commonplace that no one knows another's nature except by knowing him and knowing him intimately. Here, as elsewhere, the use of the terms 'Father' and 'Son' is significant. They point to an intimacy that transcends all others. For instance, unlike Moses and Jeremiah, Jesus never expostulates with God. Even in Gethsemane His last word is 'Not my will but thine be done'. Since the Greek words for 'know' in the great saying are *ginoskein* and *epiginoskein*, it may be asked in passing whether the Son and the Father 'know' each other 'by observation' or by 'intuition'. There is a further difference between Matthew and Luke. The former puts the saying into a context of sorrow. Jesus has just been upbraiding the cities of Galilee where He had done most of His mighty works because their peoples refused to accept God's revelation in Him. None the less in Matthew there is also the joy that 'babes' had welcomed the revelation, and it is of this that Luke, who wrote for Gentiles, speaks. It is true that he puts the saying into a different context, but this makes it the more unlikely that the saying is an intrusion into both Gospels. It is Jesus who mediates fellowship with God in its fullness. It is those that hear 'His sayings'—and so hear as to do them (Lk 6^{47})—who build upon immovable rock (Mt 7^{24-7}). The preceding words (v. 23),

'I never knew you', describe the fate of the others. This is another of the few texts in the Synoptists that illustrate the meaning of the word 'know' and is pertinent here. Its implication is *God* never knew you'. It recurs where the Bridegroom rejects the appeal of the Foolish Virgins (Mt 25[12]). In the Old Testament God chooses whom He will 'know'; in the New He does this through Christ. The dual use of 'reveal' in the Matthæan passage shows this (Mt 11[25, 27]). It is of His 'beloved Son' that God says 'in (him) I am well-pleased, *hear ye him*' (Mt 17[5]; cf. Lk 10[21]). It was to those who were ready both to learn and to do all His will that the Son 'willed to reveal' God. In Jesus' fellowship with His disciples there was no question of His having His way sometimes and they having theirs at others, as in fellowships among men, but of His having always His own way, after the Old Testament manner of God. Over against the texts where the word 'know' denotes fellowship there is the text where an 'unclean spirit' says 'I know thee who thou art, the Holy One of God' (Mk 1[24] *e*; cf. 34 *e*; Ac 19[25]). The demons knew *that* Jesus was holy, but they did not know Jesus. There are many men like them.

In the rest of the New Testament books the relevant passages are almost all Pauline or Johannine. The writer of the Epistle to the Hebrews, who keeps closely to one set of subjects and only by a kind of accident refers to other parts of the Christian message, quotes Jeremiah's prophecy that under the New Covenant men will 'know' God, using both *ginoskein* and *eidenai* as in LXX (He 8[11] *e*). On the other hand, in one of his warnings against apostasy he writes, 'We know him that said, Retribution belongeth unto me, I will recompense' (He 10[30] *e*). There is a terrible side to fellowship with God. Of course the *idea* of fellowship is often present without the word 'know', as when the writer says that Jesus calls believers His 'brethren' and 'children' (He 2[11-13]). In order that 'he might be a merciful and faithful high priest' 'it behoved him in all things to be made like unto his brethren' (He 2[17]). Paul too, of course, implies the *idea* that Christians are in fellowship with God through Christ multitudes of times. One text may serve as example—'For by grace have ye been saved through faith; and that not of yourselves: it is the gift of God' (Eph 2[8]). 'Grace' and 'faith' just describe the two sides of the distinctive Christian fellowship. Under the *word* 'know' men are said to 'know not God' in several Pauline contexts—as in the Old Testament, the Gentiles 'know not God' (Gal 4[8] *e*; 1 Th 4[5] *e*);

nominal Christians, who do not practise their knowledge, do not 'know' Him (Tit 1¹⁶ *e*); retribution awaits those who, hearing the Gospel, refuse thereby to 'know God' (2 Th 1⁸ *e*); by a Divine irony 'the foolishness of preaching' is wiser than 'the wisdom of the world', for the former, and not the latter, teaches men how 'to know God' (1 Co 1²¹). By a verbal contradiction the Gentiles are said, as in the Book of Wisdom, to 'know God' through the Creation, but, because they turned their backs on this knowledge, they have 'become fools' (Ro 1²¹ᶠ). On the other hand, the true Christian is a man who 'knows God'. He has come to 'know' Him because God has 'sent forth the Spirit of his Son into (his) heart' (Gal 4⁶, ⁹; cf. 1 Co 2¹³ᶠ *e*). In other words, he knows God because he knows Christ through the Spirit. This leads to the two passages where Paul speaks of 'knowing' Christ (Ph 3¹⁰; 2 Ti 1¹² *e*; cf. 2 Co 5¹⁶). In 2 Timothy 1¹², written at the end of his life, he says that, 'knowing whom (he has) believed', he knows that the Christ, to whom he has been faithful in his sufferings, will Himself be faithful to their fellowship 'in that day'. In Philippians 3⁸⁻¹¹, written in the midst of his apostolate, he describes, on the other hand, his own purpose in the whole of life—'For the excellency of the knowledge of Christ Jesus (his) Lord' he has 'suffered the loss of all things', and his one aim is still 'to know him'—and this includes 'knowing the power of his resurrection, and fellowship of his sufferings', in order that, having suffered for others as Christ did on the Cross, he may 'by any means attain unto the resurrection from the dead'. Christ's resurrection is the Alpha and Paul's the Omega of this account of 'knowing Christ'. The inadequacy of the English word 'know' is here immeasurable. The text introduces too Paul's use of the phrase 'the *knowledge* (that a Christian has) of Christ Jesus' (Ph 3⁸). Here the term is *gnosis*. It occurs also in 2 Corinthians 2¹⁴ᶠ, where Paul, quoting a frequent Old Testament phrase for the sacrifice of incense, says that his life sheds the 'sweet fragrance' of the 'knowledge' of God everywhere —a fragrance of which every man about him is aware, either for weal or woe. There are two other relevant passages under *gnosis* (2 Co 10⁵; Eph 3¹⁹), of which the second, which speaks of a 'love that passeth knowledge', has already been quoted. In all the passages the context relates both God and Christ to a Christian's 'knowledge'. It is the same with Paul's four relevant passages under *epignosis*. They all belong to Colossians and Ephesians. In one 'the new man' is being 'renewed unto knowledge after the image of him that created him' (Col 3¹⁰). In another 'the knowledge of the Son of God' is one of a series of opulent phrases that culminate in 'the measure of the stature of the fulness of Christ' (Eph 3¹³). The other two instances occur in passages where Paul struggles to put into words his prayers for his fellow-Christians (Eph 1¹⁷; Col 1⁹ᶠ). In both 'power' goes with 'knowledge'. In these climacteric passages the beggarliness of the English word 'knowledge' is once more plain. Other phrases, such as 'the light of the knowledge of the glory of God in the face of Jesus Christ' (2 Co 4⁶) might be added, for these, in view of the discussion above, may be said to *imply* that the Christian is a man who 'knows God'—and is continuously to '*grow* in the grace and knowledge (*gnosis*) of our Lord and Saviour Jesus Christ'. The last phrase is from the Second Epistle of Peter (3¹⁸), whose writer, rather unexpectedly, alone shares with Paul this use of *gnosis* and *epignosis*. His use of the word 'grow' suggests that already there began to be Christians who were content to learn no more than the alphabet of faith. Their progeny has been legion. This writer has *epignosis* four times (2 P 1²ᶠ, ⁸, 2²⁰). He seems to distinguish *gnosis* from *epignosis*, for while *gnosis* is one rung in his ladder of Christian qualities, *epignosis* seems to include them all (2 P 1⁵⁻⁸).

So far nothing has been said under the Epistles of the passages where God is said to 'know' men. These are rare in Paul. There seem to be two chief reasons. First, it is the *unspoken* axiom of the *kerugma* that God seeks to 'know' every man. If this were not so, there would be no gospel. Christ's ambassadors need to 'beseech' men to be 'reconciled' to God, for the reluctance for fellowship is on *their* side, not His. Secondly, the main expression of the truth that God 'knows' believers in Christ is the term 'elect', which was examined in the last chapter. While God *seeks* to know every man, He *chooses* to know those who 'believe on the Lord Jesus Christ'. Both in the seeking and the choosing He takes the initiative. In one passage Paul corrects himself to say this—'Now that ye have come to know God, or rather to be known of God' (Gal 4⁹). If, as is likely, the phrase 'Then shall I know even as I have been known' (1 Co 13¹²) refers to the fellowship between Paul and God, there too the precedence is with God. The phrase occurs in the Hymn of Love. Earlier in the Epistle Paul had written, 'If any man love God, the same is known of him' (1 Co 8³). Probably in the phrase 'as unknown and well known' (2 Co 6⁹) the Apostle means that men do not know him but God does. The text 'The Lord knoweth them that are his' (2 Ti 2⁹) does not fall here, for the context implies that 'know' has one of its attenuated meanings, 'discriminate'. But there are enough texts to show that, as in the Old Testament, it is God who chooses men for fellowship with Him, and not they who choose Him, though He chooses them on a new condition, faith in Christ.

In the Fourth Gospel the word 'know' occurs once in its personal sense in the Prologue, in a short epitome of the writer's theology—'He was in the world, and the world was made by him, and the world *knew* him not. He came home (cf. Jn 19²⁷) and his ain folk received him not. But as many as received him, to them he gave (the) right to become children of God' (Jn 1¹⁰⁻¹²). Here three things are noticeable—that the word 'receive' interprets the word 'know'; that the doctrine that God is the Father of believers is implied; and that the Greek word for 'right' is *exousia*, which is usually rendered 'authority'—i.e. one man's rightful control of other men—but implies here that children have a 'right' that is correlative to a father's.

In the first part of the Gospel proper (1¹⁹–4⁵⁴) 'know' is not used in its full personal sense. 'Know not' occurs both of the people's ignorance of Jesus before He 'manifested his glory' (1²⁶ *e*; 2¹¹) and of the Baptist's ignorance of Him until God gave the appointed sign of the Spirit (1³¹ *e*, ³³ *e*). Nicodemus' words 'We know that thou art a teacher come from God' (3² *e*) mark the first step toward a deeper knowledge—a step that Nicodemus seems to have taken but that 'the Jews' resolutely, though insincerely, refused to take.

The main subject of the second part of this Gospel (chh. 5–12) is, 'Ye will not come to me that ye may have life' (5⁴⁰)—i.e. 'Ye *will* not know me' (cf. 17³). The relevant uses of the word 'know' occur in three passages. In the first (7²⁷⁻²⁹ *e*) Jesus says, in effect: 'You know that I am a man called Jesus who comes from Nazareth, but you are refusing to recognize that God has sent me, and so to know Him whom I know.' It is the challenge that rings throughout these chapters, the full sense of 'know' appearing for the first time. In the second passage (8¹²⁻⁵⁹) the phrase 'Ye know not whence I came or whither I go' is set over against 'I know whence I came and whither I go' (8¹⁴ *e*). The first phrase only superficially contradicts 7²⁸ for the question now is about the deeper knowledge. Presently Jesus says, 'Ye know neither me nor my Father: if ye knew me ye would know my Father also' (8^{19} *e*), and again, at the conclusion of the whole passage, 'Ye have not known (my Father), but I know him, and if I should say, I know him not, I shall be like unto you, a liar; but I know him and keep his word' (8^{55} *e*). In the third passage (10$^{1-18}$), under the figure of a shepherd and his sheep (10$^{4f,\ 14f,\ 27}$), the writer introduces those who *do* 'know' Jesus. There was a true fellowship between a Judæan shepherd and his sheep. He knew, month by month, where the few 'green pastures' lay and led them there. He was their one defence against a 'wolf', and he would die to save them (10^{11f})—yet they must do all *his* will. This Shepherd is to 'lay down (his) life for the sheep' because He and the Father 'know' each other (10$^{12-15}$). This third passage is a foil to the other two. Those who know Jesus are set over against those who refuse to know Him. The chief burden of chapters 5-12 is that Jesus says to the Jews: 'I know the Father for I am the Son; men may know Him through Me; you refuse to know Him for you refuse to know Me.'

In the third part of the Gospel (chh. 13-21) the relevant passages for the present purpose all fall before Gethsemane and the subject now is 'These Eleven know Me and God through Me'. There is again a development in the succession of passages. The first relevant text occurs before Judas has gone out into the night —'I speak not of you all: I know whom I chose: but that the Scripture may be fulfilled, He that eateth my bread lifted up his heel against me' (13^{18} *e*). Here Jesus uses two metaphors—the metaphor of the intimate fellowship of the common meal, and the metaphor of the treachery of the backward kick. Two implications are notable—that Jesus, like God in the Old Testament, chooses the men who shall share His fellowship (cf. 15^{16}), and that a man may refuse the fellowship. After the traitor come the questioners (14$^{5-9}$, *eidenai* and *ginoskein*). When Jesus says to Thomas, 'If ye had known me, ye would have known my Father also: from henceforth ye know him and have seen him', Philip interjects: 'Lord, show us the Father, and it sufficieth us.' Jesus replies: 'Have I been so long time with you and dost thou not know *me*, Philip? he that hath seen me hath seen the Father.' It is the Son's unique claim—to know Him is to know God. Through Him too the disciples are to 'know the Spirit of truth'— whom 'the world does not know'—by an inward fellowship (14^{17}). The next two texts refer to those who 'know not him that sent' Jesus because they have refused to know Jesus (15²¹ᶠ ᵉ, 16³). The two remaining passages both belong to Jesus' prayer for His 'friends' (15¹⁵) in chapter 17. The second comes at the end, but it may be quoted first for it is the basis of the whole prayer—'O righteous Father, the world knew thee not, but I knew thee: and *these* knew that thou didst send me; and I made known unto them thy name (i.e. thy nature as 'Father') and will make it known; that the love wherewith thou lovedst me may be in them and I in them' (17²⁶). This epitomizes the Gospel under the fellowship of love. The other text comes near the beginning of the prayer (17³). The context speaks of the 'glory' of the Son's 'hour', the 'glory' being the manifestation of His 'authority'. In the text itself the writer, as often, uses the epexegetic 'and', whose meaning must be interpreted by the context. As the whole Gospel shows, 'and' here means 'through'. 'This is life eternal that (those whom thou hast given me) should know thee, the only true God, and (i.e. through) him whom thou didst send, Jesus Christ'. Here the New Testament doctrine of fellowship with God culminates. 'To know God and enjoy Him for ever' is not 'the chief end of man'; it is his only end.

In the First Epistle of John it may be noted that *eidenai* (*15*) is not used in any relevant text. 1 Jn 5¹³ and ¹⁹ come nearest. On the other hand *ginoskein* (*24*) is often relevant. It is used of 'knowing' God three times (1 Jn 4⁶ᶠ, 5²⁰) and of 'knowing' the Father once (1 Jn 2¹³)—of 'knowing' Christ (though not under that term) three times (1 Jn 2¹³, 5²⁰)—and of 'knowing' the Spirit twice (1 Jn 4². ⁶). To 'know not' God is used of 'the world' and of some within the church (1 Jn 3¹. ⁶, 4⁸). To 'know God' and to sin are the opposites of opposites (1 Jn 3⁶; cf. 2¹³). To 'know' God is both to 'keep his commandments' (1 Jn 2³ᶠ), and to 'love' Him (1 Jn 4⁷ᶠ)—an inevitable conjunction and the ultimate definition of the intimacy of this fellowship. To 'know' God is to be 'of (*ek*) God' (1 Jn 4⁶ᶠ)—i.e. the believer's life springs from the life of God. The words for 'knowledge', *gnosis* and *epignosis*, occur neither in the Gospel nor Epistle. Again, God is not said to 'know' men in either, and only once to 'know' Christ (Jn 10¹⁵). In the Epistle Christ is not said either to 'know' God or to 'know' believers. This late writer, taking all these as matter of course, concentrates on two truths—'Believers know Christ and thereby know God; others know neither'. In other words, the writer assuming, as he now can, that 'No one knoweth the Son save the Father,

THE FELLOWSHIP OF GOD WITH MAN IN CHRIST 205

neither doth any know the Father save the Son' concentrates on the third phrase in the Synoptic verse—'He to whomsoever the Son willeth to reveal him' (Mt 11^{27}). The Gospel and Epistle of John only draw out the meaning of the word 'know' in the Matthæan passage.

Of the group of New Testament phrases that gather round the phrase 'in Christ', two, 'in the LORD' and 'in God', are fairly common in the Old Testament. The first, which is much the commoner, is occasionally found outside the Psalter (e.g. Gn 15^6 JE; Pr 3^5; Is 26^{3f}, 45^{25}; Jer 3^{23}; Zeph 3^2), but the great majority of its examples belong to that book. 'In God' is most frequent in its Elohistic division (Ps 41–72). The two phrases accompany certain verbs and their cognate nouns. The true Hebrew 'trusts in the LORD' (Gn 15^6; Zeph 3^2; Ps 4^5, 64^{10}; Pr 3^5), 'rejoices in the LORD' (Ps 35^9, 104^{34}; Is 29^{19}), 'exults', 'boasts', and 'delights in the LORD' (1 S 2^1; Ps 34^2, 37^4; Is 63^{14}), 'hopes' and 'rests in the LORD' (Ps 31^{24}, 37^7, 38^{15}). In the Prophets 'in the LORD' is the true Israel's 'justification', her 'glory', her 'salvation', and her 'strength' (Is 45^{25}; Jer 3^{23}; Zech 12^5). Some of the same words recur under 'in God' (e.g. Ps 25^2, 42^5, 44^8). But the one English preposition 'in' renders four Hebrew prepositions. Three of them are relatively rare. Of two of these, l^e (e.g. Ps 31^{24}, 37^7, 42^5) and 'el (e.g. Ps 4^5, 56^3; Pr 3^5), the primary meaning is 'toward', but, if they retain their original distinction, the first would denote 'looking toward' and the second 'moving toward' the LORD. 'el, however, may sometimes be a scribal variant for 'al, the third Hebrew preposition (e.g. Ps 37^4, 146^5; Is 63^{14}). Its primary meaning is 'upon' and it retains this when used symbolically. It denotes the ground or basis of hope and trust. The last of the four prepositions is the prefix b^e, and it is so much the commonest that it may be called the usual Hebrew term (e.g. Gn 15^6; 1 S 2^1; Ps 26^1, 44^8, 56^{10}, 78^{22}; Is 29^9; Jer 3^{23}). Its primary meaning is 'in (a given place)', but it is so bewilderingly versatile that it is impossible to show that this concept is everywhere present. This appears clearly in the long article upon it in the *Oxford Hebrew Lexicon*. The editors interpret the Hebrew phrase 'in the LORD' to mean 'through the LORD' in some passages (e.g. Ps 18^{30}, 44^6; Hos 1^7), but they also devote a section of their article to the use of b^e 'with certain classes of verbs, though the explanation of its use may be sometimes doubtful', and among these classes are verbs of 'trusting' and 'rejoicing' which are pertinent here. They show, however, that b^e occasionally means 'on', in the literal sense, as in 'on the altar' (Gn 8[20]) and 'on his head' (Is 59[17]), and 'on' may be used in a symbolic way in such phrases as 'trust on the LORD' and 'rejoice on the LORD', which would then mean that the true Hebrew *based* his trust and joy on his God. It seems clear that the translators of LXX took the phrase in this way, for, while they occasionally translate by a dative noun without a preposition (e.g. Gn 15[6]) or use *dia*, 'through' (e.g. Is 29[19]; Jer 3[23]) or 'from' (Is 45[25]), their customary renderings are by *epi* (with dative), 'upon', and *en*, 'in', and the former is the more frequent. They generally use *epi* to render the first three Hebrew prepositions, and, while for b^e they use *epi* and *en* indiscriminately, *epi* easily outnumbers *en*. Both are used to render b^e in 'A righteous man shall delight himself in (*en*) the LORD and shall (set his) hope upon (*epi*) him' (Ps 65[10]). There are other instances for *en* in 1 S 2[1]; Ps 34[2]; Zec 12[5], and for *epi* in Ps 31[1], 35[9], 64[10]; Zeph 3[2]. There is the same variation, with the same preference for *epi*, under 'in God'. The two prepositions occur side by side to render this phrase in Psalm 56[3f] and 78[22], but in most of the other texts *epi* is used. It seems plain that for the LXX translators the dominant idea was that a true man's 'faith' and 'joy' and so on were based or grounded or founded on God. In the Apocrypha *en* occurs in Wis 5[15], but *epi* in Wis 12[2] and 2 Mac 2[18], 7[40]. In the Old Testament passages where 'in the LORD' or 'in God' occurs in the English versions, neither the Hebrew original nor the LXX translation justifies the mystical interpretation found under 'in Christ' and its synonyms in the New Testament. The typical text is 'The LORD is my rock and my fortress . . . *in him* will I trust' (Ps 18[2]). There is safety *on* a rock and *in* a fortress.

In the New Testament the phrase 'in God' occurs about eleven times. The passages can be put in an ascending series. In Paul's speech at Athens he uses the phrase 'in him we live and move and have our being' (Ac 17[28]) in a sense that his philosophic hearers would understand. It does not require the idea of a personal and conscious fellowship with a personal God any more than the accompanying quotation from Greek poets, 'For we are also his offspring'. Then there are the texts where Paul 'waxes bold' and 'boasts' and 'rejoices' 'in God' (1 Th 2[2]; Ro 2[17], 5[11]).

These are parallel to Old Testament phrases and may be interpreted as alternatives for 'on (*epi*) God', which occurs in three similar texts (Lk 1⁴⁷; 1 Ti 4¹⁰, 6¹⁷; cf. Ac 14³). The distinctive New Testament idea begins to appear in the passages where God and Christ are put together—as in the text, 'Your life is hid with Christ in God' (Col 3³; cf. Eph 3⁹), and in the salutations of two Epistles (1 Th 1¹; 2 Th 1¹; cf. Jude 1). Last, there are three Johannine passages (Jn 3²¹; 1 Jn 4¹⁵ᶠ, 5²⁰). These belong to the final New Testament exposition of what the phrase 'in Christ' means and will be taken under it.

The phrase 'in (the) Lord' is much more frequent (55). The omission of the article has a multitude of precedents in LXX. Only one text occurs outside Paul (Rev 14¹³), but this is a warning against the conclusion that the Apostle monopolized the idea. 'In *the* Lord' is rare. The phrase 'in Christ Jesus, *the* Lord of us' occurs four times (Ro 6²³, 8³⁹; 1 Co 15³¹; Eph 3¹²). Another text runs 'The faith in *the* Lord Jesus which is in you' (Eph 1¹⁵). 'In Lord Jesus' (without the article) occurs in Ro 14¹⁴; Ph 2¹⁹; 1 Th 4¹; and 'in Lord Jesus Christ' in 2 Th 3¹². This leads to the question: 'When "in (the) Lord" is used *simpliciter*, does it refer to Christ or God?' Sometimes it certainly means 'in Christ', for in Ro 16¹⁻¹⁶ 'in Lord' occurs six times, 'in Christ' three times, and 'in Christ Jesus' once, clearly as synonyms. In the context of almost all the other texts where 'in (the) Lord' occurs there is a reference to Christ, which makes it at least probable that 'in Lord' means 'in Christ'. There is no passage where this cannot be so. Perhaps the following texts may be counted doubtful—1 Co 1³¹ (with 2 Co 10¹⁷), 11¹¹; Eph 5⁸, 6¹, ¹⁰; Ph 2²⁴, 4¹⁰; 1 Th 3⁸; 2 Th 3⁴. This leaves forty-five on the other side. But in the early Thessalonian salutations there is the two-fold phrase 'In God (the) Father and (the) Lord Jesus Christ' (1 Th 1¹; 2 Th 1¹). This shows that quite soon it was discerned that to be 'in Christ' is to be 'in God'. In the order of experience 'in Christ' came first, but in the order of thought 'in God' has precedence.

'In (the) Lord' is used some fifteen times as an adjective and about forty as an adverb. Under the adverbial use there are a few passages where the phrase *might* be taken to mean 'founded *on* the Lord', as in the Old Testament. For instance, a Christian is to 'boast in the Lord' (1 Co 1³¹; 2 Co 10¹⁷; quoted from Jer 9²³) or 'in Christ Jesus our Lord' (1 Co 15³¹); he 'has confidence in the Lord' (2 Th 3⁴; Gal 5¹⁰), and 'rejoices in the Lord' (Ph 3¹).

Epi, 'on', indeed occurs once, in the phrase 'speaking boldly in the Lord' (Ac 14³). But this is an artificial exegesis in some other adverbial phrases—e.g. 'know and am persuaded in the Lord' (Ro 14¹⁴), 'toiled in the Lord' (Ro 16¹²), 'called in the Lord' (1 Co 7²²), 'doors opened in the Lord' (2 Co 2¹²), 'to witness in the Lord' (Philem 20). This is even clearer in the adjectival use, where the singularity of the phrases reaches its height—e.g. 'the love of God in Christ Jesus our Lord' (Ro 8³⁹), 'the elect in the Lord' (Ro 16¹³), 'not empty in the Lord' (1 Co 15⁵⁸), 'prisoner in the Lord' (Eph 4¹), 'fellow-servant in the Lord' (Col 4⁷).

The peculiarity of the use of the phrase needs to be exactly noted. In some of its instances the adverbial use has parallels in English. We may say, for instance, that a son 'trusts in his father' or 'delights in his father'—with the Old Testament meaning. Not many English verbs, however, admit such phrases. In the Greek of the New Testament their multiplicity is such that they require the comprehensive idea that the Christian '*lives in the Lord*'. There are no English parallels for the adjectival use. We may say that a man *is* 'in love' but not that he is 'in his beloved'. The peculiarity under 'in (the) Lord' is that *one person* is said to be '*in another person*'. In the New Testament the fellowship of Christ with the believer is so intimate that it is *normal* to describe the Christian as a man who is 'in (the) Lord'—one *person* in another.

The phrase 'in Christ' sometimes occurs *simpliciter*, but there is a cluster of longer phrases that contain it. The texts which teach that *God* is 'in Christ' (*10*) are not directly pertinent here. The list of phrases that describe the believer as 'in Christ' is as follows—'in Christ' (*22–19* in Paul); 'in the Christ' (*2*—both in Paul); 'in Christ Jesus' (*43*—all in Paul); 'in Jesus Christ' (*2*—both in Paul); 'in Jesus Christ our Lord', 'in the Lord Jesus Christ', and 'in our Lord Jesus Christ' (*6*—all in Paul); 'in his Son Jesus Christ' (*1*—1 Jn 5²⁰). To these there may be added 'in (the) Lord Jesus' (*4*—all in Paul), and 'in Jesus' (*3*—*1* in Paul). There are also the texts where 'in him' and 'in whom' mean 'in Christ', and the passages in the Fourth Gospel, discussed below, where Jesus uses the phrase 'in me'. It does not seem likely that any distinction was consciously and consistently made in the meaning of the phrases, unless it be that 'Lord' is added to emphasize the authority of Christ. The New Testament Epistles, in their doctrinal parts, are much like sermons. Has any later

THE FELLOWSHIP OF GOD WITH MAN IN CHRIST 209

preacher consistently made any nice distinctions when he has used the names 'Christ', 'Christ Jesus', 'Jesus Christ', and so on? Possibly the rare phrase 'in Jesus' is an exception. It may be added that Paul sometimes (*8*) uses phrases like 'Christ in you' without any sense of contradiction. He can use 'them that are in Christ Jesus' and 'Christ in you' in one passage for the same people (Ro 8$^{1, 10}$). Peter too has, in effect, both phrases in two verses (1 P 3^{15f}). To use a quite inadequate but not wholly inadmissible comparison, is the air that men breathe within or without them?

It will be seen that the uses of the phrases are overwhelmingly Pauline, and it is easy to deduce that the truth that they teach was Paul's *peculium*. But there is a good deal to be said on the other side. The phrases occur in the letters to the churches at Rome and Colossæ, where Paul had not preached. The Colossian use may be discounted since Colossæ was probably evangelized from Ephesus. But in the Epistle to the Roman church, which Paul had not founded or even visited when he wrote, he uses the phrases twelve times—or, if chapter 16 be omitted, eight times —and he takes it for granted that the Romans were used to them. It is increasingly allowed that the writer of First Peter, even if he were not Peter himself, is not a *mere* Paulinist, and of the three texts where he uses 'in Christ' (1 P 3^{16}, 5$^{10, 14}$) two, which speak of 'your good way-of-life in Christ' and 'the God of all grace, who called you into his eternal glory in Christ', have their own *nuances*. In Acts 4^2 'in Jesus' may mean 'through Jesus', but the Seer of the Apocalypse calls himself '(your) fellow-sharer in the tribulation and kingship and patience in Jesus' (Rev 1^9), and in the First Epistle of John there is the claim 'We are in the true (God), in his Son Jesus Christ' (5^{20}). The variation of phrase only illustrates the ubiquity of the idea. None of the phrases occurs in the Epistle to the Hebrews, whose vocabulary is peculiar elsewhere too, but it is arguable that when the writer calls Jesus by the societary name 'the High Priest of our confession' (He 3^1), he means that all Christians are 'in Him'. Finally, there are the texts where Jesus uses the phrase 'in me' in the chapters that are the summit of the teaching of the Fourth Gospel (Jn 13–17). While its writer no doubt knew some, at least, of Paul's Epistles, he was a man who was master of his own mind and, even if he borrowed from Paul at this point and was not drawing to its climax a doctrine common to all the Churches, he would not accept even Paul's phrase without assaying its truth. It is certain that by the end of the first century at latest the doctrine summed in the phrase 'in Christ' was universal in the Church.

Before pursuing the investigation of the use of the phrases further it is important to note that this book, like its predecessors, seeks to deal with the New Testament doctrine of the individual, and not of the Church. Yet in human life 'persons live on persons', and the individual and the society to which he belongs always involve each other. This truth finds its finest example in the organic interdependence of the Christian and the Church. None the less, here as elsewhere, the individual and the society may, for the convenience of study, be taken separately, so long as it is always remembered that in fact they do not exist separately, but are as interdependent as the convex and concave of a curve. When Paul writes 'to the saints and faithful brethren *in Christ* at Colossæ', he means 'to the church in Colossæ' (Col 1^2; cf. Eph 1^1, 6^{21}), providing a definition of the 'church', to be put alongside 'the body of Christ', 'a temple of God', 'a spiritual house', 'a holy priesthood', and, in effect, 'the bride of Christ' and 'the vine' (1 Co 12^{27}, 3^{16}; 1 P 2^5; Eph 5^{25}; Jn 15^1). Paul uses the phrase 'the church(es) . . . *in Christ*' four times (Gal 1^{22}; 1 Th 1^1, 2^{14}; 2 Th 1^1) and calls the Church 'a holy temple *in the Lord*' (Eph 2^{21}). The phrases do not happen to occur with the other definitions of the Church, and, indeed, it would not be natural to add 'in Christ' to all of them—for instance, to 'the body of Christ'. Again, in 1 Co 12^{12-7}, the several members, such as the ear and hand, are not '*in* the body' but 'of (*ek*) the body'. There is no Scriptural warrant for claiming that 'in Christ' means 'in the body of Christ' or 'in the church of Christ'. What the New Testament requires is that every individual Christian is 'a man *in Christ*' (2 Co 12^2; cf. Ro 16^7), and that the Christian society is 'a holy temple *in the Lord*' (Eph 2^{21}), both of them in what is sometimes called 'a mystical sense', and that therefore they are organically indivisible. For instance, in the Fourth Gospel Jesus says, both to the individual disciples and to the group, 'Abide in me' for 'I am the vine' (15^{4f}). There were eleven of them, yet they were already one in Him, though imperfectly (cf. 17^{21f}). This being always kept in mind, we may turn to a fuller list of the phrases where the New Testament writers use 'in Christ' and its synonyms to describe individual Christians.

Of the uses of the phrases in this way about thirty-five are

THE FELLOWSHIP OF GOD WITH MAN IN CHRIST 211

adverbial and forty adjectival. A few may be either (e.g. Ro 15⁷; 1 Co 15³¹; Col 1²; 1 P 5¹⁰). Under the adverbial use it is curious that 'rejoice (*chairein*) in Christ' does not occur, but the list of accompanying verbs is long and varied. For instance, the Christian 'speaks truth in Christ' (Ro 9¹), is 'approved in Christ' (Ro 16¹⁰), is 'sanctified in Christ Jesus' (1 Co 1⁴), 'falls asleep in Christ' (1 Co 15¹⁸), 'speaks in Christ' (2 Co 2¹⁷), 'has freedom in Christ Jesus' (Gal 2⁴), is 'justified in Christ' (Gal 2¹⁷), is 'faithful in Christ Jesus' (Eph 1¹), 'hopes' and 'believes in Christ' (Eph 1¹¹ᶠ), 'sits in the heavenly (places) in Christ Jesus' (Eph 2⁶), is 'created in Christ Jesus' (Eph 2¹⁰), 'boasts in Christ Jesus' (Ph 1²⁶), 'salutes every saint in Christ Jesus' (Ph 4²¹), 'commends and exhorts in (the) Lord Jesus Christ' (2 Th 3¹²). Paul 'begets' his converts 'in Christ Jesus' (1 Co 4¹⁵). To add one summarizing phrase, the Christian 'lives to God in Christ Jesus' (Ro 6¹¹). One Person enspheres another person! Such phrases as 'a bird lives in the air' and 'a fish lives in the sea' are not analagous for air and sea are not persons, yet they may help at one point—

> *Does the fish soar to find the ocean,*
> *The eagle plunge to find the air?*

As the original meaning of *pneuma* was 'air', it might have been expected that the customary phrase would have been 'in (the) Spirit',² but it was not the Spirit who became man and 'for our salvation came down from heaven'. However instinctively, the first Christians coined the strange phrase 'in Christ' just because the Son 'became man'. A true man lives '*in*' the Man—not

---

² The doctrine of the Spirit in His relation to man is, of course, another great example of the doctrine of fellowship, but this was examined in *The Bible Doctrine of Man*. It reaches its climax in the doctrine that every Christian 'receives' the Spirit and that the Spirit 'in-dwells' every Christian. Here it may be noted that it is at least doubtful whether the New Testament Christians habitually thought of themselves as men who lived 'in (the realm of) the Spirit'. The phrase 'in Spirit' is indeed common and 'in the Spirit', 'in Holy Spirit' and 'in the Holy Spirit' also occur, but, while the Greek preposition is *en*, as in 'in Christ', this is a chameleon word and often means 'with' or 'through' or 'by', as the English versions show (e.g. Ro 1²⁵; 1 Co 4²¹, 6², 14²¹). Among the thirty-five or forty texts where the phrases occur the only passages where the meaning *must* be 'in the realm of the Spirit' are those where John the Seer says 'I was in the Spirit' (e.g. Rev 1¹⁰), and these do not refer to the normal life of Christians. Paul does indeed say '*Ye* are not in flesh but in Spirit if so be that God's Spirit dwells in you' (Ro 8⁹), but this is exceptional and the context suggests that the phrase may be interpreted by 'according to (*kata*) Spirit' (v. 5). In the great majority of texts it is possible and even preferable to render by 'with' or 'through' or 'by'. It is far otherwise with the phrase 'in Christ'. The phrase 'in the Spirit' does not occur in the Old Testament.

'potentially', but in fact. One Person is the realm of another's life!

Of the forty examples of the adjectival use of the phrases only about a quarter are predicative—e.g. 'If any (man) *is in Christ* there is a new creation' (2 Co 5¹⁷). Sometimes the copulative verb, *einai* or *ginesthai* ('be' or 'become'), is expressed (1 Th 2¹⁴; Ro 16⁷; 1 Co 1³⁰; Gal 3¹⁴), but more often it is what the grammarians call 'understood'. Under the attributive uses it is possible to differentiate. First, certain Christian *experiences* are said to be 'in Christ'—e.g. 'redemption in Christ Jesus' (Ro 3²⁴), 'eternal life in Christ Jesus our Lord' (Ro 6²³), 'grace in Christ Jesus' (2 Ti 2¹), 'peace in Christ' (1 P 5¹⁴), 'faith in Christ Jesus' (Gal 3²⁶), 'tribulation and kingship and patience in Jesus' (Rev 1⁹). Next come phrases *where an experience is implied*—e.g. 'to him be glory in the Church and in Christ Jesus' (Eph 3²¹; cf. 1 P 5¹⁰), 'the gospel of life in Christ Jesus' (2 Ti 1¹), 'the prize of the upward calling of God in Christ Jesus' (Ph 3¹⁴), and 'my love be with you all in Christ Jesus' (1 Co 16²⁴). As with the adverbial uses these texts require that a Christian's life—or, in Peter's phrase, 'good way of life' (1 P 3¹⁶)—, both as it is now and as it is to be hereafter, is lived 'in Christ'. But there are also passages where the phrases do not describe a Christian's experiences and hopes but the *Christian himself*—e.g. 'my fellow-workers in Christ' (Ro 16³), 'all the saints in Christ Jesus' (Ph 1¹), 'the dead in Christ' (1 Th 4¹⁶), 'I know a man in Christ' (2 Co 12²), 'all one in Christ Jesus' (Gal 3²⁸), 'those in Christ Jesus' (Ro 8¹). No doubt an exigent grammarian would say that here the copulative verb is 'implied', and the English versions render the last text, for instance, by 'them *that are* in Christ Jesus', but probably the first Christians were as little aware of any hiatus as an Englishman is when he speaks of 'the man in the street'. Indeed, the nearest English analogy may perhaps be found in phrases like 'an *in*-land town', 'an *in*-door game', 'an *in*-ward sigh'. To say that the first Christians were '*in*-Christ men' would be justifiable. The strange phrase shows the uniqueness of the idea. No justice is done to it in the Apostles' and Nicene Creeds. Today it is so strange that, in spite of their familiarity with it in the New Testament, neither English Christians nor even their preachers have found it a place in their customary vocabulary. It has been seen that there are no true antecedents in the Old Testament and Apocrypha for the New Testament use of '*in (the) Lord*'. There *could be* no antecedents for '*in Christ*', as 'Christ' was for Christians a personal name (though not only this) and men knew no such person until Jesus came. 'In Christ' was a unique phrase, made to describe a unique experience. It is unique still.

So far it has been *assumed* that these phrases rightly belong to a chapter on *fellowship*. This assumption is justified on an examination of the long series of texts, or even of those that have been quoted. There are, indeed, two classes of exceptions. First, there are the passages where the teaching is not that the believer is 'in Christ', but that God is 'in Christ'. There is, however, a connexion between the two ideas, for 'God was in Christ reconciling the world unto Himself' and reconciliation is the renewal of fellowship (2 Co 5^{19}). Possibly two texts where the phrase is 'in *the* Christ' stand apart (1 Co 15^{22}; 2 Co 2^{14}). Second, there are the texts where 'all things' are said to be 'in Christ'. These will be discussed presently. While 'all *things*', of course, are not capable of fellowship, since fellowship is a function of *persons*, it will be found that fellowship has much to do with the phrase 'all things are in (Christ)'. Apart from these two kinds of exceptions, it will be found that, when the context is examined, every text where these phrases occur, involves the idea that the Christian lives in fellowship with Christ. A comment may be made about the concept '*life* in Christ' (Ro 6^{11}, 8^2; 2 Ti 3^{12}; 1 P 3^{16}; cf. Jn 1^4). This implies a *continuous* fellowship, and a continuous fellowship is sometimes conscious and sometimes subconscious. In a true home, for instance, there is continuous fellowship—conscious in the sharing of a meal or the keeping of birthdays, but subconscious when the father's mind is set on his 'job', the mother's on cooking a meal, the children's on their lessons. But, even when subconscious, the fellowship is strong and 'makes all the difference' —as appears if it is shattered. Fellowship is healthy when the conscious and subconscious feed each other. Similarly, the Christian's fellowship with Christ is conscious in prayer and worship, at any rate when these are what they ought to be and may be, but subconscious when, for instance, he is engrossed in a novel. Yet, since the fellowship is continuous, some passages in some novels will nauseate him. It is not possible here to examine the long series of passages in order to show how the contexts everywhere imply fellowship, but a number of the terms used, *even if taken in isolation*, have no meaning apart from it. For instance, 'grace' and 'love' and 'blessing' and 'faith' and 'peace', for which texts have been quoted, are all functions of fellowship, as are 'kindliness' (Eph 2^7) and 'consolation' (Ph 2^1) and 'salvation' (1 Ti 2^{10}).

Some of the texts show that the Christians, being in fellowship with Christ, were thereby in fellowship with each other. This leads to the doctrine of the Church, but, as already noted, as far as possible this book keeps to the doctrine of the individual. Yet there is an interpretation of the phrases under discussion which, applying them to baptism, thereby refers them to the Church, and this needs to be noticed. It is said that a person is 'in Christ' if he has been 'incorporated into the body of Christ'—that is, into the Church—by baptism. This leads to two passages about baptism where 'in Christ Jesus' and 'in Christ' occur. In one Paul writes 'For ye are all sons of God through faith in Christ Jesus, for as many (of you) as were baptized clothed yourselves with Christ' (Gal 3^{27}). Here, as usual, Paul is thinking of believers' baptism, as the term 'faith' shows, and it is not a question of 'baptism *or* fellowship', but of 'fellowship *and* baptism'. As with every genuine symbol, the symbol of baptism expresses and enhances and nourishes the experience. It is the same with the second passage (Col 2 $^{9\text{-}12}$). Here Paul begins with the fontal truth that 'the fulness of the Godhead makes its home in (Christ) bodily' and then goes on to say two or perhaps three times that Christians are 'in Christ'. 'In baptism' Christians were 'buried with (Christ), in whom (or, in which) they were also raised with (him) *through faith* in (of) the in-working of God who raised (Christ) from (the dead)'. Paul will not omit 'faith'. The claim that for Paul baptism is an element in the full exposition of 'in Christ' and its fellow-phrases is to be maintained, even though the connexion is only explicit twice, so long as it is remembered that it is individual believers' baptism that he has in mind. It could not be maintained if the experience and the symbol fell asunder. This happened in the early Middle Ages, for instance, when, the king of a northern tribe having accepted Christianity, his subjects were baptized *en masse*. The rite had ceased to be a true symbol and had sunk into a form. Again, even if the baptism of infants goes back to New Testament times, Paul could not have written the two texts about infants. He would have had to omit 'faith', for with him 'faith' and 'grace' are the two sides of the *conscious* and *willing* fellowship of Christians with Christ. As to the whole series of texts under 'in Christ' and its parallel phrases, it is impossible to apply them to infants. This is so whatever interpretation is given to infant baptism, for Paul speaks of those who *are* in conscious and willing fellowship with Christ, not of those who *will be*.

Four longer passages may be chosen to illustrate less sporadically what Paul means by 'in Christ'. The eighth chapter of Romans is one of these. It begins with 'those *in Christ Jesus*' and ends with 'the love of God *in Christ Jesus* our Lord' (Ro $8^{1,\ 39}$). 'We are in Christ' and 'God is in Christ' are the key to the chapter. Four principal points may be briefly noted. First, the man 'in Christ', being rid of the slavery of sin, is free and able to do what he ought to do and be what he ought to be (vv. 2–4). When two *men* are in fellowship and one gets all his own way, the other grows weak; but when Christ and a man are in fellowship, the man grows strong. Next, the Apostle relates the doctrine to the Spirit (vv. 9–17). Here falls the classical text for the doctrine of the Christian's assurance of sonship (vv. 15f), which is the climax of the doctrine of fellowship. Third, there is a description of salvation 'by hope' (vv. 18–30). The Christian's 'adoption' is to be completed by 'the redemption of (his) body' (v. 23). Elsewhere Paul says that this will happen at the Parousia (e.g. 1 Co 15^{52}). But it is through the body that man is linked with the universe of *things*. Paul, therefore, connects 'the sufferings of this present time' with the 'groaning and travailing in pain' of 'the whole creation' (vv. 18–22). His doctrine here will be gathered under a passage in Colossians, but it may be noted in passing that 'travail' is always a symbol of agony *and* hope (cf. Jn 16^{21f}). Fourth, there is *Quis separabit?* (vv. 31–9). So long as a Christian is faithful to his fellowship with Christ, nothing can 'separate (him) from the love of God in Christ Jesus our Lord'. As well try to break the bond of gravitation! The whole chapter expounds the phrase 'those in Christ Jesus' with which it opens.

The second passage (Eph $1^{3\text{-}14}$) is a compressed but triumphant account of God's 'blessings . . . *in Christ*'. It begins with the election unto holiness 'before the foundation of the world' of those who 'have their redemption *in Christ*', and it ends with 'the seal of the Spirit' set on those who 'hope *in Christ*', assuring them that in 'the fulness of the times' they will so live as to glorify God for ever. The idea '*God* is in Christ' occurs three times (vv. 6, 9, 11), and the idea '*We* are in Christ' five times (vv. 3, 4, 7, 12, 13). The phrase 'to sum up' or 'recapitulate all things in Christ' (v. 10) will be taken with a parallel text in Colossians. In the third long passage (Eph 2) Paul celebrates the consequences of what God 'wrought *in Christ*' for 'the church which is his body' (Eph 1[20, 22]). The whole chapter falls under the contrast between 'what you used to be' and 'what you are'. The phrase 'in Christ Jesus' or an equivalent occurs seven times and integrates the whole passage. Christians 'sit with (God) in the heavenly (places) *in Christ Jesus*' (v. 6); they are God's 'work-of-art created *in Christ Jesus*' (v. 10); '*in Christ Jesus*' the 'alienated' Gentiles are 'brought nigh' both to God and to their fellow-citizens the Jews (vv. 12f); Christ has 'created *in himself* of the twain one new man (kind)' (v. 15); '*in him*' the 'several buildings' of the one Temple, 'fitly framed together, grow into a holy sanctuary *in the Lord, in whom* ye also are builded together into a habitation of God in (the) Spirit' (vv. 21f).

The fourth passage (Col 1[9-23]) has much in common with the two from Ephesians. It belongs to a letter addressed to the 'holy and faithful brethren *in Christ*' at Colossæ, who are further described under the phrase '*in whom* we have our redemption, the forgiveness of our sins'—i.e. our 'reconciliation'—(Col 1[2, 14]; cf. Eph 1[1, 7]). The church, the society of the reconciled, is 'the body' of Christ (Col 1[18]; cf. Eph 1[22])—and so on. The *differentia* of the passage is that in it Paul states more fully than elsewhere his doctrine of 'the reconciliation of *all things*'—i.e. of the universe —to God (vv. 15–20). It involves his theodicy. With the help of other passages this may be outlined. The starting-point of the Apostle's thought is found in the phrases 'the first-born of all creation' and 'the whole fulness (of God) was pleased to dwell *in him*' (vv. 15, 19). Christ is 'before' the universe, and 'in him', 'through him' and 'unto him' it was 'created'. This is the *fons et origo* of Paul's theodicy. The next element in it is expressed in Ro 8[20-2]. Here Paul universalizes a text in Genesis (3[16-18]). When man sinned God brought the reluctant universe 'into subjection to vanity' in order that, sharing in man's 'bondage', it might one day share in 'the liberty of the glory of the children of God' (Ro 8[20-2]). Paul speaks here as though the universe of things were alive, for it 'groans and travails', and as though it has a will of its own, for it passes from an enforced bondage to freedom! The ruling idea is that man and his universe go together. Even in the epoch of sin, however, the universe 'holds together *in (Christ)*'. From its creation to its

THE FELLOWSHIP OF GOD WITH MAN IN CHRIST 217

'restitution' (Ac 3²¹) He is master of the situation. He cannot tolerate sin and pain and confusion in His universe, and, if so cold a word may be allowed, He has His plan for its redemption. The plan begins with the 'reconciliation' *of man* to God—that is, with the renewal of their fellowship—even though this costs the Cross. When Christ has completed this renewal through the Spirit in the Church, He will redeem man's body and with it the universe of things to which the body belongs. Apparently this will be by fiat 'in a moment' when 'the trumpet sounds' (1 Co 15⁵²). Once more God 'will speak—and it is done' (Ps 30⁹). While in the creation man is the Omega, in the re-creation he is the Alpha. The sequence of ideas is—'If any one is *in Christ*, there is a new creation', 'God was *in Christ*, reconciling (the) world (*kosmos*) unto himself', 'We beseech (you) on behalf of Christ, Be ye reconciled to God' (2 Co 5¹⁷, ¹⁹ᶠ). Similarly, the statement that it is God's 'purpose *in* (*Christ*)' to 'recapitulate all things *in Christ*' is a splendid interlude in a passage that begins with the *largesse* of God's 'grace' to Christians '*in the Beloved*' and resumes this theme with '*in him, in whom* also we were made a heritage' (Eph 1⁶⁻¹¹). So too it is on the destruction of 'the last enemy', death, by the resurrection of all '*in Christ*' that 'the end comes', and the Son, who has all the while been Master of the universe, restores it perfected to God (1 Co 15²²⁻⁶). Paul's theodicy is consistent. It would not be pertinent here to discuss the difficulties of the astounding doctrine that the fate of the universe depends upon the redemption of man. The relevant point is that for Paul the healing of the breach that sin has made in the fellowship of God with man is the 'one thing needful' for the perfecting of an imperfect universe. All else is sequel and complement. When mankind is '*in Christ*', 'all things' will once more be 'very good' (Gn 1³¹).

> *The world's great age begins anew,*
> *The golden years return.*

'John', used here for the writer or writers of the Fourth Gospel and the Johannine Epistles, has the same doctrine as Paul but with a different emphasis, and this shows itself in a difference of terminology. For instance, where Paul says 'God is in Christ', John has 'I am in the *Father* and the *Father* in me'; where Paul speaks of Christians as 'in Christ' and of Christ as 'in' Christians, John has 'Ye in me and I in you', meaning 'the *Son*' by 'I'; Paul uses 'in Christ' as an adverb with many verbs, but John has one dominant verb, 'abide (*menein*)', using it (in several ways) forty times in the Gospel and twenty-six in the first two Epistles.[3]

In the Fourth Gospel the relevant passages, as would be expected, almost all fall in the chapters whose main subject is 'Christ and His Own' (Jn 13–17). The few earlier texts are scattered. They illustrate two words put together in the Prologue —'*In* (the Word) was *life*, and the life was the *light* of men' (1⁴). Under 'life' there is the text, 'He that eateth my flesh and drinketh my blood *abideth in me and I in him*'—for 'life' has its origin in the Father and passes through the Son to the believer (6⁵⁶). The fontal text under 'light' is 'I am the light of the world' (8¹², 9⁵). In the Bible 'light' does not denote the 'dry light of reason', but the 'truth' by which men *live*. There 'light' is always 'light *to use in living*'—as men use the light of the sun in living. 'I am the light of the world' implies invitation as well as illumination. Just as the sun invites the eye to use its light, Jesus invites men to use His—that is, He invites men to share in the fellowship of 'life'. Most of His hearers shut their eyes, preferring darkness, but some, 'doing the *truth*', came 'to the light that (their) works might be made manifest that they have been wrought *in God*' (3²¹). As Jesus said, 'If ye *abide in* my word, ye shall know the truth, and the truth shall emancipate you' (8³¹f). There is only one more text in the chapters of Rejection (5–12). It occurs in one of the passages where Jesus appeals to His 'works'—saying in effect, 'Are they not alight with God?'—and uses for the first time the phrase 'the Father is *in* me, and I *in* the Father' (10³⁷f). If, seeing His 'works' men acknowledge that 'the Father hath sent' Him (10³⁶), they will go on to 'know and understand' what this means—that the Father is *in* Him and He *in* the Father.

In the Upper Room the phrases under discussion do not occur till Judas, who 'loves darkness rather than light', has gone out into the night (Jn 13³⁰). Jesus had washed his feet in vain. The first passage where the phrases occur (14¹⁰⁻²⁰) begins with Philip's question, asked on behalf of all, 'Lord, shew us the Father and it sufficeth us' (v. 10). The passage implies that the disciples do not

---

[3] With one doubtful exception (Jn 9²²) John uses 'Christ' in two ways: (*a*) In the controversy with the Jews under the question 'Is (the Baptist or) this Jesus *the* Christ?' (cf. Jn 20³¹), and (*b*) in the phrase 'Jesus Christ'. When this is used—even in John 17³ and 1 John 1³, 2¹—the writer is thinking of what Jesus was and did when He was 'in the flesh' (cf. 1 Jn 4²). He never uses 'Christ', as Paul did, as the *personal* name of the *Risen* Lord.

yet know that 'I am *in* the Father and the Father *in* me' but believe 'for the very works' sake' that the Father 'abides *in* (the Son)'—that is, believe that God 'sent' Jesus and that He 'came forth from God' (17⁸, 16³⁰). It is 'in that day'—when 'the Spirit of truth' has come and, 'abiding with' them, is '*in*' them—that they will go on to 'know that I am *in* my Father and ye *in* me and I *in* you' (14¹⁷⁻²⁰).

Yet there had long been a fellowship between Jesus and His disciples, even though they had not understood its implications. Its issue, typified by the Feet-washing, is that they are 'already clean' (15³; cf. 13¹⁰). The word 'abide' (*menein*) chimes again and again. The exact meaning of the verb is 'to remain where one is' and not 'to remain where one has been' (e.g. in 1³²f, 2¹²; Lk 9⁴, 24²⁹), though the latter idea may be involved as well (e.g. Jn 1³⁹f, 11⁶, 21²²). The Eleven are 'branches' whom the Husbandman has 'cleansed' (15²), and who will remain 'clean' if from now onward they 'abide in' the Vine. A tree's branches are 'in' it in the sense that they share its *life*. When *persons* are compared to branches, the sharing is by fellowship, and this means that it depends upon the continuity of mutual consent. In true disciples' fellowship with Jesus they love Him so much that they let Him have all His own way and so 'abide *in* (his) love' (15¹⁰), they '*in*' Him and He '*in*' them (vv. 4f). If 'His words abide *in*' them, this is a guarantee that when they pray they will not ask amiss but will 'bear much fruit' (vv. 7f). This account of fellowship expounds what is meant by the Synoptic and Pauline phrase 'the new covenant *in* my blood', for, while the Eleven had long been in fellowship in Jesus, this fellowship had been incomplete. It is to be completed 'now' through the Cross (cf. 12³¹). The two verses that close the passage about the Vine compare the Father's 'love' for the Son and the Son's 'love' for the disciples. The verses delineate a dual reciprocity in 'love'—between the Father and the Son, and between the Son and the disciples—i.e. there is unity through fellowship between the Father and the Son, and there is unity through fellowship between the Son and the disciples, for love is the bond of fellowship. As the Son shows that He 'abides' in the Father's love for him by 'keeping the Father's commandments', so the disciples will show that they 'abide' in the Son's love for them by 'keeping the Son's commandments'. In both fellowships love shows itself in complete and willing obedience.

At this point three marks of the whole discourse may be noted. First, while John does not use the word 'church' except in one Epistle (3 Jn 6, 9f), the *idea* of the Church is present throughout the passage, notably in the parable of the Vine. As everywhere in the New Testament, the individual Christian and the society of Christians imply and complement each other. Second, the same ideas, expressed in the same phrases, recur throughout the chapters. Yet, third, there is first an emphasis on one idea, then on another, and then on another. The first idea is summed in the phrase, 'These have believed that *Thou didst send me*'. This refers to the past. The second idea is epitomized in the phrase '*Abide in me*'. This refers to the present, and presupposes an experience that springs from 'believing'. Everything that Paul says under 'in Christ' is included in this one phrase. The third leading idea is central in Christ's prayer (ch. 17) and falls under the phrase '*that they may all be one, even as thou, Father, (art) in me, and I in thee, that they also may be in us*' (17^{21}; cf. v. 11). Occurring in a prayer, this refers to the future. It also elucidates the second phrase as the second elucidates the first. In so far as the prayer is answered in the Church, 'the world', which has so far rejected Christ, will come to follow the disciples' first step and 'believe' that God did 'send' Him—that is, the Church is to share 'the glory' of the Son's Mission (vv. 1f, 22f). Its unity, in so far as it is real, is like the unity between the Father and the Son—not, of course, at all points, for the unity of the Trinity is transcendent and unique—but at the point of fellowship. Indeed, to say that the fellowship of the Church, when 'perfected into one', is *like* the fellowship between the Father and the Son is inadequate; it is a kind of extension of that fellowship, as the phrase 'I in them and thou in me', for instance, shows (v. 23). The fellowship within the Godhead is to pervade the Church. To discuss the doctrine of the Church, however, does not fall under the present subject. Its members, each for himself, believe 'that thou didst send me' (vv. 8, 25). As complement and antecedent to this there are the declarations 'I manifested thy name' and 'made known unto them thy name' (vv. 6, 26). In the Bible to know a person's name is to know the person (v. 3). Persons only know each other by fellowship, and only know each other intimately by the fellowship of 'love'. The Son has taught and will teach His disciples to 'know' the Father 'that the *love* wherewith thou lovest me may be in them and (so) I in them' (v. 26). The meaning of the phrase 'to know God' has already been discussed. The two phrases 'I in them and they in me' and 'I in them and thou in me' are its exposition. In the prayer the adverbial use of 'in thee' and 'in me' finally falls away; even the phrase 'Abide in me' is absent; ultimately all is predicative—'Thou *art* in me', 'I *am* in thee', 'I *am* in them', 'They *are* in me', 'They *are* in thee'. This is the summit of the Bible doctrine of fellowship.

It will be seen that, though Paul and John use different phrases, their teaching is the same. Both speak of a fellowship that begins in time but is intrinsically eternal, for it is fellowship with God. Paul, however, writing to help churches that, like himself, are in the thick of history, nowhere integrates the whole doctrine but uses the phrase 'in Christ' as occasion requires. The writer of the Fourth Gospel, writing apparently in old age and 'looking before and after', does just this. Indeed, the chief subject of the final discourse in this Gospel is to expound the full meaning of a verse in the prologue—'As many as received him, to them he gave the right to become *children of God*' (Jn 1[12]). Under this phrase John joins hands with Paul.

The phrases under discussion are not used in the Second and Third Epistles of John, though they are implied (2 Jn 3f, 6, 9; 3 Jn 3f). The passages in the First Epistle are almost all adverbial, falling under the phrases 'abide in him' and its corollary 'walk (*peripatein*) in him'—that is, the writer here approximates to the Pauline emphasis on the present and shows what the doctrine means for Christians *now*—though, again like Paul, he does not omit the past and future. The phrase 'abide in him' occurs to mean 'abide in Christ' or 'in the Son' (e.g. 1 Jn 2[5f], 3[5f]); once the phrase is 'in the Son and in the Father' (2[24]); 'abide in God' is also found (4[12f, 15f]); in yet another text the meaning may either be 'in the Son' or 'in God' (3[24]). A man who so 'abides' will '*walk* even as (Christ) walked' (2[6])—that is, he will 'walk in the light as God is in the light' (1[7]) for he 'abides in the light' (2[10]). The Second and Third Epistles use the alternatives, 'to walk in the *truth*' (2 Jn 4; 3 Jn 3f) and 'in his commandments' or 'teaching' (2 Jn 6, 9). Again, since 'God is *love*', to 'abide in God' is to 'abide in love' (1 Jn 3[16]). This means that the believer abides in the love of God for him, not that he abides in his love for God (cf. v. 19). The parallel sometimes suggested with the English phrase 'he is in love' is no true parallel for this means that a man is engrossed in his own love for another, not in another's love for him. 'Eternal *life*' too is 'in the Son of God' (5¹¹). This Epistle also makes explicit a doctrine of the *Spirit* that is implicit both in Paul and the Fourth Gospel—'Hereby we know that we abide in (God), and he in us, because he hath given us of his Spirit' (4¹³; cf. 3²⁴). The range of the phrases is the whole of the inward and outward life of the Christian. Finally, at the beginning of the First Epistle to 'walk *in* the light' is to 'have *fellowship*' with God and with one another (1 Jn 1⁵⁻⁷); at its end 'to *know* him that is true' is to 'be *in* him that is true, *in* his Son Jesus Christ' (5²⁰). This Epistle, therefore, explicitly identifies the three expressions discussed at length in this chapter—'fellowship', 'to know God', and 'to be in Christ'.

The doctrine of fellowship has not always been given its due place in systems of Christian theology. A Methodist writer may be allowed to say that John Wesley restored it to its New Testament place in theology and that Charles Wesley spread it abroad in song. The latter even wrote a few controversial hymns (!) about it, for when the early Methodists claimed, under their doctrine of 'Assurance', that they '*knew* him whom they had believed', they were dubbed 'enthusiasts' and challenged with the question: '*How* do you know?' Charles Wesley replied with such lines as these:

> *For us who have our sight,*
> *Ye fain would judges be,*
> *And make us think we have no light*
> *Because you cannot see,*

and

> *But us you never can persuade*
> *That honey is not sweet.*

This means that he appealed to a self-authenticating experience. Today some might call it 'existential'. There are now a number of writers who maintain that ultimately there is only one ground for believing in a personal God, speaking of a 'Divine encounter' in which Person meets and challenges person. This is an appeal to experience and not to argument. All *arguments* for the existence of God, they claim, are ancillary at best and only teach men *about* Him. When God meets a man, it is a self-authenticating experience—i.e. the man knows *that God is* because *he knows God*. The appeal is not to what is called the 'merely subjective', for, like every other instance of fellowship, it posits the *reality* of two 'subjects' who are each other's '*objects*'. When these writers are told that their claim has no value for those who have no such experience, they say two things—first, 'If you say that this certainty is an illusion, you must give some more likely account of the perennial phenomenon that there are many men who claim to "know" God'; and second, 'Are you quite sure that you have never encountered God?' Even in the Old Testament men know that there is a God because, in differing ways and degrees, they are aware of Him. But in the New Testament there is something more. There is the belief that Christians know *Christ* and thereby know God, or, better, that they know 'God in Christ'. *This* belief distinguishes Christians from other theists. It is true that in the New Testament there is a historical sequence—first, Jesus 'in the days of his flesh'; then, the Risen Christ; then, the gift of the Spirit; finally the conviction that through the Spirit the Christian knows God in Christ. But in the New Testament there is no argumentative answer to the question: 'On what grounds do you identify the unseen Person whom you say you know with the Jesus that some saw after the Resurrection?' Or, as theists who are not Christians might put it: 'We agree that you know God, but why bring in Christ?' In the New Testament there is only the answer: 'We know that we know Jesus Christ.' The early Christians argued *from* this conviction and rightly reached the doctrine of the Trinity, but they never argued *to* it. The existential experience precedes the doctrine.[4] The New Testament *differentia* is the assertion of a self-authenticating fellowship with *Christ*. While the early Christians believed that God confronts and challenges the sinner in judgement and in grace, for them His challenge was made in Christ and the emphasis is on grace rather than judgement—that is, on the 'good news'. '*Our* fellowship is with the Father *and* (this is so because it is) with his Son Jesus Christ' (1 Jn 1³).

---

[4] Similarly, there are young Christians today, who are suspicious of what they call 'academic theology', yet who say 'Jesus *is* our Friend'—that is, they know Him and He them. They usually add: 'He is our Lord.' But they have not yet faced the question that ensues: 'If the unseen Jesus is your Friend, and if He has been the Friend of so many people in so many centuries, who then is He?'

INDEX OF HEBREW, GREEK AND ENGLISH TERMS

(*References to cognates are usually included under those to principal terms*)

abide: 210, 218ff
accept: 146f, 153, 166
adokimos: 154, 168, 171
adoption: 31, 130, 176, 215
agape: 39, 52ff, 61, 65, 87, 92ff, 165f, 190, 197
agapetos: 158
agchisteuein: 45
'ahab: 11, 30ff, 53, 190
akouein: 182
alight: 118
'all things': 213, 216; see 'creation'
allagma: 42
almsgiving: 38f, 65, 190
altar: 43
'amad: 150, 156
anakainosis: 79
anger: 14f, 41, 43f, 69
anienai: 41, 67
anistanai: 181
antidikos: 116
antikeimenos: 107f, 116
aphienai: 40ff, 66
aphorme: 131
apistos: 163
Apocalyptic: 71f, 109
apodokimazein: 114, 154, 168
apotelein: 135
apothein: 154, 167f
apotithenai: 138
appeal: 48, 81ff
approve: 114f, 166
archegos: 75
'ashar: 29, 49
atrophy: 145, 150, 155, 157, 162, 164, 171, 182, 184
'azar: 43, 83

bachan: 100f, 105
bachar: 143ff, 152
baptism: 79, 128ff, 140, 214
bara': 26, 80
barak: 29, 49, 86
barunein: 155, 168
Beatitudes: 87f, 90
believers: 8, 56f, 60f, 62f, 67, 72f, 96, 98, 125f, 126ff, 131ff, 135ff, 161, 163f, 166f, 172, 175ff, 180, 185, 188f, 199, 201f, 204f, 211, 214, 215ff
berith: 193
blessedness: 5, 6, 49ff, 87, 89, 158
blessing: 28f, 48ff, 52, 86ff, 105, 106, 113, 152, 176, 213
body: 131, 132, 137f
boethein: 44, 83

called: 161f, 164, 174, 176, 180
chabar: 188
chaddesh: 26
chairein: 211
chamal: 25
chanan: 35
charis: 1, 5, 33ff, 57ff, 68, 87, 130, 197
charizesthai: 35, 60, 62, 67f
chasid: 13f, 17f, 20f, 39, 66
chastise: see 'discipline'
chazeq: 148, 155
chen: 6, 8ff, 33, 35, 39, 57, 65, 194
chesed: 6, 10ff, 14, 21, 32, 35, 37ff, 65
choice (God's): see 'elect'
'Christ in you': 209
Church: 58, 63, 120, 130, 210, 214, 216, 220
cleanse: 19, 24, 25, 27, 42, 127, 135
comfort: 5, 28, 47, 81ff
compassion: 14, 25, 27, 39f, 65f, 72
conversion: 127ff, 132, 136ff, 140
covenant: 9ff, 14, 19, 22, 24, 30, 32, 36f, 40, 52, 56, 77f, 144, 164, 178f, 180f, 193, 199, 219
crave: 131, 133f, 135ff
creation: 173, 181, 215ff
Creeds: 212
Cross: 119, 123, 200, 217, 219

daimon: 51
death: 18, 217
deesis: 37
dektos: 153, 166
deleazein: 135
design (God's): 172ff, 176, 177ff, 180, 182, 186
desire: 131
determinism: 150, 177
Devil: see 'Satan'
devout: see *chasid, hosios, eulabes, eusebes*
diabolos: 107ff, 116f
diaterein: 156, 169f, 181
diatheke: 193
diatithenai: 156
didonai: 156
dikaiosune: 38, 39, 66
dikaioun: 139
diligence: 166
discipline: 7, 102, 103ff, 155f, 191
dokimazein: 105ff, 111, 113ff, 115, 135, 168, 171
dross: 101, 155
dull: 148f
dunatos: 152

INDEX OF TERMS

echthros: 116
egeirein: 156, 169f, 181
eidenai: 196, 197ff, 203, 204
einai: 212
eirene: 52, 53, 89ff
ekduesthai: 138
eklegein, eklektos: 152f, 158ff, 165f, 176f
elect, election: 7, 16, 30ff, 35, 64, 65, 75, 143ff, 151ff, 157ff, 161ff, 170, 172, 186, 201f
eleos: 6, 10, 14f, 33, 35ff, 38, 39, 46, 64ff
encounter: 222f
enduesthai: 138
enkainizein: 26, 79f
enthumeisthai: 46
entole: 193
epangelein: 178f
epiboulos: 107f
epiginoskein: 171, 196, 197f, 200f, 204
epikataratos: 158
epistasthai: 196
epithumia: 131, 133ff
eros: 52, 91, 98
etazein: 105f, 113
euarestos: 158f, 166
eucharistein: 61
eudaimonia: 51, 89
eudokein: 153f, 158, 166
eulabes: 124
eulogein: 49f, 86f
eulogetos: 158
eusebes: 124
exairein: 45, 69, 181
exelkein: 135
exilaskesthai: 41, 68
existential: 222f
exoudenein: 154
exousia: 202
exouthenein: 168

faith: see 'believers'
faithfulness: 11, 144f, 152, 164
farewells: 58, 59f, 62, 90
favour: 8, 9f, 33ff, 57f, 64, 146
fear: 16
fellowship: 7, 16, 24, 40, 56f, 61, 67f, 187ff, 213ff
flesh: 131ff, 136ff, 218
foreknow: 173ff, 180, 185
foreordain: 173ff, 176, 184f
forgiveness: 5, 6, 15f, 23, 24, 29, 40ff, 43f, 63, 65, 66ff, 128, 135
freedom: 142ff, 148, 150f, 152, 157, 164, 167, 170, 175, 176f, 179, 183f, 186, 215
friendship: 91f, 187, 190ff, 196, 204

general grace: 124, 126
gennan: 130
Gentiles: 11, 23, 36, 38, 55, 71, 73, 85f, 124f, 126, 145, 162, 169, 170ff, 174, 179, 181f, 184, 186, 198, 199

gerundive: 158ff, 166
ginesthai: 212
ginoskein: 196, 197ff, 200f, 203, 204
go'el: 21f, 41, 45, 69f, 85
good pleasure: 146f, 153f, 159, 166f, 176, 199
grace: 1, 5, 7, 8f, 34, 56, 57ff, 90f, 111, 122, 123, 124ff, 187, 199, 213, 214, 217 223

habit: 171
hagios: 39, 66, 164f
hairein: 152
happiness: 28f, 49, 50f, 87ff
harden: 27, 148, 149, 155, 169, 182, 184
hate: 32
heaven: 116
hell: 115, 143
help: 28, 46f, 81ff, 93
hilaschesthai: 40ff, 68f
histanai: 156
hithhallek: 158f
holiness: 5, 6, 95, 122, 144
holos: 130
holy: 26f, 95
homilia: 188
horizein: 175
hosios: 13, 37, 39, 66, 153
hygiainein: 52
hypakouein: 182
hyperoran: 154, 182
hypertrophy: 150

ignorance: 109f, 139, 169, 171, 175
'in Christ': 2, 7, 57, 188, 205ff
'in God': 205ff
'in Jesus': 208f
'in the Lord': 205ff
individual: 18, 26, 154, 156, 157, 178, 179f, 183f, 186 195f, 197, 210ff, 220

JHVH: 2
justification: 5, 6, 60, 139, 176

kabed: 148, 155
kapporeth: 42, 43, 68
katharos: 42, 130
keli: 183
kerugma: 5, 73, 201
kipper: 16, 19f, 40, 41f
kletos: 164f
'know' (God): 7, 24, 78, 171, 187f, 192ff, 220
koinonia: 7, 188ff
kosmos: 77, 118, 217
krisis: 151f
ktisis: 26, 80f, 128

INDEX OF TERMS

lipainein: 155, 168
logizesthai: 129, 138
long-suffering: 184f
love: 5, 6, 30ff, 50, 52ff, 56, 59, 90, 91ff, 187, 190, 197, 201, 204, 213, 219ff
luein: 40, 41, 45f
lust: 133f
lutroun: 42, 44f, 69ff

ma'as: 147f, 154f, 167f
makarios: 49, 50f, 87ff
mastix: 110, 119
menein: 218f
mercy: 5, 6, 10, 13f, 26, 36ff, 43, 59, 64ff, 68, 186, 194
merit: 37
metanoein: 46
miqra: 164
miracle faith: 72f, 75
misein: 154
mizbeach: 43n.
morphe: 79

nacham: 27f, 46ff
nasa': 15, 40f
nasah: 100, 104, 112
nathan: 151, 156f
natzal: 20f, 45
nekroun: 138
'new birth': 24, 77ff, 130, 131
'new creation': 5, 6, 24ff, 48, 79f, 128ff, 131, 140
nouthetein: 109, 119, 120f

oiktirmos: 14, 39f, 65f
olive: 186
opportunity: 157, 162, 168f, 182, 185
original sin: 139
over-rule: 109, 156, 170, 186

pachunein: 155, 168
padah: 21, 41, 44f, 69
paideuein: 109f, 111, 119f, 121f
paradidonai: 156, 170
parakalein: 5, 6, 27, 46ff, 81ff
parakletos: 81, 84f, 158
paramuthein: 85
Patriarchs: 143, 180
peace: 5, 6, 20, 29f, 51f, 59, 89f, 213
peculiar: 144
peirazein: 104f, 111ff, 117, 135
peripatein: 221
phaidesthai: 25
Pharaoh: 148f, 150, 156, 172, 178, 181ff
Pharisees: 112, 125, 157, 160, 177, 191
phaulesthai: 154
philia: 52f, 54, 91f, 188, 190f
pistos: 164, 166
pity: 5, 9, 14f, 25, 64f
pleonexia: 134
pneuma: 79, 211

poiema: 80
poneros: 117
poor: 12f, 37f
poroun: 169
potter: 142f, 151, 181ff
praxis: 132
predestination: 159, 175f, 180
pre-incarnate Christ: 126
prevenient: 61, 124, 126
proginoskein: 175
pro-orizein: 175
propitiation: 16, 40, 41f, 43, 44
proschein: 25
prosdechesthai: 40, 153, 166
protithenai: 172f, 176
prove: 100
punishment: 16, 17, 101, 103, 110f, 122, 147, 149, 193
purge: 19f, 24, 42, 145
purify: 19, 101
puroun: 106f, 111, 115, 167

qara': 164
qasheh: 148, 155
qodesh: 164
qum: 150, 156, 181

rabdos: 110, 119
rachamim: 14, 35, 39f
rainein: 25
ransom: 21, 69
rantizein: 79
ratzah: 146f, 153
rea': 191
reconciliation: 5, 6
reconsider: 46, 81
refine: 19
rejection: 147f, 149ff, 154f, 164, 167ff, 175, 178ff, 218
remnant: 145, 173, 183f
repentance: 15, 27f, 31f, 38, 40, 46, 66f, 75, 143, 149
reprobate: 148, 157, 171f
resurrection: 18, 25
retribution: 103, 110, 147, 168, 199f
rhema: 182
righteousness: 11f, 14, 17, 31f, 36, 38ff, 51, 122, 125, 141, 143f, 180ff
'righteousness in sinners': 7, 124, 140
rod: 103f, 110, 119f, 121
ruach: 25f, 79
rue: 27, 46ff
ruesthai: 44, 45, 69

saint: 13, 20, 90
salach: 15f, 40f, 68
salutations: 58, 59f, 62, 65, 90, 207
sarx: see 'flesh'
Satan (and Devil): 7, 90, 102f, 107ff, 112f, 115ff, 121, 123, 131

INDEX OF TERMS

save, salvation: 5, 6, 16ff, 44ff, 56, 64, 69ff, 89, 147, 160ff, 166f, 175, 177, 214, 215
Saviour: 76f
scourge: see 'whip'
sebomenos: 124
segullah: 144
select: 152, 160, 163
shalom: 29f, 51f, 89
shamen: 149f, 155
shebet: 103f, 110, 119
Shekinah: 43
sig: 154
sin: 1, 7, 8, 18ff, 25f, 31f, 36, 57, 66, 90, 124ff, 170ff
sin in believers: 7, 126ff
skandalon: 163
skeuos: 183
skleros: 155, 168f
sklerotrachelos: 155, 168f
soma: see 'body'
sophia: 191
sovereignty (of God): 141ff, 149, 150f, 157, 162, 167, 170, 177, 179, 183, 186
sozein: 44f, 51f, 71ff
Spirit: 19, 20, 22, 25ff, 58ff, 62f, 67, 78ff, 84f, 89, 90f, 93, 95f, 117, 118, 126, 130, 136f, 179, 188f, 200, 202, 203f, 211, 215, 219, 222f
spirit, evil: 102f, 107, 112, 199
stereoun: 155, 168
stiff-necked: 148, 149, 155f, 168f
stone: 161, 163f
stumbling-block: 163
suntheke: 193
supplication: 9, 37

tahor: 39
tassein: 175
techinnah: 9, 37
temptation: 7, 100ff, 131, 132, 134f
terein: 170

test: 100ff, 171
thanks: 35, 57, 61
thlipsis: 114
thusiasterion: 43n.
tithenai: 176
tob: 152
tom: 39
travail: 215
trial: 7, 100ff
truth: 7
tuphloun: 169
tzaraph: 100, 101, 106f

universalism: 14, 23, 32, 38, 54, 56f, 60, 86, 93, 186; also see 'Gentiles'
utensil: 183

veil: 169
vessel: 183f
vine: 210, 219f

walk: 159, 193, 196, 221f
water: 25
weakness: 131ff, 138, 139, 176f
well-pleasing: 158f
whip: 110, 119f, 121, 123
wisdom: 30, 32, 34, 50, 110f, 152, 171, 188, 197
woes: 87
works: 62
wrath: 38, 44, 55, 74, 171, 184f

xenos: 164

yadaʿ: 192, 197
yakach: 103
yasar: 103f, 109f, 119
yashaʿ: 16ff, 44
yashar: 39

zaqaq: 19
zaraq: 25

INDEX OF TEXTS
THE OLD TESTAMENT

Genesis
1...80
1^1...80
1^{1f}...26
1^{27}...139
1^{28}...49
3$^{16-18}$...216
4^1...194
5...173
5^{22}...148, 196
5^{24}...148
6^3...196
6^{6f}...27
6^8...33
6^9...148
8^{20}...206
9$^{8-17}$...11
9^{20}...11
11...173
12...143
12^{21}...9
14...148
14^{20}...49
15^6...143, 205, 206
15^{15}...29
17^1...143
17^{19}...173
18^{19}...192
18^{26}...41
19^{19}...35, 38
21^{23}...10, 38
22^1...100
22^7...53
23^{16}...105
24^{40}...148
24^{64}...118
24^{67}...53
25^{23}...173
26^{31}...52
27^{38}...49
28$^{11-22}$...173
29^6...52
30^{27}...9, 33
32^{20}...40, 41
33^{10}...146
33^{11}...36
37^4...53
38^8...181
39^{21}...12
40^{21}...16
42^{15f}...100
43^{27}...52
47^{25}...33
48^5...148
48^{16}...21

Exodus
2^6...25
3^8...45
3^{19}...148
3^{21}...33
4^{18}...29
4^{21}...148
4^{22}...31
5^2...192
7^3...183
7^{14}...155
8^{15}...148, 155
8^{32}...155
8^{33}...148
9^{12}...149
9^{16}...156, 181
9^{16f}...150
9^{34}...148
9^{35}...148
10^1...148
10^{17}...15, 40
11^3...33
12^{22}...78
12^{27}...45
13^{13}...21
14^8...149
15^2...16
15^{13}...12
16$^{1-13}$...10
16^4...100
17$^{1-7}$...100
19^6...164
20^6...11
20^8...21
20^{20}...100
21^8...70
21^{19f}...110
21^{30}...42
24^8...78
25^{37}...42
28^{19}...39
29$^{33, 36}$...42
29^{37}...42
30^{10}...42
30^{12}...42
31$^{1-9}$...10
32^9...148
32$^{12-14}$...27
32^{32}...15, 41
32^{32f}...26
33^3...148, 155
33^5...155
33^{10}...33
33^{11}...191, 196
33^{12}...194

33$^{12-17}$...9, 195
33$^{12-23}$...192
33$^{12-28}$...194
33^{13}...194
33^{16}...194
33^{17}...194
33^{19}...14, 181
33$^{20-3}$...191
34^6...9, 10, 15, 36, 39
34^7...15
34^9...40, 148
34^{10}...10
34^{20}...45

Leviticus
1^3...146
4^{20}...40
5^1...15
6^2...188
7^{18}...146
14$^{4-7}$...20
16^2...42
16^{13}...42
16^{14}...42
16^{15}...42
16^{22}...15
19^{18}...53, 54
25^9...42
25^{27ff}...21
25^{35}...45
26^{15}...148
26^{43}...154
26^{43f}...148

Numbers
3$^{46-51}$...21
5^8...42
6^{25}...9
6^{26}...29
11^{29}...25
13^{20}...149
14^{11ff}...16
14^{19}...40
14^{20}...15
14^{26}...100
14^{31}...147
15^{25}...40
21^3...151
21^{34}...151
22^{22}...102, 107
22^{32}...107
30$^{6-18}$...40
35...45
35^{31f}...42
36...45

INDEX OF TEXTS

Deuteronomy
2^{24}...151
2^{30}...149
3^{23}...9
4^{31}...14
4^{31-40}...144
4^{34}...104
4^{37}...32, 53, 143
6^{5}...53, 54
6^{10ff}...149
6^{16}...100
6^{19}...169
6^{25}...38
7^{2}...36, 151
7^{6-11}...144
7^{7-11}...32
7^{8}...44
7^{9-12}...11
7^{14}...49
7^{19}...104
8^{2}...100
8^{5}...103
8^{16}...100
9^{6}...155
9^{9}...40
9^{13}...155
10^{12-22}...143, 144
10^{15}...164
11^{28}...192
12^{29f}...151
13^{5}...100
13^{6-11}...151
13^{17}...14
15^{4-18}...29
15^{25}...151
17^{5}...143
18^{5}...143
20^{4}...44
21^{8}...42
22^{7}...44
23^{5}...32
23^{14}...151
25^{7}...181
28...151
28^{1}...151
28^{7}...151
28^{15}...151
28^{25}...151
28^{3-12}...49
$29^{2}-30^{20}$...144
32^{4}...39
32^{15}...149, 155
32^{36}...45, 47
32^{39}...45
32^{43}...42
33^{29}...16, 49
34^{15}...155
34^{19}...155

Joshua
2^{12}...10

11^{20}...149
24^{19}...41

Judges
1^{15}...49
1^{24}...11
2^{10}...192
2^{11-23}...17
2^{18}...47
2^{22}...100, 108
3^{7-11}...17
3^{9-15}...17
4^{1-3}...17
6^{33}...29
6^{38}...100
9^{8ff}...183
9^{38}...147
14^{11}...164
17^{4}...101, 106
21^{22}...9

Ruth
$1-4$...45
2^{2}...9
2^{10}...9
2^{13}...9

1 Samuel
2^{1}...205, 206
2^{12}...192
3^{7}...192
3^{14}...42
5^{7}...148
6^{6}...149
8^{7}...154
9^{13}...164
10^{24}...147
12^{3}...41
14^{45}...21
15^{3}...25
15^{11}...27, 46
15^{13}...49
15^{23-6}...147
15^{29}...46
16^{1}...154
16^{8-10}...143
16^{22}...33
17^{37}...45
17^{39}...100
19^{5}...9
20^{8-14}...10
20^{17}...53
23^{21}...49
25^{8}...33
29^{4}...102, 146

2 Samuel
4^{9}...21, 45
6^{1}...152
6^{21}...143
7^{14}...102, 104

7^{15}...12
7^{19}...31
7^{20}...192
9^{1}...10
9^{3}...10
9^{7}...10
10^{2}...10
12^{24}...32
13^{15}...53
14^{22}...33
15^{11}...164
15^{25}...33
16^{17}...10
19^{22}...102
21^{3}...41
21^{6}...145
23^{17}...68
24^{1}...102
24^{14}...14, 39
24^{16}...47

1 Kings
1^{29}...164
1^{41}...164
2^{28}...163
5^{4}...102, 107
8^{23}...11
8^{28}...37
8^{30-9}...15
8^{38-54}...9
10^{1}...100
10^{9}...32
11^{11}...193
11^{14}...102, 107
11^{23}...102, 107
11^{25}...102, 107
12^{11}...103, 109
12^{11ff}...103
14^{16}...151
17^{22}...70
19^{18}...172
22^{21ff}...107

2 Kings
1^{2-6}...116
4^{35}...70
5^{21}...118
17^{4}...149
17^{15}...148
17^{20}...148
18^{29-35}...45

1 Chronicles
15^{22}...103
16^{13}...145
21^{1}...102, 107
28^{11-20}...42
29^{3}...164
29^{17}...101, 146

INDEX OF TEXTS

2 Chronicles
10^7...146
13^3...152
13^{17}...152
20^7...190
32^{11-17}...45
32^{30}...13
32^{32}...13

Ezra
9^{8-10}...10
10^{11}...146

Nehemiah
1^6...11
9^7...143
9^{14}...146
9^{16}...9
13^{14}...13
13^{26}...32

Esther
1^8...146
2^9...11
2^{17}...11, 52
4^8...9
5^8...33
5^{10}...33
7^4...107
8^1...107
8^7...35, 67

Job
1-42...141
1...107
1^6...108
1^9...9
1^{11}...192
2...108
2^9...102
2^{11}...47
4...47
5...47
5^{17}...148
6^{14}...10
7^{18}...101, 105
8^{20}...148
9^{34}...104
12^{11}...100
14^6...146
16^2...47, 81
17^7...169
18^{21}...192
19^{21}...9
19^{25}...21
21^9...104, 110
23^{10}...101
24^1...192
33^{24}...41
33^{26}...146
34^8...188

34^{13}...13
34^{24}...150
34^{26}...101
37^{13}...11, 104
42^6...154
42^9...40

Psalms
1^1...49
1^{1f}...29
2^9...104
2^{10}...109
3^8...49
4^3...13
4^5...205
4^8...29
5^5...32
5^{12}...29
5^{13}...146
6^2...36
6^4...12
6^9...37
7^9...101, 105
7^{13}...183
11^{4f}...101
11^{6-8}...53
12^6...101, 106
13^4...15
14^7...32
15^2...148
15^4...148
15^7...145
15^{32}...145
16^{10}...18, 66
17^3...101, 105, 106
17^{14}...29
18^1...39
18^2...206
18^{17}...45
18^{27}...44
18^{30}...101, 205
18^{33}...150
18^{50}...12
19^1...182
19^{14}...146
20^{1-6}...44
22^4...47
22^{11}...9
22^{20}...45
23^4...28
23^6...12
24^{3-6}...18
24^5...38
25^2...205
25^6...14
25^7...12
25^{10}...11
25^{11}...40
25^{22}...21, 45
26^1...205
26^{1f}...100

26^2...101
26^3...159
26^{11}...21
27^1...18
28^2...9
28^6...9
28^9...49
29^{11}...29
30^1...145
30^4...14
30^5...146
30^9...217
30^{12}...145
31^1...206
31^5...21
31^7...12
31^{14ff}...13
31^{14-16}...18
31^{24}...205
32^1...15, 29
32^4...16
32^5...41
32^{10}...13
34^2...205, 206
34^6...18
35^9...205, 206
37^4...205
37^7...205
37^{11}...37
37^{21}...9
37^{26}...9, 14
37^{28}...14, 32
38^{1f}...103
38^{15}...205
38^{18}...103
38^{20}...107
39^8...21
40^{11}...39
40^{13}...45
41-72...205
41^2...49
42^5...205
44^3...146
44^6...205
44^8...205
44^{26}...13
45^2...34
45^6...104
46^8...178
49^{6f}...41
49^{14f}...18
50^{23}...52
51...25, 30, 48, 78, 80
51^1...9, 12, 14, 26
51^2...20, 26
51^5...20
51^{5ff}...20
51^7...20, 26, 80
51^9...26
51^{10}...20, 79
51^{11}...26, 188

INDEX OF TEXTS

Psalms—contd.
51^{12}...26
51^{14}...20
51^{19}...146
53^5...148, 154
56^3...205
56^{3f}...206
56^{10}...205
56^{13}...159
57^1...9
59^{16}...12
64^{10}...205, 206
65^{1-3}...42
65^{1-4}...145
65^3...20
65^{10}...206
66^{10-12}...101
66^{10}...106
66^{11}...108
67...29
67^7...29
68^{19}...49
69^{5-13}...20
69^{14}...45
69^{18}...21
71^2...12
71^{13}...107
71^{21}...28, 47
72^3...30
72^7...30
72^{12}...45
72^{14}...45
76^{10}...186
77^8...13
77^{15}...45
78^{18}...100
78^{22}...205, 206
78^{38}...42
78^{41}...100
78^{54}...100
78^{59}...148
78^{63}...152
78^{67}...148
78^{70}...143
79^6...192
79^8...16
79^9...20, 42
84^{11}...33, 34
85^1...146
85^4...20
85^{7f}...20
85^{10}...30
86^2...13
86^5...13, 15, 40
86^{15}...36
86^{17}...28, 47
88^1...18
89...12
89^1...12
89^{17}...146
89^{32}...104

89^{38}...148
90^{13}...27, 45
91^{14-16}...17
94^{10}...103, 109
94^{12}...103
94^{19}...47
95^{8f}...104
95^8...169
95^9...100, 101, 105
96^5...50
97^{10}...14
99^8...16, 40
103^2...50
103^3...15, 40
103^8...9, 39
103^{12}...16
103^{13}...15, 39
103^{17}...11
105^{19}...101
105^{26}...143
106^5...145
106^{14}...100
106^{23}...145
106^{45}...27
109^4...107
109^6...102, 107
109^{16}...11
109^{20}...107
109^{29}...107
113^{7f}...150
116^3...18
116^5...14
116^6...18
116^9...159
116^{13}...14, 18
118^{22}...163
119^{40}...101, 106
119^{52}...47
119^{76}...28, 47
119^{82}...28
119^{108}...146
119^{165}...30
119^{170}...21
119^{176}...21
122^5...30
122^6...30
125^5...30
130^1...26
130^4...16, 40
130^7...12, 13
130^{7f}...21
135^{14}...47
136...12
137^3...29
137^7...29
137^8...29
137^9...29
139^1...192
139^{23}...105
139^{23f}...101
141^5...11

143^{10}...46
145^8...9
145^{17}...13
146^5...205
146^8...32
147^{11}...146
147^{14}...30
149^4...146
149^5...14

Proverbs
1^{2f}...108
1^9...34
1^{11}...188
1^{22}...109
2^{12}...45
3^4...33
3^5...205
3^8...39
3^{11f}...122
3^{12}...32
3^{17}...30
3^{18}...49
3^{22}...34
3^{24}...33
3^{34}...58
4^6...53
4^8...53
4^9...34
4^{13}...103
5^{12}...103
5^{19}...34
5^{23}...103, 109
6^{16-19}...32
6^{23}...103
6^{35}...42
7^5...34
7^{18}...52
8^{10}...103, 104, 152
8^{17}...32, 53
8^{21}...53
8^{33}...103, 104
8^{35}...146
9^{10}...196
10^{29}...39
11^{17}...39
12^1...53
12^2...34, 146
12^{10}...14
12^{22}...146
13^8...42
13^{18}...104
13^{24}...104
14^{21}...36
15^9...32
15^{17}...34
15^{32}...104
15^{33}...103
16^6...42
16^7...146
16^{13}...146

INDEX OF TEXTS

Proverbs—contd.
16^{14}...41
16^{15}...146
16^{20}...49
16^{22}...103
17^3...101
17^8...34
18^{22}...33
19^{18}...109
19^{22}...10
20^{28}...11, 38
21^3...145
21^{18}...42
21^{21}...39
22^1...34
22^{11}...39
22^{15}...104, 110
23^{11}...21
24^{32}...104
25^{4ff}...154
25^{10}...34
26^2...9
27^{21}...101
28^{14}...155
28^{23}...9
28^{24}...188
29^3...53
30^5...101
30^7...34
31^{26}...10
31^{30}...9

Ecclesiastes
9^{7-10}...146
9^{11}...34
9^{18}...183
10^{12}...34

Isaiah
1^1...149
1^3...195
1^{14}...41
1^{22}...154
1^{23}...88
1^{25}...101, 107
1^{27}...21
2^{2-4}...23
2^9...41
3^9...150
3^{12}...49
5^{24}...148
6^{1-8}...19
6^7...42
6^{9f}...155, 168, 169, 171
6^{9-13}...145
6^{10}...149, 155, 169
6^{11-13}...155
7^{10-12}...100
7^{17}...47
8^{11}...103
8^{13-15}...163

9^6...30
9^{16}...152
10^5...109
10^{12}...109
11^9...23
12^1...28, 46
13^{18}...39
14^1...145
19^{19-25}...23
19^{20}...45
19^{21}...195
19^{25}...49
24^{14}...42
26^3...30
26^{3f}...205
26^{19}...18
27^9...19, 42
28^{16}...100, 163
28^{18}...42
29...142
29^9...205
29^{16}...142
29^{19}...205, 206
29^{22}...21
30^7...47
30^{12}...148
30^{18}...49
30^{19}...36
31^7...147
32^{17}...30
33^8...40
33^{24}...31
35^3...122
35^9...69
37^{35}...44
40...11
$40-66$...21, 69, 147
40^1...28
40^{1-8}...47
40^2...17, 18, 28, 147
40^{27}...17
41^7...101, 106
41^8...145, 188, 190
41^{14}...45
41^{18-20}...169
$41^{18}-43^{13}$...21
42^1...147, 161, 166
42^6...23
42^{14}...45
42^{18-20}...22, 169
42^{19}...22
42^{21-5}...22
43^1...45
43^{1-13}...22
43^{1-14f}...69
43^{10}...195
43^{11}...17
43^{14}...70
43^{16}...70
43^{20}...145
43^{25}...22, 26

44^2...147
44^6...45
44^{6-8}...22
44^{6-23}...22
44^{9-20}...22
44^{21-3}...22
44^{21f}...70
44^{22}...22
44^{24}...45, 70
45^4...145
45^8...17
45^9...142
45^{25}...205, 206
46^4...41
47^4...45
48^{10}...101
48^{17}...45
48^{18}...30
48^{22}...30
49^1...14, 173
49^5...173
49^{5-13}...147
49^6...23
49^7...45, 145
49^8...19, 166
49^{13}...15, 28
49^{25f}...44
50^2...45
50^7...47
51^3...47
51^5...17
51^8...32
51^{9-11}...69
51^{12}...28, 47
52^3...9, 70
52^{7-10}...17
52^9...28
52^{13}...76
52^{15}...19, 182
52^{13}-53^{12}...19, 23
53...77, 98
53^1...82
53^{1-9}...19
53^3...42
53^{11}...22, 25, 81
53^{12}...20, 81
54^5...45
54^8...45
54^{10}...12, 30
54^{11}...47
54^{13}...30
55^2...66
55^6...154
55^7...15, 16 40
55^{12}...29
56^{1-8}...147
56^{20f}...22
57^1...13
57^{18}...47
58^2...146
59^1...44

INDEX OF TEXTS

Isaiah—contd.
59^{17}...206
60^{10}...146
60^{17f}...30
60^{18}...17
61^{1ff}...28, 147
61^{2}...166
61^{10}...17
62^{5}...152
62^{10-12}...22
62^{11}...17
63^{4}...70
63^{6-10}...27
63^{7}...48
63^{7-19}...12
63^{8f}...70
63^{9}...45, 70
63^{10}...27, 30, 149
63^{10f}...26
63^{11}...26, 70
63^{12f}...27
63^{14}...26, 205
63^{15}...14, 39
63^{17}...27, 149
63^{18}...26, 27
64^{8}...142
65^{9}...145
65^{11}...51
65^{15}...145
65^{22}...145
66^{11}...47
66^{12f}...47
66^{13}...28

Jeremiah
1^{5}...173, 193, 195
1^{8}...45
1^{25}...183
1^{41}...181
2^{2}...13
2^{3}...48
2^{8}...195
2^{19}...150
2^{30}...109
3^{12}...13, 39
3^{17}...154
3^{23}...205, 206
4^{22}...195
4^{28}...27, 46
5^{1}...15
5^{3}...155
5^{7}...15, 40
5^{20}...147
6^{14}...30
6^{15}...152
6^{19}...148, 154
6^{23}...14
6^{27}...101, 105
6^{28-30}...101
6^{30}...148, 154
7^{9}...195

7^{26}...149
7^{29}...148, 154
8...24
8^{9}...148, 154
9^{3}...196
9^{6}...196
9^{7}...101, 105, 107
9^{23}...207
9^{24}...195
9^{36}...195
10^{9}...101, 106
10^{14}...101
10^{25}...195
11^{7}...39
11^{20}...101
12^{3}...101, 195
12^{8}...32
12^{15}...39
13^{14}...14
14^{19f}...154
15^{5}...25
15^{19-21}...21
15^{20}...44
15^{21}...45
16^{5}...30, 33
16^{13}...33
17^{10}...101
18...42, 183
18^{5ff}...142
18^{10}...27
18^{23}...42
22^{16}...195, 196
22^{20}...52
24^{7}...195
25^{4}...105
29^{11}...30
30^{9}...150
30^{16}...144
30^{24}...144
30^{25}...144
31...142
31^{1}...24
31^{2}...33
31^{3}...12, 31
31^{9}...9, 32
31^{13}...28
31^{18}...103
31^{31}...178
31^{31-4}...19, 24
31^{33}...24
31^{33f}...48
31^{34}...68, 195, 196
31^{37}...148
33^{3}...19
33^{8}...19
33^{9}...29
33^{24}...143, 148
33^{26}...148
36^{7}...35
42^{9f}...27
45^{1ff}...142

45^{9}...142
50^{20}...21
51^{12}...148

Lamentations
1^{2}...47
1^{16f}...47
1^{21}...47
3^{1}...47
3^{22}...12

Ezekiel
5^{6}...148
5^{11}...154
11^{19}...24
12^{2}...34
13^{10}...30
14^{10}...15
14^{16-29}...45
14^{22f}...28
16^{5}...25
16^{23}...52
16^{63}...41
20^{5}...144
20^{13}...148
20^{16}...148
20^{38}...144
20^{39-41}...147
20^{40-4}...145
20^{42}...144
24^{14}...27
31^{16}...152
34^{10}...45
34^{22}...44
34^{25}...30
36...25
36^{16-36}...24
36^{22-8}...24
36^{25}...79
36^{25-7}...78
36^{25-8}...19
36^{26f}...48, 79
36^{29}...25
37...25, 79
37^{23}...19
37^{26}...30
38^{16}...195
39^{25}...39
43^{18}...25

Daniel
1^{9}...11, 34
1^{12}...100
4^{32}...45, 70
9^{24}...41, 42
11^{3}...146
11^{16}...146
11^{35}...101
11^{36}...146
12^{2}...18

INDEX OF TEXTS

Hosea
1^6...14, 39
1^7...205
1^{9f}...164
2^1...14
2^7...52
2^{14}...194
2^{19}...14
2^{23}...39, 164
3^1...30
4^1...11
4^6...148, 154
5^2...109
5^3...193
5^4...194
6^4...13
6^6...13, 196
7^{13}...21
8^2...194
8^8...183
8^{13}...147
9^{15}...31
9^{17}...148
11^1...31
11^8...151, 156
13^{4f}...194
13^{14}...21
14^4...31
14^8...31

Joel
2^{14}...27
2^{28}...25

Amos
1-2...149
2^4...147, 154
2^{11}...152
3^2...144, 193
3^3...193
4^{11}...20
5^{12}...42
5^{22}...147
7^2...40
7^3...27, 46
7^6...27, 46
9^6...178

Jonah
3^9...27
4^{11}...23

Micah
1^8...196
4^{10}...45
6^7...147
6^8...11, 53
7^2...13
7^{18}...15, 16
7^{19}...16, 39
7^{20}...11

Nahum
1^7...193

Habakkuk
1^6...181

Zephaniah
1^7...164

3^1...70
3^2...205, 206

Haggai
2^6...30
2^{23}...143

Zechariah
1^{-3-17}...47
3^1...107
3^{1-6}...102
3^2...20
4^7...34
6^{14}...34
7^{3-14}...149
7^9...11
8^{14}...27
8^{17}...32
11^{13}...105
11^{15}...183
11^{16}...150
12^5...205, 206
12^{10}...34
13^9...101

Malachi
1^8...146
2^5...30
2^6...30, 195
2^{13}...147
2^{14}...188
3^{2f}...101
3^3...19, 154
3^{10}...49, 101
3^{15}...29, 101, 105
3^{17}...164

APOCRYPHA

1 Esdras
2^{2f}...156
2^{8f}...156
4^7...41
4^{24}...52
4^{25}...53
4^{35-40}...50
5^{58}...50
6^{15}...157
8^4...34
8^{25}...50
8^{53}...43
8^{73-90}...110
8^{77}...157
11^{13-20}...43

2 Esdras
1-16...172, 180

Add. Esther
4^{17}...37
13^{17}...43
14^6...157
15^{16}...85

16^3...188
22^1...45
22^9...45

Wisdom
1^1...53
1^2...105
1^{2f}...106
1^{5f}...111
1^9...106
2...153
2^{10}...38
2^{12}...111
2^{13}...197
2^{16}...50
2^{17}...105, 108
2^{18}...46
2^{21}...169
2^{24}...105, 108
3...153
3^1...108, 153
3^3...52
3^{4f}...110
3^5...105

3^{5f}...106, 111
3^6...153
3^9...35, 37, 38, 54, 153
3^{11}...154
3^{13}...50
3^{14}...35, 153
3^{18}...85
4^6...106
4^{10}...54, 159
4^{15}...35, 153
4^{18}...155
4^{19}...155
4^{26}...35
5^2...45
5^{15}...206
6^3...106
6^{5f}...106
6^{10}...39
6^{11}...39, 111
6^{12}...53
6^{17}...111
6^{18f}...39
6^{21}...106
6^{23}...188

INDEX OF TEXTS

Wisdom—*contd.*
6^{24}...45
6^{25}...111
7^{14}...53, 111, 191
7^{22f}...53
7^{27}...39, 53, 191
7^{29}...54
8^2...52, 53
8^{18}...53, 188, 191
8^{21}...34, 35
9^4...154
9^{10}...159
9^{13}...196
9^{17}...196
9^{18}...45
10^6...46
10^9...46
10^{15}...39
10^{17}...39
11^9...38, 105, 110
11^{9f}...106
11^{10}...106
11^{21}...156
11^{21}-12^{11}...36
11^{23-6}...54
11^{24}...54
11^{25}...156
11^{26}...53, 54
12^2...110, 206
12^{3ff}...36
12^7...196
12^{21f}...110
12^{22}...38
12^{26}...105
13^3...196
13^{11}...183
14-19...55
14^7...49, 50
14^{22}...52, 197
15^{1-3}...36
15^6...52, 53
15^7...183
15^{19}...49
16^7...45
16^{26}...53, 54
17^1...109, 111
18^1...39, 50
18^{1-14}...38
18^2...35
18^5...39
18^7...45
18^9...39
18^{21f}...43
19^5...105
19^{12}...85
19^{22}...154
37^{19}...109
37^{21}...34

Sirach
Prologue^3...111
Prologue^{10}...111
Prologue^{12}...48
Prologue^{21}...111
1^{23}...52
1^{26}...110
2^1...105
2^5...106, 153
2^{7-17}...38
2^{10}...154
2^{11}...36, 40, 41, 45
2^{15f}...53
2^{16}...154
3^3...43
3^8...50
3^{17}...153
3^{26f}...156
3^{30}...39, 44
3^{31}...34
4^{10}...54
4^{11-19}...54
4^{14}...54
4^{17}...105, 111
4^{21}...34
4^{23}...45
4^{24}...111
4^{25}...110
4^{26}...37
5^{4-7}...38
5^{5f}...44
5^6...40
6^{10}...188
6^{18}...110
6^{20}...110, 111
7^9...153
7^{10}...39
7^{19}...35
7^{21}...53
7^{23}...35, 110
7^{33}...35
7^{35}...53
8^4...110
8^8...111
8^{19}...34
10^1...111
10^3...111
10^4...156
10^{22}...38
11^{17}...154
11^{22}...50
11^{28}...50
12^1...35
12^3...35, 67
12^{13f}...36
13^{1f}...188
13^{14}...110
13^{18}...52
14^{1f}...50
14^{20}...50
15^{13}...53
16^{6-14}...88
16^{11}...156
16^{24f}...111
17^{22}...35
17^{24}...47
17^{25}...44
17^{29}...44
18^{1-14}...38
18^4...36
18^{12}...44
18^{17}...35
18^{20}...43, 106
19^{15}...108
20^{13}...34
20^{23}...35
20^{28}...44
20^{29}...169
21^5...37
21^{11-21}...111
21^{16}...35
21^{24}...110
21^{27}...108
22^3...110
22^6...110
24^{15}...153
24^{16f}...35
25^{7-12}...50
25^{23}...50
26^1...50
26^4...38
26^5...108
26^{13-15}...35
27^5...106, 183
27^7...104
28^2...41
28^5...44
28^9...108
28^{19}...50
29^{15}...35
29^{17}...46
30^1...53
30^6...35
31^{8f}...50
31^{10}...106
31^{22}...155
31^{26}...106
32^{10}...35
32^{14}...54
33^1...105
33^{7-15}...151
33^{24}...110
34^9...105
34^{15f}...50
34^{19}...44
35^1...45
35^3...43, 154
35^7...153
35^{12}...153
35^{13}...37
35^{16}...37, 154
35^{17}...47
35^{17-20}...38
35^{19}...37

INDEX OF TEXTS

Sirach—contd.
36^1...36
36^5...196
36^{12}...36
36^{13}...40
36^{15}...156
36^{16}...40, 154
36^{17}...37
37^{24}...50
37^{27}...105
38^2...45
38^8...52
38^{17}...108
38^{28}...183
38^{34}...37
39^{13}...39
39^{14}...50
39^{24}...39
39^{18}...45, 153
40^{22}...35
40^{27-9}...50
41^4...53
41^{16}...106
41^{17}...34
41^{18}...188
41^{24}...34
42^8...106
44^{16}...159
44^{20}...104
44^{23}...196
44^{44}...52
45^1...54
45^4...153
45^6...153
45^7...50
45^{16}...44, 153
45^{23}...44
45^{23f}...52
46^1...45, 153
46^{7-11}...44
46^{13}...54
47^{2ff}...153
47^{13}...52
47^{16}...52
47^{22}...38, 153
48^{11}...196
48^{20}...36, 45
49^6...153
50^{22-4}...38
51^1...45
51^2...108
51^{2f}...45
51^6...108
51^{11}...37
51^{16}...11
51^{23-30}...111

Baruch
1^2...34
2^{14}...34, 37
2^{30}...155

3^2...36
3^{13f}...52
3^{27f}...152
4...45
4^{4ff}...50
4^{13}...110
4^{15}...36
4^{16}...53
4^{20}...37
4^{22}...45
4^{36-59}...50
5...45
5^4...52

Song of the Three Holy Children
9...157
11...157
12...37
$28-34$...49
$35-59$...49
$60-8$...49
$64f$...39
$67f$...38

Tobit
1^4...152
1^{13}...34
3^8...51, 108
3^{10}...53
3^{14}...50
4^{7-16}...39
4^{9f}...44
4^{10}...46
4^{11}...46
4^{14}...110
6^{17}...36, 45
7^{11}...36
7^{12}...36
7^{15}...36
7^{16}...38
7^{17}...36
7^{18}...34
8^4...36
8^{15}...50
8^{15-17}...50
8^{17}...50
10^{12}...53
12^{17}...52
13^2...36
13^5...36
13^9...36
13^{10}...54
13^{12}...54
13^{14}...52, 54, 110
13^{18}...49
14^4...52
14^5...36

Judith
2^{15}...153

5^8...196
6^{19}...36
7^{15}...52
7^{3c}...37
8^{15}...105
8^{17}...45
8^{19}...35
8^{20}...196
8^{23}...34
8^{25-7}...105
8^{35}...52
9^4...54
9^6...152
9^{11}...45
10^8...34
12^{10}...165
13^{14}...38
13^{17f}...50
13^{18}...49, 50
15^{10}...154
16^{15}...43

Susanna
5^1...105
6^0...50
6^2...45
6^3...53

1 Maccabees
1^{35f}...108
2^{21}...43, 68
2^{42}...14, 39
2^{52}...104
2^{59}...45
2^{60}...46
2^{69}...50
3^6...45
3^7...50
3^{29}...35
3^{44}...40
4^1...153
4^{11}...45
4^{30}...50
4^{44}...37
5^{53}...46
5^{54}...52
7^{13-17}...39
7^{37}...37, 152
9^5...153
9^{33}...46
9^{35}...48
10^{27}...37
10^{28-34}...41
10^{60}...34
11^{49}...37
12^{10}...105
13^{46}...38
14^{25}...35
16^2...46
16^3...38

238 INDEX OF TEXTS

2 Maccabees
1-15...82
1^1...52
1^4...52
1^5...37
1^{17}...50, 157
1^{24}...36
1^{25}...153
1^{26}...153
1^{35}...35
2^7...37, 43
2^{18}...36, 178, 206
2^{22}...43
3^8...173
3^{11}...108
3^{21}...36
3^{31-3}...35, 43, 67
3^{38}...107
4^3...106
4^{25}...188
4^{34}...46, 48
5^{18-20}...152
6^1...38
6^{12}...110
6^{16}...38, 110
6^{21}...48
7^1...110
7^5...46, 48
7^6...46, 48
7^9ff...70
7^{21}...48
7^{22}...67
7^{24}...50
7^{27}...36
7^{37}...43
7^{40}...206
8^2...40
8^{16}...48
8^{29}...36
9^{12}...37
9^{18}...48
9^{25-7}...48
10^4...110, 157
10^{26}...43
10^{46}...108
11^6...45
11^9...36
11^{15}...46
12^3...46
12^{42}...48
12^{43}...43
12^{45}...35, 43
13^3...45
13^{12}...36, 48
13^{14}...48
14^{26}...108
14^{27}...108
15^8...48
15^{8-10}...85
15^{39}...35

THE NEW TESTAMENT

Matthew
2^8...113
2^{18}...81
3^8...81
4^1...117
4^9...119
5^{3-12}...87
5^4...81, 83
5^7...65
5^9...90
5^{10f}...161
5^{27-32}...134
5^{29}...69
5^{44}...93
6^{2-4}...65
6^2...83
6^3...88
6^5...83
6^{10}...88
6^{13}...112, 117
6^{14f}...67
6^{16}...83
6^{19-34}...134
6^{25}...134
6^{32}...134
7^{14}...162
7^{23}...198
7^{24-7}...198
8^{25}...72
9^{13}...65
9^{27}...65
10^{11}...113
10^{11-15}...89
10^{17}...120
10^{34f}...89
10^{35}...89
10^{37}...91
11^{25}...199
11^{27}...198, 199, 205
12^{18}...93, 161, 166
12^{31}...66
13^5...168
13^{14f}...169
13^{39}...116, 118
14^{22-4}...130
14^{30}...72
15^{25}...83
16^{17}...88
16^{18}...132, 163
16^{21-3}...163
16^{22}...68
16^{23}...118, 163
17^5...166, 199
18^{32f}...67
18^{33}...65
21^{42}...161
22^7...162
22^8...161
22^{9f}...161
22^{14}...161, 165
22^{24}...181
23^{10}...188
23^{23}...65
23^{24}...120
23^{35}...125
24^{12}...92
24^{20f}...127
25^{12}...199
25^{34}...86
25^{40}...192
25^{41}...116
26^{28}...66
26^{53}...83
27^{49}...73
28^{10}...192

Mark
1^{12f}...117
1^4...66
1^8...79
1^{11}...93, 158, 165
1^{18}...66
1^{24}...119, 199
1^{30f}...73
1^{34}...66, 199
1^{40}...81
1^{44}...66
2^{5-10}...66
2^{5-11}...72
2^{10}...67
2^{26}...173
3^5...169
3^{22}...116
3^{22-6}...116
3^{23}...118
3^{27}...118, 183
3^{28}...66
3^{29}...118
3^{36}...73
4^4...116
4^8...116
4^{10}...116
4^{13}...66
4^{15}ff...183
5^{10}...81
5^{12}...81
5^{17}...81
5^{19}...65
5^{25}...72
5^{28}...72
5^{34}...72, 89
6^{41}...86
6^{45}...162
6^{52}...169

INDEX OF TEXTS

Mark—contd.
6^{56}...72, 81
7^{32}...81
8^7...86
8^{11}...112
8^{17}...169
8^{31}...168
8^{32f}...119
8^{34}...163
8^{35-8}...71
9^7...93, 158
9^{12}...168
9^{14}...170
9^{22}...83
9^{24}...83
9^{34}...90
9^{50}...90
10^2...112
10^6...80
10^{16}...86
10^{21}...92
10^{26}...71
10^{34}...120
10^{44}...69
10^{45}...69
10^{47f}...65
10^{52}...72
11^{9f}...86
11^{16}...183
11^{25}...66
12^6...93, 158
12^{10}...168
12^{13-16}...112
12^{16}...181
12^{20-3}...92
12^{30}...98
13^{13}...72
13^{20}...72, 132, 161
13^{22}...161
13^{27}...161
14^{10f}...170
14^{16}...170
14^{22}...86
14^{24}...77
14^{36}...161
14^{38}...112, 132
14^{44}...92
14^{61}...86
15^{30f}...73

Luke
1^{30}...57
1^{34}...194
1^{42}...86
1^{47}...76, 207
1^{50}...65
1^{54}...65
1^{64}...86
1^{68}...70
1^{69}...71, 75
1^{71}...75
1^{72}...65

1^{74}...69
1^{75}...66
1^{77}...66, 75, 89
1^{78}...65
1^{79}...89
2^{11}...76, 89, 169
2^{14}...89, 167
2^{15ff}...173
2^{25}...83
2^{29}...89
2^{30}...76, 89
2^{38}...70
2^{40-52}...57
3^6...76
3^{18}...181
3^{22}...89
4^{9f}...116
4^{12}...111
4^{18}...66
4^{19}...166
4^{22}...57
4^{24}...166
5^{10}...188
6^{13}...161
6^{20-6}...87
6^{24}...83
6^{27-36}...93
6^{28}...87
6^{32-4}...57
6^{36}...65
6^{47}...198
7^5...92
7^{12-15}...72
7^{16}...83
7^{21}...67
7^{23}...88
7^{34}...92, 191
7^{42}...92
7^{42f}...67, 68
7^{45}...91
7^{47}...92
7^{47-50}...73
7^{50}...89
8^{12}...73
8^{28-36}...72
8^{48}...89
8^{50}...72
9^4...219
9^{21ff}...160
9^{35}...160
9^{57-62}...162
10^1...118
10^{5-16}...89
10^{17f}...118
10^{18f}...116
10^{19}...118
10^{21}...167, 199
10^{22}...78, 198
10^{23}...88
10^{25}...112
10^{25f}...93

10^{37}...65
11^4...66, 67, 112
11^{5-8}...191
11^{16}...112
11^{21}...89
11^{27f}...88
11^{42}...92, 93
11^{43}...92
11^{54}...112
12^4...92, 191
12^{15}...134
12^{32}...167
12^{37-43}...88
12^{46}...163
12^{49-53}...89
12^{52}...89
13^{16}...116
13^{23}...71
13^{23-30}...162
13^{29}...162
14^{14f}...87
14^{15-24}...88
14^{16-24}...162
14^{23}...162
15^2...116
15^7...116
15^{28}...83
16^{13}...92
16^{25}...81, 83
17^9...57
17^{13}...65
17^{19}...72
17^{25}...168
18^7...161
18^9...168
18^{13}...68
18^{38}...65
19^9...75
19^{9f}...71, 73
19^{38}...89
19^{42}...89
20^{13}...93
21^{28}...70
22^3...118
22^{17}...61
22^{19}...61
22^{28}...112, 119
22^{31}...117, 119
23^{11}...168
23^{12}...191
23^{16}...121
23^{22}...121
23^{29}...88
23^{35}...161
23^{39}...72
24^{21}...70
24^{29}...219
24^{30}...86
24^{39}...132
24^{47}...66
24^{53}...86

240 INDEX OF TEXTS

John
1^{19-454}...202
1^{3}...80
1^{3f}...126
1^{4}...213, 218
1^{12}...221
1^{14-18}...58
1^{16}...60
1^{19-34}...79
1^{26}...202
1^{31}...202
1^{33}...202
1^{39f}...219
2^{11}...202
2^{12}...219
3^{2}...202
3^{3-7}...79
3^{6-8}...79
3^{8}...79
3^{16}...56, 60, 95
3^{17}...74
3^{21}...190, 207, 218
3^{29}...191
4^{22}...76
4^{42}...77
5-12...202, 203, 218
5^{20}...92
5^{34}...74
5^{40}...202
6^{6}...112
6^{56}...218
6^{70}...118, 160
7^{27-9}...202
7^{28}...202
8^{12}...218
8^{12-59}...202
8^{14}...202
8^{31f}...218
8^{32}...197
8^{36}...197
8^{44}...117, 119
8^{55}...203
9^{2}...72
9^{5}...218
9^{22}...218
10^{1-18}...203
10^{4f}...203
10^{9}...74
10^{11f}...203
11^{3}...73
11^{6}...219
11^{11}...191
11^{12}...74
11^{19}...85
11^{23f}...85
11^{31}...85
12^{13}...86
12^{25-31}...119
12^{27}...74
12^{31}...219
12^{32f}...219

12^{40f}...169
13-17...189, 209, 218
13-21...207
13^{1}...96, 189
13^{2}...118
13^{7}...130
13^{10}...130, 219
13^{13}...191
13^{17}...188
13^{18}...160, 203
13^{27}...118
13^{30}...218
13^{34}...96, 97
14^{5-9}...203
14^{10}...218
14^{10-20}...218
14^{15}...97
14^{16}...84
14^{16f}...85
14^{17}...203
14^{17-20}...219
14^{21}...96
14^{21-4}...97
14^{23}...96
14^{26}...85
14^{26f}...91
14^{31}...95
15^{1}...210
15^{2}...219
15^{3}...219
15^{3f}...130
15^{4}...186, 219
15^{4f}...210
15^{7}...219
15^{9f}...96
15^{10}...130, 219
15^{12f}...96
15^{12}...97
15^{13-15}...191
15^{14f}...92
15^{15}...204
15^{16}...160, 203
15^{19}...160
15^{21f}...204
15^{26}...85
16^{2}...161
16^{3}...204
16^{7ff}...85
16^{12f}...191
16^{21f}...215
16^{23}...91
16^{27}...92
16^{30}...219
17...204, 220
17^{1f}...220
17^{2}...132
17^{3}...78, 202, 204, 218
17^{6}...170, 220
17^{8}...219, 220
17^{11}...170, 220
17^{21}...221

17^{21f}...210
17^{21-3}...190
17^{22f}...220
17^{23}...96, 220
17^{24}...95, 96
17^{25}...220
17^{26}...96, 220
19^{1}...120
19^{12}...191
19^{26}...92
19^{27}...202
20^{17}...192
20^{19}...91
20^{21}...91
20^{23}...66
20^{26}...91
20^{29}...88
20^{31}...218
21^{12}...113
21^{15-17}...92
21^{22}...219

Acts
1^{2}...160
1^{24}...160
2^{7}...124
2^{17}...182
2^{21}...78
2^{23}...175
2^{27}...66
2^{38}...66, 67
2^{40}...73, 82
2^{42}...189
2^{46}...88
2^{47}...57
3^{12f}...175
3^{14}...67
3^{21}...217
3^{23}...175
3^{25f}...86
4^{2}...209
4^{9}...73
4^{11}...168
4^{12}...73, 75
4^{17}...175
2^{27}...93
4^{28}...175
4^{33}...58
4^{36}...83
5^{3}...118
5^{9}...111
5^{31}...66, 67, 76
6^{5}...160
6^{8}...58
7^{10}...57
7^{22}...122
7^{25}...175
7^{26}...89
7^{27}...168
7^{35}...70
7^{39}...168

INDEX OF TEXTS

Acts—contd.
7^{42}...170
7^{46}...58
7^{51}...169
8^{22}...66
8^{31}...82
9^{15}...165, 183
9^{31}...83
10^{1f}...124
10^{2}...124
10^{4}...65
10^{11}...183
10^{31}...65
10^{34}...69
10^{34f}...124
10^{35}...87, 166
10^{36}...91
11^{14}...71, 73
11^{23}...58, 82, 173
12^{11}...69
12^{20}...89
13^{10}...118, 119
13^{15}...83
13^{17}...160
13^{23}...76
12^{26}...75
13^{27}...160
13^{34}...66
13^{42}...82
13^{43}...58
13^{46}...168, 175
13^{47}...75
13^{48}...124, 175
13^{50}...134
14^{3}...58, 207, 208
14^{9}...73
14^{22}...82
14^{26}...58
15^{1f}...73
15^{7}...160
15^{10}...111
15^{11}...58, 73
15^{25}...158, 160
15^{31}...83
15^{40}...58
16^{1-3}...91
16^{5}...168
16^{9}...82, 83
16^{14}...124
16^{15}...81
16^{17}...71, 75
16^{22}...119
16^{30}...71
16^{30f}...73
16^{35}...119
16^{38}...119
17^{4}...124
17^{17}...124
17^{26-9}...125
17^{28}...206
17^{30}...139, 182

18^{6}...186
18^{17}...124
18^{27}...58
19^{9}...169, 182
19^{11}...191
19^{25}...199
20^{1f}...82
20^{12}...82
20^{19}...43
20^{24}...58
20^{31}...121
20^{32}...58
22^{3}...122
22^{24}...120
23^{6ff}...91
24^{3}...61
24^{4}...82, 83
24^{20f}...91
24^{27}...57
25^{3-9}...58
26^{2}...88
26^{5}...175
26^{17}...69
26^{18}...118
27^{13}...173
27^{17}...183
27^{20}...73
27^{24}...67
27^{31}...73
27^{34}...75
28^{14}...81
28^{17}...168, 169
28^{18}...76
28^{19}...162
28^{27}...82

Romans
1^{1}...165
1^{3}...132
1^{4f}...62
1^{5}...63
1^{6f}...165
1^{7}...59, 90, 96, 158, 165
1^{8}...61
1^{11}...63
1^{16}...175
1^{18}...170
1^{18-27}...171
1^{18-32}...159, 170, 171, 174
1^{20}...80, 182
1^{20-3}...174
1^{21}...161
1^{21f}...200
1^{24}...170
1^{25}...86, 211
1^{26}...170
1^{28}...114, 168, 170, 171
1^{31}...65
1^{32}...171
2^{5}...169
2^{14-16}...174

2^{16}...174
2^{17}...206
2^{18}...114
3...180
3^{8-10}...97
3^{9f}...125
3^{12}...181
3^{17}...91
3^{20-4}...60
3^{22f}...181
3^{24}...60, 61, 70, 214
3^{25}...68
4^{4}...62
4^{5-9}...88
4^{7}...66
4^{13-20}...179
4^{16}...61
4^{25}...170
5^{1}...90
5^{2}...61, 62
5^{5}...62, 96
5^{8}...95
5^{9}...74
5^{11}...206
5^{12-21}...61
5^{13}...139
5^{15}...60, 63
5^{17f}...60
5^{18f}...81
5^{20f}...59
5^{20}...61
5^{21}...62
6^{1}...137, 138
6^{2}...129
6^{3}...129
6^{3f}...128
6^{4}...61
6^{5}...129
6^{6}...128, 129, 137
6^{8}...128, 137
6^{11}...129, 138, 211
6^{12}...137, 139
6^{13}...137
6^{14}...62
6^{15}...137
6^{17}...61
6^{18}...137
6^{19}...138
6^{20}...137
6^{22}...137
6^{23}...63, 207, 212
7...26, 131
7^{14}...133
7^{23}...139
7^{24}...69
8...62
8^{1}...209, 212, 215
8^{1-9}...132
8^{2}...213
8^{2-4}...215
8^{5}...211

INDEX OF TEXTS

Romans—contd.
8^6...90
8^8...131
8^9...131, 211
8^{9-17}...215
8^{10}...132, 209
8^{11}...131
8^{12}...170
8^{12f}...137
8^{13}...132
8^{15f}...215
8^{20-2}...216
8^{21f}...80
8^{23}...70, 73, 215
8^{24}...74
8^{26-30}...159
8^{26-38}...174
8^{28}...97, 173
8^{28-30}...174
8^{29}...175
8^{29f}...175, 176
8^{31-9}...68, 215
8^{32}...25, 60
8^{33}...174
8^{35}...96
8^{37}...96
8^{39}...94, 96, 207, 208, 215
9-11...7, 159, 177, 184, 186
9^1...211
9^{1-5}...178
9^{4f}...178
9^6...180
9^8...178
9^{8-13}...180
9^{11}...173, 179, 180
9^{12f}...185
9^{13}...180
9^{14}...180
9^{14-18}...181
9^{15}...65, 66
9^{15-18}...65
9^{17}...183
9^{17f}...184
9^{18}...169, 182
9^{19f}...185
9^{19-24}...181
9^{19-29}...184
9^{21-3}...183
9^{22}...184
9^{23}...65
9^{24-33}...182
9^{27}...74, 172
9^{27-9}...184
9^{30f}...182
9^{30-2}...185
10...183
10^1...75, 166, 167
10^{1f}...178
10^3...181
10^{3ff}...180
10^9...74

10^{9f}...181
10^{10}...75
10^{11}...75
10^{13}...74
10^{16-21}...182
10^{19-21}...182
11^1...48
11^{1f}...178
11^{2-4}...185
11^{2-5}...172
11^{4-8}...182
11^5...64
11^6...62
11^7...182
11^{14}...74
11^{22}...186
11^{25-36}...186
11^{26}...74, 178
11^{28}...158, 186
11^{30-2}...65, 184
12^1...66, 82
12^{1f}...159
12^2...79, 114
12^{4ff}...63
12^{6ff}...62
12^8...65, 83
12^{13}...190
12^{14}...87
12^{19}...97
13^{11}...75
13^{14}...139
13^{18}...91
14^{14}...207, 208
14^{18}...159
14^{19}...90
14^{22}...88, 114
15^{4f}...83
15^7...211
15^9...65
15^{13}...90
15^{15}...63
15^{26f}...167, 190
15^{27}...133
15^{29}...87
15^{30}...62, 84, 96
15^{31}...69
15^{33}...90
16^{1-16}...207
16^3...212
16^{5-12}...158
16^7...210, 212
16^{7-11}...129
16^{10}...114, 211
16^{12}...208
16^{13}...208
16^{16}...91, 92
16^{18}...86
16^{20}...59, 90, 118

1 Corinthians
1^1...165

1^2...165
1^4...60, 61, 120, 211
1^{10-17}...159
1^{11}...63
1^{12}...133
1^{15}...63
1^{18-25}...177
1^{21}...167, 200
1^{23}...163
1^{24}...165
1^{26-8}...176
1^{28}...132, 168
1^{30}...70, 176, 212
1^{31}...176, 207
2^2...175
2^{10-13}...62
2^{12}...60, 68, 118
2^{13f}...200
3^1...133
3^{1-3}...132, 133
3^3...133
3^9...97
3^{10}...60, 63
3^{13}...115, 144
3^{15}...115, 122
3^{16}...210
3^{19-21}...121
4^4...97
4^{14}...121
4^{15}...122, 211
4^{19-21}...121
4^{21}...211
5^5...117, 120
6^2...211
6^{11}...128
6^{14}...181
6^{15}...138
7^{11}...66
7^{15}...90
7^{20}...165
7^{22}...208
7^{25}...65
8...64
8^3...201
9^9...189
9^{11}...63
9^{22}...74
9^{26f}...168
9^{27}...114
10^{1-6}...167
10^4...126
10^9...111
10^{11}...121
10^{13}...111
10^{16-20}...190
10^{16-21}...189
11^{11}...207
11^{19}...114
11^{28}...114
11^{32}...114
12...63

INDEX OF TEXTS

1 Corinthians—contd.
12-14...90
12^{4ff}...63
12^{4-11}...62
12^{12-17}...210
12^{13}...63
12^{15f}...139
12^{27}...210
12^{27-30}...63
12^{28}...63
13...59, 63, 97
13^{2}...177
13^{12}...201
14^{1}...63
14^{21}...211
15^{10}...62
15^{18}...211
15^{18-22}...215
15^{22}...213
15^{22-6}...217
15^{24}...73
15^{26}...73
15^{27}...61
15^{31}...207, 211
15^{52}...215, 217
15^{58}...208
16^{22}...92
16^{24}...212

2 Corinthians
1^{3}...66, 86
1^{3ff}...82
1^{3-6}...84
1^{6}...75
1^{6f}...190
1^{10}...69
2^{2}...210, 212
2^{7}...63, 82
2^{7-10}...68
2^{8}...82
2^{9}...114
2^{10}...63
2^{11}...116, 117
2^{12}...208
2^{14}...61, 213
2^{14f}...200
2^{15}...74
2^{17}...211
3^{2-11}...78
3^{3}...79, 133
3^{6}...78
3^{14}...169
4^{1}...65
4^{4}...169
4^{6}...201
4^{7}...183
4^{11}...132
4^{14f}...61
4^{16}...79
5^{8}...167

5^{14}...84, 96
5^{16}...200
5^{17}...80, 81, 128, 212, 216
5^{19}...213
5^{19f}...217
5^{20}...84
5^{21}...80
6^{1}...60, 84
6^{1-10}...97
6^{2}...75, 83, 166
6^{9}...122, 197, 201
6^{14f}...190
7^{1}...97, 158
7^{4}...83
7^{6}...83
7^{10}...75
7^{13}...82
8^{4}...83, 190
8^{9}...60, 63
8^{17}...83
8^{23}...190
9^{5}...82
9^{5f}...87
9^{7}...92
9^{8}...61
9^{13}...190
9^{15}...61
10^{1}...84
10^{4}...133
10^{5}...200
10^{10}...168
10^{17}...207
10^{18}...114
11^{3}...115
11^{4}...116
11^{14}...117
11^{24}...120
11^{25}...119
11^{31}...86
12^{2}...116
12^{7}...117, 132
12^{7-9}...112, 131
12^{8}...83
12^{9}...62
13^{3}...114
13^{5}...114
13^{5-7}...113, 114, 168
13^{11}...83, 90, 94
13^{14}...59, 60, 62, 189

Galatians
1^{4}...69
1^{6}...60
1^{15}...60, 173
1^{22}...210
2^{4}...211
2^{9}...63, 190
2^{17}...211
2^{20}...95, 128, 132, 170
3^{9}...86, 87
3^{10}...158

3^{13}...158
3^{14}...87, 212
3^{14-22}...178, 179
3^{18}...68
3^{21}...212
3^{22}...68
3^{24f}...122
3^{26}...212
3^{27}...128, 138, 214
3^{28}...212
4^{8}...199
4^{8f}...78
4^{9}...200, 201
4^{14}...113, 168
4^{15}...88
4^{23}...178
4^{28}...179
5^{4}...62
5^{10}...207
5^{12-26}...136
5^{13}...136
5^{14}...97
5^{16f}...136
5^{19-21}...132
5^{22}...90
5^{24}...128, 136
6^{1}...62
6^{4}...114
6^{6}...190
6^{14}...128
6^{15}...80
6^{16}...65
6^{18}...62

Ephesians
1^{1}...210, 211, 216
1^{3}...176, 215
1^{3-14}...159, 176, 215
1^{4}...176
1^{5-7}...60, 176
1^{6}...60, 62, 215, 216
1^{6-11}...217
1^{7}...61, 66, 70, 215, 216
1^{9}...176, 215
1^{10}...215, 216
1^{11}...173, 176, 215
1^{11f}...211
1^{12}...215
1^{12f}...216
1^{13}...62, 75, 176, 215
1^{14}...70
1^{15}...176, 207, 216
1^{15-23}...176
1^{17}...201
1^{18}...61, 165
1^{20}...216
1^{21f}...216
1^{22}...216
2...216
2^{2}...118
2^{2f}...184

INDEX OF TEXTS

Ephesians—contd.
2^{4f}...65
2^{5-8}...61, 74
2^6...211
2^7...60, 61, 214
2^8...74, 131, 199
2^{10}...80, 211
2^{15}...80
2^{21}...210
3^8...63
3^9...207
3^{11}...173
3^{12}...207
3^{13}...201
3^{19}...197, 200
3^{20f}...76
4^1...165, 208
4^4...62, 165
4^7...61, 62
4^{17-19}...169
4^{22}...138
4^{24}...139
4^{29}...61
4^{30}...70
4^{32}...63, 68
4^{32f}...67
5^1...158, 175
5^6...184
5^8...207
5^{10}...159
5^{20}...61
5^{25}...210
5^{28}...76
6^1...207
6^{10}...207
6^{10-12}...119
6^{11}...117
6^{17}...76
6^{21}...210

Philippians
1^1...212
1^5...190
1^{10}...114
1^{15}...167
1^{19}...75
1^{26}...11
1^{28f}...75
1^{29}...60, 68
2^1...66, 83, 85, 189
2^{1-11}...68
2^9...60
2^{10}...116
2^{12}...75, 97
2^{13}...167
2^{19}...207
2^{22}...114
2^{24}...207
2^{27}...65
3^1...207
3^8...200

3^{8-11}...200
3^{10}...78, 189, 200
3^{14}...165, 212
4^7...59, 90
4^9...90
4^{10}...207
4^{15}...190
4^{18}...159, 166
4^{21}...211
4^{23}...62
4^{24}...66

Colossians
1^2...59, 128
1^{2f}...59
1^6...60
1^{9f}...201
1^{12}...61
1^{13}...69
1^{13f}...95
1^{14}...67, 70
1^{15}...80
1^{15-17}...182
1^{16f}...96, 126
1^{19f}...167
1^{20}...90
1^{23}...167
1^{24}...123
1^{28}...121
2^2...82
2^{5f}...168
2^{9f}...138
2^{12}...128
2^{13}...60, 68
2^{16}-3^{17}...138
2^{19}...138
2^{20}...129
2^{20-3}...138
3^3...207
3^5...132, 139
3^{5-9}...138
3^{5-11}...128
3^6...184
3^7...138
3^8...139
3^{10}...79, 80, 96, 201
3^{12}...66, 96, 139
3^{13}...63, 67
3^{14f}...90
3^{15}...61
3^{16}...121
4^8...82
4^{18}...59

1 Thessalonians
1^1...59, 129, 207
1^4...96, 166
1^{10}...69
2^2...206
2^{3f}...83
2^4...113

2^{10}...66
2^{11}...85
2^{13}...166
2^{16}...74
3^5...116
3^7...82
3^8...207
4^1...82, 84, 207
4^{1-8}...128
4^4...183
4^5...199
4^{10}...82
4^{18}...82
5^3...89
5^{8f}...75
5^9...75
5^{11}...82
5^{12}...121
5^{14}...82, 85, 121
5^{21}...114
5^{23}...90

2 Thessalonians
1^1...207, 210
1^8...200
1^{11}...165, 167
1^{12}...60
2^4...116
2^7...83
1^{10}...74
2^{11f}...82
2^{13}...75, 96
2^{16}...60, 61, 83, 96
3^2...69
3^3...118
3^4...207
3^{12}...207, 211
3^{15}...121
3^{16}...90

1 Timothy
1^1...76
1^2...65, 90
1^{11}...88
1^{12}...61
1^{13}...65
1^{14}...60, 61
1^{15}...60, 74
1^{16}...65
1^{19}...168
1^{20}...117, 121
2^{3-5}...76
2^4...74
2^6...70
2^{10}...214
3^7...117
3^{11}...116
4^4...61
4^{10}...77, 207
4^{13}...83
4^{14}...63

INDEX OF TEXTS

1 Timothy—contd.
4^{16}...74
5^{1}...82
5^{14f}...116
5^{22}...188
6^{2}...82
6^{9}...113
6^{14f}...88
6^{17}...207

2 Timothy
1^{2}...65
1^{3}...61
1^{9f}...77
1^{9}...60, 62, 74, 173
1^{10}...77
1^{12}...200
2^{1}...212
2^{9}...202
2^{10}...75
2^{15}...114
2^{19}...168
2^{19-21}...183
2^{23}...122
2^{25}...122
3^{3}...116
3^{4}...92
3^{8}...114, 168
3^{10}...173
3^{12}...213
3^{15}...75
3^{16}...122
4^{2}...136
4^{8}...97
4^{18}...74
4^{22}...62

Titus
1^{1}...212
1^{3}...76
1^{3f}...77
1^{6}...63
1^{8}...66
1^{9}...82
1^{16}...168, 200
1^{18}...114
2^{10}...77
2^{11}...60, 76
2^{12}...122
2^{13}...77, 88
2^{14}...70
3^{4}...77, 92
3^{5}...65, 74, 79
3^{5-7}...62
3^{6}...77
3^{7}...61
3^{10}...121

Philemon
5^{f}...190
9^{f}...82

1^{7}...190
2^{0}...208
2^{5}...62

Hebrews
1^{2}...125, 176
1^{9}...94
1^{14}...75
2^{3}...75
2^{9}...58, 60
2^{10}...75, 123
2^{11}...192
2^{11-13}...199
2^{14}...119, 132, 188
2^{14f}...118
2^{15}...123
2^{17}...65, 68, 94, 199
2^{18}...83
3^{1}...165, 209
3^{8}...169, 182
3^{8-11}...111
3^{9}...111, 114
3^{13}...82, 169
3^{15}...169
4^{7}...169, 182
4^{13}...80
4^{16}...58, 65, 83
5^{7}...74
5^{7-10}...75
5^{8f}...123
6^{1-12}...75
6^{4}...79
6^{4ff}...70
6^{5}...172
6^{6}...79, 80
6^{7f}...86
6^{8}...114, 168
6^{9}...97, 158
6^{10}...94, 97
6^{14}...86, 87
6^{18}...83
7^{1}...87
7^{6f}...87
7^{16}...133
7^{25}...74
7^{26}...66
8^{6}...78
8^{8-10}...77
8^{11}...199
8^{12}...68
$9-11$...179
9^{2}...173
9^{5}...68
9^{11}...80
9^{12}...70
9^{14f}...78
9^{15}...70
9^{18}...80
9^{22}...66
9^{28}...75, 76
10^{5-7}...167

10^{18}...67
10^{19}...95
10^{20}...80
10^{24}...94
10^{28f}...66
10^{29}...58, 62
10^{30}...199
10^{35-9}...179
10^{38}...167
11...179
11^{3}...125
11^{5f}...159
11^{6}...125
11^{7}...75
11^{13}...179
11^{17}...112
11^{17-19}...113
11^{20f}...86
11^{29}...111
11^{31}...89
11^{32}...125
11^{33}...125
11^{35}...70
11^{36}...111, 113
11^{37}...123
11^{39f}...179
12^{1f}...179
12^{2}...75, 125
12^{4}...70
12^{4-13}...122
12^{5}...83
12^{6}...94, 96, 120
12^{11}...122
12^{12f}...122
12^{14}...91
12^{15}...28
12^{16}...159, 180
12^{16f}...168
12^{17}...87, 114
12^{24}...78
12^{26}...125
13^{6}...83
13^{8}...97
13^{9}...25
13^{13}...97
13^{16}...190
13^{20}...78, 90
13^{21}...159
13^{22}...83
13^{25}...58

James
1^{2}...113, 114
1^{2f}...113, 114
1^{12}...88, 97, 113, 135, 179
1^{13}...112
1^{14}...113
1^{14f}...135
1^{16}...97, 158
1^{18}...80
1^{21}...74, 138

INDEX OF TEXTS

James—contd.
1^{25}...88
2^5...97, 164
2^8...97
2^{13}...65
2^{14}...74
2^{23}...92, 190
3^9...86
3^{17}...65
4^{1f}...139
4^4...91, 191
4^{5f}...58
4^7...117, 119
4^{12}...74
5^{11}...65, 86, 88
5^{15}...66, 74
5^{20}...74

1 Peter
1^1...164
1^2...58, 90, 175
1^3...65, 86, 130
1^5...76, 210
1^{6f}...113, 114, 115
1^7...114
1^8...97
1^{9f}...76
1^{10f}...58
1^{10-12}...126
1^{12}...164
1^{13}...58
1^{14}...176
1^{18f}...70
1^{20}...175
1^{23}...130
2^1...138
2^2...76, 130
2^4...168
2^{4-7}...161
2^{4-10}...163
2^5...161
2^7...168
2^{10}...65
2^{11}...84, 97, 136, 158
2^{13}...80
2^{19f}...58
3^7...58, 183
3^9...87
3^{14}...88
3^{15f}...209
3^{16}...209, 212, 213
3^{21}...74
4^2...136
4^9...80
4^{10}...58, 63
4^{12}...113, 114, 115
4^{12-14}...97, 113
4^{18}...74
5^1...82
5^5...58
5^8...116, 117
5^{9f}...168
5^{10}...58, 209, 211, 212
5^{12}...58
5^{14}...92, 209, 212

2 Peter
1-3...72, 166
1^1...72, 76
1^2...58
1^{2f}...201
1^4...189
1^{5-8}...201
1^8...201
1^{10}...165, 166
1^{11}...72, 76
1^{17}...158
2^4...170
2^7...69
2^9...113, 170
2^{20}...72, 76, 201
3^1...97
3^2...72, 76
3^3...136
3^4...180
3^{15}...72, 76
3^{17}...175
3^{18}...58, 72, 76, 201

1 John
1^3...189, 212, 218
1^4...189
1^5...95, 189
1^{5-7}...190, 222
1^{6f}...189
1^7...95, 221
1^8...127, 136
1^9...66, 135
1^{10}...127
1^{10-12}...202
2^1...84, 218
2^2...68
2^{3f}...78
2^{3-5}...170
2^{5f}...97, 221
2^6...221
2^7...97, 158
2^{10}...221
2^{10f}...97
2^{11}...169
2^{12}...66
2^{13}...204
2^{13f}...78, 118
1^{15-17}...97
2^{24}...221
2^{25}...179
2^{29}...130
3^1...96, 119, 204
3^{5f}...221
3^6...204
3^8...118, 119
3^9...130
3^{10}...97, 118, 119
3^{16}...136, 221
3^{16ff}...97
3^{19}...221
3^{23}...97
3^{24}...221, 222
4^2...204, 218
4^{7f}...204
4^{7-5^3}...94
4^6...204
4^{6f}...204
4^7...96, 130
4^8...94, 204
4^{10}...68, 97, 95
4^{11}...96
4^{12-15}...96
4^{12f}...221
4^{13}...95, 222
4^{14}...77, 95, 97
4^{15f}...207, 221
4^{16}...94, 96
4^{16f}...96
4^{17}...95
4^{19}...96, 97
5^1...130
5^{1-3}...96
5^4...130
5^{11}...222
5^{13}...204
5^{18}...118, 130, 170
5^{19}...118, 204
5^{20}...204, 207, 208, 209, 222

2 John
3...58, 65, 90
3^f...221
4...221
6...221
9...221
11...188

3 John
3^f...221
6...220
9^f...220
14...191

Jude
1...96, 165, 207
1-25...72
2...65
3...72, 82, 97
4...58
5...72, 74
9...115
16...136
21...65
23...72, 74
25...72, 76

INDEX OF TEXTS

Revelation
1^3...88
1^{4f}...58, 90
1^5...94
1^{5f}...94
1^9...209, 212
2^4...94
2^9...113
2^{10}...113, 116, 117
2^{19}...94
2^{27}...120
3^9...94
3^{10}...112, 113
3^{10f}...113
3^{14}...80
3^{19}...92, 122
5^{5f}...91
5^{12f}...87
6^4...89
6^{9f}...161
7^{10}...72, 76
7^{10-12}...87
12^5...120
12^9...115, 116
12^{10}...72, 76
12^{11}...94
13^{10f}...97
14^{13}...207
15^4...66
16^5...66
16^{15}...88
17^{14}...164
18^9...115
18^{18}...115
19^1...72
19^{1f}...76
19^8...132
19^{15}...120
20^6...88
20^9...94
20^{10}...116, 118
21^4...73
22^7...88
22^{14}...88
22^{21}...58

www.ingramcontent.com/pod-product-compliance
Lightning Source LLC
Chambersburg PA
CBHW050851230426
43667CB00012B/2246